ISBN 978-0-260-85564-0
PIBN 10977131

HOW TO USE THIS INDEX

In order to get maximum usage from this index, the researcher should keep the following guidelines in mind:

1. Coverage is limited to the 83rd General Assembly House floor debate (January 12, 1983—January 9, 1985)..

2. Reference is by bill number only. Citations to Public Acts which are given in the Illinois Revised Statutes and in other sources, can be converted to bill numbers by consulting the appropriate Public Act as it appears in the session laws. Those who need access to debate by subject or sponsor should check the indexes in the Legislative Synopsis and Digest for reference to pertinent bill numbers.

3. The purpose of this index is to lead the user to discussion of legislative intent or reasons for particular activity, and not to serve as a record of all action. This means that there are no references to stages in the bills' progress which did not involve debate. Many bills, for example, are not amended on second reading. The Secretary indicates that there are no committee amendments, the presiding officer asks if there are floor amendments, is informed that there are none, and the bill is moved to third reading. There will be no citation to second reading debate on such bills since the floor proceedings contain no more information that the Senate Journal or the Legislative Synopsis and Digest. Some bills were put on an agreed bill list and passed in a single roll call without separate discussion; these will not have citations to debate on third reading (final passage stage). No concurrences are often adopted without debate and will therefore not be indexed.

4. Within the limitations of the preceding guidelines, debate was indexed for all House and Senate bills where it existed. Coverage for resolutions was more selective, since most of them are ceremonial and perfunctory in nature. Debate was indexed for all House and Senate constitutional amendment resolutions and for resolutions which involved controversy (usually investigations of problems or expression of sentiments which were not universally accepted).

HOW TO USE THIS INDEX

In order to get maximum usage from this index, the researcher should keep the following guidelines in mind:

1. Coverage is limited to the 83rd General Assembly House floor debate (January-12, 1983-January 9, 1985).

2. Reference is by bill number only. Citations to Public Acts which are given in the Illinois Revised Statutes and in other sources, can be converted to bill numbers by consulting the appropriate Public Act as it appears in the session laws. Those who need access to debate by subject or sponsor should check the indexes in the Legislative Synopsis and Digest for reference to pertinent bill numbers.

3. The purpose of this index is to lead the user to discussion of legislative intent or reasons for particular activity, and not to serve as a record of all action. This means that there are no references to stages in the bills' progress which did not involve debate. Many bills, for example, are not amended on second reading. The Secretary indicates that there are no committee amendments, the presiding officer asks if there are floor amendments, is informed that there are none, and the bill is moved to third reading. There will be no citation to second reading debate on such bills since the floor proceedings contain no more information that the Senate Journal or the Legislative Synopsis and Digest. Some bills were put on an agreed bill list and passed in a single r lb call without separate discussion; these will not have citations to debate on third reading (final passage stage). Noncon-currences are often adopted without debate and will therefore not be indexed.

4. Within the limitations of the preceding guidelines, debate was indexed for all House and Senate bills where it existed. Coverage for resolutions was more selective, since most of them are ceremonial and perfunctory in nature. Debate was indexed for all House and Senate constitutional amendment resolutions and for resolutions which involved controversy (usually investigations of problems or expression of sentiments which were not universally accepted).

TO LOCATE DEBATE FOR A BILL

1. Consult the bill number index. If there are entries under the bill, they will refer to date and pages.

2. Turn to the "Conversion Table: Legislative Day to Date" in order to convert the date to legislative day numbers.

3. Turn to Microfiche Frame Locations to determine on which fiche the citation is located. This table gives the microfiche number for each legislative day.

Please note the microfiche are numbered sequentially in the upper right corner of the heading. The heading shows the number of the legislative day and date of the first legislative day on that particular fiche. There is no correlation between sequential fiche numbers and the legislative day contained on the fiche.

On the days for which there are both regular and special sessions, debates for the special sessions appear after the regular sessions for that day.

TABLE OF CONTENTS

REGULAR SESSION:
  HOUSE BILLS...1
  SENATE BILLS..235
  HOUSE RESOLUTIONS.......................................327
  HOUSE JOINT RESOLUTIONS.................................332
  HOUSE JOINT RESOLUTIONS CONSTITUTIONAL AMENDMENTS.......335
  SENATE JOINT RESOLUTIONS................................336
  JOINT SESSION RESOLUTIONS...............................339
  EXECUTIVE ORDER...339

ORDER OF BUSINESS...340

CONVERSION TABLE: LEGISLATIVE DAY TO DATE...................379

MICROFICHE FRAME LOCATIONS..................................382

APPENDIX A. ILLINOIS DOCUMENT DEPOSITORY LIBRARIES.........384

APPENDIX B. ADDITIONAL LIBRARIES RECEIVING LEGISLATIVE
             MATERIALS ON MICROFICHE..................... .388

BILL NUMBER	DATE	PAGE	ACTION
HB-0001	01/13/83	4	FIRST READING
	03/22/83	26	SECOND READING
	04/07/83	44	THIRD READING
HB-0002	01/13/83	4	FIRST READING
HB-0003	01/13/83	4	FIRST READING
	05/23/83	4	SECOND READING
	05/23/83	10	OUT OF RECORD
HB-0004	01/13/83	4	FIRST READING
	05/06/83	35	OTHER
HB-0005	01/13/83	4	FIRST READING
	05/03/83	8	OTHER
HB-0006	01/13/83	4	FIRST READING
	03/15/83	52	SECOND READING
	04/21/83	48	THIRD READING
HB-0007	01/13/83	4	FIRST READING
	05/13/83	6	SECOND READING
	05/17/83	162	THIRD READING
HB-0008	01/13/83	5	FIRST READING
	04/05/83	9	SECOND READING
	04/06/83	44	THIRD READING
HB-0009	01/13/83	5	FIRST READING
	05/13/83	7	SECOND READING
	05/17/83	177	THIRD READING
HB-0010	01/13/83	5	FIRST READING
HB-0011	01/13/83	5	FIRST READING
	04/14/83	70	SECOND READING
	04/21/83	48	THIRD READING
HB-0012	01/13/83	5	FIRST READING
	03/09/83	9	SECOND READING
	03/16/83	20	THIRD READING
HB-0013	01/13/83	5	FIRST READING
HB-0014	01/13/83	5	FIRST READING
	05/06/83	35	OTHER
HB-0015	01/13/83	5	FIRST READING
	04/04/84	23	MOTION
	05/10/84	81	SECOND READING
	05/24/84	275	OTHER

BILL NUMBER	DATE	PAGE	ACTION
HB-0016	01/13/83	5	FIRST READING
	05/25/83	296	SECOND READING
HB-0017	01/13/83	5	FIRST READING
	04/19/83	23	SECOND READING
	04/19/83	24	HELD ON SECOND
	04/19/83	64	SECOND READING
	04/20/83	25	THIRD READING
HB-0018	01/13/83	5	FIRST READING
	04/19/83	11	SECOND READING
	04/20/83	34	THIRD READING
	05/06/83	12	RECALLED
	05/06/83	15	SECOND READING
	05/06/83	21	HELD ON SECOND
	05/12/83	183	SECOND READING
	05/25/83	179	THIRD READING
	06/28/83	155	CONCURRENCE
HB-0019	01/13/83	5	FIRST READING
HB-0020	01/13/83	5	FIRST READING
	03/02/83	5	SECOND READING
	03/03/83	10	THIRD READING
	06/28/83	6	CONCURRENCE
HB-0021	01/13/83	5	FIRST READING
	03/23/83	19	HELD ON SECOND
	03/24/83	8	SECOND READING
	04/05/83	25	THIRD READING
	04/05/83	50	MOTION
	04/05/83	51	RECALLED
	04/06/83	34	SECOND READING
	04/07/83	47	THIRD READING
	10/20/83	38	VETO MESSAGE
HB-0022	01/13/83	5	FIRST READING
	04/15/83	25	SECOND READING
	04/21/83	50	THIRD READING
	05/06/83	36	OTHER
	06/28/83	155	CONCURRENCE
	06/28/83	156	CONCURRENCE
	06/28/83	156	OUT OF RECORD
	10/19/83	204	VETO MESSAGE
HB-0023	01/13/83	6	FIRST READING
	05/06/83	35	OTHER
HB-0024	01/13/83	6	FIRST READING
	04/19/83	11	SECOND READING
	04/21/83	53	THIRD READING

1/14/91 - 11/2/83 - Sew

BILL NUMBER	DATE	PAGE	ACTION
HB-0024 (cont'd)	05/06/83	36	OTHER
	05/24/83	117	THIRD READING
HB-0025	01/13/83	6	FIRST READING
	03/16/83	8	SECOND READING
	03/23/83	37	THIRD READING
	06/28/83	8	CONCURRENCE
HB-0026	01/13/83	6	FIRST READING
	02/24/83	5	SECOND READING
	03/01/83	6	THIRD READING
	06/28/83	156	CONCURRENCE
	06/30/83	166	CONFERENCE
	06/30/83	168	OUT OF RECORD
	07/01/83	275	CONFERENCE
HB-0027	01/13/83	6	FIRST READING
	03/22/83	25	SECOND READING
	03/23/83	33	THIRD READING
HB-0028	01/13/83	6	FIRST READING
	03/02/83	42	SECOND READING
	03/08/83	20	THIRD READING
	06/24/83	230	NON-CONCURRENCE
	06/30/83	133	CONFERENCE
	06/30/83	138	OUT OF RECORD
	06/30/83	148	CONFERENCE
HB-0029	01/13/83	6	FIRST READING
	05/03/83	7	OTHER
HB-0030	01/13/83	6	FIRST READING
	05/03/83	7	OTHER
HB-0031	01/13/83	6	FIRST READING
	05/03/83	7	OTHER
HB-0032	01/13/83	6	FIRST READING
	05/13/83	17	SECOND READING
	05/27/83	93	THIRD READING
HB-0033	01/13/83	6	FIRST READING
	03/23/83	18	SECOND READING
	03/24/83	17	THIRD READING
	06/28/83	9	CONCURRENCE
HB-0034	01/13/83	6	FIRST READING
	05/03/83	7	OTHER
HB-0035	01/13/83	6	FIRST READING
	05/03/83	7	OTHER

BILL NUMBER	DATE	PAGE	ACTION
HB-0036	01/13/83	7	FIRST READING
	03/23/83	20	SECOND READING
	03/24/83	42	RECALLED
	03/24/83	60	OTHER
	04/05/83	31	THIRD READING
HB-0037	01/13/83	7	FIRST READING
	05/03/83	7	OTHER
HB-0038	01/13/83	7	FIRST READING
	05/03/83	7	OTHER
HB-0039	01/13/83	7	FIRST READING
	05/03/83	7	OTHER
HB-0040	01/13/83	7	FIRST READING
	05/03/83	7	OTHER
HB-0041	01/13/83	7	FIRST READING
	02/24/83	5	SECOND READING
	03/01/83	6	THIRD READING
	06/28/83	10	CONCURRENCE
	10/20/83	42	VETO MESSAGE
HB-0042	01/13/83	7	FIRST READING
HB-0043	01/13/83	7	FIRST READING
	04/06/83	8	SECOND READING
	04/06/83	35	SECOND READING
	04/14/83	31	RECALLED
	04/28/83	19	SECOND READING
	05/05/83	8	THIRD READING
	06/28/83	157	CONCURRENCE
HB-0044	01/13/83	7	FIRST READING
	05/03/83	7	OTHER
HB-0045	01/13/83	7	FIRST READING
	03/14/83	6	SECOND READING
	03/16/83	23	THIRD READING
HB-0046	01/13/83	7	FIRST READING
	04/05/83	10	SECOND READING
	04/07/83	49	THIRD READING
HB-0047	01/13/83	7	FIRST READING
HB-0048	01/13/83	7	FIRST READING
	05/03/83	7	OTHER
HB-0049	01/13/83	7	FIRST READING

BILL NUMBER	DATE	PAGE	ACTION
HB-0049 (cont'd)	03/23/83	20	SECOND READING
	03/24/83	43	THIRD READING
HB-0050	01/13/83	7	FIRST READING
	02/24/83	5	SECOND READING
	03/01/83	11	THIRD READING
HB-0051	01/13/83	8	FIRST READING
	05/04/83	53	OTHER
HB-0052	01/13/83	8	FIRST READING
	02/24/83	5	SECOND READING
	03/03/83	17	THIRD READING
HB-0053	01/13/83	8	FIRST READING
HB-0054	01/13/83	8	FIRST READING
	04/14/83	70	SECOND READING
	04/19/83	7	SECOND READING
	04/21/83	19	THIRD READING
HB-0055	01/13/83	8	FIRST READING
	03/23/83	20	SECOND READING
	03/23/83	18	THIRD READING
HB-0056	01/13/83	8	FIRST READING
	04/13/83	9	SECOND READING
HB-0057	01/13/83	8	FIRST READING
	03/02/83	6	SECOND READING
	03/23/83	50	THIRD READING
	03/23/83	54	OTHER
	04/06/83	57	RECALLED
HB-0058	01/13/83	8	FIRST READING
	04/28/83	5	SECOND READING
	05/10/83	6	THIRD READING
HB-0059	01/13/83	8	FIRST READING
	04/28/83	116	OTHER
HB-0060	01/13/83	8	FIRST READING
	05/11/83	6	SECOND READING
	05/12/83	185	THIRD READING
	06/28/83	158	CONCURRENCE
HB-0061	01/13/83	20	FIRST READING
	05/11/83	2	SECOND READING
	05/17/83	99	THIRD READING
	06/28/83	11	CONCURRENCE

BILL NUMBER	DATE	PAGE	ACTION
HB-0062	01/13/83	20	FIRST READING
	02/24/83	5	SECOND READING
	03/01/83	17	THIRD READING
	03/01/83	19	OTHER
	03/03/83	11	THIRD READING
HB-0063	01/13/83	20	FIRST READING
	05/06/83	36	OTHER
HB-0064	01/13/83	20	FIRST READING
	05/03/83	24	SECOND READING
	05/05/83	10	THIRD READING
	06/28/83	159	CONCURRENCE
HB-0065	01/13/83	20	FIRST READING
	05/06/83	35	OTHER
HB-0066	01/13/83	20	FIRST READING
HB-0067	01/13/83	21	FIRST READING
	04/05/83	11	SECOND READING
	04/07/83	50	THIRD READING
	10/18/83	10	VETO MESSAGE
HB-0068	01/13/83	21	FIRST READING
	03/02/83	6	SECOND READING
	03/02/83	9	OUT OF RECORD
	03/02/83	26	SECOND READING
	03/14/83	10	RECALLED
	03/14/83	34	SECOND READING
	03/15/83	23	THIRD READING
	03/15/83	29	OTHER
HB-0069	01/13/83	21	FIRST READING
	03/09/83	9	SECOND READING
	03/10/83	11	THIRD READING
HB-0070	01/13/83	21	FIRST READING
HB-0071	01/13/83	21	FIRST READING
HB-0072	01/13/83	21	FIRST READING
HB-0073	01/13/83	21	FIRST READING
	05/18/83	38	SECOND READING
	05/23/83	94	THIRD READING
HB-0074	01/13/83	21	FIRST READING
	04/15/83	26	SECOND READING
	04/21/83	65	THIRD READING

PROGRAM-LRTRNMST
08/20/85
LEGISLATIVE INFORMATION SYSTEM
HOUSE OF REPRESENTATIVES
PAGE 7

MASTER TRANSCRIPT INDEX

BILL NUMBER	DATE	PAGE	ACTION
HB-0075	01/13/83	21	FIRST READING
	05/03/83	35	OTHER
HB-0076	01/13/83	21	FIRST READING
	03/08/83	17	SECOND READING
	03/09/83	14	THIRD READING
	06/28/83	12	CONCURRENCE
HB-0077	01/25/83	2	FIRST READING
	03/08/83	18	SECOND READING
	03/09/83	15	THIRD READING
HB-0078	01/25/83	2	FIRST READING
	04/21/83	6	SECOND READING
	05/05/83	13	THIRD READING
HB-0079	01/25/83	2	FIRST READING
	03/08/83	25	MOTION
	03/14/83	6	OUT OF RECORD
	03/15/83	5	SECOND READING
	04/05/83	32	THIRD READING
HB-0080	01/25/83	2	FIRST READING
	03/08/83	18	SECOND READING
	03/09/83	16	THIRD READING
HB-0081	01/27/83	1	FIRST READING
	04/05/83	24	SECOND READING
	04/07/83	56	THIRD READING
HB-0082	01/27/83	1	FIRST READING
	04/14/83	11	SECOND READING
	05/27/83	221	THIRD READING
	05/27/83	223	OUT OF RECORD
HB-0083	01/27/83	1	
HB-0084	01/27/83	1	FIRST READING
	04/15/83	14	SECOND READING
	04/15/83	101	RECALLED
	04/21/83	22	THIRD READING
	10/18/83	94	VETO MESSAGE
HB-0085	01/27/83	1	FIRST READING
	04/05/83	11	SECOND READING
	05/05/83	16	THIRD READING
HB-0086	01/27/83	1	FIRST READING
	02/23/83	3	SECOND READING
	03/01/83	4	THIRD READING

PROGRAM-LRTRNMST
08/20/85
LEGISLATIVE INFORMATION SYSTEM
HOUSE OF REPRESENTATIVES
PAGE 8

MASTER TRANSCRIPT INDEX

BILL NUMBER	DATE	PAGE	ACTION
HB-0087	01/27/83	1	FIRST READING
	04/19/83	12	SECOND READING
HB-0088	01/27/83	1	FIRST READING
	03/09/83	30	SECOND READING
	03/14/83	36	THIRD READING
HB-0089	01/27/83	1	FIRST READING
	05/13/83	18	SECOND READING
HB-0090	01/27/83	2	FIRST READING
	04/28/83	19	SECOND READING
	05/05/83	20	THIRD READING
HB-0091	01/27/83	2	FIRST READING
	05/22/84	8	MOTION
	05/23/84	5	SECOND READING
	05/25/84	148	THIRD READING
HB-0092	01/27/83	2	FIRST READING
	05/06/83	35	OTHER
HB-0093	01/27/83	2	FIRST READING
	03/02/83	43	SECOND READING
	03/03/83	12	THIRD READING
HB-0094	01/27/83	2	FIRST READING
	05/03/83	4	TABLED
HB-0095	01/27/83	2	FIRST READING
	05/03/83	4	TABLED
HB-0096	01/27/83	2	FIRST READING
	05/11/83	5	SECOND READING
HB-0097	01/27/83	2	FIRST READING
	03/08/83	5	SECOND READING
	03/09/83	20	THIRD READING
	06/30/83	88	CONCURRENCE
HB-0098	01/27/83	2	FIRST READING
HB-0099	01/27/83	2	FIRST READING
	05/03/83	26	SECOND READING
	05/05/83	21	THIRD READING
HB-0100	01/27/83	2	FIRST READING
HB-0101	01/27/83	2	FIRST READING
	05/06/83	35	OTHER

BILL NUMBER	DATE	PAGE	ACTION
HB-0102	01/27/83	2	FIRST READING
	05/06/83	35	OTHER
HB-0103	01/27/83	2	FIRST READING
HB-0104	01/27/83	3	FIRST READING
	03/08/83	18	SECOND READING
	03/09/83	8	SECOND READING
	03/14/83	8	THIRD READING
	03/14/83	10	OUT OF RECORD
	03/15/83	9	THIRD READING
	06/28/83	163	CONCURRENCE
	07/01/83	158	CONFERENCE
HB-0105	01/27/83	3	FIRST READING
HB-0106	01/27/83	3	FIRST READING
	03/09/83	13	TABLED
HB-0107	01/27/83	3	FIRST READING
	04/06/83	42	SECOND READING
	04/07/83	58	THIRD READING
HB-0108	01/27/83	3	FIRST READING
	04/06/83	12	SECOND READING
	04/07/83	59	THIRD READING
	06/28/83	12	CONCURRENCE
HB-0109	01/27/83	3	FIRST READING
	05/03/83	31	OTHER
HB-0110	01/27/83	3	FIRST READING
HB-0111	01/27/83	3	FIRST READING
HB-0112	01/27/83	3	FIRST READING
	04/26/83	16	SECOND READING
	05/05/83	30	THIRD READING
	06/28/83	161	CONCURRENCE
	07/01/83	266	CONFERENCE
HB-0113	01/27/83	3	FIRST READING
HB-0114	01/27/83	3	FIRST READING
	03/23/83	21	SECOND READING
	03/24/83	44	THIRD READING
	06/28/83	6	CONCURRENCE
	07/01/83	263	CONFERENCE
HB-0115	01/27/83	3	FIRST READING
	04/21/83	46	SECOND READING

BILL NUMBER	DATE	PAGE	ACTION
HB-0115 (cont'd)	05/19/83	255	SECOND READING
	05/23/83	95	THIRD READING
HB-0116	01/27/83	3	FIRST READING
	04/21/83	46	SECOND READING
	05/19/83	256	SECOND READING
	05/23/83	96	THIRD READING
HB-0117	01/27/83	3	FIRST READING
	04/14/83	70	SECOND READING
	04/21/83	48	THIRD READING
HB-0118	01/27/83	3	FIRST READING
	04/14/83	71	SECOND READING
	04/21/83	48	THIRD READING
HB-0119	01/27/83	4	FIRST READING
	04/14/83	5	SECOND READING
	04/15/83	33	THIRD READING
HB-0120	01/27/83	4	FIRST READING
	04/15/83	14	SECOND READING
	04/19/83	29	THIRD READING
HB-0121	01/27/83	4	FIRST READING
	04/14/83	71	SECOND READING
	04/21/83	48	THIRD READING
HB-0122	01/27/83	4	FIRST READING
	04/20/83	11	SECOND READING
	04/21/83	23	THIRD READING
HB-0123	01/27/83	4	FIRST READING
	04/21/83	46	SECOND READING
	05/19/83	257	SECOND READING
	05/23/83	96	THIRD READING
HB-0124	01/27/83	4	FIRST READING
	04/15/83	15	SECOND READING
	04/19/83	30	THIRD READING
HB-0125	01/27/83	4	FIRST READING
	04/15/83	15	SECOND READING
	04/19/83	30	THIRD READING
HB-0126	01/27/83	4	FIRST READING
	04/15/83	16	SECOND READING
	04/19/83	31	THIRD READING
HB-0127	01/27/83	4	FIRST READING
	04/20/83	11	SECOND READING

BILL NUMBER	DATE	PAGE	ACTION
HB-0127 (cont'd)	04/21/83	24	THIRD READING
	06/24/83	198	NON-CONCURRENCE
HB-0128	01/27/83	4	FIRST READING
	04/21/83	47	SECOND READING
	05/19/83	257	SECOND READING
	05/23/83	96	THIRD READING
HB-0129	01/27/83	4	FIRST READING
	04/21/83	47	SECOND READING
	05/19/83	257	SECOND READING
	05/23/83	96	THIRD READING
HB-0130	01/27/83	4	FIRST READING
	04/21/83	47	SECOND READING
	05/19/83	258	SECOND READING
	05/23/83	96	THIRD READING
HB-0131	01/27/83	4	FIRST READING
	04/14/83	71	SECOND READING
	04/21/83	48	THIRD READING
HB-0132	01/27/83	4	FIRST READING
	04/21/83	47	SECOND READING
	05/19/83	258	SECOND READING
	05/23/83	96	THIRD READING
HB-0133	01/27/83	4	FIRST READING
	05/19/83	258	SECOND READING
	05/23/83	96	THIRD READING
	04/25/84	20	MOTION
	04/26/84	70	CONCURRENCE
HB-0134	01/27/83	5	FIRST READING
	05/19/83	259	SECOND READING
	05/23/83	96	THIRD READING
	06/24/83	198	NON-CONCURRENCE
HB-0135	01/27/83	5	FIRST READING
	05/19/83	259	SECOND READING
	05/23/83	96	THIRD READING
HB-0136	01/27/83	5	FIRST READING
HB-0137	01/27/83	5	FIRST READING
	03/24/83	6	HELD ON SECOND
	04/05/83	9	SECOND READING
	04/15/83	33	RECALLED
	05/19/83	259	SECOND READING
	05/23/83	96	THIRD READING

BILL NUMBER	DATE	PAGE	ACTION
HB-0138	01/27/83	5	FIRST READING
	04/14/83	71	SECOND READING
	04/21/83	48	THIRD READING
HB-0139	01/27/83	5	FIRST READING
	03/23/83	18	SECOND READING
	03/24/83	19	THIRD READING
HB-0140	01/27/83	5	FIRST READING
	03/23/83	18	SECOND READING
	03/24/83	19	THIRD READING
HB-0141	01/27/83	5	FIRST READING
HB-0142	01/27/83	5	FIRST READING
	05/19/83	220	SECOND READING
	05/23/83	96	THIRD READING
HB-0143	01/27/83	5	FIRST READING
	04/14/83	71	SECOND READING
	04/21/83	48	THIRD READING
HB-0144	01/27/83	5	FIRST READING
	05/19/83	220	SECOND READING
	05/23/83	96	THIRD READING
HB-0145	01/27/83	5	FIRST READING
	04/15/83	17	SECOND READING
	04/19/83	31	THIRD READING
HB-0146	01/27/83	5	FIRST READING
	03/15/83	57	TABLED
HB-0147	01/27/83	5	FIRST READING
	05/19/83	260	SECOND READING
	05/23/83	96	THIRD READING
	06/24/83	225	NON-CONCURRENCE
HB-0148	01/27/83	6	FIRST READING
	05/19/83	260	SECOND READING
	05/23/83	96	THIRD READING
HB-0149	01/27/83	6	FIRST READING
	05/19/83	261	SECOND READING
	05/23/83	96	THIRD READING
HB-0150	01/27/83	6	FIRST READING
	05/19/83	261	SECOND READING
	05/23/83	96	THIRD READING
HB-0151	01/27/83	6	FIRST READING

PROGRAM-LRTRNMST
08/20/85
LEGISLATIVE INFORMATION SYSTEM
HOUSE OF REPRESENTATIVES
PAGE   13

MASTER TRANSCRIPT INDEX

BILL NUMBER	DATE	PAGE	ACTION
HB-0151 (cont'd)	05/19/83	261	SECOND READING
	05/23/83	96	THIRD READING
HB-0152	01/27/83	6	FIRST READING
	04/14/83	71	SECOND READING
	04/21/83	48	THIRD READING
HB-0153	01/27/83	6	FIRST READING
	05/19/83	262	SECOND READING
	05/23/83	97	THIRD READING
HB-0154	01/27/83	6	FIRST READING
	05/19/83	262	SECOND READING
	05/23/83	57	THIRD READING
HB-0155	01/27/83	6	FIRST READING
	05/19/83	262	SECOND READING
	05/23/83	97	THIRD READING
HB-0156	01/27/83	6	FIRST READING
	05/19/83	262	SECOND READING
	05/23/83	97	THIRD READING
HB-0157	01/27/83	6	FIRST READING
	05/19/83	263	SECOND READING
	05/23/83	97	THIRD READING
	06/24/83	226	NON-CONCURRENCE
HB-0158	01/27/83	6	FIRST READING
	04/15/83	17	SECOND READING
	04/19/83	32	THIRD READING
HB-0159	01/27/83	6	FIRST READING
	04/15/83	18	SECOND READING
	04/19/83	32	THIRD READING
HB-0160	01/27/83	6	FIRST READING
	04/15/83	18	SECOND READING
	04/19/83	33	THIRD READING
HB-0161	01/27/83	6	FIRST READING
HB-0162	01/27/83	6	FIRST READING
	04/14/83	71	SECOND READING
	04/21/83	48	THIRD READING
HB-0163	01/27/83	6	FIRST READING
	04/14/83	71	SECOND READING
	04/21/83	48	THIRD READING
HB-0164	01/27/83	7	FIRST READING

PROGRAM-LRTRNMST
08/20/85
LEGISLATIVE INFORMATION SYSTEM
HOUSE OF REPRESENTATIVES
PAGE   14

MASTER TRANSCRIPT INDEX

BILL NUMBER	DATE	PAGE	ACTION
HB-0164 (cont'd)	04/14/83	71	SECOND READING
	04/21/83	48	THIRD READING
HB-0165	01/27/83	7	FIRST READING
	05/19/83	266	SECOND READING
	05/23/83	97	THIRD READING
HB-0166	01/27/83	7	FIRST READING
	04/15/83	19	SECOND READING
	04/21/83	67	THIRD READING
HB-0167	01/27/83	7	FIRST READING
	04/14/83	71	SECOND READING
	04/21/83	48	THIRD READING
HB-0168	01/27/83	7	FIRST READING
	04/14/83	71	SECOND READING
	04/21/83	48	THIRD READING
HB-0169	01/27/83	7	FIRST READING
	03/23/83	21	SECOND READING
	04/05/83	36	THIRD READING
HB-0170	02/02/83	1	FIRST READING
	03/23/83	21	SECOND READING
	03/24/83	45	THIRD READING
HB-0171	02/02/83	1	FIRST READING
	03/22/83	25	SECOND READING
	03/23/83	35	THIRD READING
	06/28/83	55	CONCURRENCE
HB-0172	02/02/83	1	FIRST READING
	03/23/83	21	SECOND READING
	03/24/83	63	THIRD READING
HB-0173	02/02/83	1	FIRST READING
	05/06/83	35	OTHER
HB-0174	02/02/83	1	FIRST READING
	05/13/83	18	SECOND READING
	05/17/83	103	THIRD READING
HB-0175	02/02/83	1	FIRST READING
HB-0176	02/02/83	1	FIRST READING
	05/11/83	13	SECOND READING
	05/13/83	2	THIRD READING
HB-0177	02/02/83	1	FIRST READING
	05/06/83	35	OTHER

PROGRAM-LRTRNMST
08/20/85
LEGISLATIVE INFORMATION SYSTEM
HOUSE OF REPRESENTATIVES
PAGE 15

MASTER TRANSCRIPT INDEX

BILL NUMBER	DATE	PAGE	ACTION
HB-0178	02/02/83	1	FIRST READING
	03/02/83	5	OUT OF RECORD
	03/08/83	4	SECOND READING
	03/09/83	18	THIRD READING
HB-0179	02/02/83	1	FIRST READING
HB-0180	02/02/83	2	FIRST READING
HB-0181	02/02/83	2	FIRST READING
	05/06/83	35	OTHER
HB-0182	02/02/83	2	FIRST READING
	05/06/83	35	OTHER
HB-0183	02/02/83	2	FIRST READING
HB-0184	02/02/83	2	FIRST READING
HB-0185	02/02/83	2	FIRST READING
	05/06/83	35	OTHER
HB-0186	02/02/83	2	FIRST READING
	05/11/83	4	SECOND READING
	05/17/83	104	HELD ON SECOND
	05/17/83	105	THIRD READING
	06/28/83	129	CONCURRENCE
	07/01/83	3	CONFERENCE
	10/19/83	4	VETO MESSAGE
	10/19/83	4	OUT OF RECORD
	10/19/83	5	VETO MESSAGE
	10/19/83	6	OUT OF RECORD
	10/20/83	3	VETO MESSAGE
HB-0187	02/02/83	2	FIRST READING
	03/23/83	21	SECOND READING
	05/17/83	106	THIRD READING
HB-0188	02/02/83	2	FIRST READING
	04/20/83	4	SECOND READING
HB-0189	02/02/83	2	FIRST READING
	05/03/83	33	OTHER
HB-0190	02/02/83	2	FIRST READING
	05/03/83	8	OTHER
HB-0191	02/02/83	2	FIRST READING
	05/03/83	33	OTHER
HB-0192	02/02/83	3	FIRST READING

PROGRAM-LRTRNMST
08/20/85
LEGISLATIVE INFORMATION SYSTEM
HOUSE OF REPRESENTATIVES
PAGE 16

MASTER TRANSCRIPT INDEX

BILL NUMBER	DATE	PAGE	ACTION
HB-0192 (cont'd)	05/03/83	33	OTHER
HB-0193	02/02/83	3	FIRST READING
	05/03/83	33	OTHER
HB-0194	02/02/83	3	FIRST READING
	05/03/83	33	OTHER
HB-0195	02/03/83	1	FIRST READING
	04/19/83	24	SECOND READING
	04/27/83	9	THIRD READING
HB-0196	02/08/83	8	FIRST READING
	04/14/83	71	SECOND READING
	04/21/83	49	THIRD READING
HB-0197	02/08/83	8	FIRST READING
	05/19/83	117	SECOND READING
HB-0198	02/08/83	8	FIRST READING
	03/09/83	30	SECOND READING
	03/14/83	36	THIRD READING
HB-0199	02/08/83	8	FIRST READING
	03/09/83	30	SECOND READING
	03/14/83	36	THIRD READING
HB-0200	02/08/83	8	FIRST READING
	05/11/83	12	SECOND READING
	05/17/83	115	THIRD READING
HB-0201	02/08/83	8	FIRST READING
HB-0202	02/08/83	9	FIRST READING
	05/03/83	32	OTHER
HB-0203	02/08/83	9	FIRST READING
	04/06/83	12	SECOND READING
	04/27/83	4	THIRD READING
HB-0204	02/08/83	9	FIRST READING
	04/28/83	20	SECOND READING
	05/05/83	31	THIRD READING
HB-0205	02/08/83	9	FIRST READING
	02/24/83	6	SECOND READING
	03/03/83	17	THIRD READING
	06/28/83	163	CONCURRENCE
	10/18/83	12	VETO MESSAGE
HB-0206	02/08/83	9	FIRST READING

MASTER TRANSCRIPT INDEX

BILL NUMBER	DATE	PAGE	ACTION
HB-0206 (cont'd)	05/05/83	6	OTHER
HB-0207	02/08/83	9	FIRST READING
	05/26/83	291	SECOND READING
	05/27/83	197	RECALLED
	05/27/83	200	THIRD READING
HB-0208	02/08/83	9	FIRST READING
	03/15/83	5	SECOND READING
	03/15/83	5	HELD ON SECOND
	04/05/83	12	SECOND READING
	04/07/83	61	THIRD READING
HB-0209	02/08/83	9	FIRST READING
HB-0210	02/08/83	9	FIRST READING
HB-0211	02/08/83	9	FIRST READING
	05/03/83	35	OTHER
HB-0212	02/08/83	9	FIRST READING
	05/06/83	35	OTHER
HB-0213	02/08/83	9	FIRST READING
	03/03/83	10	SECOND READING
	03/09/83	60	THIRD READING
	06/28/83	13	CONCURRENCE
HB-0214	02/08/83	9	FIRST READING
	05/06/83	35	OTHER
HB-0215	02/08/83	9	FIRST READING
HB-0216	02/08/83	10	FIRST READING
HB-0217	02/08/83	10	FIRST READING
	05/06/83	35	OTHER
HB-0218	02/08/83	10	FIRST READING
HB-0219	02/08/83	10	FIRST READING
HB-0220	02/08/83	10	FIRST READING
	05/19/83	118	SECOND READING
	05/19/83	118	TABLED
HB-0221	02/08/83	10	FIRST READING
HB-0222	02/08/83	10	FIRST READING
HB-0223	02/08/83	10	FIRST READING

MASTER TRANSCRIPT INDEX

BILL NUMBER	DATE	PAGE	ACTION
HB-0223 (cont'd)	04/06/83	13	SECOND READING
	04/07/83	61	THIRD READING
HB-0224	02/08/83	10	FIRST READING
	02/24/83	6	SECOND READING
	03/03/83	17	THIRD READING
HB-0225	02/08/83	10	FIRST READING
	03/08/83	19	SECOND READING
	03/09/83	29	THIRD READING
HB-0226	02/08/83	10	FIRST READING
	04/19/83	12	SECOND READING
	04/27/83	35	THIRD READING
HB-0227	02/09/83	2	FIRST READING
	03/09/83	9	SECOND READING
	03/10/83	14	THIRD READING
	06/28/83	13	CONCURRENCE
HB-0228	02/09/83	2	FIRST READING
	04/20/83	4	SECOND READING
HB-0229	02/09/83	2	FIRST READING
	05/06/83	35	OTHER
HB-0230	02/09/83	2	FIRST READING
	03/24/83	10	SECOND READING
	04/05/83	37	THIRD READING
	04/05/83	46	OTHER
	05/06/83	13	RECALLED
HB-0231	02/09/83	2	FIRST READING
	05/03/83	8	OTHER
HB-0232	02/09/83	2	FIRST READING
	05/03/83	8	OTHER
HB-0233	02/09/83	2	FIRST READING
	03/08/83	19	SECOND READING
	03/14/83	32	SECOND READING
	04/14/83	32	THIRD READING
HB-0234	02/09/83	2	FIRST READING
	05/19/83	224	SECOND READING
	05/25/83	180	THIRD READING
	06/28/83	170	CONCURRENCE
	10/20/83	43	VETO MESSAGE
HB-0235	02/09/83	2	FIRST READING
	03/15/83	5	SECOND READING

BILL NUMBER	DATE	PAGE	ACTION
HB-0235 (cont'd)	03/23/83	54	THIRD READING
	06/28/83	176	CONCURRENCE
HB-0236	02/09/83	2	FIRST READING
	03/15/83	52	SECOND READING
	04/21/83	49	THIRD READING
HB-0237	02/09/83	3	FIRST READING
	05/03/83	33	OTHER
HB-0238	02/09/83	3	FIRST READING
	05/13/83	80	SECOND READING
	05/17/83	119	THIRD READING
HB-0239	02/09/83	3	FIRST READING
	05/13/83	19	SECOND READING
	05/10/84	10	SECOND READING
HB-0240	02/09/83	3	FIRST READING
	04/20/83	11	SECOND READING
	04/21/83	24	THIRD READING
	06/28/83	14	CONCURRENCE
HB-0241	02/09/83	3	FIRST READING
	05/13/83	19	SECOND READING
	05/17/83	120	THIRD READING
HB-0242	02/09/83	3	FIRST READING
	04/06/83	13	SECOND READING
	04/07/83	67	THIRD READING
	06/28/83	14	CONCURRENCE
HB-0243	02/09/83	3	FIRST READING
	05/10/84	12	SECOND READING
	05/16/84	63	THIRD READING
	06/21/84	81	CONCURRENCE
HB-0244	02/09/83	3	FIRST READING
	05/18/83	53	SECOND READING
HB-0245	02/09/83	3	FIRST READING
	05/18/83	57	SECOND READING
HB-0246	02/09/83	3	FIRST READING
	03/16/83	12	SECOND READING
	03/23/83	62	THIRD READING
HB-0247	02/09/83	3	FIRST READING
	05/13/83	20	SECOND READING
	05/17/83	121	THIRD READING
	06/28/83	177	CONCURRENCE

BILL NUMBER	DATE	PAGE	ACTION
HB-0247 (cont'd)	10/19/83	4	VETO MESSAGE
HB-0248	02/09/83	3	FIRST READING
HB-0249	02/09/83	3	FIRST READING
HB-0250	02/09/83	4	FIRST READING
	05/11/83	14	SECOND READING
	05/18/83	270	THIRD READING
HB-0251	02/09/83	6	FIRST READING
	05/06/83	35	OTHER
HB-0252	02/09/83	6	FIRST READING
	05/20/83	123	SECOND READING
	05/24/83	186	THIRD READING
	06/24/83	227	NON-CONCURRENCE
HB-0253	02/09/83	6	FIRST READING
	05/06/83	35	OTHER
HB-0254	02/09/83	6	FIRST READING
HB-0255	02/09/83	6	FIRST READING
	03/23/83	21	SECOND READING
	04/05/83	12	SECOND READING
	04/14/83	46	THIRD READING
HB-0256	02/09/83	6	FIRST READING
HB-0257	02/09/83	6	FIRST READING
	03/22/83	26	SECOND READING
	04/13/83	20	THIRD READING
HB-0258	02/09/83	6	FIRST READING
	04/15/83	104	OTHER
HB-0259	02/09/83	7	FIRST READING
	05/03/83	5	OTHER
HB-0260	02/16/83	2	FIRST READING
	05/03/83	35	OTHER
HB-0261	02/16/83	2	FIRST READING
	05/11/83	15	SECOND READING
	05/18/83	272	THIRD READING
	06/28/83	179	CONCURRENCE
HB-0262	02/16/83	2	FIRST READING
	03/09/83	13	TABLED

BILL NUMBER	DATE	PAGE	ACTION
HB-0263	02/16/83	2	FIRST READING
HB-0264	02/16/83	2	FIRST READING
	04/05/83	16	SECOND READING
	04/13/83	29	THIRD READING
	06/28/83	180	CONCURRENCE
HB-0265	02/16/83	2	FIRST READING
	03/14/83	32	SECOND READING
	03/15/83	30	THIRD READING
	06/29/83	227	CONCURRENCE
HB-0266	02/16/83	2	FIRST READING
	03/24/83	11	SECOND READING
	04/15/83	54	THIRD READING
HB-0267	02/16/83	2	FIRST READING
	04/06/83	15	SECOND READING
	04/14/83	55	THIRD READING
	06/28/83	15	CONCURRENCE
HB-0268	02/16/83	2	FIRST READING
	03/24/83	11	SECOND READING
	04/05/83	47	THIRD READING
	06/28/83	16	CONCURRENCE
HB-0269	02/16/83	2	FIRST READING
	04/27/83	53	OTHER
HB-0270	02/16/83	2	FIRST READING
	05/11/83	6	SECOND READING
	05/17/83	123	HELD ON SECOND
	05/17/83	161	THIRD READING
	06/29/83	27	CONCURRENCE
HB-0271	02/16/83	3	FIRST READING
HB-0272	02/16/83	3	FIRST READING
	05/19/83	80	SECOND READING
HB-0273	02/16/83	3	FIRST READING
	03/15/83	6	SECOND READING
	03/16/83	24	THIRD READING
	06/30/83	95	CONCURRENCE
HB-0274	02/16/83	3	FIRST READING
	03/09/83	10	TABLED
HB-0275	02/16/83	3	FIRST READING
HB-0276	02/16/83	3	FIRST READING

BILL NUMBER	DATE	PAGE	ACTION
HB-0276 (cont'd)	04/28/83	22	SECOND READING
HB-0277	02/16/83	3	FIRST READING
	04/28/83	23	SECOND READING
HB-0278	02/16/83	3	FIRST READING
	05/03/83	13	SECOND READING
HB-0279	02/16/83	3	FIRST READING
	05/03/83	14	SECOND READING
HB-0280	02/16/83	3	FIRST READING
	05/13/83	21	SECOND READING
HB-0281	02/16/83	3	FIRST READING
	05/13/83	166	SECOND READING
HB-0282	02/16/83	3	FIRST READING
	04/28/83	23	SECOND READING
HB-0283	02/16/83	4	FIRST READING
	05/13/83	23	SECOND READING
HB-0284	02/16/83	4	FIRST READING
	05/13/83	24	SECOND READING
HB-0285	02/16/83	4	FIRST READING
	05/13/83	25	SECOND READING
HB-0286	02/16/83	4	FIRST READING
	03/23/83	32	SECOND READING
	03/24/83	20	THIRD READING
	06/28/83	17	CONCURRENCE
HB-0287	02/16/83	4	FIRST READING
HB-0288	02/16/83	4	FIRST READING
	05/04/84	8	MOTION
	05/04/84	10	OUT OF RECORD
	05/04/84	16	MOTION
HB-0289	02/16/83	4	FIRST READING
	05/19/83	118	SECOND READING
HB-0290	02/16/83	4	FIRST READING
HB-0291	02/16/83	4	FIRST READING
	04/06/83	16	SECOND READING
	04/14/83	57	RECALLED
	04/14/83	58	THIRD READING

PROGRAM-LRTRNMST
08/20/85
LEGISLATIVE INFORMATION SYSTEM
HOUSE OF REPRESENTATIVES
PAGE   23

MASTER TRANSCRIPT INDEX

BILL NUMBER	DATE	PAGE	ACTION
HB-0292	02/16/83	4	FIRST READING
	03/09/83	11	SECOND READING
	03/10/83	16	THIRD READING
	10/18/83	13	VETO MESSAGE
HB-0293	02/16/83	4	FIRST READING
	04/06/83	17	SECOND READING
	04/13/83	10	THIRD READING
HB-0294	02/16/83	4	FIRST READING
HB-0295	02/16/83	4	FIRST READING
	04/06/83	7	SECOND READING
	04/06/83	9	OTHER
	04/13/83	10	HELD ON SECOND
	04/21/83	7	SECOND READING
	04/27/83	44	THIRD READING
HB-0296	02/16/83	4	FIRST READING
	03/09/83	8	SECOND READING
	03/10/83	7	THIRD READING
HB-0297	02/16/83	4	FIRST READING
	03/15/83	6	SECOND READING
	03/16/83	28	THIRD READING
HB-0298	02/16/83	10	FIRST READING
HB-0299	02/16/83	10	FIRST READING
	03/22/83	5	SECOND READING
	03/23/83	63	THIRD READING
HB-0300	02/16/83	10	FIRST READING
	04/13/83	14	SECOND READING
	04/27/83	44	THIRD READING
HB-0301	02/16/83	10	FIRST READING
	03/03/83	17	TABLED
HB-0302	02/16/83	10	FIRST READING
	03/23/83	29	SECOND READING
	04/13/83	38	THIRD READING
HB-0303	02/16/83	10	FIRST READING
	05/06/83	35	OTHER
HB-0304	02/16/83	11	FIRST READING
	05/06/83	35	OTHER
HB-0305	02/16/83	11	FIRST READING
	03/09/83	11	SECOND READING

PROGRAM-LRTRNMST
08/20/85
LEGISLATIVE INFORMATION SYSTEM
HOUSE OF REPRESENTATIVES
PAGE   24

MASTER TRANSCRIPT INDEX

BILL NUMBER	DATE	PAGE	ACTION
HB-0305 (cont'd)	03/10/83	22	THIRD READING
HB-0306	02/16/83	11	FIRST READING
	05/06/83	35	OTHER
HB-0307	02/16/83	11	FIRST READING
	03/23/83	30	SECOND READING
	04/13/83	39	THIRD READING
	10/20/83	110	VETO MESSAGE
HB-0308	02/16/83	11	FIRST READING
	04/06/83	4	SECOND READING
	04/14/83	24	THIRD READING
HB-0309	02/16/83	11	FIRST READING
	05/03/83	12	OTHER
HB-0310	02/16/83	11	FIRST READING
	05/06/83	35	OTHER
HB-0311	02/17/83	2	FIRST READING
	03/14/83	5	SECOND READING
	03/15/83	20	THIRD READING
HB-0312	02/17/83	2	FIRST READING
	05/19/83	119	SECOND READING
	05/25/83	59	THIRD READING
	10/18/83	99	VETO MESSAGE
	10/20/83	27	VETO MESSAGE
HB-0313	02/17/83	2	FIRST READING
HB-0314	02/17/83	3	FIRST READING
HB-0315	02/17/83	3	FIRST READING
	04/28/83	24	SECOND READING
	05/18/84	134	SECOND READING
HB-0316	02/17/83	3	FIRST READING
	05/03/83	2	OTHER
HB-0317	02/17/83	3	FIRST READING
	04/05/83	17	SECOND READING
	04/13/83	40	THIRD READING
HB-0318	02/17/83	3	FIRST READING
	03/22/83	5	SECOND READING
	03/23/83	68	THIRD READING
HB-0319	02/17/83	3	FIRST READING
	03/09/83	12	SECOND READING

BILL NUMBER	DATE	PAGE	ACTION
HB-0369 (cont'd)	05/04/83	10	THIRD READING
HB-0370	02/24/83	2	FIRST READING
HB-0371	02/24/83	3	FIRST READING
	05/06/83	35	OTHER
HB-0372	02/24/83	3	FIRST READING
	03/16/83	14	SECOND READING
	03/22/83	8	THIRD READING
HB-0373	02/24/83	3	FIRST READING
	03/16/83	15	SECOND READING
	03/22/83	17	THIRD READING
	06/28/83	19	CONCURRENCE
HB-0374	02/24/83	3	FIRST READING
	03/23/83	30	SECOND READING
	03/24/83	37	THIRD READING
HB-0375	02/24/83	3	FIRST READING
	05/23/83	10	SECOND READING
	05/23/83	16	OUT OF RECORD
	05/25/83	143	SECOND READING
	05/26/83	164	THIRD READING
HB-0376	02/24/83	3	FIRST READING
	03/16/83	6	SECOND READING
	03/23/83	36	THIRD READING
HB-0377	02/24/83	3	FIRST READING
	04/19/83	13	SECOND READING
	05/04/83	13	THIRD READING
HB-0378	02/24/83	3	FIRST READING
HB-0379	02/24/83	3	FIRST READING
	04/21/83	7	SECOND READING
	05/04/83	14	THIRD READING
HB-0380	02/24/83	3	FIRST READING
	04/19/83	14	SECOND READING
	05/04/83	15	THIRD READING
	06/24/83	229	NON-CONCURRENCE
	07/01/83	284	CONFERENCE
HB-0381	02/24/83	3	FIRST READING
	04/14/83	13	SECOND READING
	05/04/83	15	THIRD READING
HB-0382	02/24/83	3	FIRST READING

BILL NUMBER	DATE	PAGE	ACTION
HB-0383	02/24/83	3	FIRST READING
	03/14/83	33	SECOND READING
	03/14/83	34	OUT OF RECORD
	03/14/83	37	SECOND READING
	03/15/83	41	THIRD READING
HB-0384	02/24/83	4	FIRST READING
	03/23/83	31	SECOND READING
	03/24/83	38	RECALLED
	03/24/83	39	THIRD READING
	06/27/83	169	CONCURRENCE
HB-0385	02/24/83	4	FIRST READING
	05/11/83	15	SECOND READING
	05/18/83	282	THIRD READING
	06/29/83	236	CONCURRENCE
HB-0386	02/24/83	4	FIRST READING
	03/14/83	5	SECOND READING
	03/16/83	18	THIRD READING
HB-0387	02/24/83	4	FIRST READING
	04/06/83	20	SECOND READING
	04/27/83	55	RECALLED
	04/28/83	25	SECOND READING
	05/04/83	19	THIRD READING
HB-0388	02/24/83	4	FIRST READING
HB-0389	02/24/83	4	FIRST READING
	05/06/83	35	OTHER
HB-0390	02/24/83	4	FIRST READING
	03/14/83	30	SECOND READING
	03/15/83	22	THIRD READING
	06/29/83	30	CONCURRENCE
	10/18/83	14	VETO MESSAGE
HB-0391	02/24/83	4	FIRST READING
	05/11/83	15	SECOND READING
	05/18/83	283	THIRD READING
HB-0392	02/24/83	11	FIRST READING
	04/15/83	12	TABLED
HB-0393	02/24/83	11	FIRST READING
HB-0394	02/24/83	11	FIRST READING
	05/03/83	27	SECOND READING
	05/03/83	31	TABLED

PROGRAM-LRTRNMST
08/20/85

LEGISLATIVE INFORMATION SYSTEM
HOUSE OF REPRESENTATIVES

PAGE   23

MASTER TRANSCRIPT INDEX

BILL NUMBER	DATE	PAGE	ACTION
HB-0292	02/16/83	4	FIRST READING
	03/09/83	11	SECOND READING
	03/10/83	16	THIRD READING
	10/18/83	13	VETO MESSAGE
HB-0293	02/16/83	4	FIRST READING
	04/06/83	17	SECOND READING
	04/13/83	20	THIRD READING
HB-0294	02/16/83	4	FIRST READING
HB-0295	02/16/83	4	FIRST READING
	04/06/83	7	SECOND READING
	04/06/83	9	OTHER
	04/13/83	10	HELD ON SECOND
	04/21/83	7	SECOND READING
	04/27/83	44	THIRD READING
HB-0296	02/16/83	4	FIRST READING
	03/09/83	8	SECOND READING
	03/10/83	7	THIRD READING
HB-0297	02/16/83	4	FIRST READING
	03/15/83	6	SECOND READING
	03/16/83	28	THIRD READING
HB-0298	02/16/83	10	FIRST READING
HB-0299	02/16/83	10	FIRST READING
	03/22/83	5	SECOND READING
	03/23/83	63	THIRD READING
HB-0300	02/16/83	10	FIRST READING
	04/13/83	14	SECOND READING
	04/27/83	44	THIRD READING
HB-0301	02/16/83	10	FIRST READING
	03/03/83	17	TABLED
HB-0302	02/16/83	10	FIRST READING
	03/23/83	29	SECOND READING
	04/13/83	38	THIRD READING
HB-0303	02/16/83	10	FIRST READING
	05/06/83	35	OTHER
HB-0304	02/16/83	11	FIRST READING
	05/06/83	35	OTHER
HB-0305	02/16/83	11	FIRST READING
	03/09/83	11	SECOND READING

PROGRAM-LRTRNMST
08/20/85

LEGISLATIVE INFORMATION SYSTEM
HOUSE OF REPRESENTATIVES

PAGE   24

MASTER TRANSCRIPT INDEX

BILL NUMBER	DATE	PAGE	ACTION
HB-0305 (cont'd)	03/10/83	22	THIRD READING
HB-0306	02/16/83	11	FIRST READING
	05/06/83	35	OTHER
HB-0307	02/16/83	11	FIRST READING
	03/23/83	30	SECOND READING
	04/13/83	39	THIRD READING
	10/20/83	110	VETO MESSAGE
HB-0308	02/16/83	11	FIRST READING
	04/06/83	4	SECOND READING
	04/14/83	24	THIRD READING
HB-0309	02/16/83	11	FIRST READING
	05/03/83	12	OTHER
HB-0310	02/16/83	11	FIRST READING
	05/06/83	35	OTHER
HB-0311	02/17/83	2	FIRST READING
	03/14/83	5	SECOND READING
	03/15/83	20	THIRD READING
HB-0312	02/17/83	2	FIRST READING
	05/19/83	119	SECOND READING
	05/25/83	59	THIRD READING
	10/18/83	99	VETO MESSAGE
	10/20/83	27	VETO MESSAGE
HB-0313	02/17/83	2	FIRST READING
HB-0314	02/17/83	3	FIRST READING
HB-0315	02/17/83	3	FIRST READING
	04/28/83	24	SECOND READING
	05/18/84	134	SECOND READING
HB-0316	02/17/83	3	FIRST READING
	05/03/83	2	OTHER
HB-0317	02/17/83	3	FIRST READING
	04/05/83	17	SECOND READING
	04/13/83	40	THIRD READING
HB-0318	02/17/83	3	FIRST READING
	03/22/83	5	SECOND READING
	03/23/83	68	THIRD READING
HB-0319	02/17/83	3	FIRST READING
	03/09/83	12	SECOND READING

MASTER TRANSCRIPT INDEX

BILL NUMBER	DATE	PAGE	ACTION
HB-0319 (cont'd)	03/14/83	14	THIRD READING
	03/14/83	29	OUT OF RECORD
	03/23/83	73	RECALLED
	03/24/83	47	MOTION
	03/24/83	48	RECALLED
	04/07/83	7	SECOND READING
	04/15/83	59	THIRD READING
HB-0320	02/17/83	3	FIRST READING
	03/09/83	8	SECOND READING
	03/10/83	9	THIRD READING
	06/28/83	185	CONCURRENCE
	07/02/83	109	CONFERENCE
	10/19/83	220	MOTION
	11/03/83	24	CONFERENCE
HB-0321	02/17/83	3	FIRST READING
	05/11/83	12	SECOND READING
	05/17/83	123	THIRD READING
	06/28/83	186	CONCURRENCE
	06/28/83	190	OUT OF RECORD
	06/28/83	203	CONCURRENCE
HB-0322	02/17/83	3	FIRST READING
HB-0323	02/17/83	3	FIRST READING
HB-0324	02/17/83	3	FIRST READING
	05/03/83	7	OTHER
HB-0325	02/17/83	3	FIRST READING
HB-0326	02/17/83	3	FIRST READING
HB-0327	02/17/83	3	FIRST READING
	03/02/83	42	SECOND READING
	03/03/83	14	THIRD READING
	03/24/83	24	MOTION
	03/24/83	25	CONCURRENCE
HB-0328	02/17/83	28	FIRST READING
	06/25/83	2	MOTION
	05/10/84	13	SECOND READING
	05/10/84	15	HELD ON SECOND
	05/16/84	245	SECOND READING
HB-0329	02/17/83	29	FIRST READING
	04/05/83	23	SECOND READING
	04/06/83	46	THIRD READING
HB-0330	02/17/83	29	FIRST READING

MASTER TRANSCRIPT INDEX

BILL NUMBER	DATE	PAGE	ACTION
HB-0331	02/17/83	29	FIRST READING
	04/06/83	19	SECOND READING
	04/15/83	68	THIRD READING
HB-0332	02/17/83	29	FIRST READING
	04/06/83	19	SECOND READING
	04/15/83	69	THIRD READING
HB-0333	02/17/83	29	FIRST READING
	03/16/83	13	SECOND READING
	03/23/83	81	THIRD READING
	06/28/83	195	OUT OF RECORD
	06/28/83	215	CONCURRENCE
	10/19/83	6	VETO MESSAGE
HB-0334	02/17/83	29	FIRST READING
HB-0335	02/17/83	29	FIRST READING
HB-0336	02/17/83	29	FIRST READING
	05/19/83	124	SECOND READING
	05/19/83	250	MOTION
	05/24/83	198	THIRD READING
	12/12/84	7	MOTION
	12/12/84	38	MOTION
	01/09/85	11	MOTION
	01/09/85	13	CONCURRENCE
HB-0337	02/17/83	29	FIRST READING
	03/14/83	33	SECOND READING
	04/15/83	69	THIRD READING
HB-0338	02/17/83	29	FIRST READING
	05/13/83	26	SECOND READING
	05/13/83	29	HELD ON SECOND
	05/18/83	58	SECOND READING
	05/10/84	15	SECOND READING
	05/10/84	15	HELD ON SECOND
	05/18/84	151	SECOND READING
	05/22/84	103	THIRD READING
HB-0339	02/17/83	29	FIRST READING
HB-0340	02/17/83	29	FIRST READING
	03/15/83	57	SECOND READING
	03/16/83	33	THIRD READING
HB-0341	02/17/83	29	FIRST READING
HB-0342	02/17/83	29	FIRST READING

BILL NUMBER	DATE	PAGE	ACTION
HB-0342 (cont'd)	03/10/83	7	TABLED
HB-0343	02/17/83	30	FIRST READING
	05/13/83	29	SECOND READING
	05/17/83	125	THIRD READING
HB-0344	02/17/83	30	FIRST READING
	04/14/83	71	SECOND READING
	04/21/83	49	THIRD READING
HB-0345	02/17/83	30	FIRST READING
	05/11/83	15	SECOND READING
	05/18/83	279	THIRD READING
	06/24/83	233	NON-CONCURRENCE
	07/01/83	113	CONFERENCE
HB-0346	02/17/83	30	FIRST READING
	03/15/83	4	SECOND READING
	03/16/83	16	THIRD READING
HB-0347	02/17/83	30	FIRST READING
	04/19/83	13	SECOND READING
	04/27/83	45	THIRD READING
HB-0348	02/23/83	2	FIRST READING
HB-0349	02/23/83	17	FIRST READING
	04/06/83	43	SECOND READING
	04/15/83	82	THIRD READING
	06/28/83	198	CONCURRENCE
	10/19/83	126	VETO MESSAGE
HB-0350	02/23/83	18	FIRST READING
	02/24/83	8	MOTION
	03/09/83	12	SECOND READING
	03/10/83	24	THIRD READING
HB-0351	02/23/83	18	FIRST READING
	04/15/83	27	SECOND READING
	04/28/83	105	THIRD READING
	06/28/83	190	CONCURRENCE
HB-0352	02/23/83	18	FIRST READING
	03/15/83	7	SECOND READING
	03/16/83	38	THIRD READING
HB-0353	02/23/83	18	FIRST READING
HB-0354	02/23/83	18	FIRST READING
HB-0355	02/23/83	18	FIRST READING

BILL NUMBER	DATE	PAGE	ACTION
HB-0355 (cont'd)	03/15/83	7	SECOND READING
	03/16/83	39	THIRD READING
HB-0356	02/23/83	18	FIRST READING
	03/22/83	27	SECOND READING
	03/24/83	31	THIRD READING
HB-0357	02/23/83	18	FIRST READING
	04/05/83	18	SECOND READING
	04/15/83	89	THIRD READING
HB-0358	02/23/83	18	FIRST READING
HB-0359	02/23/83	18	FIRST READING
	05/13/83	58	SECOND READING
	05/17/83	128	THIRD READING
HB-0360	02/23/83	18	FIRST READING
	03/15/83	4	SECOND READING
	03/16/83	17	THIRD READING
HB-0361	02/23/83	18	FIRST READING
	04/26/83	17	SECOND READING
	04/28/83	106	THIRD READING
HB-0362	02/23/83	18	FIRST READING
	05/13/83	59	SECOND READING
HB-0363	02/23/83	18	FIRST READING
HB-0364	02/23/83	19	FIRST READING
HB-0365	02/23/83	19	FIRST READING
HB-0366	02/23/83	19	FIRST READING
	04/06/83	20	SECOND READING
	05/04/83	9	THIRD READING
	10/18/83	95	VETO MESSAGE
HB-0367	02/23/83	21	FIRST READING
	05/11/83	7	SECOND READING
	05/24/83	203	THIRD READING
	06/24/83	228	NON-CONCURRENCE
HB-0368	02/23/83	21	FIRST READING
	05/11/83	8	SECOND READING
	05/24/83	216	THIRD READING
	06/24/83	228	NON-CONCURRENCE
HB-0369	02/24/83	2	FIRST READING
	04/06/83	20	SECOND READING

PROGRAM-LRTRNMST
08/20/85

LEGISLATIVE INFORMATION SYSTEM
HOUSE OF REPRESENTATIVES

PAGE   29

MASTER TRANSCRIPT INDEX

BILL NUMBER	DATE	PAGE	ACTION
HB-0369 (cont'd)	05/04/83	10	THIRD READING
HB-0370	02/24/83	2	FIRST READING
HB-0371	02/24/83	3	FIRST READING
	05/06/83	35	OTHER
HB-0372	02/24/83	3	FIRST READING
	03/16/83	14	SECOND READING
	03/22/83	8	THIRD READING
HB-0373	02/24/83	3	FIRST READING
	03/16/83	15	SECOND READING
	03/22/83	17	THIRD READING
	06/28/83	19	CONCURRENCE
HB-0374	02/24/83	3	FIRST READING
	03/23/83	30	SECOND READING
	03/24/83	37	THIRD READING
HB-0375	02/24/83	3	FIRST READING
	05/23/83	10	SECOND READING
	05/23/83	16	OUT OF RECORD
	05/24/83	143	SECOND READING
	05/26/83	164	THIRD READING
HB-0376	02/24/83	3	FIRST READING
	03/16/83	6	SECOND READING
	03/23/83	36	THIRD READING
HB-0377	02/24/83	3	FIRST READING
	04/19/83	13	SECOND READING
	05/04/83	13	THIRD READING
HB-0378	02/24/83	3	FIRST READING
HB-0379	02/24/83	3	FIRST READING
	04/21/83	7	SECOND READING
	05/04/83	14	THIRD READING
HB-0380	02/24/83	3	FIRST READING
	04/19/83	14	SECOND READING
	05/04/83	15	THIRD READING
	06/24/83	229	NON-CONCURRENCE
	07/01/83	284	CONFERENCE
HB-0381	02/24/83	3	FIRST READING
	04/14/83	13	SECOND READING
	05/04/83	15	THIRD READING
HB-0382	02/24/83	3	FIRST READING

PROGRAM-LRTRNMST
08/20/85

LEGISLATIVE INFORMATION SYSTEM
HOUSE OF REPRESENTATIVES

PAGE   30

MASTER TRANSCRIPT INDEX

BILL NUMBER	DATE	PAGE	ACTION
HB-0383	02/24/83	3	FIRST READING
	03/14/83	33	SECOND READING
	03/14/83	34	OUT OF RECORD
	03/14/83	37	SECOND READING
	03/15/83	41	THIRD READING
HB-0384	02/24/83	4	FIRST READING
	03/23/83	31	SECOND READING
	03/24/83	38	RECALLED
	03/24/83	39	THIRD READING
	06/27/83	169	CONCURRENCE
HB-0385	02/24/83	4	FIRST READING
	05/11/83	15	SECOND READING
	05/18/83	282	THIRD READING
	06/29/83	236	CONCURRENCE
HB-0386	02/24/83	4	FIRST READING
	03/14/83	5	SECOND READING
	03/16/83	18	THIRD READING
HB-0387	02/24/83	4	FIRST READING
	04/06/83	20	SECOND READING
	04/27/83	55	RECALLED
	04/28/83	25	SECOND READING
	05/04/83	19	THIRD READING
HB-0388	02/24/83	4	FIRST READING
HB-0389	02/24/83	4	FIRST READING
	05/06/83	35	OTHER
HB-0390	02/24/83	4	FIRST READING
	03/14/83	30	SECOND READING
	03/15/83	22	THIRD READING
	06/29/83	30	CONCURRENCE
	10/18/83	14	VETO MESSAGE
HB-0391	02/24/83	4	FIRST READING
	05/11/83	15	SECOND READING
	05/18/83	283	THIRD READING
HB-0392	02/24/83	11	FIRST READING
	04/15/83	12	TABLED
HB-0393	02/24/83	11	FIRST READING
HB-0394	02/24/83	11	FIRST READING
	05/03/83	27	SECOND READING
	05/03/83	31	TABLED

PROGRAM-LRTRNMST
08/20/85

LEGISLATIVE INFORMATION SYSTEM
HOUSE OF REPRESENTATIVES

PAGE   31

MASTER TRANSCRIPT INDEX

BILL NUMBER	DATE	PAGE	ACTION
HB-0395	02/24/83	12	FIRST READING
	05/13/83	167	SECOND READING
	05/18/83	283	THIRD READING
HB-0396	02/24/83	12	FIRST READING
	03/09/83	13	TABLED
HB-0397	02/24/83	12	FIRST READING
HB-0398	02/24/83	12	FIRST READING
	04/14/83	13	SECOND READING
	05/04/83	22	THIRD READING
HB-0399	02/24/83	12	FIRST READING
	05/03/83	5	OTHER
HB-0400	02/24/83	12	FIRST READING
	03/15/83	8	SECOND READING
	03/22/83	21	THIRD READING
	06/28/83	145	CONCURRENCE
HB-0401	02/24/83	12	FIRST READING
	04/14/83	13	SECOND READING
	05/04/83	24	THIRD READING
HB-0402	02/24/83	12	FIRST READING
	05/25/83	304	SECOND READING
	05/25/83	304	HELD ON SECOND
HB-0403	02/24/83	12	FIRST READING
	04/14/83	14	SECOND READING
	05/04/83	25	THIRD READING
HB-0404	02/24/83	12	FIRST READING
	03/23/83	19	SECOND READING
	03/24/83	23	THIRD READING
	06/28/83	20	CONCURRENCE
HB-0405	02/24/83	12	FIRST READING
	05/06/83	35	OTHER
HB-0406	02/24/83	12	FIRST READING
	04/06/83	20	SECOND READING
	05/04/83	38	THIRD READING
	06/28/83	4	CONCURRENCE
	06/30/83	115	CONFERENCE
	10/20/83	5	VETO MESSAGE
HB-0407	02/24/83	13	FIRST READING
	05/06/83	35	OTHER

PROGRAM-LRTRNMST
08/20/85

LEGISLATIVE INFORMATION SYSTEM
HOUSE OF REPRESENTATIVES

PAGE   32

MASTER TRANSCRIPT INDEX

BILL NUMBER	DATE	PAGE	ACTION
HB-0408	02/24/83	13	FIRST READING
	04/05/83	19	SECOND READING
	05/04/83	43	THIRD READING
HB-0409	02/24/83	13	FIRST READING
	04/21/83	8	SECOND READING
	05/04/83	44	THIRD READING
HB-0410	02/24/83	13	FIRST READING
HB-0411	02/24/83	13	FIRST READING
	03/14/83	7	SECOND READING
	03/15/83	43	THIRD READING
HB-0412	02/24/83	13	FIRST READING
	04/06/83	21	SECOND READING
	05/04/83	46	THIRD READING
	10/19/83	213	VETO MESSAGE
HB-0413	02/24/83	13	FIRST READING
	05/05/83	6	OTHER
HB-0414	02/24/83	13	FIRST READING
	03/01/83	20	MOTION
	03/09/83	30	SECOND READING
	03/14/83	36	THIRD READING
HB-0415	02/24/83	13	FIRST READING
	03/16/83	7	SECOND READING
	03/22/83	6	THIRD READING
	06/29/83	41	CONCURRENCE
HB-0416	02/24/83	13	FIRST READING
	03/15/83	4	SECOND READING
	03/16/83	19	THIRD READING
HB-0417	02/24/83	13	FIRST READING
	04/06/83	21	SECOND READING
	05/04/83	47	THIRD READING
	06/28/83	147	CONCURRENCE
	10/20/83	46	VETO MESSAGE
HB-0418	02/24/83	13	FIRST READING
HB-0419	02/24/83	13	FIRST READING
HB-0420	02/24/83	14	FIRST READING
HB-0421	02/24/83	14	FIRST READING
HB-0422	02/24/83	14	FIRST READING

PROGRAM-LRTRNMST
08/20/85
LEGISLATIVE INFORMATION SYSTEM
HOUSE OF REPRESENTATIVES
PAGE 33

MASTER TRANSCRIPT INDEX

BILL NUMBER	DATE	PAGE	ACTION
HB-0422 (cont'd)	04/06/83	22	SECOND READING
	05/05/83	33	THIRD READING
HB-0423	02/24/83	14	FIRST READING
HB-0424	02/24/83	14	FIRST READING
	05/13/83	59	SECOND READING
	05/13/83	61	HELD ON SECOND
	05/19/83	128	SECOND READING
	05/19/83	129	HELD ON SECOND
	05/19/83	249	SECOND READING
	05/24/83	118	THIRD READING
HB-0425	02/24/83	14	FIRST READING
HB-0426	02/24/83	14	FIRST READING
	04/06/83	5	SECOND READING
	04/14/83	26	THIRD READING
HB-0427	02/24/83	14	FIRST READING
	03/15/83	8	SECOND READING
	03/16/83	40	THIRD READING
	06/28/83	22	CONCURRENCE
HB-0428	02/24/83	14	FIRST READING
	05/13/83	187	SECOND READING
	05/18/83	285	THIRD READING
HB-0429	02/24/83	14	FIRST READING
	04/14/83	14	SECOND READING
	05/05/83	36	THIRD READING
HB-0430	03/01/83	2	FIRST READING
HB-0431	03/01/83	2	FIRST READING
	05/06/83	35	OTHER
HB-0432	03/01/83	2	FIRST READING
	05/06/83	35	OTHER
HB-0433	03/01/83	2	FIRST READING
	04/28/83	6	SECOND READING
	05/10/83	13	THIRD READING
HB-0434	03/01/83	2	FIRST READING
	05/26/83	306	FIRST READING
HB-0435	03/01/83	3	FIRST READING
	05/04/84	35	MOTION
HB-0436	03/01/83	3	FIRST READING

PROGRAM-LRTRNMST
08/20/85
LEGISLATIVE INFORMATION SYSTEM
HOUSE OF REPRESENTATIVES
PAGE 34

MASTER TRANSCRIPT INDEX

BILL NUMBER	DATE	PAGE	ACTION
HB-0437	03/01/83	3	FIRST READING
HB-0438	03/01/83	3	FIRST READING
	04/14/83	71	SECOND READING
	04/21/83	49	THIRD READING
	06/28/83	24	CONCURRENCE
HB-0439	03/01/83	3	FIRST READING
	04/21/83	9	SECOND READING
	05/05/83	37	THIRD READING
	10/19/83	133	VETO MESSAGE
HB-0440	03/01/83	3	FIRST READING
	04/21/83	47	SECOND READING
	04/27/83	51	THIRD READING
	06/28/83	24	CONCURRENCE
HB-0441	03/01/83	3	FIRST READING
	04/28/83	6	SECOND READING
	05/05/83	48	RECALLED
	05/05/83	50	THIRD READING
	06/28/83	26	CONCURRENCE
	10/18/83	15	VETO MESSAGE
	10/19/83	72	VETO MESSAGE
HB-0442	03/01/83	3	FIRST READING
HB-0443	03/01/83	23	FIRST READING
	04/06/83	42	SECOND READING
	05/05/83	51	THIRD READING
HB-0444	03/01/83	23	FIRST READING
HB-0445	03/01/83	23	FIRST READING
HB-0446	03/01/83	24	FIRST READING
	04/05/83	19	SECOND READING
	05/05/83	53	THIRD READING
	06/29/83	42	CONCURRENCE
HB-0447	03/01/83	24	FIRST READING
	03/22/83	6	SECOND READING
	04/05/83	48	RECALLED
	05/10/83	77	THIRD READING
HB-0448	03/01/83	24	FIRST READING
HB-0449	03/01/83	24	FIRST READING
HB-0450	03/01/83	24	FIRST READING
	04/14/83	7	SECOND READING

PROGRAM-LRTRNMST
08/20/85

LEGISLATIVE INFORMATION SYSTEM
HOUSE OF REPRESENTATIVES

PAGE   35

MASTER TRANSCRIPT INDEX

BILL NUMBER	DATE	PAGE	ACTION
HB-0450 (cont'd)	04/19/83	33	THIRD READING
	06/28/83	30	CONCURRENCE
HB-0451	03/01/83	24	FIRST READING
	04/05/83	9	SECOND READING
	04/06/83	47	THIRD READING
HB-0452	03/01/83	4	FIRST READING
	05/11/83	6	SECOND READING
	05/18/83	216	THIRD READING
HB-0453	03/01/83	5	FIRST READING
HB-0454	03/01/83	25	FIRST READING
	04/07/83	12	SECOND READING
	04/15/83	27	SECOND READING
	05/10/83	81	THIRD READING
HB-0455	03/01/83	25	FIRST READING
	04/06/83	23	SECOND READING
	05/10/83	91	THIRD READING
	06/28/83	31	CONCURRENCE
HB-0456	03/01/83	25	FIRST READING
	05/11/83	8	SECOND READING
HB-0457	03/02/83	3	FIRST READING
HB-0458	03/02/83	3	FIRST READING
HB-0459	03/02/83	3	FIRST READING
	04/13/83	11	SECOND READING
	04/27/83	54	RECALLED
	04/28/83	26	SECOND READING
	05/10/83	101	THIRD READING
	06/28/83	34	CONCURRENCE
HB-0460	03/02/83	3	FIRST READING
HB-0461	03/02/83	3	FIRST READING
	04/21/83	9	SECOND READING
	05/10/83	104	THIRD READING
HB-0462	03/02/83	3	FIRST READING
	04/05/83	9	SECOND READING
	04/07/83	33	THIRD READING
HB-0463	03/02/83	4	FIRST READING
	05/19/83	129	SECOND READING
HB-0464	03/02/83	4	FIRST READING

PROGRAM-LRTRNMST
08/20/85

LEGISLATIVE INFORMATION SYSTEM
HOUSE OF REPRESENTATIVES

PAGE   36

MASTER TRANSCRIPT INDEX

BILL NUMBER	DATE	PAGE	ACTION
HB-0465	03/02/83	4	FIRST READING
	04/13/83	8	SECOND READING
	04/14/83	28	THIRD READING
	06/25/83	74	NON-CONCURRENCE
	07/01/83	257	CONFERENCE
HB-0466	03/02/83	4	FIRST READING
	05/03/83	16	SECOND READING
	05/10/83	10	THIRD READING
HB-0467	03/02/83	4	FIRST READING
	04/21/83	9	SECOND READING
	05/10/83	105	THIRD READING
HB-0468	03/02/83	4	FIRST READING
	05/11/83	8	SECOND READING
HB-0469	03/02/83	4	FIRST READING
	05/11/83	8	SECOND READING
HB-0470	03/02/83	4	FIRST READING
	04/14/83	71	SECOND READING
	04/21/83	49	THIRD READING
	06/28/83	199	CONCURRENCE
HB-0471	03/02/83	4	FIRST READING
	05/13/83	79	SECOND READING
	05/27/83	94	THIRD READING
HB-0472	03/02/83	4	FIRST READING
HB-0473	03/02/83	4	FIRST READING
	05/03/83	35	OTHER
HB-0474	03/02/83	4	FIRST READING
	05/13/83	60	SECOND READING
HB-0475	03/02/83	47	FIRST READING
	04/26/83	4	SECOND READING
	04/28/83	95	THIRD READING
	06/28/83	201	CONCURRENCE
HB-0476	03/02/83	47	FIRST READING
HB-0477	03/02/83	47	FIRST READING
	04/15/83	28	SECOND READING
	05/10/83	108	THIRD READING
HB-0478	03/02/83	47	FIRST READING
HB-0479	03/02/83	47	FIRST READING

BILL NUMBER	DATE	PAGE	ACTION
HB-0479 (cont'd)	04/20/83	4	SECOND READING
HB-0480	03/02/83	47	FIRST READING
HB-0481	03/02/83	47	FIRST READING
	05/18/83	32	SECOND READING
	05/23/83	99	THIRD READING
HB-0482	03/02/83	47	FIRST READING
	04/06/83	5	SECOND READING
	04/07/83	36	THIRD READING
	10/19/83	125	VETO MESSAGE
HB-0483	03/02/83	48	FIRST READING
	04/06/83	5	SECOND READING
	04/07/83	37	THIRD READING
HB-0484	03/02/83	48	FIRST READING
HB-0485	03/02/83	48	FIRST READING
	04/26/83	4	SECOND READING
	04/28/83	97	THIRD READING
HB-0486	03/02/83	48	FIRST READING
	04/07/83	26	SECOND READING
	04/13/83	59	TABLED
HB-0487	03/02/83	48	FIRST READING
	05/13/83	169	SECOND READING
	05/18/83	288	THIRD READING
	06/28/83	16	CONCURRENCE
	10/18/83	100	VETO MESSAGE
HB-0488	03/02/83	48	FIRST READING
	04/06/83	24	SECOND READING
	05/10/83	116	THIRD READING
	06/28/83	37	CONCURRENCE
	10/18/83	102	VETO MESSAGE
	10/18/83	103	OUT OF RECORD
	10/18/83	110	VETO MESSAGE
HB-0489	03/02/83	48	FIRST READING
	05/11/83	9	SECOND READING
HB-0490	03/02/83	48	FIRST READING
	05/25/83	299	SECOND READING
HB-0491	03/02/83	48	FIRST READING
	03/10/83	7	TABLED
HB-0492	03/02/83	48	FIRST READING

BILL NUMBER	DATE	PAGE	ACTION
HB-0492 (cont'd)	05/03/83	31	OTHER
HB-0493	03/02/83	48	FIRST READING
	05/06/83	35	OTHER
HB-0494	03/02/83	48	FIRST READING
	05/13/83	61	SECOND READING
HB-0495	03/02/83	48	FIRST READING
	04/15/83	28	SECOND READING
	05/10/83	120	THIRD READING
HB-0496	03/02/83	48	FIRST READING
HB-0497	03/03/83	2	FIRST READING
HB-0498	03/03/83	2	FIRST READING
	04/14/83	71	SECOND READING
	04/21/83	49	THIRD READING
	06/28/83	35	CONCURRENCE
HB-0499	03/03/83	2	FIRST READING
	04/13/83	9	SECOND READING
	04/15/83	34	THIRD READING
HB-0500	03/03/83	2	FIRST READING
	04/28/83	112	SECOND READING
	05/05/83	7	THIRD READING
HB-0501	03/03/83	2	FIRST READING
	04/19/83	7	SECOND READING
	04/21/83	46	THIRD READING
HB-0502	03/03/83	2	FIRST READING
	05/13/83	170	SECOND READING
	05/18/83	289	THIRD READING
HB-0503	03/03/83	2	FIRST READING
	05/13/83	170	SECOND READING
	05/20/83	7	THIRD READING
HB-0504	03/03/83	2	FIRST READING
	04/13/83	8	SECOND READING
	04/14/83	28	THIRD READING
HB-0505	03/03/83	2	FIRST READING
	04/14/83	71	SECOND READING
	04/21/83	49	THIRD READING
HB-0506	03/03/83	2	FIRST READING
	04/13/83	15	HELD ON SECOND

BILL NUMBER	DATE	PAGE	ACTION
HB-0506 (cont'd)	04/14/83	8	SECOND READING
	04/19/83	34	RECALLED
	04/27/83	55	RECALLED
	04/28/83	96	SECOND READING
	05/10/83	14	RECALLED
	05/20/83	103	THIRD READING
HB-0507	03/03/83	2	FIRST READING
	04/19/83	29	SECOND READING
	05/10/83	121	THIRD READING
HB-0508	03/03/83	2	FIRST READING
HB-0509	03/03/83	2	FIRST READING
	05/11/83	9	SECOND READING
HB-0510	03/03/83	3	FIRST READING
	04/06/83	5	SECOND READING
	04/07/83	38	THIRD READING
HB-0511	03/03/83	3	FIRST READING
	04/06/83	25	SECOND READING
	05/05/83	55	RECALLED
	05/10/83	122	THIRD READING
HB-0512	03/03/83	3	FIRST READING
	05/05/83	2	SECOND READING
	05/13/83	2	THIRD READING
HB-0513	03/03/83	3	FIRST READING
HB-0514	03/03/83	3	FIRST READING
	04/15/83	29	SECOND READING
	05/03/83	36	SECOND READING
	05/10/83	122	THIRD READING
	06/27/83	169	CONCURRENCE
	06/27/83	170	OUT OF RECORD
	06/27/83	174	CONCURRENCE
	06/30/83	156	CONFERENCE
	06/30/83	160	OUT OF RECORD
HB-0515	03/03/83	21	FIRST READING
	05/03/83	6	OTHER
HB-0516	03/03/83	21	FIRST READING
	05/11/83	16	SECOND READING
	05/20/83	10	THIRD READING
	06/24/83	232	NON-CONCURRENCE
	07/01/83	203	CONFERENCE
HB-0517	03/03/83	21	FIRST READING

BILL NUMBER	DATE	PAGE	ACTION
HB-0517 (cont'd)	04/13/83	14	SECOND READING
	05/10/83	123	THIRD READING
HB-0518	03/03/83	21	FIRST READING
HB-0519	03/03/83	21	FIRST READING
	04/28/83	27	SECOND READING
	05/10/83	125	THIRD READING
HB-0520	03/03/83	21	FIRST READING
	04/06/83	6	SECOND READING
	04/07/83	39	THIRD READING
	06/28/83	36	CONCURRENCE
HB-0521	03/03/83	21	FIRST READING
	05/06/83	35	OTHER
HB-0522	03/03/83	21	FIRST READING
	04/20/83	12	SECOND READING
	04/28/83	99	THIRD READING
HB-0523	03/03/83	21	FIRST READING
HB-0524	03/03/83	21	FIRST READING
	04/06/83	25	SECOND READING
	05/10/83	128	THIRD READING
HB-0525	03/03/83	21	FIRST READING
HB-0526	03/03/83	21	FIRST READING
HB-0527	03/03/83	21	FIRST READING
	05/06/83	35	OTHER
HB-0528	03/03/83	22	FIRST READING
	04/06/83	26	SECOND READING
	05/10/83	129	THIRD READING
HB-0529	03/08/83	2	FIRST READING
HB-0530	03/08/83	2	FIRST READING
	04/06/83	33	SECOND READING
	04/07/83	40	THIRD READING
HB-0531	03/08/83	2	FIRST READING
	04/14/83	15	SECOND READING
	05/11/83	191	THIRD READING
	02/08/84	26	CONCURRENCE
HB-0532	03/08/83	2	FIRST READING
	04/07/83	27	SECOND READING

BILL NUMBER	DATE	PAGE	ACTION
HB-0533	03/08/83	3	FIRST READING
	04/07/83	27	SECOND READING
HB-0534	03/08/83	3	FIRST READING
	04/27/83	53	OTHER
HB-0535	03/08/83	3	FIRST READING
HB-0536	03/08/83	3	FIRST READING
	04/26/83	17	TABLED
HB-0537	03/08/83	27	FIRST READING
	05/03/83	36	SECOND READING
	05/10/83	132	THIRD READING
	06/29/83	46	CONCURRENCE
	10/19/83	109	VETO MESSAGE
HB-0538	03/08/83	27	FIRST READING
	05/03/83	36	SECOND READING
	05/10/83	132	THIRD READING
HB-0539	03/08/83	27	FIRST READING
	05/13/83	62	SECOND READING
	05/27/83	201	THIRD READING
HB-0540	03/08/83	27	FIRST READING
HB-0541	03/08/83	27	FIRST READING
	04/14/83	16	SECOND READING
	04/15/83	98	THIRD READING
	06/29/83	88	CONCURRENCE
	10/18/83	60	MOTION
	11/04/83	84	CONFERENCE
HB-0542	03/08/83	27	FIRST READING
	04/14/83	16	SECOND READING
	04/15/83	98	THIRD READING
	06/29/83	88	CONCURRENCE
	10/19/83	91	VETO MESSAGE
HB-0543	03/08/83	27	FIRST READING
	04/15/83	37	SECOND READING
	04/20/83	7	THIRD READING
	06/29/83	88	CONCURRENCE
	07/02/83	43	CONFERENCE
	10/19/83	155	VETO MESSAGE
HB-0544	03/08/83	27	FIRST READING
	05/19/83	130	SECOND READING
HB-0545	03/08/83	28	FIRST READING

BILL NUMBER	DATE	PAGE	ACTION
HB-0546	03/08/83	28	FIRST READING
	04/14/83	71	SECOND READING
	04/21/83	49	THIRD READING
	06/28/83	39	CONCURRENCE
HB-0547	03/08/83	28	FIRST READING
	04/14/83	64	SECOND READING
	04/15/83	99	THIRD READING
	05/12/83	187	CONCURRENCE
HB-0548	03/08/83	28	FIRST READING
	05/13/83	171	SECOND READING
	05/20/83	27	THIRD READING
HB-0549	03/08/83	28	FIRST READING
HB-0550	03/08/83	28	FIRST READING
	05/11/83	10	SECOND READING
HB-0551	03/08/83	28	FIRST READING
	05/13/83	81	SECOND READING
	05/13/83	81	OUT OF RECORD
	05/13/83	92	SECOND READING
	05/02/84	8	SECOND READING
	05/03/84	13	THIRD READING
HB-0552	03/08/83	28	FIRST READING
	04/15/83	31	SECOND READING
	04/28/83	27	SECOND READING
	05/10/83	134	THIRD READING
HB-0553	03/08/83	28	FIRST READING
	04/19/83	14	SECOND READING
	05/13/83	180	RECALLED
	05/17/83	131	THIRD READING
	05/17/83	139	OUT OF RECORD
	05/26/83	96	RECALLED
	05/26/83	96	THIRD READING
	11/04/83	6	CONCURRENCE
	11/04/83	6	OUT OF RECORD
	11/04/83	9	CONCURRENCE
HB-0554	03/08/83	28	FIRST READING
	05/11/83	10	SECOND READING
	05/17/83	139	THIRD READING
	05/26/83	95	THIRD READING
HB-0555	03/08/83	28	FIRST READING
	04/19/83	15	SECOND READING
	05/10/83	135	THIRD READING

PROGRAM-LRTRNMST
08/20/85

LEGISLATIVE INFORMATION SYSTEM
HOUSE OF REPRESENTATIVES

PAGE 43

MASTER TRANSCRIPT INDEX

BILL NUMBER	DATE	PAGE	ACTION
HB-0556	03/08/83	28	FIRST READING
	05/13/83	172	SECOND READING
	05/20/83	11	RECALLED
	05/23/83	104	THIRD READING
	06/30/83	154	CONCURRENCE
	06/30/83	156	CONCURRENCE
	06/30/83	156	OUT OF RECORD
	10/18/83	61	MOTION
	10/20/83	116	CONFERENCE
HB-0557	03/08/83	28	FIRST READING
	05/11/83	11	SECOND READING
	05/25/83	208	RECALLED
	05/25/83	210	THIRD READING
	12/12/84	5	MOTION
	12/12/84	35	MOTION
	12/12/84	93	CONCURRENCE
HB-0558	03/08/83	29	FIRST READING
	04/19/83	15	SECOND READING
	05/17/83	142	HELD ON SECOND
	05/17/83	142	THIRD READING
	06/28/83	33	CONCURRENCE
	07/01/83	4	CONFERENCE
HB-0559	03/08/83	29	FIRST READING
	05/03/83	7	OTHER
HB-0560	03/08/83	29	FIRST READING
	05/03/83	32	OTHER
HB-0561	03/08/83	29	FIRST READING
	05/13/83	81	SECOND READING
	05/13/83	91	OUT OF RECORD
	05/13/83	95	SECOND READING
	05/13/83	96	OUT OF RECORD
	05/13/83	97	SECOND READING
	05/13/83	101	HELD ON SECOND
	05/19/83	131	SECOND READING
	05/26/83	174	THIRD READING
	06/30/83	95	CONCURRENCE
	10/20/83	47	VETO MESSAGE
HB-0562	03/08/83	29	FIRST READING
	04/14/83	17	SECOND READING
	04/19/83	36	THIRD READING
HB-0563	03/08/83	29	FIRST READING
	04/14/83	18	SECOND READING
	04/19/83	42	THIRD READING

PROGRAM-LRTRNMST
08/20/85

LEGISLATIVE INFORMATION SYSTEM
HOUSE OF REPRESENTATIVES

PAGE 44

MASTER TRANSCRIPT INDEX

BILL NUMBER	DATE	PAGE	ACTION
HB-0564	03/08/83	29	FIRST READING
	04/06/83	27	SECOND READING
	04/19/83	50	THIRD READING
	06/29/83	47	CONCURRENCE
	10/18/83	20	VETO MESSAGE
HB-0565	03/08/83	29	FIRST READING
	05/03/83	9	OTHER
HB-0566	03/08/83	29	FIRST READING
	05/03/83	9	OTHER
HB-0567	03/08/83	29	FIRST READING
HB-0568	03/08/83	29	FIRST READING
	05/03/83	9	OTHER
HB-0569	03/08/83	29	FIRST READING
	10/19/83	60	SECOND READING
	10/19/83	61	OUT OF RECORD
	10/19/83	172	SECOND READING
	04/04/84	20	THIRD READING
	04/04/84	21	OUT OF RECORD
	05/25/84	168	THIRD READING
HB-0570	03/08/83	30	FIRST READING
HB-0571	03/09/83	3	FIRST READING
	04/05/83	23	SECOND READING
	04/07/83	41	THIRD READING
HB-0572	03/09/83	3	FIRST READING
	05/13/83	92	SECOND READING
	05/23/83	16	SECOND READING
	05/23/83	20	OUT OF RECORD
	05/25/83	286	SECOND READING
HB-0573	03/09/83	3	FIRST READING
	05/03/83	37	SECOND READING
	05/10/83	141	THIRD READING
	06/24/83	234	NON-CONCURRENCE
	06/30/83	121	CONFERENCE
HB-0574	03/09/83	4	FIRST READING
	04/21/83	10	SECOND READING
	05/10/83	143	THIRD READING
HB-0575	03/09/83	4	FIRST READING
HB-0576	03/09/83	4	FIRST READING
	04/14/83	71	SECOND READING

BILL NUMBER	DATE	PAGE	ACTION
HB-0576 (cont'd)	04/20/83	13	OTHER
	04/27/83	51	THIRD READING
	06/28/83	40	CONCURRENCE
HB-0577	03/09/83	65	FIRST READING
	04/28/83	112	SECOND READING
	05/05/83	7	THIRD READING
	06/28/83	199	CONCURRENCE
HB-0578	03/09/83	65	FIRST READING
HB-0579	03/09/83	65	FIRST READING
	04/05/83	20	SECOND READING
	04/19/83	56	THIRD READING
	06/28/83	41	CONCURRENCE
	10/20/83	11	VETO MESSAGE
HB-0580	03/09/83	65	FIRST READING
	04/26/83	18	SECOND READING
	04/26/83	18	HELD ON SECOND
	05/23/83	21	SECOND READING
HB-0581	03/09/83	65	FIRST READING
	04/14/83	18	SECOND READING
	04/19/83	61	THIRD READING
HB-0582	03/09/83	65	FIRST READING
	04/28/83	28	SECOND READING
	05/10/83	147	THIRD READING
HB-0583	03/09/83	65	FIRST READING
HB-0584	03/09/83	65	FIRST READING
	04/13/83	12	SECOND READING
	05/10/83	151	THIRD READING
	06/28/83	4	CONCURRENCE
	07/01/83	5	CONFERENCE
HB-0585	03/09/83	65	FIRST READING
HB-0586	03/09/83	65	FIRST READING
	05/03/83	9	OTHER
HB-0587	03/09/83	65	FIRST READING
HB-0588	03/09/83	65	FIRST READING
	05/03/83	12	OTHER
HB-0589	03/09/83	65	FIRST READING
	05/03/83	16	SECOND READING
	05/10/83	15	THIRD READING

BILL NUMBER	DATE	PAGE	ACTION
HB-0589 (cont'd)	12/12/84	5	MOTION
	12/12/84	32	MOTION
	12/12/84	99	CONCURRENCE
HB-0590	03/09/83	65	FIRST READING
	05/03/83	9	OTHER
HB-0591	03/09/83	66	FIRST READING
	05/03/83	9	OTHER
HB-0592	03/09/83	66	FIRST READING
	05/03/83	12	OTHER
HB-0593	03/09/83	66	FIRST READING
	05/03/83	12	OTHER
HB-0594	03/09/83	66	FIRST READING
	05/03/83	12	OTHER
HB-0595	03/09/83	66	FIRST READING
	05/03/83	12	OTHER
HB-0596	03/09/83	66	FIRST READING
	04/07/83	28	SECOND READING
HB-0597	03/09/83	66	FIRST READING
HB-0598	03/09/83	66	FIRST READING
	05/02/84	9	SECOND READING
	05/03/84	42	THIRD READING
	06/28/84	6	CONCURRENCE
	06/30/84	12	CONFERENCE
HB-0599	03/09/83	66	FIRST READING
	04/07/83	28	SECOND READING
HB-0600	03/09/83	66	FIRST READING
HB-0601	03/09/83	66	FIRST READING
HB-0602	03/09/83	66	FIRST READING
HB-0603	03/09/83	66	FIRST READING
	04/14/83	71	SECOND READING
	04/21/83	49	THIRD READING
	06/28/83	43	CONCURRENCE
HB-0604	03/09/83	66	FIRST READING
	04/05/83	20	HELD ON SECOND
	04/06/83	28	SECOND READING
	05/10/83	157	THIRD READING

BILL NUMBER	DATE	PAGE	ACTION
HB-0605	03/09/83	67	FIRST READING
	04/06/83	28	SECOND READING
	05/10/83	160	THIRD READING
HB-0606	03/09/83	67	FIRST READING
	04/28/83	28	SECOND READING
	04/28/83	!9	HELD ON SECOND
	04/28/83	12	SECOND READING
	05/10/83	1 2	THIRD READING
	06/29/83	:4	CONCURRENCE
	07/01/83	1:1	CONFERENCE
	10/19/83	2 7	VETO MESSAGE
HB-0607	03/09/83	67	FIRST READING
	04/05/83	21	SECOND READING
	05/10/83	171	THIRD READING
HB-0608	03/09/83	67	FIRST READING
HB-0609	03/09/83	67	FIRST READING
	04/13/83	15	SECOND READING
	05/10/83	171	THIRD READING
	06/29/83	55	CONCURRENCE
HB-0610	03/09/83	67	FIRST READING
	04/06/83	29	SECOND READING
	05/10/83	175	THIRD READING
HB-0611	03/09/83	67	FIRST READING
HB-0612	03/09/83	67	FIRST READING
HB-0613	03/09/83	67	FIRST READING
	05/11/83	11	SECOND READING
	05/17/83	143	THIRD READING
HB-0614	03/09/83	67	FIRST READING
	05/11/83	11	SECOND READING
	05/17/83	145	THIRD READING
HB-0615	03/09/83	67	FIRST READING
	05/13/83	93	SECOND READING
	05/17/83	146	THIRD READING
	10/18/83	21	VETO MESSAGE
	10/19/83	7	VETO MESSAGE
HB-0616	03/09/83	67	FIRST READING
	05/11/83	12	SECOND READING
	05/27/83	96	THIRD READING
HB-0617	03/09/83	67	FIRST READING

BILL NUMBER	DATE	PAGE	ACTION
HB-0618	03/09/83	67	FIRST READING
HB-0619	03/09/83	68	FIRST READING
	04/28/83	29	SECOND READING
	05/11/83	19	THIRD READING
HB-0620	03/09/83	68	FIRST READING
	04/28/83	32	SECOND READING
	05/11/83	30	THIRD READING
	06/29/83	157	CONCURRENCE
	10/19/83	110	VETO MESSAGE
HB-0621	03/09/83	68	FIRST READING
	05/06/83	4	MOTION
	05/13/83	93	SECOND READING
	05/17/83	147	THIRD READING
	06/29/83	)5	CONCURRENCE
HB-0622	03/09/83	68	FIRST READING
	04/05/83	22	HELD ON SECOND
	04/07/83	28	SECOND READING
	05/11/83	31	THIRD READING
	10/18/83	24	VETO MESSAGE
HB-0623	03/09/83	68	FIRST READING
	05/03/83	6	OTHER
HB-0624	03/10/83	3	FIRST READING
HB-0625	03/10/83	3	FIRST READING
	04/05/83	22	SECOND READING
	05/11/83	35	THIRD READING
HB-0626	03/10/83	3	FIRST READING
	04/06/83	7	SECOND READING
	04/07/83	42	THIRD READING
HB-0627	03/10/83	3	FIRST READING
	04/19/83	17	SECOND READING
	05/11/83	38	THIRD READING
HB-0628	03/10/83	3	FIRST READING
	04/14/83	10	SECOND READING
	04/21/83	25	THIRD READING
	06/28/83	201	CONCURRENCE
	10/19/83	12	VETO MESSAGE
HB-0629	03/10/83	3	FIRST READING
	04/14/83	72	SECOND READING
	04/21/83	49	THIRD READING

PROGRAM-LRTRNMST
08/20/85
LEGISLATIVE INFORMATION SYSTEM
HOUSE OF REPRESENTATIVES
PAGE   49

MASTER TRANSCRIPT INDEX

BILL NUMBER	DATE	PAGE	ACTION
HB-0630	03/10/83	4	FIRST READING
	05/13/83	94	SECOND READING
	05/17/83	149	THIRD READING
HB-0631	03/10/83	4	FIRST READING
	04/14/83	18	SECOND READING
	05/11/83	39	THIRD READING
HB-0632	03/10/83	4	FIRST READING
	04/14/83	18	SECOND READING
	05/11/83	46	THIRD READING
HB-0633	03/10/83	4	FIRST READING
	04/14/83	19	SECOND READING
	05/11/83	48	THIRD READING
HB-0634	03/10/83	4	FIRST READING
	05/11/83	114	OTHER
HB-0635	03/10/83	4	FIRST READING
	05/13/83	173	SECOND READING
	05/23/83	106	THIRD READING
HB-0636	03/10/83	4	FIRST READING
HB-0637	03/10/83	4	FIRST READING
	04/14/83	19	SECOND READING
	04/27/83	56	RECALLED
	05/13/83	94	SECOND READING
	05/17/83	150	THIRD READING
	05/26/83	57	MOTION
	05/26/83	60	THIRD READING
	05/26/83	60	MOTION
HB-0638	03/10/83	4	FIRST READING
	04/19/83	17	SECOND READING
	05/11/83	49	THIRD READING
HB-0639	03/10/83	4	FIRST READING
	04/14/83	72	SECOND READING
	04/21/83	49	THIRD READING
HB-0640	03/10/83	4	FIRST READING
HB-0641	03/10/83	4	FIRST READING
	05/03/83	7	OTHER
HB-0642	03/10/83	4	FIRST READING
HB-0643	03/10/83	4	FIRST READING
	05/13/83	172	SECOND READING

PROGRAM-LRTRNMST
08/20/85
LEGISLATIVE INFORMATION SYSTEM
HOUSE OF REPRESENTATIVES
PAGE   50

MASTER TRANSCRIPT INDEX

BILL NUMBER	DATE	PAGE	ACTION
HB-0643(cont'd)	05/20/83	20	THIRD READING
	06/29/83	23	CONCURRENCE
	07/01/83	123	CONFERENCE
	10/18/83	26	VETO MESSAGE
HB-0644	03/10/83	4	FIRST READING
	04/19/83	17	SECOND READING
	05/11/83	50	THIRD READING
	10/18/83	28	VETO MESSAGE
HB-0645	03/10/83	4	FIRST READING
	04/05/83	10	SECOND READING
	04/07/83	42	THIRD READING
	06/24/83	229	NON-CONCURRENCE
	07/01/83	6	CONFERENCE
	10/18/83	32	VETO MESSAGE
	10/20/83	104	VETO MESSAGE
HB-0646	03/10/83	5	FIRST READING
	04/28/83	41	SECOND READING
	05/11/83	62	THIRD READING
	06/25/83	84	CONCURRENCE
	06/30/83	139	CONFERENCE
HB-0647	03/10/83	5	FIRST READING
	04/28/83	41	SECOND READING
	05/11/83	62	THIRD READING
	07/01/83	7	CONFERENCE
HB-0648	03/10/83	5	FIRST READING
HB-0649	03/10/83	28	FIRST READING
HB-0650	03/10/83	28	FIRST READING
HB-0651	03/10/83	28	FIRST READING
HB-0652	03/10/83	28	FIRST READING
	05/13/83	96	SECOND READING
	05/17/83	154	THIRD READING
HB-0653	03/10/83	28	FIRST READING
	04/28/83	41	SECOND READING
	05/11/83	63	THIRD READING
HB-0654	03/10/83	28	FIRST READING
	05/13/83	101	SECOND READING
	05/17/83	158	THIRD READING
HB-0655	03/10/83	28	FIRST READING
	04/28/83	42	SECOND READING

BILL NUMBER	DATE	PAGE	ACTION
HB-0655 (cont'd)	05/11/83	69	THIRD READING
HB-0656	03/10/83	29	FIRST READING
HB-0657	03/10/83	29	FIRST READING
	05/13/83	101	SECOND READING
	05/17/83	154	THIRD READING
	10/18/83	36	VETO MESSAGE
HB-0658	03/10/83	29	FIRST READING
	05/06/83	35	OTHER
HB-0659	03/10/83	29	FIRST READING
	05/13/83	15	SECOND READING
	05/11/83	76	THIRD READING
	05/11/83	145	MOTION
HB-0660	03/10/83	29	FIRST READING
	05/06/83	35	OTHER
HB-0661	03/10/83	29	FIRST READING
	05/03/83	8	OTHER
HB-0662	03/10/83	29	FIRST READING
	05/13/83	173	SECOND READING
	05/20/83	27	THIRD READING
	10/18/83	103	VETO MESSAGE
HB-0663	03/10/83	29	FIRST READING
	05/13/83	102	SECOND READING
	05/18/83	222	THIRD READING
	06/29/83	56	CONCURRENCE
HB-0664	03/10/83	29	FIRST READING
HB-0665	03/10/83	29	FIRST READING
HB-0666	03/10/83	29	FIRST READING
	05/13/83	105	SECOND READING
	05/18/83	224	THIRD READING
HB-0667	03/10/83	29	FIRST READING
	04/20/83	24	SECOND READING
	04/21/83	26	THIRD READING
	06/28/83	44	CONCURRENCE
HB-0668	03/10/83	29	FIRST READING
HB-0669	03/10/83	30	FIRST READING
	04/15/83	20	SECOND READING
	04/28/83	100	THIRD READING

BILL NUMBER	DATE	PAGE	ACTION
HB-0669 (cont'd)	06/29/83	63	CONCURRENCE
HB-0670	03/14/83	4	FIRST READING
	05/13/83	105	SECOND READING
	05/18/83	228	THIRD READING
	06/28/83	44	CONCURRENCE
HB-0671	03/14/83	4	FIRST READING
	05/23/83	22	SECOND READING
	05/27/83	146	THIRD READING
HB-0672	03/14/83	43	FIRST READING
	04/15/83	12	TABLED
HB-0673	03/14/83	43	FIRST READING
	05/13/83	106	SECOND READING
	05/18/83	228	THIRD READING
HB-0674	03/14/83	44	FIRST READING
	04/19/83	18	SECOND READING
	05/11/83	85	RECALLED
	05/18/83	230	THIRD READING
HB-0675	03/14/83	44	FIRST READING
	04/14/83	19	SECOND READING
	05/11/83	91	THIRD READING
HB-0676	03/14/83	44	FIRST READING
	04/28/83	42	SECOND READING
	05/11/83	94	THIRD READING
HB-0677	03/14/83	44	FIRST READING
HB-0678	03/14/83	44	FIRST READING
HB-0679	03/14/83	44	FIRST READING
	05/06/83	35	OTHER
HB-0680	03/14/83	44	FIRST READING
HB-0681	03/14/83	44	FIRST READING
HB-0682	03/14/83	44	FIRST READING
	04/07/83	30	SECOND READING
	04/21/83	10	SECOND READING
	05/11/83	108	THIRD READING
	06/28/83	51	CONCURRENCE
	10/19/83	25	VETO MESSAGE
HB-0683	03/14/83	44	FIRST READING

BILL NUMBER	DATE	PAGE	ACTION
HB-0684	03/14/83	44	FIRST READING
	04/28/83	42	SECOND READING
	05/11/83	97	THIRD READING
	06/28/83	52	CONCURRENCE
HB-0685	03/14/83	44	FIRST READING
	04/26/83	5	SECOND READING
	04/28/83	101	THIRD READING
HB-0686	03/14/83	44	FIRST READING
	05/03/83	55	OTHER
HB-0687	03/14/83	45	FIRST READING
	04/19/83	8	SECOND READING
	04/21/83	27	THIRD READING
	06/28/83	51	CONCURRENCE
	07/02/83	144	CONFERENCE
HB-0688	03/14/83	45	FIRST READING
	05/11/83	17	SECOND READING
	05/20/83	28	THIRD READING
HB-0689	03/14/83	45	FIRST READING
	05/11/83	17	SECOND READING
	05/20/83	31	THIRD READING
HB-0690	03/14/83	45	FIRST READING
	05/13/83	175	SECOND READING
	05/20/83	31	THIRD READING
	06/28/83	204	CONCURRENCE
	07/01/83	15	CONFERENCE
	07/01/83	16	OUT OF RECORD
	07/01/83	168	CONFERENCE
	07/01/83	174	OUT OF RECORD
	07/02/83	28	CONFERENCE
HB-0691	03/14/83	45	FIRST READING
	04/14/83	20	SECOND READING
	05/11/83	98	THIRD READING
	06/29/83	14	CONCURRENCE
	07/01/83	16	CONFERENCE
HB-0692	03/14/83	45	FIRST READING
	05/03/83	9	OTHER
HB-0693	03/14/83	45	FIRST READING
	05/03/83	9	OTHER
HB-0694	03/14/83	45	FIRST READING
	04/14/83	20	SECOND READING
	05/11/83	103	THIRD READING

BILL NUMBER	DATE	PAGE	ACTION
HB-0695	03/14/83	45	FIRST READING
	04/28/83	93	SECOND READING
	05/11/83	106	THIRD READING
	10/19/83	221	MOTION
	11/03/83	2	CONCURRENCE
	11/03/83	3	OUT OF RECORD
	11/03/83	7	CONCURRENCE
HB-0696	03/15/83	3	FIRST READING
	05/11/83	18	SECOND READING
	05/20/83	33	THIRD READING
HB-0697	03/15/83	3	FIRST READING
	04/13/83	13	SECOND READING
	05/11/83	114	THIRD READING
HB-0698	03/15/83	3	FIRST READING
	04/19/83	10	SECOND READING
	04/21/83	27	THIRD READING
HB-0699	03/15/83	62	FIRST READING
HB-0700	03/15/83	62	FIRST READING
	05/13/83	107	SECOND READING
	05/18/83	237	THIRD READING
	06/29/83	15	CONCURRENCE
	07/01/83	19	CONFERENCE
HB-0701	03/15/83	62	FIRST READING
	04/15/83	32	SECOND READING
	05/11/83	118	THIRD READING
	10/18/83	38	VETO MESSAGE
HB-0702	03/15/83	62	FIRST READING
	05/13/83	107	SECOND READING
	05/18/83	242	THIRD READING
HB-0703	03/15/83	62	FIRST READING
	05/13/83	108	SECOND READING
	05/27/83	207	THIRD READING
	04/11/84	31	SECOND READING
	05/24/84	300	RECALLED
	05/25/84	122	OTHER
HB-0704	03/15/83	62	FIRST READING
	05/13/83	110	SECOND READING
	05/16/84	241	SECOND READING
	05/24/84	276	THIRD READING
HB-0705	03/15/83	62	FIRST READING

BILL NUMBER	DATE	PAGE	ACTION
HB-0706	03/15/83	62	FIRST READING
HB-0707	03/15/83	62	FIRST READING
	05/04/83	54	OTHER
HB-0708	03/15/83	62	FIRST READING
	04/19/83	18	SECOND READING
	05/11/83	120	THIRD READING
	06/29/83	66	CONCURRENCE
HB-0709	03/15/83	62	FIRST READING
	04/19/83	19	SECOND READING
	05/11/83	121	THIRD READING
	06/29/83	67	CONCURRENCE
HB-0710	03/15/83	62	FIRST READING
	04/28/83	43	SECOND READING
	05/11/83	122	THIRD READING
HB-0711	03/15/83	62	FIRST READING
	04/14/83	72	SECOND READING
	04/20/83	14	SECOND READING
	04/21/83	28	THIRD READING
HB-0712	03/15/83	62	FIRST READING
HB-0713	03/15/83	63	FIRST READING
	04/28/83	43	SECOND READING
HB-0714	03/15/83	63	FIRST READING
	04/21/83	47	SECOND READING
	04/27/83	51	THIRD READING
	06/27/83	170	CONCURRENCE
	06/30/83	158	CONFERENCE
HB-0715	03/15/83	63	FIRST READING
HB-0716	03/15/83	63	FIRST READING
	04/20/83	14	SECOND READING
	04/21/83	31	THIRD READING
HB-0717	03/15/83	63	FIRST READING
	04/20/83	20	SECOND READING
	04/21/83	32	THIRD READING
HB-0718	03/15/83	63	FIRST READING
	04/13/83	9	SECOND READING
	04/14/83	29	THIRD READING
HB-0719	03/15/83	63	FIRST READING
	05/13/83	111	SECOND READING

BILL NUMBER	DATE	PAGE	ACTION
HB-0719 (cont'd)	05/18/83	252	THIRD READING
HB-0720	03/15/83	63	FIRST READING
	05/06/83	4	MOTION
	05/13/83	111	SECOND READING
	05/27/83	157	RECALLED
	05/27/83	160	THIRD READING
	06/24/83	232	NON-CONCURRENCE
	10/18/83	62	MOTION
	11/04/83	21	CONFERENCE
HB-0721	03/15/83	63	FIRST READING
	04/28/83	9	SECOND READING
	05/10/83	16	THIRD READING
	06/29/83	227	CONCURRENCE
	06/29/83	228	OUT OF RECORD
	06/30/83	3	CONCURRENCE
	10/18/83	38	VETO MESSAGE
HB-0722	03/15/83	63	FIRST READING
	04/19/83	19	SECOND READING
	05/11/83	128	THIRD READING
	06/30/83	102	CONCURRENCE
HB-0723	03/15/83	63	FIRST READING
	04/28/83	47	SECOND READING
	04/28/83	47	HELD ON SECOND
	05/13/83	115	SECOND READING
	05/18/83	253	THIRD READING
HB-0724	03/15/83	63	FIRST READING
HB-0725	03/15/83	64	FIRST READING
HB-0726	03/15/83	64	FIRST READING
	05/13/83	159	SECOND READING
	05/20/83	128	THIRD READING
HB-0727	03/15/83	64	FIRST READING
	05/13/83	176	SECOND READING
	05/13/83	177	HELD ON SECOND
	05/18/83	31	SECOND READING
	05/20/83	34	THIRD READING
HB-0728	03/15/83	64	FIRST READING
	04/14/83	72	SECOND READING
	04/21/83	49	THIRD READING
HB-0729	03/15/83	64	FIRST READING
	04/14/83	72	SECOND READING
	04/21/83	49	THIRD READING

BILL NUMBER	DATE	PAGE	ACTION
HB-0730	03/15/83	64	FIRST READING
	04/14/83	21	SECOND READING
	05/11/83	129	THIRD READING
	06/28/83	53	CONCURRENCE
	10/20/83	124	VETO MESSAGE
HB-0731	03/15/83	64	FIRST READING
	05/13/83	115	SECOND READING
	05/20/83	129	THIRD READING
	10/20/83	30	VETO MESSAGE
HB-0732	03/15/83	64	FIRST READING
	05/03/83	6	OTHER
HB-0733	03/15/83	64	FIRST READING
HB-0734	03/15/83	64	FIRST READING
	04/27/83	53	OTHER
HB-0735	03/15/83	64	FIRST READING
HB-0736	03/15/83	64	FIRST READING
	04/19/83	9	SECOND READING
	04/21/83	33	THIRD READING
HB-0737	03/15/83	65	FIRST READING
	05/03/83	31	OTHER
HB-0738	03/15/83	65	FIRST READING
HB-0739	03/15/83	65	FIRST READING
HB-0740	03/15/83	65	FIRST READING
	04/19/83	9	SECOND READING
	04/21/83	34	THIRD READING
	06/28/83	54	CONCURRENCE
	06/28/83	54	OUT OF RECORD
HB-0741	03/16/83	5	FIRST READING
	05/13/83	116	SECOND READING
	05/26/83	197	RECALLED
	05/26/83	198	THIRD READING
	06/29/83	69	CONCURRENCE
	06/29/83	71	OUT OF RECORD
	06/29/83	210	CONCURRENCE
HB-0742	03/16/83	5	FIRST READING
	04/21/83	11	SECOND READING
	05/11/83	137	THIRD READING
	06/29/83	235	CONCURRENCE

BILL NUMBER	DATE	PAGE	ACTION
HB-0743	03/16/83	5	FIRST READING
	04/19/83	20	SECOND READING
	05/11/83	137	THIRD READING
	10/18/83	110	VETO MESSAGE
	10/20/83	128	VETO MESSAGE
HB-0744	03/16/83	5	FIRST READING
	04/21/83	11	SECOND READING
	05/20/83	136	THIRD READING
	10/19/83	13	VETO MESSAGE
HB-0745	03/16/83	5	FIRST READING
	04/15/83	20	SECOND READING
	04/20/83	21	SECOND READING
	04/21/83	35	THIRD READING
HB-0746	03/16/83	5	FIRST READING
HB-0747	03/16/83	51	FIRST READING
	04/28/83	47	SECOND READING
	05/11/83	140	THIRD READING
	06/29/83	71	CONCURRENCE
	10/18/83	39	VETO MESSAGE
HB-0748	03/16/83	51	FIRST READING
	05/03/83	35	OTHER
HB-0749	03/16/83	51	FIRST READING
	05/03/83	37	SECOND READING
	05/11/83	141	THIRD READING
	06/28/83	55	CONCURRENCE
HB-0750	03/16/83	51	FIRST READING
	04/21/83	47	SECOND READING
	04/27/83	51	THIRD READING
HB-0751	03/16/83	52	FIRST READING
	05/11/83	18	SECOND READING
	05/19/83	100	THIRD READING
	06/29/83	73	CONCURRENCE
HB-0752	03/16/83	52	FIRST READING
	05/06/83	35	OTHER
HB-0753	03/16/83	52	FIRST READING
	05/13/83	118	SECOND READING
	05/24/83	134	THIRD READING
	06/28/83	56	CONCURRENCE
HB-0754	03/16/83	52	FIRST READING
	04/14/83	22	SECOND READING

BILL NUMBER	DATE	PAGE	ACTION
HB-0754 (cont'd)	04/27/83	56	RECALLED
	04/28/83	48	SECOND READING
	05/11/83	157	THIRD READING
	06/28/83	57	CONCURRENCE
	10/18/83	40	VETO MESSAGE
	10/19/83	227	MOTION
	10/19/83	2'9	VETO MESSAGE
HB-0755	03/16/83	-2	FIRST READING
	04/14/83	0	SECOND READING
	04/21/83	15	THIRD READING
	06/29/83	'5	CONCURRENCE
HB-0756	03/16/83	52	FIRST READING
	05/03/83	17	SECOND READING
	05/10/83	17	THIRD READING
HB-0757	03/16/83	52	FIRST READING
	04/28/83	113	SECOND READING
	05/05/83	7	THIRD READING
	06/28/83	205	CONCURRENCE
HB-0758	03/16/83	52	FIRST READING
	04/14/83	22	SECOND READING
	05/11/83	161	THIRD READING
	06/29/83	73	CONCURRENCE
HB-0759	03/16/83	52	FIRST READING
	05/06/83	35	OTHER
HB-0760	03/16/83	52	FIRST READING
HB-0761	03/16/83	52	FIRST READING
	05/03/83	38	SECOND READING
	05/11/83	162	THIRD READING
HB-0762	03/16/83	52	FIRST READING
	05/02/84	9	SECOND READING
	05/03/84	43	THIRD READING
HB-0763	03/22/83	4	FIRST READING
	04/26/83	4	SECOND READING
	05/10/83	19	THIRD READING
HB-0764	03/22/83	4	FIRST READING
	04/19/83	21	SECOND READING
	05/11/83	163	THIRD READING
HB-0765	03/22/83	4	FIRST READING
	05/19/83	140	SECOND READING
	05/20/83	139	THIRD READING

BILL NUMBER	DATE	PAGE	ACTION
HB-0765 (cont'd)	05/20/83	142	OUT OF RECORD
HB-0766	03/22/83	35	FIRST READING
	05/03/83	4	OTHER
HB-0767	03/22/83	41	FIRST READING
	05/19/83	142	SECOND READING
	05/19/83	153	HELD ON SECOND
	05/24/83	165	SECOND READING
	05/26/83	205	THIRD READING
HB-0768	03/22/83	41	FIRST READING
	04/14/83	22	SECOND READING
	05/11/83	163	THIRD READING
	06/28/83	58	CONCURRENCE
	10/19/83	95	VETO MESSAGE
HB-0769	03/22/83	41	FIRST READING
	04/19/83	21	SECOND READING
	05/20/83	142	RECALLED
	05/20/83	143	THIRD READING
HB-0770	03/22/83	41	FIRST READING
	05/19/83	153	SECOND READING
	05/19/83	163	HELD ON SECOND
	05/23/83	29	SECOND READING
HB-0771	03/22/83	41	FIRST READING
	04/14/83	23	SECOND READING
	04/27/83	57	RECALLED
	04/28/83	50	SECOND READING
	05/11/83	172	THIRD READING
HB-0772	03/22/83	41	FIRST READING
	04/21/83	47	SECOND READING
	04/27/83	52	THIRD READING
	06/25/83	76	CONCURRENCE
	06/30/83	116	CONFERENCE
HB-0773	03/22/83	42	FIRST READING
	04/28/83	9	SECOND READING
	05/10/83	20	THIRD READING
HB-0774	03/22/83	42	FIRST READING
	05/23/83	30	SECOND READING
HB-0775	03/22/83	42	FIRST READING
	04/28/83	51	SECOND READING
	05/11/83	173	THIRD READING
	06/30/83	110	CONCURRENCE
	10/20/83	106	VETO MESSAGE

BILL NUMBER	DATE	PAGE	ACTION
HB-0776	03/22/83	42	FIRST READING
	04/14/83	10	SECOND READING
	04/21/83	36	THIRD READING
HB-0777	03/22/83	42	FIRST READING
HB-0778	03/22/83	42	FIRST READING
	04/27/83	53	OTHER
HB-0779	03/22/83	42	FIRST READING
	04/27/83	53	OTHER
HB-0780	03/22/83	42	FIRST READING
	04/27/83	53	OTHER
HB-0781	03/22/83	42	FIRST READING
	04/28/83	113	SECOND READING
	05/05/83	7	THIRD READING
HB-0782	03/22/83	42	FIRST READING
	04/28/83	10	SECOND READING
	05/10/83	21	THIRD READING
	06/28/83	61	CONCURRENCE
HB-0783	03/22/83	42	FIRST READING
HB-0784	03/22/83	42	FIRST READING
	04/28/83	51	SECOND READING
	05/11/83	187	THIRD READING
HB-0785	03/22/83	42	FIRST READING
	05/03/83	9	OTHER
HB-0786	03/22/83	42	FIRST READING
	05/03/83	9	OTHER
HB-0787	03/22/83	42	FIRST READING
	04/15/83	24	SECOND READING
	05/20/83	34	THIRD READING
HB-0788	03/22/83	43	FIRST READING
	05/03/83	9	OTHER
HB-0789	03/22/83	43	FIRST READING
	05/03/83	13	OTHER
HB-0790	03/22/83	43	FIRST READING
	05/03/83	13	OTHER
HB-0791	03/22/83	43	FIRST READING
	04/28/83	52	SECOND READING

BILL NUMBER	DATE	PAGE	ACTION
HB-0791 (cont'd)	05/11/83	174	THIRD READING
	10/18/83	116	VETO MESSAGE
HB-0792	03/22/83	43	FIRST READING
	05/03/83	24	OTHER
HB-0793	03/22/83	43	FIRST READING
	04/15/83	21	SECOND READING
	04/19/83	35	THIRD READING
HB-0794	03/22/83	43	FIRST READING
HB-0795	03/22/83	43	FIRST READING
HB-0796	03/23/83	85	FIRST READING
	04/19/83	22	SECOND READING
	05/11/83	188	THIRD READING
HB-0797	03/23/83	85	FIRST READING
	04/20/83	6	SECOND READING
HB-0798	03/23/83	85	FIRST READING
	04/28/83	52	SECOND READING
	05/11/83	192	THIRD READING
	06/27/83	171	CONCURRENCE
	07/01/83	287	CONFERENCE
	10/18/83	41	VETO MESSAGE
HB-0799	03/23/83	85	FIRST READING
	05/23/83	30	SECOND READING
	05/23/83	35	HELD ON SECOND
	05/24/83	255	SECOND READING
	05/26/83	211	THIRD READING
	10/18/83	122	VETO MESSAGE
HB-0800	03/23/83	85	FIRST READING
	04/27/83	32	OTHER
HB-0801	03/23/83	85	FIRST READING
	04/28/83	10	SECOND READING
	05/10/83	23	THIRD READING
	10/19/83	96	VETO MESSAGE
HB-0802	03/23/83	85	FIRST READING
	05/13/83	120	SECOND READING
HB-0803	03/23/83	85	FIRST READING
	04/21/83	47	SECOND READING
	04/27/83	52	THIRD READING
	10/19/83	14	VETO MESSAGE

BILL NUMBER	DATE	PAGE	ACTION
HB-0804	03/23/83	86	FIRST READING
HB-0805	03/23/83	86	FIRST READING
	05/11/83	18	SECOND READING
	05/23/83	106	RECALLED
	05/23/83	108	THIRD READING
	06/29/83	74	CONCURRENCE
HB-0806	03/23/83	86	FIRST READING
	04/28/83	53	SECOND READING
	05/11/83	193	THIRD READING
HB-0807	03/23/83	86	FIRST READING
HB-0808	03/23/83	86	FIRST READING
	05/03/83	6	OTHER
HB-0809	03/23/83	86	FIRST READING
	05/06/83	35	OTHER
	05/10/84	16	SECOND READING
	05/16/84	53	RECALLED
	05/16/84	55	HELD ON SECOND
	05/18/84	134	SECOND READING
	05/24/84	277	THIRD READING
HB-0810	03/23/83	86	FIRST READING
	04/21/83	47	SECOND READING
	04/27/83	52	THIRD READING
	06/28/83	62	CONCURRENCE
HB-0811	03/23/83	86	FIRST READING
	05/18/83	50	SECOND READING
	05/20/83	146	THIRD READING
HB-0812	03/23/83	86	FIRST READING
	04/28/83	53	SECOND READING
	05/11/83	194	THIRD READING
HB-0813	03/23/83	86	FIRST READING
	04/28/83	53	SECOND READING
	05/11/83	195	THIRD READING
	06/29/83	17	CONCURRENCE
	07/01/83	272	CONFERENCE
HB-0814	03/23/83	86	FIRST READING
	04/19/83	22	SECOND READING
	05/12/83	11	THIRD READING
	10/20/83	12	VETO MESSAGE
HB-0815	03/23/83	86	FIRST READING
	04/21/83	12	SECOND READING

BILL NUMBER	DATE	PAGE	ACTION
HB-0815 (cont'd)	05/12/83	12	THIRD READING
HB-0816	03/23/83	86	FIRST READING
HB-0817	03/23/83	86	FIRST READING
	05/13/83	120	SECOND READING
	05/20/83	147	THIRD READING
HB-0818	03/23/83	86	FIRST READING
	04/21/83	47	SECOND READING
	04/27/83	52	THIRD READING
	06/28/83	62	CONCURRENCE
HB-0819	03/23/83	87	FIRST READING
HB-0820	03/23/83	87	FIRST READING
	04/28/83	53	SECOND READING
	05/12/83	3	RECALLED
	05/12/83	3	THIRD READING
HB-0821	03/23/83	87	FIRST READING
	05/13/83	121	SECOND READING
	05/20/83	157	THIRD READING
	05/26/83	291	THIRD READING
HB-0822	03/23/83	87	FIRST READING
	05/03/83	12	OTHER
HB-0823	03/23/83	87	FIRST READING
	04/28/83	10	SECOND READING
	05/10/83	26	THIRD READING
HB-0824	03/23/83	87	FIRST READING
HB-0825	03/23/83	87	FIRST READING
	05/13/83	121	SECOND READING
	05/20/83	160	THIRD READING
	05/01/84	45	SECOND READING
	05/24/84	70	THIRD READING
HB-0826	03/23/83	87	FIRST READING
	04/21/83	15	SECOND READING
	05/12/83	13	THIRD READING
HB-0827	03/23/83	87	FIRST READING
HB-0828	03/23/83	87	FIRST READING
	04/28/83	14	SECOND READING
	05/10/83	39	THIRD READING
HB-0829	03/23/83	87	FIRST READING

BILL NUMBER	DATE	PAGE	ACTION
HB-0830	03/23/83	88	FIRST READING
	04/28/83	54	SECOND READING
	05/12/83	18	THIRD READING
HB-0831	03/23/83	88	FIRST READING
	04/20/83	22	SECOND READING
	04/21/83	37	THIRD READING
HB-0832	03/23/83	88	FIRST READING
	04/15/83	13	TABLED
HB-0833	03/23/83	88	FIRST READING
	05/13/83	177	SECOND READING
	05/20/83	35	THIRD READING
	10/20/83	55	VETO MESSAGE
HB-0834	03/23/83	88	FIRST READING
	04/19/83	10	SECOND READING
	04/21/83	37	RECALLED
	04/28/83	103	THIRD READING
HB-0835	03/23/83	88	FIRST READING
	04/21/83	12	SECOND READING
	05/12/83	20	THIRD READING
	06/28/83	125	CONCURRENCE
	10/18/83	123	VETO MESSAGE
HB-0836	03/23/83	88	FIRST READING
	04/21/83	12	SECOND READING
	05/12/83	20	THIRD READING
HB-0837	03/24/83	3	FIRST READING
	05/06/83	35	OTHER
HB-0838	03/24/83	3	FIRST READING
	04/19/83	22	SECOND READING
	05/12/83	21	THIRD READING
HB-0839	03/24/83	3	FIRST READING
	05/13/83	122	SECOND READING
	05/20/83	172	THIRD READING
HB-0840	03/24/83	3	FIRST READING
	05/13/83	123	SECOND READING
	05/20/83	179	THIRD READING
HB-0841	03/24/83	4	FIRST READING
HB-0842	03/24/83	4	FIRST READING
	05/13/83	177	SECOND READING
	05/13/83	178	HELD ON SECOND
HB-0842(cont'd)	05/18/83	2	SECOND READING
	05/20/83	37	THIRD READING
	06/28/83	129	CONCURRENCE
	10/20/83	55	VETO MESSAGE
HB-0843	03/24/83	4	FIRST READING
	05/25/83	299	SECOND READING
HB-0844	03/24/83	67	FIRST READING
	05/13/83	123	SECOND READING
	05/20/83	179	THIRD READING
HB-0845	03/24/83	67	FIRST READING
	05/13/83	125	SECOND READING
	05/20/83	181	THIRD READING
HB-0846	03/24/83	67	FIRST READING
HB-0847	03/24/83	67	FIRST READING
HB-0848	03/24/83	67	FIRST READING
	05/13/83	125	SECOND READING
	05/20/83	183	THIRD READING
HB-0849	03/24/83	67	FIRST READING
	05/13/83	126	SECOND READING
	05/20/83	184	THIRD READING
	06/29/83	75	CONCURRENCE
HB-0850	03/24/83	68	FIRST READING
HB-0851	03/24/83	68	FIRST READING
HB-0852	03/24/83	68	FIRST READING
HB-0853	03/24/83	68	FIRST READING
	05/13/83	178	SECOND READING
	05/20/83	37	THIRD READING
	06/28/83	66	CONCURRENCE
HB-0854	03/24/83	68	FIRST READING
	05/13/83	126	SECOND READING
	05/27/83	10	THIRD READING
	05/27/83	180	THIRD READING
	06/29/83	76	CONCURRENCE
HB-0855	03/24/83	68	FIRST READING
HB-0856	03/24/83	68	FIRST READING
	05/13/83	126	SECOND READING
	05/27/83	133	MOTION

PROGRAM-LRTRNMST
08/20/85
LEGISLATIVE INFORMATION SYSTEM
HOUSE OF REPRESENTATIVES
PAGE 67

MASTER TRANSCRIPT INDEX

BILL NUMBER	DATE	PAGE	ACTION
HB-0856 (cont'd)	05/27/83	136	THIRD READING
HB-0857	03/24/83	68	FIRST READING
HB-0858	03/24/83	68	FIRST READING
	05/03/83	4	OTHER
HB-0859	03/24/83	68	FIRST READING
	04/20/83	23	SECOND READING
	04/21/83	39	THIRD READING
	06/28/83	66	CONCURRENCE
HB-0860	03/24/83	68	FIRST READING
	04/21/83	6	SECOND READING
	05/10/83	40	RECALLED
	05/10/83	41	THIRD READING
HB-0861	03/24/83	68	FIRST READING
HB-0862	03/24/83	68	FIRST READING
	05/13/83	178	SECOND READING
	05/20/83	38	THIRD READING
	06/29/83	78	CONCURRENCE
HB-0863	03/24/83	69	FIRST READING
	05/19/83	163	SECOND READING
	05/20/83	185	RECALLED
	05/20/83	185	THIRD READING
HB-0864	03/24/83	69	FIRST READING
	05/13/83	127	SECOND READING
HB-0865	03/24/83	69	FIRST READING
	05/03/83	12	OTHER
HB-0866	03/24/83	69	FIRST READING
	04/20/83	23	SECOND READING
	04/21/83	41	THIRD READING
HB-0867	03/24/83	69	FIRST READING
	04/20/83	23	SECOND READING
	04/21/83	41	THIRD READING
HB-0868	03/24/83	69	FIRST READING
	04/20/83	23	SECOND READING
	04/21/83	42	THIRD READING
HB-0869	03/24/83	69	FIRST READING
	04/26/83	19	SECOND READING
	05/12/83	23	THIRD READING

PROGRAM-LRTRNMST
08/20/85
LEGISLATIVE INFORMATION SYSTEM
HOUSE OF REPRESENTATIVES
PAGE 68

MASTER TRANSCRIPT INDEX

BILL NUMBER	DATE	PAGE	ACTION
HB-0870	03/24/83	69	FIRST READING
	04/21/83	47	SECOND READING
	04/27/83	52	THIRD READING
HB-0871	03/24/83	69	FIRST READING
	05/06/83	36	OTHER
HB-0872	03/24/83	69	FIRST READING
	05/13/83	127	SECOND READING
	05/20/83	190	THIRD READING
HB-0873	03/24/83	69	FIRST READING
	04/21/83	13	SECOND READING
	05/12/83	23	THIRD READING
HB-0874	03/24/83	69	FIRST READING
HB-0875	03/24/83	69	FIRST READING
HB-0876	03/24/83	69	FIRST READING
	05/06/83	36	OTHER
	04/10/84	3	SECOND READING
	04/24/84	7	THIRD READING
	06/21/84	84	CONCURRENCE
HB-0877	03/24/83	70	FIRST READING
	05/06/83	36	OTHER
	05/09/84	2	SECOND READING
	05/16/84	6	SECOND READING
	05/17/84	231	THIRD READING
	06/26/84	91	CONCURRENCE
	06/26/84	94	OUT OF RECORD
	06/26/84	103	CONCURRENCE
	06/30/84	68	CONFERENCE
HB-0878	03/24/83	70	FIRST READING
	05/06/83	36	OTHER
HB-0879	03/24/83	70	FIRST READING
HB-0880	03/24/83	70	FIRST READING
	04/20/83	23	SECOND READING
	04/21/83	43	THIRD READING
HB-0881	03/24/83	70	FIRST READING
	05/13/83	130	SECOND READING
	05/26/83	216	THIRD READING
HB-0882	03/24/83	70	FIRST READING
	05/13/83	128	SECOND READING
	05/24/83	102	THIRD READING

BILL NUMBER	DATE	PAGE	ACTION
HB-0883	03/24/83	70	FIRST READING
	04/28/83	12	SECOND READING
	04/28/83	13	RECALLED
	05/10/83	42	THIRD READING
HB-0884	04/05/83	2	FIRST READING
	05/13/83	131	SECOND READING
	05/24/83	217	THIRD READING
	06/29/83	88	CONCURRENCE
	10/19/83	162	VETO MESSAGE
HB-0885	04/05/83	2	FIRST READING
HB-0886	04/05/83	2	FIRST READING
	05/13/83	179	SECOND READING
	05/23/83	109	RECALLED
	05/23/83	109	OUT OF RECORD
	05/23/83	175	RECALLED
	05/24/83	226	THIRD READING
HB-0887	04/05/83	2	FIRST READING
HB-0888	04/05/83	2	FIRST READING
	04/07/83	70	MOTION
	04/15/83	37	SECOND READING
	04/20/83	8	THIRD READING
	06/29/83	88	CONCURRENCE
	07/02/83	45	CONFERENCE
	10/19/83	160	VETO MESSAGE
HB-0889	04/05/83	3	FIRST READING
	05/13/83	31	MOTION
HB-0890	04/05/83	3	FIRST READING
	05/13/83	51	MOTION
HB-0891	04/05/83	3	FIRST READING
	05/13/83	52	MOTION
HB-0892	04/05/83	3	FIRST READING
	05/13/83	53	MOTION
HB-0893	04/05/83	3	FIRST READING
	05/13/83	54	MOTION
HB-0894	04/05/83	3	FIRST READING
	05/13/83	54	MOTION
HB-0895	04/05/83	3	FIRST READING
	05/13/83	54	MOTION

BILL NUMBER	DATE	PAGE	ACTION
HB-0896	04/05/83	3	FIRST READING
	05/13/83	54	MOTION
HB-0897	04/05/83	3	FIRST READING
	05/13/83	54	MOTION
HB-0898	04/05/83	3	FIRST READING
	05/13/83	54	MOTION
HB-0899	04/05/83	4	FIRST READING
	05/13/83	54	MOTION
HB-0900	04/05/83	4	FIRST READING
	05/13/83	54	MOTION
HB-0901	04/05/83	4	FIRST READING
	05/13/83	54	MOTION
HB-0902	04/05/83	4	FIRST READING
	05/13/83	54	MOTION
HB-0903	04/05/83	4	FIRST READING
	05/13/83	54	MOTION
HB-0904	04/05/83	4	FIRST READING
	05/13/83	54	MOTION
HB-0905	04/05/83	4	FIRST READING
	05/13/83	54	MOTION
HB-0906	04/05/83	4	FIRST READING
	05/13/83	54	MOTION
HB-0907	04/05/83	4	FIRST READING
	05/13/83	54	MOTION
HB-0908	04/05/83	4	FIRST READING
	05/13/83	54	MOTION
HB-0909	04/05/83	5	FIRST READING
	05/13/83	54	MOTION
HB-0910	04/05/83	5	FIRST READING
	04/27/83	33	TABLED
HB-0911	04/05/83	5	FIRST READING
	05/13/83	55	MOTION
HB-0912	04/05/83	5	FIRST READING
	05/13/83	55	MOTION

PROGRAM-LRTRNMST
08/20/85
LEGISLATIVE INFORMATION SYSTEM
HOUSE OF REPRESENTATIVES
PAGE 71

MASTER TRANSCRIPT INDEX

BILL NUMBER	DATE	PAGE	ACTION
HB-0913	04/05/83	5	FIRST READING
	05/13/83	55	MOTION
HB-0914	04/05/83	5	FIRST READING
	05/13/83	55	MOTION
HB-0915	04/05/83	5	FIRST READING
	05/13/83	55	MOTION
HB-0916	04/05/83	5	FIRST READING
	05/13/83	55	MOTION
HB-0917	04/05/83	5	FIRST READING
	05/13/83	55	MOTION
HB-0918	04/05/83	5	FIRST READING
	05/13/83	55	MOTION
HB-0919	04/05/83	6	FIRST READING
	05/13/83	55	MOTION
HB-0920	04/05/83	6	FIRST READING
	05/13/83	55	MOTION
HB-0921	04/05/83	6	FIRST READING
	05/11/83	13	SECOND READING
	05/13/83	2	THIRD READING
	06/24/83	233	NON-CONCURRENCE
	06/30/83	132	CONFERENCE
HB-0922	04/05/83	6	FIRST READING
	05/03/83	17	SECOND READING
	05/10/83	43	RECALLED
	05/13/83	179	SECOND READING
	05/20/83	50	THIRD READING
	06/28/83	67	CONCURRENCE
HB-0923	04/05/83	6	FIRST READING
	04/28/83	113	SECOND READING
	05/05/83	7	THIRD READING
HB-0924	04/05/83	6	FIRST READING
	05/13/83	180	SECOND READING
	05/20/83	53	THIRD READING
	06/28/83	68	CONCURRENCE
HB-0925	04/05/83	6	FIRST READING
	04/28/83	55	SECOND READING
	05/12/83	26	THIRD READING
HB-0926	04/05/83	6	FIRST READING

PROGRAM-LRTRNMST
08/20/85
LEGISLATIVE INFORMATION SYSTEM
HOUSE OF REPRESENTATIVES
PAGE 72

MASTER TRANSCRIPT INDEX

BILL NUMBER	DATE	PAGE	ACTION
HB-0926 (cont'd)	05/13/83	181	SECOND READING
	05/20/83	54	THIRD READING
HB-0927	04/05/83	6	FIRST READING
	05/24/83	169	SECOND READING
HB-0928	04/05/83	6	FIRST READING
	05/13/83	132	SECOND READING
	05/19/83	165	SECOND READING
	05/24/83	62	THIRD READING
HB-0929	04/05/83	7	FIRST READING
	05/13/83	133	SECOND READING
	05/13/83	135	OUT OF RECORD
	05/19/83	165	SECOND READING
	05/19/83	168	HELD ON SECOND
	05/23/83	35	SECOND READING
	05/24/83	110	THIRD READING
	10/20/83	13	VETO MESSAGE
HB-0930	04/05/83	7	FIRST READING
	04/28/83	12	SECOND READING
	05/10/83	43	THIRD READING
	06/29/83	29	CONCURRENCE
HB-0931	04/05/83	7	FIRST READING
HB-0932	04/05/83	7	FIRST READING
	05/03/83	38	SECOND READING
	05/12/83	26	THIRD READING
	06/29/83	100	CONCURRENCE
	10/18/83	124	VETO MESSAGE
	10/20/83	102	VETO MESSAGE
HB-0933	04/05/83	7	FIRST READING
	04/19/83	23	SECOND READING
	05/12/83	27	THIRD READING
	05/12/83	30	OUT OF RECORD
	05/24/83	64	RECALLED
	05/24/83	66	THIRD READING
	10/20/83	57	VETO MESSAGE
HB-0934	04/05/83	7	FIRST READING
	05/13/83	135	SECOND READING
	05/24/83	66	THIRD READING
HB-0935	04/05/83	7	FIRST READING
	04/21/83	47	SECOND READING
	04/27/83	52	THIRD READING
HB-0936	04/05/83	7	FIRST READING

PROGRAM-LRTRNMST
08/20/85
LEGISLATIVE INFORMATION SYSTEM
HOUSE OF REPRESENTATIVES
PAGE   73

MASTER TRANSCRIPT INDEX

BILL NUMBER	DATE	PAGE	ACTION
HB-0937	04/05/83	7	FIRST READING
HB-0938	04/05/83	7	FIRST READING
HB-0939	04/05/83	58	FIRST READING
HB-0940	04/05/83	58	FIRST READING
	05/13/83	136	SECOND READING
	05/24/83	68	THIRD READING
HB-0941	04/05/83	58	FIRST READING
	05/13/83	136	SECOND READING
	05/24/83	69	RECALLED
HB-0942	04/05/83	58	FIRST READING
HB-0943	04/05/83	58	FIRST READING
HB-0944	04/05/83	58	FIRST READING
	04/28/83	69	SECOND READING
	05/12/83	30	THIRD READING
HB-0945	04/05/83	58	FIRST READING
	04/21/83	13	SECOND READING
	05/12/83	31	THIRD READING
HB-0946	04/05/83	59	FIRST READING
	04/26/83	20	SECOND READING
	05/12/83	32	THIRD READING
	10/20/83	14	VETO MESSAGE
HB-0947	04/05/83	59	FIRST READING
	05/03/83	18	SECOND READING
	05/10/83	45	THIRD READING
HB-0948	04/05/83	59	FIRST READING
	05/13/83	137	SECOND READING
	05/24/83	70	THIRD READING
HB-0949	04/05/83	59	FIRST READING
	04/26/83	6	SECOND READING
	04/28/83	104	THIRD READING
HB-0950	04/05/83	59	FIRST READING
HB-0951	04/05/83	59	FIRST READING
HB-0952	04/05/83	59	FIRST READING
	05/18/83	2	SECOND READING
	05/20/83	55	RECALLED
	05/20/83	56	THIRD READING

PROGRAM-LRTRNMST
08/20/85
LEGISLATIVE INFORMATION SYSTEM
HOUSE OF REPRESENTATIVES
PAGE   74

MASTER TRANSCRIPT INDEX

BILL NUMBER	DATE	PAGE	ACTION
HB-0952 (cont'd)	12/12/84	5	MOTION
	12/12/84	34	MOTION
	12/12/84	101	CONCURRENCE
HB-0953	04/05/83	59	FIRST READING
	05/03/83	32	OTHER
HB-0954	04/05/83	59	FIRST READING
	05/03/83	38	SECOND READING
	05/12/83	37	THIRD READING
HB-0955	04/05/83	59	FIRST READING
	05/03/83	32	OTHER
HB-0956	04/05/83	59	FIRST READING
	04/26/83	6	SECOND READING
	04/28/83	105	THIRD READING
HB-0957	04/05/83	59	FIRST READING
	04/28/83	69	SECOND READING
	05/12/83	38	THIRD READING
HB-0958	04/05/83	59	FIRST READING
	04/28/83	15	SECOND READING
	05/10/83	46	THIRD READING
	10/19/83	26	VETO MESSAGE
HB-0959	04/05/83	59	FIRST READING
	05/13/83	137	SECOND READING
HB-0960	04/05/83	59	FIRST READING
	05/03/83	18	SECOND READING
	05/10/83	47	THIRD READING
	06/28/83	68	CONCURRENCE
	10/18/83	42	VETO MESSAGE
HB-0961	04/05/83	66	FIRST READING
	05/23/83	188	SECOND READING
	05/24/83	78	THIRD READING
HB-0962	04/05/83	60	FIRST READING
	05/06/83	36	OTHER
HB-0963	04/05/83	60	FIRST READING
	05/13/83	137	SECOND READING
	05/24/83	82	THIRD READING
	06/29/83	17	CONCURRENCE
	10/18/83	63	MOTION
	11/02/83	230	CONFERENCE
HB-0964	04/05/83	60	FIRST READING

BILL NUMBER	DATE	PAGE	ACTION
HB-0964 (cont'd)	05/13/83	137	SECOND READING
	05/24/83	84	THIRD READING
HB-0965	04/05/83	60	FIRST READING
	04/28/83	15	SECOND READING
	05/10/83	51	THIRD READING
	10/19/83	27	VETO MESSAGE
HB-0966	04/05/83	60	FIRST READING
	04/20/83	24	SECOND READING
	04/21/83	43	THIRD READING
HB-0967	04/05/83	60	FIRST READING
	04/20/83	24	SECOND READING
	04/21/83	44	THIRD READING
HB-0968	04/05/83	60	FIRST READING
HB-0969	04/05/83	60	FIRST READING
HB-0970	04/05/83	60	FIRST READING
	05/05/83	2	SECOND READING
	05/13/83	2	THIRD READING
HB-0971	04/05/83	60	FIRST READING
	05/03/83	5	OTHER
HB-0972	04/05/83	60	FIRST READING
	05/13/83	138	SECOND READING
	05/24/83	85	THIRD READING
HB-0973	04/05/83	60	FIRST READING
	05/06/83	36	OTHER
HB-0974	04/05/83	60	FIRST READING
	04/21/83	14	SECOND READING
	05/12/83	45	THIRD READING
	10/19/83	30	VETO MESSAGE
HB-0975	04/05/83	61	FIRST READING
	04/28/83	70	SECOND READING
	05/12/83	50	THIRD READING
	06/28/83	69	CONCURRENCE
	10/20/83	107	VETO MESSAGE
HB-0976	04/05/83	61	FIRST READING
	04/28/83	70	SECOND READING
	05/12/83	53	THIRD READING
	05/12/83	55	RECALLED
HB-0977	04/05/83	61	FIRST READING

BILL NUMBER	DATE	PAGE	ACTION
HB-0977 (cont'd)	05/03/83	39	SECOND READING
	05/12/83	61	RECALLED
	05/12/83	62	THIRD READING
HB-0978	04/05/83	61	FIRST READING
HB-0979	04/05/83	61	FIRST READING
HB-0980	04/05/83	61	FIRST READING
	05/03/83	12	OTHER
HB-0981	04/05/83	61	FIRST READING
HB-0982	04/05/83	61	FIRST READING
HB-0983	04/05/83	61	FIRST READING
HB-0984	04/05/83	61	FIRST READING
HB-0985	04/05/83	61	FIRST READING
	05/13/83	181	SECOND READING
	05/24/83	228	THIRD READING
	06/29/83	91	CONCURRENCE
HB-0986	04/05/83	61	FIRST READING
	04/28/83	70	SECOND READING
	05/12/83	63	THIRD READING
HB-0987	04/05/83	61	FIRST READING
HB-0988	04/05/83	61	FIRST READING
	04/21/83	47	SECOND READING
	04/27/83	52	THIRD READING
HB-0989	04/05/83	62	FIRST READING
	05/06/83	36	OTHER
HB-0990	04/05/83	62	FIRST READING
	05/06/83	36	OTHER
HB-0991	04/05/83	62	FIRST READING
	05/06/83	36	OTHER
HB-0992	04/05/83	62	FIRST READING
	05/06/83	36	OTHER
HB-0993	04/05/83	62	FIRST READING
	05/06/83	36	OTHER
HB-0994	04/05/83	62	FIRST READING

BILL NUMBER	DATE	PAGE	ACTION
HB-0995	04/05/83	62	FIRST READING
	05/13/83	138	SECOND READING
	05/25/83	203	THIRD READING
HB-0996	04/05/83	62	FIRST READING
	05/13/83	182	SECOND READING
	05/20/83	57	THIRD READING
HB-0997	04/05/83	62	FIRST READING
	04/21/83	47	SECOND READING
	04/27/83	52	THIRD READING
	06/28/83	71	CONCURRENCE
HB-0998	04/05/83	62	FIRST READING
	05/04/83	55	OTHER
HB-0999	04/05/83	62	FIRST READING
	04/21/83	47	SECOND READING
	04/27/83	52	THIRD READING
HB-1000	04/05/83	62	FIRST READING
	05/13/83	138	SECOND READING
	05/24/83	86	THIRD READING
HB-1001	04/05/83	62	FIRST READING
	05/13/83	139	SECOND READING
	05/26/83	218	THIRD READING
	06/29/83	92	CONCURRENCE
HB-1002	04/05/83	62	FIRST READING
	04/28/83	71	SECOND READING
	05/12/83	67	THIRD READING
	06/28/83	206	CONCURRENCE
	07/01/83	204	CONFERENCE
HB-1003	04/05/83	62	FIRST READING
	04/28/83	15	SECOND READING
	05/10/83	52	THIRD READING
HB-1004	04/05/83	63	FIRST READING
	05/23/84	11	SECOND READING
	05/24/84	116	THIRD READING
	05/24/84	118	OUT OF RECORD
	05/24/84	133	THIRD READING
HB-1005	04/05/83	63	FIRST READING
HB-1006	04/05/83	63	FIRST READING
HB-1007	04/05/83	63	FIRST READING
	05/13/83	139	SECOND READING

BILL NUMBER	DATE	PAGE	ACTION
HB-1007 (cont'd)	05/13/83	139	HELD ON SECOND
	05/04/84	38	MOTION
HB-1008	04/05/83	63	FIRST READING
HB-1009	04/05/83	63	FIRST READING
	05/13/83	140	SECOND READING
	05/25/83	290	RECALLED
	05/25/83	291	OUT OF RECORD
	05/25/83	292	SECOND READING
	05/27/83	208	THIRD READING
HB-1010	04/05/83	63	FIRST READING
HB-1011	04/05/83	63	FIRST READING
HB-1012	04/05/83	63	FIRST READING
HB-1013	04/05/83	63	FIRST READING
HB-1014	04/05/83	63	FIRST READING
HB-1015	04/05/83	63	FIRST READING
HB-1016	04/05/83	63	FIRST READING
HB-1017	04/05/83	64	FIRST READING
	04/28/83	113	SECOND READING
	05/05/83	7	THIRD READING
	06/29/83	100	CONCURRENCE
HB-1018	04/05/83	64	FIRST READING
	05/03/83	12	OTHER
HB-1019	04/05/83	64	FIRST READING
	05/03/83	5	OTHER
HB-1020	04/05/83	64	FIRST READING
	05/13/83	182	SECOND READING
	05/20/83	58	THIRD READING
HB-1021	04/05/83	64	FIRST READING
HB-1022	04/05/83	64	FIRST READING
HB-1023	04/05/83	64	FIRST READING
	05/13/83	161	SECOND READING
	05/24/83	88	THIRD READING
	10/20/83	164	VETO MESSAGE
HB-1024	04/05/83	64	FIRST READING

BILL NUMBER	DATE	PAGE	ACTION
HB-1024 (cont'd)	04/28/83	72	SECOND READING
	05/12/83	70	RECALLED
	05/12/83	86	SECOND READING
	05/12/83	87	THIRD READING
	06/25/83	74	NON-CONCURRENCE
	06/25/83	111	MOTION
	06/29/83	223	CONCURRENCE
	06/29/83	226	OUT OF RECORD
	06/30/83	114	CONCURRENCE
	10/18/83	45	VETO MESSAGE
HB-1025	04/05/83	64	FIRST READING
HB-1026	04/05/83	64	FIRST READING
	05/13/83	140	SECOND READING
	05/25/83	28	THIRD READING
HB-1027	04/05/83	64	FIRST READING
HB-1028	04/05/83	64	FIRST READING
HB-1029	04/05/83	64	FIRST READING
	04/28/83	113	SECOND READING
	05/05/83	7	THIRD READING
HB-1030	04/05/83	65	FIRST READING
	05/06/83	36	OTHER
HB-1031	04/05/83	65	FIRST READING
	10/19/83	230	MOTION
HB-1032	04/05/83	65	FIRST READING
	04/28/83	72	SECOND READING
	05/12/83	71	RECALLED
	05/12/83	72	THIRD READING
	10/18/83	125	VETO MESSAGE
	10/20/83	61	VETO MESSAGE
HB-1033	04/05/83	65	FIRST READING
HB-1034	04/05/83	65	FIRST READING
	05/03/83	19	SECOND READING
	05/10/83	53	THIRD READING
HB-1035	04/05/83	65	FIRST READING
HB-1036	04/05/83	65	FIRST READING
	05/13/83	141	SECOND READING
	05/25/83	31	THIRD READING
HB-1037	04/05/83	65	FIRST READING

BILL NUMBER	DATE	PAGE	ACTION
HB-1037 (cont'd)	05/10/83	3	SECOND READING
	05/13/83	2	THIRD READING
	06/28/83	131	CONCURRENCE
HB-1038	04/05/83	65	FIRST READING
	04/21/83	48	SECOND READING
	04/27/83	52	THIRD READING
HB-1039	04/05/83	65	FIRST READING
	04/28/83	15	SECOND READING
	05/10/83	54	THIRD READING
HB-1040	04/05/83	65	FIRST READING
	05/03/83	23	OTHER
HB-1041	04/05/83	65	FIRST READING
HB-1042	04/05/83	65	FIRST READING
HB-1043	04/05/83	66	FIRST READING
	04/28/83	16	SECOND READING
	05/10/83	55	THIRD READING
HB-1044	04/05/83	66	FIRST READING
HB-1045	04/05/83	66	FIRST READING
	04/28/83	73	SECOND READING
	05/12/83	75	THIRD READING
	06/29/83	18	CONCURRENCE
	06/30/83	140	CONFERENCE
	06/30/83	143	OUT OF RECORD
	06/30/83	144	MOTION
	06/30/83	145	CONFERENCE
HB-1046	04/06/83	3	FIRST READING
HB-1047	04/06/83	3	FIRST READING
HB-1048	04/06/83	3	FIRST READING
	05/19/83	168	SECOND READING
	05/19/83	169	HELD ON SECOND
	05/23/83	35	SECOND READING
	05/25/83	32	THIRD READING
HB-1049	04/06/83	3	FIRST READING
HB-1050	04/06/83	3	FIRST READING
	05/13/83	141	SECOND READING
	05/25/83	34	THIRD READING
HB-1051	04/06/83	3	FIRST READING

BILL NUMBER	DATE	PAGE	ACTION
HB-1051 (cont'd)	05/13/83	182	SECOND READING
	05/20/83	59	THIRD READING
HB-1052	04/06/83	3	FIRST READING
	05/13/83	183	SECOND READING
	05/20/83	60	THIRD READING
	06/28/83	72	CONCURRENCE
HB-1053	04/06/83	4	FIRST READING
	04/28/83	80	SECOND READING
	05/12/83	88	THIRD READING
HB-1054	04/06/83	4	FIRST READING
	05/19/83	170	SECOND READING
	05/24/83	97	RECALLED
	05/24/83	291	RECALLED
	05/26/83	63	RECALLED
	05/26/83	64	THIRD READING
	06/29/83	113	CONCURRENCE
	06/29/83	113	OUT OF RECORD
	06/29/83	175	CONCURRENCE
	07/01/83	213	CONFERENCE
	10/19/83	166	VETO MESSAGE
HB-1055	04/06/83	4	FIRST READING
	05/05/83	2	SECOND READING
	05/13/83	2	THIRD READING
HB-1056	04/06/83	4	FIRST READING
	05/13/83	142	SECOND READING
	05/25/83	65	THIRD READING
HB-1057	04/06/83	4	FIRST READING
	05/05/83	2	SECOND READING
	05/13/83	2	THIRD READING
	06/28/83	141	CONCURRENCE
HB-1058	04/06/83	4	FIRST READING
	05/06/83	36	OTHER
HB-1059	04/06/83	4	FIRST READING
	05/03/83	32	OTHER
HB-1060	04/06/83	4	FIRST READING
	05/06/83	36	OTHER
HB-1061	04/06/83	4	FIRST READING
	04/21/83	15	SECOND READING
	05/12/83	95	THIRD READING
HB-1062	04/06/83	63	FIRST READING

BILL NUMBER	DATE	PAGE	ACTION
HB-1063	04/06/83	63	FIRST READING
	05/08/84	11	SECOND READING
	05/25/84	123	OUT OF RECORD
HB-1064	04/06/83	63	FIRST READING
HB-1065	04/06/83	63	FIRST READING
	05/13/83	159	SECOND READING
	05/25/83	35	THIRD READING
	06/29/83	243	CONCURRENCE
HB-1066	04/06/83	63	FIRST READING
	04/28/83	16	SECOND READING
	05/10/83	56	THIRD READING
HB-1067	04/06/83	64	FIRST READING
	05/13/83	143	SECOND READING
	05/25/83	36	THIRD READING
	10/20/83	63	VETO MESSAGE
HB-1068	04/06/83	64	FIRST READING
	04/28/83	113	SECOND READING
	05/05/83	7	THIRD READING
HB-1069	04/06/83	64	FIRST READING
	05/06/83	36	OTHER
	04/10/84	5	SECOND READING
	04/24/84	12	RECALLED
	04/25/84	6	SECOND READING
	05/03/84	45	THIRD READING
HB-1070	04/06/83	64	FIRST READING
HB-1071	04/06/83	64	FIRST READING
	04/28/83	16	SECOND READING
	05/10/83	56	THIRD READING
HB-1072	04/06/83	64	FIRST READING
	04/28/83	16	SECOND READING
	05/10/83	63	THIRD READING
HB-1073	04/06/83	64	FIRST READING
	04/28/83	80	SECOND READING
	05/12/83	96	THIRD READING
HB-1074	04/06/83	64	FIRST READING
	04/28/83	80	SECOND READING
	05/12/83	104	THIRD READING
HB-1075	04/06/83	64	FIRST READING
	04/28/83	113	SECOND READING

PROGRAM-LRTRNMST
08/20/85
LEGISLATIVE INFORMATION SYSTEM
HOUSE OF REPRESENTATIVES

MASTER TRANSCRIPT INDEX
PAGE 83

BILL NUMBER	DATE	PAGE	ACTION
HB-1075 (cont'd)	05/05/83	7	THIRD READING
HB-1076	04/06/83	64	FIRST READING
	04/28/83	17	SECOND READING
	05/10/83	65	THIRD READING
	06/28/83	126	CONCURRENCE
	06/28/83	127	OUT OF RECORD
	06/28/83	152	CONCURRENCE
HB-1077	04/06/83	54	FIRST READING
	04/28/83	31	SECOND READING
	05/12/83	125	THIRD READING
HB-1078	04/06/83	64	FIRST READING
	05/13/83	144	SECOND READING
	05/25/83	38	THIRD READING
HB-1079	04/06/83	64	FIRST READING
	05/13/83	144	SECOND READING
	05/25/83	45	THIRD READING
	06/28/83	72	CONCURRENCE
	10/19/83	119	VETO MESSAGE
HB-1080	04/06/83	64	FIRST READING
HB-1081	04/06/83	64	FIRST READING
	05/23/83	36	SECOND READING
	05/25/83	46	THIRD READING
	06/29/83	113	CONCURRENCE
HB-1082	04/06/83	65	FIRST READING
	04/28/83	81	SECOND READING
	05/12/83	107	THIRD READING
HB-1083	04/06/83	65	FIRST READING
	04/26/83	21	SECOND READING
	05/12/83	113	THIRD READING
HB-1084	04/06/83	65	FIRST READING
	04/28/83	82	SECOND READING
	05/12/83	120	THIRD READING
HB-1085	04/06/83	65	FIRST READING
	05/13/83	183	SECOND READING
	05/20/83	62	THIRD READING
HB-1086	04/06/83	65	FIRST READING
	05/13/83	145	SECOND READING
	05/25/83	49	RECALLED
	05/25/83	53	THIRD READING

PROGRAM-LRTRNMST
08/20/85
LEGISLATIVE INFORMATION SYSTEM
HOUSE OF REPRESENTATIVES

MASTER TRANSCRIPT INDEX
PAGE 84

BILL NUMBER	DATE	PAGE	ACTION
HB-1087	04/06/83	65	FIRST READING
HB-1088	04/06/83	65	FIRST READING
HB-1089	04/06/83	65	FIRST READING
	04/26/83	21	SECOND READING
	05/12/83	121	THIRD READING
	06/28/83	151	CONCURRENCE
HB-1090	04/06/83	65	FIRST READING
	05/18/83	3	SECOND READING
	05/20/83	63	THIRD READING
	06/28/83	134	CONCURRENCE
HB-1091	04/06/83	65	FIRST READING
	04/28/83	113	SECOND READING
	05/05/83	7	THIRD READING
HB-1092	04/06/83	65	FIRST READING
	05/13/83	145	SECOND READING
	05/25/83	54	THIRD READING
	06/30/83	74	CONCURRENCE
	06/30/83	88	MOTION
HB-1093	04/06/83	65	FIRST READING
	05/03/83	9	OTHER
HB-1094	04/06/83	65	FIRST READING
	05/03/83	9	OTHER
HB-1095	04/06/83	65	FIRST READING
HB-1096	04/06/83	65	FIRST READING
HB-1097	04/06/83	65	FIRST READING
HB-1098	04/06/83	66	FIRST READING
HB-1099	04/06/83	66	FIRST READING
HB-1100	04/06/83	66	FIRST READING
	04/26/83	22	SECOND READING
	05/12/83	122	THIRD READING
HB-1101	04/06/83	66	FIRST READING
	05/13/83	184	SECOND READING
	05/20/83	66	THIRD READING
HB-1102	04/06/83	66	FIRST READING
	05/13/83	145	SECOND READING
	05/26/83	2	THIRD READING

PROGRAM-LRTRNMST
08/20/85
LEGISLATIVE INFORMATION SYSTEM
HOUSE OF REPRESENTATIVES
PAGE   85

MASTER TRANSCRIPT INDEX

BILL NUMBER	DATE	PAGE	ACTION
HB-1103	04/06/83	66	FIRST READING
HB-1104	04/06/83	66	FIRST READING
	05/13/83	146	SECOND READING
	05/13/83	148	OUT OF RECORD
	05/19/83	170	SECOND READING
	05/26/83	7	THIRD READING
HB-1105	04/06/83	66	FIRST READING
	05/13/83	149	SECOND READING
	05/26/83	9	THIRD READING
HB-1106	04/06/83	66	FIRST READING
HB-1107	04/06/83	66	FIRST READING
	05/03/83	35	OTHER
HB-1108	04/07/83	2	FIRST READING
	05/23/83	36	SECOND READING
	05/24/83	99	RECALLED
	05/25/83	291	RECALLED
	05/26/83	70	THIRD READING
	06/28/83	74	CONCURRENCE
	10/19/83	167	VETO MESSAGE
HB-1109	04/07/83	3	FIRST READING
HB-1110	04/07/83	3	FIRST READING
HB-1111	04/07/83	3	FIRST READING
	05/13/83	184	SECOND READING
	05/20/83	68	THIRD READING
HB-1112	04/07/83	3	FIRST READING
HB-1113	04/07/83	3	FIRST READING
HB-1114	04/07/83	3	FIRST READING
	05/03/83	19	SECOND READING
	05/10/83	66	THIRD READING
HB-1115	04/07/83	3	FIRST READING
	05/03/83	2	OTHER
HB-1116	04/07/83	3	FIRST READING
	05/13/83	149	SECOND READING
	05/26/83	13	THIRD READING
HB-1117	04/07/83	3	FIRST READING
	05/13/83	184	SECOND READING
	05/20/83	69	THIRD READING

PROGRAM-LRTRNMST
08/20/85
LEGISLATIVE INFORMATION SYSTEM
HOUSE OF REPRESENTATIVES
PAGE   86

MASTER TRANSCRIPT INDEX

BILL NUMBER	DATE	PAGE	ACTION
HB-1117 (cont'd)	06/27/83	171	CONCURRENCE
	07/02/83	138	CONFERENCE
HB-1118	04/07/83	3	FIRST READING
	04/28/83	82	SECOND READING
	05/12/83	123	THIRD READING
HB-1119	04/07/83	3	FIRST READING
	05/23/83	36	SECOND READING
	05/26/83	19	THIRD READING
HB-1120	04/07/83	3	FIRST READING
	05/03/83	40	SECOND READING
	05/12/83	124	THIRD READING
HB-1121	04/07/83	3	FIRST READING
	04/26/83	21	SECOND READING
	05/12/83	125	RECALLED
	05/12/83	129	THIRD READING
	06/27/83	172	CONCURRENCE
	06/27/83	174	MOTION
	06/27/83	176	CONCURRENCE
	10/20/83	6	VETO MESSAGE
HB-1122	04/07/83	3	FIRST READING
	05/03/83	8	OTHER
HB-1123	04/07/83	3	FIRST READING
	05/03/83	8	OTHER
	04/25/84	5	SECOND READING
	05/03/84	45	THIRD READING
HB-1124	04/07/83	82	FIRST READING
	05/11/83	13	SECOND READING
	05/13/83	2	THIRD READING
HB-1125	04/07/83	82	FIRST READING
	05/06/83	36	OTHER
HB-1126	04/07/83	82	FIRST READING
HB-1127	04/07/83	82	FIRST READING
HB-1128	04/07/83	82	FIRST READING
	04/03/84	4	SECOND READING
	04/24/84	13	THIRD READING
HB-1129	04/07/83	82	FIRST READING
	05/03/83	35	OTHER
HB-1130	04/07/83	83	FIRST READING

BILL NUMBER	DATE	PAGE	ACTION
HB-1130 (cont'd)	05/18/83	33	SECOND READING
	05/20/83	72	THIRD READING
	11/04/83	149	CONCURRENCE
HB-1131	04/07/83	83	FIRST READING
	05/13/83	149	SECOND READING
	05/26/83	24	THIRD READING
HB-1132	04/07/83	83	FIRST READING
HB-1133	04/07/83	83	FIRST READING
	05/13/83	149	SECOND READING
	05/26/83	96	THIRD READING
	06/28/83	73	CONCURRENCE
	10/19/83	16	VETO MESSAGE
HB-1134	04/07/83	83	FIRST READING
	05/13/83	150	SECOND READING
	05/13/83	152	HELD ON SECOND
	05/18/83	42	SECOND READING
	05/23/83	177	RECALLED
	05/26/83	97	THIRD READING
	06/28/83	132	CONCURRENCE
HB-1135	04/07/83	83	FIRST READING
HB-1136	04/07/83	83	FIRST READING
	04/28/83	84	SECOND READING
	05/12/83	135	THIRD READING
HB-1137	04/07/83	83	FIRST READING
	05/13/83	152	SECOND READING
	05/25/83	204	THIRD READING
HB-1138	04/07/83	83	FIRST READING
	05/13/83	152	SECOND READING
	05/26/83	73	THIRD READING
	06/28/83	74	CONCURRENCE
HB-1139	04/07/83	83	FIRST READING
	05/25/83	300	SECOND READING
	05/26/83	25	THIRD READING
HB-1140	04/07/83	83	FIRST READING
	04/27/83	33	OTHER
HB-1141	04/07/83	83	FIRST READING
	05/13/83	153	SECOND READING
	05/25/83	224	THIRD READING
	06/28/83	75	CONCURRENCE
	10/19/83	36	VETO MESSAGE

BILL NUMBER	DATE	PAGE	ACTION
HB-1142	04/07/83	83	FIRST READING
	05/05/83	3	SECOND READING
	05/13/83	184	SECOND READING
	05/20/83	76	THIRD READING
HB-1143	04/07/83	84	FIRST READING
	05/13/83	185	SECOND READING
	05/20/83	77	THIRD READING
	06/27/83	172	CONCURRENCE
	07/01/83	215	CONFERENCE
HB-1144	04/07/83	84	FIRST READING
	04/28/83	94	SECOND READING
	05/12/83	138	THIRD READING
	06/29/83	102	CONCURRENCE
HB-1145	04/07/83	84	FIRST READING
HB-1146	04/07/83	84	FIRST READING
HB-1147	04/07/83	84	FIRST READING
HB-1148	04/07/83	84	FIRST READING
	05/13/83	153	SECOND READING
	05/26/83	97	THIRD READING
HB-1149	04/07/83	84	FIRST READING
	05/13/83	153	SECOND READING
	05/26/83	29	THIRD READING
HB-1150	04/07/83	84	FIRST READING
HB-1151	04/07/83	84	FIRST READING
HB-1152	04/07/83	84	FIRST READING
HB-1153	04/07/83	84	FIRST READING
	05/13/83	153	SECOND READING
	05/26/83	39	THIRD READING
HB-1154	04/07/83	84	FIRST READING
	05/13/83	154	SECOND READING
	05/26/83	46	THIRD READING
HB-1155	04/07/83	84	FIRST READING
	05/13/83	154	SECOND READING
	05/24/83	229	THIRD READING
	06/29/83	244	CONCURRENCE
HB-1156	04/07/83	85	FIRST READING
	05/13/83	160	SECOND READING

BILL NUMBER	DATE	PAGE	ACTION
HB-1156 (cont'd)	05/26/83	58	RECALLED
	05/26/83	58	THIRD READING
	06/28/83	207	CONCURRENCE
	10/19/83	52	VETO MESSAGE
HB-1157	04/07/83	85	FIRST READING
	05/13/83	160	SECOND READING
	05/26/83	97	THIRD READING
HB-1158	04/07/83	85	FIRST READING
	04/28/83	17	SECOND READING
	05/10/83	67	THIRD READING
HB-1159	04/07/83	85	FIRST READING
	05/13/83	161	SECOND READING
	05/26/83	62	THIRD READING
HB-1160	04/07/83	85	FIRST READING
HB-1161	04/07/83	85	FIRST READING
	05/18/83	3	SECOND READING
	05/20/83	78	THIRD READING
HB-1162	04/07/83	85	FIRST READING
	05/13/83	162	SECOND READING
	05/26/83	226	THIRD READING
	05/27/83	18	THIRD READING
HB-1163	04/07/83	85	FIRST READING
HB-1164	04/07/83	85	FIRST READING
	05/03/83	40	SECOND READING
	05/12/83	138	THIRD READING
HB-1165	04/07/83	85	FIRST READING
	05/18/83	4	SECOND READING
	05/20/83	79	THIRD READING
HB-1166	04/07/83	85	FIRST READING
	05/13/83	178	SECOND READING
	05/26/83	97	THIRD READING
HB-1167	04/07/83	85	FIRST READING
	05/13/83	190	SECOND READING
	05/26/83	87	THIRD READING
HB-1168	04/07/83	85	FIRST READING
HB-1169	04/07/83	86	FIRST READING
	04/20/83	25	TABLED

BILL NUMBER	DATE	PAGE	ACTION
HB-1170	04/07/83	86	FIRST READING
	05/13/83	186	SECOND READING
	05/20/83	90	THIRD READING
	10/18/83	46	VETO MESSAGE
HB-1171	04/07/83	86	FIRST READING
	04/28/83	17	SECOND READING
	05/10/83	72	THIRD READING
HB-1172	04/07/83	86	FIRST READING
	04/19/83	72	TABLED
HB-1173	04/07/83	86	FIRST READING
HB-1174	04/07/83	86	FIRST READING
HB-1175	04/07/83	86	FIRST READING
HB-1176	04/07/83	86	FIRST READING
HB-1177	04/07/83	86	FIRST READING
HB-1178	04/07/83	87	FIRST READING
	05/13/83	164	SECOND READING
	05/26/83	110	RECALLED
	05/26/83	112	THIRD READING
	06/27/83	176	CONCURRENCE
	07/01/83	27	CONFERENCE
	07/02/83	27	CONFERENCE
HB-1179	04/07/83	87	FIRST READING
	04/28/83	84	SECOND READING
	05/12/83	153	RECALLED
	05/12/83	154	THIRD READING
	06/29/83	102	CONCURRENCE
	10/18/83	47	VETO MESSAGE
	10/18/83	49	OUT OF RECORD
	10/18/83	50	VETO MESSAGE
HB-1180	04/07/83	87	FIRST READING
	05/13/83	164	SECOND READING
	05/25/83	78	THIRD READING
HB-1181	04/07/83	87	FIRST READING
HB-1182	04/07/83	87	FIRST READING
	05/19/83	174	SECOND READING
	05/26/83	97	THIRD READING
	06/29/83	44	CONCURRENCE
HB-1183	04/07/83	87	FIRST READING

BILL NUMBER	DATE	PAGE	ACTION
HB-1184	04/07/83	87	FIRST READING
HB-1185	04/07/83	87	FIRST READING
HB-1186	04/07/83	87	FIRST READING
	05/17/83	22	SECOND READING
	05/02/84	43	SECOND READING
	05/24/84	8	THIRD READING
	05/24/84	11	OUT OF RECORD
	05/24/84	63	THIRD READING
HB-1187	04/07/83	87	FIRST READING
	05/19/83	174	SECOND READING
	05/26/83	118	RECALLED
	05/26/83	119	THIRD READING
HB-1188	04/07/83	87	FIRST READING
	05/17/83	23	SECOND READING
	05/02/84	44	SECOND READING
	05/18/84	110	RECALLED
	05/18/84	113	THIRD READING
HB-1189	04/07/83	88	FIRST READING
	05/17/83	23	SECOND READING
	05/26/83	121	THIRD READING
HB-1190	04/07/83	88	FIRST READING
	05/02/84	44	SECOND READING
	05/24/84	11	OUT OF RECORD
	06/26/84	132	CONCURRENCE
HB-1191	04/07/83	88	FIRST READING
	04/28/83	113	SECOND READING
	05/05/83	7	THIRD READING
HB-1192	04/07/83	88	FIRST READING
	05/03/83	20	SECOND READING
	05/10/83	73	THIRD READING
	06/27/83	173	CONCURRENCE
HB-1193	04/07/83	88	FIRST READING
HB-1194	04/07/83	88	FIRST READING
	05/03/83	10	OTHER
HB-1195	04/07/83	88	FIRST READING
	05/20/83	198	MOTION
HB-1196	04/07/83	88	FIRST READING
	05/13/83	186	SECOND READING
	05/20/83	91	RECALLED

BILL NUMBER	DATE	PAGE	ACTION
HB-1196 (cont'd)	05/20/83	93	THIRD READING
	06/28/83	76	CONCURRENCE
HB-1197	04/07/83	88	FIRST READING
HB-1198	04/07/83	88	FIRST READING
HB-1199	04/13/83	2	FIRST READING
	05/26/83	47	MOTION
	05/26/83	284	SECOND READING
	05/27/83	85	THIRD READING
HB-1200	04/13/83	2	FIRST READING
	05/03/83	7	OTHER
HB-1201	04/13/83	2	FIRST READING
	05/13/83	186	SECOND READING
	05/20/83	94	TABLED
HB-1202	04/13/83	2	FIRST READING
	05/18/83	200	SECOND READING
	05/20/83	95	THIRD READING
HB-1203	04/13/83	2	FIRST READING
	05/17/83	23	SECOND READING
	05/27/83	133	MOTION
	05/27/83	136	THIRD READING
HB-1204	04/13/83	2	FIRST READING
	05/17/83	24	SECOND READING
	05/26/83	97	THIRD READING
HB-1205	04/13/83	2	FIRST READING
	05/17/83	24	SECOND READING
	05/26/83	128	THIRD READING
	06/28/83	51	CONCURRENCE
	10/18/83	67	MOTION
	11/03/83	38	CONFERENCE
HB-1206	04/13/83	2	FIRST READING
	05/17/83	24	SECOND READING
	05/26/83	129	RECALLED
HB-1207	04/13/83	2	FIRST READING
	05/04/83	3	OTHER
HB-1208	04/13/83	2	FIRST READING
	05/13/83	186	SECOND READING
	05/20/83	4	THIRD READING
	06/28/83	77	CONCURRENCE
	10/20/83	66	VETO MESSAGE

BILL NUMBER	DATE	PAGE	ACTION
HB-1209	04/13/83	2	FIRST READING
	04/28/83	18	SECOND READING
	05/10/83	74	THIRD READING
HB-1210	04/13/83	2	FIRST READING
	05/17/84	4	SECOND READING
	05/24/84	261	THIRD READING
HB-1211	04/13/83	2	FIRST READING
	05/22/84	9	SECOND READING
	05/24/84	267	THIRD READING
	05/25/84	86	THIRD READING
HB-1212	04/13/83	5	FIRST READING
HB-1213	04/13/83	5	FIRST READING
	05/13/83	187	SECOND READING
	05/20/83	95	THIRD READING
HB-1214	04/13/83	5	FIRST READING
HB-1215	04/13/83	5	FIRST READING
	04/26/83	23	TABLED
HB-1216	04/13/83	5	FIRST READING
	05/17/83	25	SECOND READING
	05/16/84	47	SECOND READING
	05/24/84	87	RECALLED
	05/24/84	88	HELD ON SECOND
	05/24/84	271	SECOND READING
	05/24/84	272	THIRD READING
HB-1217	04/13/83	6	FIRST READING
	05/04/83	6	OTHER
HB-1218	04/13/83	6	FIRST READING
	05/03/83	2	OTHER
HB-1219	04/13/83	6	FIRST READING
	04/27/83	32	OTHER
HB-1220	04/13/83	6	FIRST READING
	05/04/83	6	OTHER
HB-1221	04/13/83	6	FIRST READING
	05/17/83	25	SECOND READING
HB-1222	04/13/83	6	FIRST READING
	05/17/83	35	SECOND READING
	05/26/83	130	THIRD READING

BILL NUMBER	DATE	PAGE	ACTION
HB-1223	04/13/83	6	FIRST READING
	05/03/83	40	SECOND READING
	05/12/83	159	THIRD READING
	10/20/83	16	VETO MESSAGE
HB-1224	04/13/83	6	FIRST READING
	05/17/83	35	SECOND READING
	05/26/83	132	THIRD READING
HB-1225	04/13/83	6	FIRST READING
	05/13/83	187	SECOND READING
	05/20/83	97	RECALLED
	05/20/83	98	THIRD READING
	06/28/83	133	CONCURRENCE
HB-1226	04/13/83	6	FIRST READING
	05/10/83	3	SECOND READING
	05/18/83	4	SECOND READING
	05/20/83	99	THIRD READING
HB-1227	04/13/83	6	FIRST READING
	05/17/83	35	SECOND READING
	05/26/83	139	THIRD READING
HB-1228	04/13/83	6	FIRST READING
	04/28/83	85	SECOND READING
	05/12/83	161	THIRD READING
HB-1229	04/13/83	6	FIRST READING
HB-1230	04/13/83	6	FIRST READING
	05/10/83	3	SECOND READING
	05/13/83	187	SECOND READING
	05/20/83	100	THIRD READING
HB-1231	04/13/83	7	FIRST READING
	05/13/83	188	SECOND READING
	05/20/83	100	THIRD READING
HB-1232	04/13/83	7	FIRST READING
	05/19/83	177	SECOND READING
	05/26/83	140	THIRD READING
HB-1233	04/13/83	7	FIRST READING
HB-1234	04/13/83	7	FIRST READING
HB-1235	04/13/83	7	FIRST READING
	05/13/83	188	SECOND READING
	05/20/83	101	THIRD READING

PROGRAM-LRTRNMST
08/20/85
LEGISLATIVE INFORMATION SYSTEM
HOUSE OF REPRESENTATIVES
PAGE 95

MASTER TRANSCRIPT INDEX

BILL NUMBER	DATE	PAGE	ACTION
HB-1236	04/13/83	7	FIRST READING
	05/17/83	36	SECOND READING
	05/27/83	133	MOTION
	05/27/83	136	THIRD READING
HB-1237	04/13/83	61	FIRST READING
	05/17/83	36	SECOND READING
	05/27/83	133	MOTION
	05/27/83	136	THIRD READING
HB-1238	04/13/83	61	FIRST READING
	05/17/83	36	SECOND READING
	05/27/83	133	MOTION
	05/27/83	136	THIRD READING
HB-1239	04/13/83	61	FIRST READING
	05/17/83	37	SECOND READING
	05/17/83	40	OUT OF RECORD
	05/17/83	41	SECOND READING
	05/26/83	141	THIRD READING
	10/19/83	15	VETO MESSAGE
HB-1240	04/13/83	62	FIRST READING
	04/28/83	87	SECOND READING
	05/12/83	171	THIRD READING
HB-1241	04/13/83	62	FIRST READING
HB-1242	04/13/83	62	FIRST READING
	04/28/83	87	SECOND READING
	05/12/83	172	THIRD READING
HB-1243	04/13/83	62	FIRST READING
	05/06/83	36	OTHER
HB-1244	04/13/83	62	FIRST READING
	04/28/83	87	SECOND READING
	05/12/83	173	THIRD READING
HB-1245	04/13/83	62	FIRST READING
	05/13/83	189	SECOND READING
	05/20/83	102	THIRD READING
HB-1246	04/13/83	62	FIRST READING
HB-1247	04/13/83	62	FIRST READING
	05/03/83	11	TABLED
HB-1248	04/13/83	62	FIRST READING
	05/05/83	3	SECOND READING
	05/13/83	2	THIRD READING

PROGRAM-LRTRNMST
08/20/85
LEGISLATIVE INFORMATION SYSTEM
HOUSE OF REPRESENTATIVES
PAGE 96

MASTER TRANSCRIPT INDEX

BILL NUMBER	DATE	PAGE	ACTION
HB-1249	04/13/83	62	FIRST READING
	05/13/83	189	SECOND READING
	05/20/83	114	THIRD READING
	06/27/83	177	CONCURRENCE
	07/01/83	217	CONFERENCE
HB-1250	04/13/83	62	FIRST READING
	05/17/83	40	SECOND READING
	05/26/83	145	THIRD READING
	06/28/83	134	CONCURRENCE
HB-1251	04/13/83	62	FIRST READING
	05/03/83	7	OTHER
HB-1252	04/13/83	62	FIRST READING
	05/03/83	21	SECOND READING
	05/10/83	75	THIRD READING
HB-1253	04/13/83	62	FIRST READING
	05/19/83	178	SECOND READING
	05/26/83	145	THIRD READING
HB-1254	04/13/83	62	FIRST READING
HB-1255	04/13/83	63	FIRST READING
	05/17/83	40	SECOND READING
	05/26/83	97	THIRD READING
	06/29/83	111	CONCURRENCE
HB-1256	04/13/83	63	FIRST READING
	05/06/83	36	OTHER
HB-1257	04/13/83	63	FIRST READING
	05/24/83	184	SECOND READING
	05/26/83	75	THIRD READING
	06/28/83	106	CONCURRENCE
	07/02/83	76	CONFERENCE
	10/19/83	168	VETO MESSAGE
HB-1258	04/13/83	63	FIRST READING
HB-1259	04/13/83	63	FIRST READING
	05/19/83	179	SECOND READING
	05/25/83	79	THIRD READING
	10/19/83	150	VETO MESSAGE
HB-1260	04/13/83	63	FIRST READING
	05/19/83	266	SECOND READING
	05/19/83	269	OUT OF RECORD
	05/24/83	256	SECOND READING
	05/25/83	83	THIRD READING

BILL NUMBER	DATE	PAGE	ACTION
HB-1260 (cont'd)	06/28/83	136	CONCURRENCE
	10/19/83	153	VETO MESSAGE
HB-1261	04/13/83	63	FIRST READING
	05/18/83	5	SECOND READING
	05/20/83	119	THIRD READING
	06/28/83	78	CONCURRENCE
HB-1262	04/13/83	63	FIRST READING
	05/17/83	41	SECOND READING
	05/26/83	148	THIRD READING
	06/28/83	82	CONCURRENCE
	10/20/83	18	VETO MESSAGE
HB-1263	04/13/83	63	FIRST READING
HB-1264	04/13/83	63	FIRST READING
	05/17/83	190	SECOND READING
	05/23/83	110	THIRD READING
	06/28/83	83	CONCURRENCE
	07/01/83	129	CONFERENCE
HB-1265	04/13/83	63	FIRST READING
HB-1266	04/13/83	63	FIRST READING
HB-1267	04/13/83	63	FIRST READING
HB-1268	04/13/83	63	FIRST READING
HB-1269	04/13/83	64	FIRST READING
	05/17/83	41	SECOND READING
HB-1270	04/13/83	64	FIRST READING
HB-1271	04/13/83	64	FIRST READING
HB-1272	04/13/83	64	FIRST READING
	05/17/83	42	SECOND READING
HB-1273	04/13/83	64	FIRST READING
HB-1274	04/13/83	64	FIRST READING
HB-1275	04/13/83	64	FIRST READING
	05/17/83	42	SECOND READING
	05/26/83	149	THIRD READING
HB-1276	04/13/83	64	FIRST READING
HB-1277	04/13/83	64	FIRST READING

BILL NUMBER	DATE	PAGE	ACTION
HB-1278	04/13/83	64	FIRST READING
HB-1279	04/13/83	64	FIRST READING
	05/06/83	36	OTHER
HB-1280	04/13/83	64	FIRST READING
	05/17/83	43	SECOND READING
	05/27/83	24	THIRD READING
	06/28/83	84	CONCURRENCE
HB-1281	04/13/83	64	FIRST READING
	05/17/83	44	SECOND READING
	05/27/83	26	THIRD READING
HB-1282	04/13/83	64	FIRST READING
	05/23/83	37	SECOND READING
	05/27/83	27	THIRD READING
HB-1283	04/13/83	65	FIRST READING
	05/13/83	191	SECOND READING
	05/23/83	111	THIRD READING
HB-1284	04/13/83	65	FIRST READING
HB-1285	04/13/83	65	FIRST READING
	05/11/83	13	SECOND READING
	05/13/83	2	THIRD READING
HB-1286	04/13/83	65	FIRST READING
	05/05/83	3	SECOND READING
	05/13/83	2	THIRD READING
HB-1287	04/13/83	65	FIRST READING
	05/13/83	191	SECOND READING
	05/23/83	112	THIRD READING
	06/28/83	127	CONCURRENCE
HB-1288	04/13/83	65	FIRST READING
	05/06/83	29	MOTION
	05/17/83	44	SECOND READING
	05/26/83	97	THIRD READING
HB-1289	04/13/83	65	FIRST READING
HB-1290	04/13/83	65	FIRST READING
	05/17/83	44	SECOND READING
	05/17/83	54	OUT OF RECORD
	05/19/83	179	SECOND READING
	05/26/83	81	THIRD READING
HB-1291	04/13/83	65	FIRST READING

BILL NUMBER	DATE	PAGE	ACTION
HB-1291(cont'd)	04/27/83	4	TABLED
HB-1292	04/13/83	65	FIRST READING
HB-1293	04/13/83	65	FIRST READING
	05/19/83	221	SECOND READING
	05/23/83	113	THIRD READING
	06/28/83	84	CONCURRENCE
	07/01/83	252	CONFERENCE
HB-1294	04/13/83	65	FIRST READING
	05/03/83	35	OTHER
HB-1295	04/13/83	65	FIRST READING
HB-1296	04/13/83	65	FIRST READING
	04/15/83	52	SECOND READING
	04/15/83	52	MOTION
	04/20/83	8	THIRD READING
HB-1297	04/13/83	66	FIRST READING
	05/13/83	55	MOTION
HB-1298	04/13/83	66	FIRST READING
	05/03/83	4	OTHER
HB-1299	04/13/83	66	FIRST READING
HB-1300	04/13/83	66	FIRST READING
	05/03/83	11	OTHER
	05/03/83	35	OTHER
HB-1301	04/13/83	66	FIRST READING
HB-1302	04/13/83	66	FIRST READING
	05/03/83	7	OTHER
	05/22/84	19	SECOND READING
	05/23/84	47	THIRD READING
	06/21/84	94	CONCURRENCE
HB-1303	04/13/83	66	FIRST READING
HB-1304	04/13/83	66	FIRST READING
HB-1305	04/13/83	66	FIRST READING
	05/17/83	55	SECOND READING
	05/25/83	86	THIRD READING
HB-1306	04/13/83	66	FIRST READING
	05/18/83	43	SECOND READING
	05/27/83	30	THIRD READING

BILL NUMBER	DATE	PAGE	ACTION
HB-1307	04/13/83	66	FIRST READING
	05/03/83	12	OTHER
HB-1308	04/13/83	66	FIRST READING
	05/11/83	13	SECOND READING
	05/13/83	2	THIRD READING
HB-1309	04/13/83	66	FIRST READING
	05/05/83	3	SECOND READING
	05/13/83	3	THIRD READING
HB-1310	04/13/83	66	FIRST READING
	05/05/83	3	SECOND READING
	05/13/83	3	THIRD READING
	06/29/83	111	CONCURRENCE
	06/29/83	112	OUT OF RECORD
	06/29/83	122	CONCURRENCE
HB-1311	04/13/83	66	FIRST READING
	05/18/83	5	SECOND READING
	05/18/83	7	HELD ON SECOND
	05/19/83	223	SECOND READING
	05/23/83	116	THIRD READING
HB-1312	04/13/83	67	FIRST READING
HB-1313	04/13/83	67	FIRST READING
	05/18/83	43	SECOND READING
	05/27/83	31	THIRD READING
HB-1314	04/13/83	67	FIRST READING
	05/18/83	43	SECOND READING
	05/18/83	44	HELD ON SECOND
	05/19/83	184	SECOND READING
	05/19/83	185	HELD ON SECOND
	05/23/83	190	SECOND READING
	05/25/83	304	SECOND READING
HB-1315	04/13/83	67	FIRST READING
	04/28/83	87	SECOND READING
	05/12/83	174	THIRD READING
HB-1316	04/13/83	67	FIRST READING
	04/28/83	88	SECOND READING
	05/12/83	179	THIRD READING
HB-1317	04/13/83	67	FIRST READING
	04/28/83	90	SECOND READING
	05/12/83	180	THIRD READING
HB-1318	04/13/83	67	FIRST READING

BILL NUMBER	DATE	PAGE	ACTION
HB-1319	04/13/83	67	FIRST READING
	04/28/83	91	SECOND READING
	05/12/83	180	THIRD READING
	11/04/83	152	CONCURRENCE
HB-1320	04/13/83	67	FIRST READING
	04/28/83	91	SECOND READING
	05/12/83	181	THIRD READING
HB-1321	04/13/83	67	FIRST READING
HB-1322	04/13/83	67	FIRST READING
HB-1323	04/13/83	67	FIRST READING
	05/13/83	192	SECOND READING
	05/23/83	120	THIRD READING
	10/18/83	49	VETO MESSAGE
HB-1324	04/13/83	67	FIRST READING
HB-1325	04/13/83	67	FIRST READING
HB-1326	04/13/83	68	FIRST READING
	05/05/83	3	SECOND READING
	05/13/83	3	THIRD READING
HB-1327	04/13/83	68	FIRST READING
HB-1328	04/13/83	68	FIRST READING
	05/18/83	44	SECOND READING
	05/18/83	45	HELD ON SECOND
	05/19/83	185	SECOND READING
	05/27/83	38	THIRD READING
	06/28/83	91	CONCURRENCE
HB-1329	04/13/83	68	FIRST READING
	05/18/83	7	SECOND READING
	05/23/83	129	THIRD READING
HB-1330	04/13/83	68	FIRST READING
	05/18/83	45	SECOND READING
	05/25/83	207	THIRD READING
	11/04/83	6	CONCURRENCE
HB-1331	04/13/83	68	FIRST READING
	05/18/83	52	SECOND READING
	05/27/83	40	THIRD READING
HB-1332	04/13/83	68	FIRST READING
	05/18/83	53	SECOND READING
	05/27/83	42	THIRD READING

BILL NUMBER	DATE	PAGE	ACTION
HB-1333	04/13/83	68	FIRST READING
	05/18/83	7	SECOND READING
	05/23/83	121	THIRD READING
	05/23/83	129	OUT OF RECORD
HB-1334	04/13/83	68	FIRST READING
	05/18/83	53	SECOND READING
	04/26/84	15	SECOND READING
	05/22/84	145	THIRD READING
	05/25/84	123	THIRD READING
HB-1335	04/13/83	68	FIRST READING
	04/27/83	57	OTHER
	05/10/84	17	SECOND READING
	05/16/84	70	THIRD READING
	05/16/84	72	OUT OF RECORD
	05/16/84	281	RECALLED
	05/18/84	114	THIRD READING
HB-1336	04/13/83	68	FIRST READING
	05/18/83	8	SECOND READING
	05/23/83	129	THIRD READING
	06/29/83	112	CONCURRENCE
	10/19/83	17	VETO MESSAGE
HB-1337	04/13/83	68	FIRST READING
	05/03/83	22	SECOND READING
	05/10/83	75	THIRD READING
	06/29/83	21	CONCURRENCE
	07/01/83	218	CONFERENCE
HB-1338	04/13/83	68	FIRST READING
	05/05/83	3	SECOND READING
	05/13/83	3	THIRD READING
HB-1339	04/13/83	69	FIRST READING
	05/03/83	41	HELD ON SECOND
	05/18/83	59	SECOND READING
	05/24/83	231	THIRD READING
	06/28/83	92	CONCURRENCE
	10/20/83	7	VETO MESSAGE
HB-1340	04/13/83	69	FIRST READING
	05/13/83	192	SECOND READING
	05/26/83	97	THIRD READING
HB-1341	04/13/83	69	FIRST READING
HB-1342	04/13/83	69	FIRST READING
	05/19/83	186	SECOND READING
	05/27/83	45	THIRD READING

PROGRAM-LRTRNMST
08/20/85
LEGISLATIVE INFORMATION SYSTEM
HOUSE OF REPRESENTATIVES
PAGE 103

MASTER TRANSCRIPT INDEX

BILL NUMBER	DATE	PAGE	ACTION
HB-1342 (cont'd)	10/19/83	18	VETO MESSAGE
HB-1343	04/13/83	69	FIRST READING
HB-1344	04/13/83	69	FIRST READING
	05/19/83	187	SECOND READING
	05/26/83	97	THIRD READING
HB-1345	04/13/83	69	FIRST READING
	05/18/83	45	SECOND READING
	05/23/83	174	RECALLED
	05/23/83	174	RECALLED
	05/24/83	232	THIRD READING
HB-1346	04/13/83	69	FIRST READING
HB-1347	04/13/83	69	FIRST READING
	05/03/83	31	OTHER
HB-1348	04/13/83	69	FIRST READING
	05/03/83	31	OTHER
	05/10/84	18	SECOND READING
	05/23/84	50	THIRD READING
	06/26/84	133	CONCURRENCE
HB-1349	04/13/83	69	FIRST READING
	05/06/83	22	MOTION
HB-1350	04/13/83	69	FIRST READING
	05/06/83	36	OTHER
HB-1351	04/13/83	69	FIRST READING
	05/13/83	192	SECOND READING
	05/23/83	130	THIRD READING
HB-1352	04/13/83	69	FIRST READING
HB-1353	04/13/83	70	FIRST READING
	05/03/83	23	OTHER
HB-1354	04/13/83	70	FIRST READING
HB-1355	04/13/83	70	FIRST READING
	05/11/83	13	SECOND READING
	05/13/83	166	THIRD READING
	06/29/83	23	CONCURRENCE
HB-1356	04/13/83	70	FIRST READING
	05/13/83	193	SECOND READING
	05/23/83	132	THIRD READING

PROGRAM-LRTRNMST
08/20/85
LEGISLATIVE INFORMATION SYSTEM
HOUSE OF REPRESENTATIVES
PAGE 104

MASTER TRANSCRIPT INDEX

BILL NUMBER	DATE	PAGE	ACTION
HB-1357	04/13/83	70	FIRST READING
HB-1358	04/13/83	70	FIRST READING
	05/18/83	45	SECOND READING
	05/27/83	46	THIRD READING
HB-1359	04/13/83	70	FIRST READING
	05/13/83	193	SECOND READING
	05/23/83	132	THIRD READING
HB-1360	04/13/83	70	FIRST READING
HB-1361	04/13/83	70	FIRST READING
HB-1362	04/13/83	70	FIRST READING
HB-1363	04/13/83	70	FIRST READING
	05/18/83	46	SECOND READING
	05/26/83	97	THIRD READING
HB-1364	04/14/83	2	FIRST READING
HB-1365	04/14/83	2	FIRST READING
	11/01/83	59	MOTION
HB-1366	04/14/83	3	FIRST READING
	05/06/83	36	OTHER
HB-1367	04/14/83	3	FIRST READING
	05/18/83	46	SECOND READING
	05/27/83	48	THIRD READING
HB-1368	04/14/83	3	FIRST READING
	05/18/83	47	SECOND READING
	05/27/83	49	THIRD READING
HB-1369	04/14/83	3	FIRST READING
	05/19/83	116	SECOND READING
	05/27/83	50	RECALLED
	05/27/83	53	THIRD READING
	06/29/83	114	CONCURRENCE
HB-1370	04/14/83	3	FIRST READING
	05/13/83	193	SECOND READING
	05/23/83	133	THIRD READING
HB-1371	04/14/83	3	FIRST READING
	05/13/83	193	SECOND READING
	05/23/83	134	RECALLED
	05/23/83	135	THIRD READING
	06/28/83	207	CONCURRENCE

PROGRAM-LRTRNMST
08/20/85

LEGISLATIVE INFORMATION SYSTEM
HOUSE OF REPRESENTATIVES

PAGE 105

MASTER TRANSCRIPT INDEX

BILL NUMBER	DATE	PAGE	ACTION
HB-1371 (cont'd)	06/30/83	164	CONFERENCE
	10/20/83	64	VETO MESSAGE
HB-1372	04/14/83	3	FIRST READING
	05/05/83	3	SECOND READING
	05/13/83	3	THIRD READING
HB-1373	04/14/83	3	FIRST READING
	05/18/83	48	SECOND READING
	05/27/83	54	THIRD READING
HB-1374	04/14/83	3	FIRST READING
	05/18/83	60	SECOND READING
	05/26/83	97	THIRD READING
HB-1375	04/14/83	3	FIRST READING
	05/06/83	36	OTHER
	06/28/84	47	CONCURRENCE
HB-1376	04/14/83	3	FIRST READING
	05/19/83	189	SECOND READING
	05/24/83	233	THIRD READING
HB-1377	04/14/83	3	FIRST READING
HB-1378	04/14/83	3	FIRST READING
	05/18/83	61	SECOND READING
	05/26/83	97	THIRD READING
	06/28/83	137	CONCURRENCE
HB-1379	04/14/83	3	FIRST READING
	05/18/83	61	SECOND READING
	05/27/83	55	THIRD READING
HB-1380	04/14/83	4	FIRST READING
HB-1381	04/14/83	4	FIRST READING
	05/05/83	3	SECOND READING
	05/13/83	193	SECOND READING
	05/23/83	136	RECALLED
	05/23/83	137	THIRD READING
HB-1382	04/14/83	4	FIRST READING
	05/18/83	61	SECOND READING
	05/27/83	56	THIRD READING
	06/29/83	21	CONCURRENCE
	07/02/83	138	CONFERENCE
	10/19/83	39	VETO MESSAGE
	10/20/83	166	VETO MESSAGE
HB-1383	04/14/83	4	FIRST READING

PROGRAM-LRTRNMST
08/20/85

LEGISLATIVE INFORMATION SYSTEM
HOUSE OF REPRESENTATIVES

PAGE 106

MASTER TRANSCRIPT INDEX

BILL NUMBER	DATE	PAGE	ACTION
HB-1383 (cont'd)	05/03/83	35	OTHER
	05/12/83	184	MOTION
	05/18/83	62	SECOND READING
	05/26/83	97	THIRD READING
HB-1384	04/14/83	4	FIRST READING
HB-1385	04/14/83	4	FIRST READING
	05/18/83	62	SECOND READING
	05/27/83	56	THIRD READING
HB-1386	04/14/83	4	FIRST READING
	05/18/83	63	SECOND READING
	05/26/83	97	THIRD READING
	06/28/83	93	CONCURRENCE
	10/18/83	58	VETO MESSAGE
HB-1387	04/14/83	4	FIRST READING
HB-1388	04/14/83	4	FIRST READING
	05/13/83	194	SECOND READING
	05/26/83	97	THIRD READING
	06/28/83	93	CONCURRENCE
	10/18/83	59	VETO MESSAGE
HB-1389	04/14/83	4	FIRST READING
	05/18/83	63	SECOND READING
	05/27/83	57	THIRD READING
HB-1390	04/14/83	4	FIRST READING
	05/11/83	13	SECOND READING
	05/13/83	3	THIRD READING
	06/28/83	94	CONCURRENCE
HB-1391	04/14/83	4	FIRST READING
	05/05/83	3	SECOND READING
	05/13/83	3	THIRD READING
HB-1392	04/14/83	4	FIRST READING
HB-1393	04/14/83	5	FIRST READING
HB-1394	04/14/83	75	FIRST READING
	05/13/83	194	SECOND READING
	05/23/83	138	THIRD READING
HB-1395	04/14/83	75	FIRST READING
	05/10/84	18	HELD ON SECOND
	05/10/84	18	SECOND READING
	05/17/84	5	SECOND READING
	05/18/84	120	THIRD READING

PROGRAM-LRTRNMST
08/20/85
LEGISLATIVE INFORMATION SYSTEM
HOUSE OF REPRESENTATIVES
PAGE 107

MASTER TRANSCRIPT INDEX

BILL NUMBER	DATE	PAGE	ACTION
HB-1396	04/14/83	75	FIRST READING
	05/18/83	63	SECOND READING
	05/27/83	204	THIRD READING
HB-1397	04/14/83	75	FIRST READING
HB-1398	04/14/83	75	FIRST READING
HB-1399	04/14/83	75	FIRST READING
	05/06/83	4	MOTION
	05/18/83	64	SECOND READING
	05/27/83	115	THIRD READING
	06/28/83	56	CONCURRENCE
	04/25/84	16	MOTION
	04/26/84	77	MOTION
	04/26/84	81	CONFERENCE
	06/29/84	50	VETO MESSAGE
HB-1400	04/14/83	75	FIRST READING
	05/18/83	8	SECOND READING
	05/23/83	140	THIRD READING
HB-1401	04/14/83	75	FIRST READING
HB-1402	04/14/83	75	FIRST READING
	05/18/83	64	SECOND READING
	05/27/83	218	THIRD READING
	06/29/83	262	CONCURRENCE
	10/19/83	19	VETO MESSAGE
HB-1403	04/14/83	76	FIRST READING
HB-1404	04/14/83	76	FIRST READING
	05/18/83	64	SECOND READING
	05/27/83	61	RECALLED
	05/27/83	62	THIRD READING
HB-1405	04/14/83	76	FIRST READING
	05/18/83	65	SECOND READING
	05/27/83	219	THIRD READING
HB-1406	04/14/83	76	FIRST READING
	05/05/83	5	OTHER
HB-1407	04/14/83	76	FIRST READING
HB-1408	04/14/83	76	FIRST READING
	05/03/83	5	OTHER
HB-1409	04/14/83	76	FIRST READING
	05/03/83	22	SECOND READING

PROGRAM-LRTRNMST
08/20/85
LEGISLATIVE INFORMATION SYSTEM
HOUSE OF REPRESENTATIVES
PAGE 108

MASTER TRANSCRIPT INDEX

BILL NUMBER	DATE	PAGE	ACTION
HB-1409 (cont'd)	05/10/83	77	THIRD READING
	06/29/83	115	CONCURRENCE
HB-1410	04/14/83	76	FIRST READING
	05/19/83	189	SECOND READING
	05/24/83	100	RECALLED
	05/26/83	83	THIRD READING
HB-1411	04/14/83	76	FIRST READING
HB-1412	04/14/83	76	FIRST READING
	05/18/83	65	SECOND READING
	05/26/83	97	THIRD READING
HB-1413	04/14/83	76	FIRST READING
	05/18/83	39	SECOND READING
	05/23/83	141	THIRD READING
	06/29/83	116	CONCURRENCE
HB-1414	04/14/83	76	FIRST READING
	05/18/83	66	SECOND READING
	05/18/83	68	HELD ON SECOND
	05/25/83	305	SECOND READING
	05/27/83	220	THIRD READING
	06/29/83	118	CONCURRENCE
HB-1415	04/14/83	76	FIRST READING
HB-1416	04/14/83	76	FIRST READING
HB-1417	04/14/83	77	FIRST READING
HB-1418	04/14/83	77	FIRST READING
HB-1419	04/14/83	77	FIRST READING
HB-1420	04/14/83	77	FIRST READING
HB-1421	04/14/83	77	FIRST READING
HB-1422	04/14/83	77	FIRST READING
	05/03/83	3	OTHER
HB-1423	04/14/83	77	FIRST READING
HB-1424	04/14/83	77	FIRST READING
HB-1425	04/14/83	77	FIRST READING
	05/18/83	68	SECOND READING
HB-1426	04/14/83	77	FIRST READING

PROGRAM-LRTRNMST
08/20/85

LEGISLATIVE INFORMATION SYSTEM
HOUSE OF REPRESENTATIVES

PAGE 109

MASTER TRANSCRIPT INDEX

BILL NUMBER	DATE	PAGE	ACTION
HB-1426 (cont'd)	05/18/83	69	SECOND READING
	05/26/83	98	THIRD READING
HB-1427	04/14/83	77	FIRST READING
	05/18/83	69	SECOND READING
	04/11/84	30	SECOND READING
	04/26/84	10	THIRD READING
	06/26/84	137	CONCURRENCE
HB-1428	04/14/83	77	FIRST READING
	05/18/83	69	SECOND READING
HB-1429	04/14/83	77	FIRST READING
HB-1430	04/14/83	77	FIRST READING
HB-1431	04/14/83	78	FIRST READING
HB-1432	04/14/83	78	FIRST READING
HB-1433	04/14/83	78	FIRST READING
	05/18/83	8	SECOND READING
	05/23/83	142	THIRD READING
HB-1434	04/14/83	78	FIRST READING
	05/18/83	70	SECOND READING
HB-1435	04/14/83	78	FIRST READING
	05/03/83	5	OTHER
HB-1436	04/14/83	78	FIRST READING
	05/18/83	71	SECOND READING
HB-1437	04/14/83	78	FIRST READING
	05/18/83	71	SECOND READING
	05/26/83	98	THIRD READING
	06/28/83	97	CONCURRENCE
HB-1438	04/14/83	78	FIRST READING
	04/28/83	113	OTHER
HB-1439	04/14/83	78	FIRST READING
HB-1440	04/14/83	78	FIRST READING
HB-1441	04/14/83	78	FIRST READING
HB-1442	04/14/83	78	FIRST READING
	05/24/83	257	SECOND READING
	05/24/83	259	OUT OF RECORD
	05/24/83	269	SECOND READING

PROGRAM-LRTRNMST
08/20/85

LEGISLATIVE INFORMATION SYSTEM
HOUSE OF REPRESENTATIVES

PAGE 110

MASTER TRANSCRIPT INDEX

BILL NUMBER	DATE	PAGE	ACTION
HB-1442 (cont'd)	05/26/83	238	RECALLED
	05/26/83	240	THIRD READING
HB-1443	04/14/83	79	FIRST READING
HB-1444	04/14/83	79	FIRST READING
	05/13/83	195	SECOND READING
	05/23/83	145	THIRD READING
HB-1445	04/14/83	79	FIRST READING
	05/18/83	72	SECOND READING
HB-1446	04/14/83	79	FIRST READING
	05/03/83	7	OTHER
HB-1447	04/14/83	79	FIRST READING
	05/03/83	7	OTHER
HB-1448	04/14/83	79	FIRST READING
	04/11/84	7	SECOND READING
	05/22/84	150	THIRD READING
	06/26/84	139	CONCURRENCE
HB-1449	04/14/83	79	FIRST READING
	05/05/83	3	SECOND READING
	05/13/83	3	THIRD READING
HB-1450	04/14/83	79	FIRST READING
	05/05/83	3	SECOND READING
	05/13/83	3	THIRD READING
HB-1451	04/14/83	79	FIRST READING
	05/05/83	3	SECOND READING
	05/13/83	3	THIRD READING
HB-1452	04/14/83	79	FIRST READING
HB-1453	04/14/83	79	FIRST READING
	05/18/83	72	SECOND READING
HB-1454	04/14/83	79	FIRST READING
	05/18/83	72	SECOND READING
HB-1455	04/14/83	79	FIRST READING
	05/18/83	72	SECOND READING
	05/18/83	73	OUT OF RECORD
	05/19/83	190	SECOND READING
	05/19/83	203	HELD ON SECOND
	05/25/83	294	SECOND READING
	05/27/83	102	THIRD READING

MASTER TRANSCRIPT INDEX

BILL NUMBER	DATE	PAGE	ACTION
HB-1456	04/14/83	79	FIRST READING
HB-1457	04/14/83	79	FIRST READING
HB-1458	04/14/83	80	FIRST READING
HB-1459	04/14/83	80	FIRST READING
HB-1460	04/14/83	80	FIRST READING
	05/18/83	73	SECOND READING
	05/27/83	103	RECALLED
	05/27/83	106	OUT OF RECORD
HB-1461	04/14/83	80	FIRST READING
HB-1462	04/14/83	80	FIRST READING
	05/10/83	3	SECOND READING
	05/13/83	3	THIRD READING
HB-1463	04/14/83	80	FIRST READING
	05/18/83	8	SECOND READING
	05/23/83	150	THIRD READING
HB-1464	04/14/83	80	FIRST READING
HB-1465	04/14/83	80	FIRST READING
HB-1466	04/14/83	80	FIRST READING
	05/18/83	74	SECOND READING
	05/25/83	214	THIRD READING
HB-1467	04/14/83	80	FIRST READING
	05/13/83	195	SECOND READING
	05/23/83	151	THIRD READING
HB-1468	04/14/83	80	FIRST READING
HB-1469	04/14/83	80	FIRST READING
	05/06/83	36	OTHER
HB-1470	04/14/83	80	FIRST READING
	05/13/83	195	SECOND READING
	05/23/83	152	THIRD READING
	06/29/83	177	CONCURRENCE
	06/30/83	15	CONFERENCE
HB-1471	04/14/83	80	FIRST READING
HB-1472	04/14/83	80	FIRST READING
HB-1473	04/14/83	80	FIRST READING

MASTER TRANSCRIPT INDEX

BILL NUMBER	DATE	PAGE	ACTION
HB-1473(cont'd)	05/18/83	74	SECOND READING
	05/27/83	10	THIRD READING
	05/27/83	180	THIRD READING
	10/19/83	50	VETO MESSAGE
HB-1474	04/14/83	81	FIRST READING
	05/01/84	37	SECOND READING
	05/23/84	51	THIRD READING
	06/27/84	24	CONCURRENCE
	06/30/84	16	CONFERENCE
HB-1475	04/14/83	81	FIRST READING
HB-1476	04/14/83	81	FIRST READING
HB-1477	04/14/83	81	FIRST READING
	05/19/83	203	SECOND READING
HB-1478	04/14/83	81	FIRST READING
HB-1479	04/14/83	81	FIRST READING
HB-1480	04/14/83	81	FIRST READING
	05/19/83	203	SECOND READING
HB-1481	04/14/83	81	FIRST READING
HB-1482	04/14/83	81	FIRST READING
HB-1483	04/14/83	81	FIRST READING
	05/10/83	3	SECOND READING
	05/23/83	153	THIRD READING
HB-1484	04/14/83	81	FIRST READING
	05/18/83	75	SECOND READING
HB-1485	04/14/83	81	FIRST READING
	05/19/83	204	SECOND READING
	05/27/83	106	THIRD READING
HB-1486	04/14/83	81	FIRST READING
	05/18/83	9	SECOND READING
	05/25/83	210	THIRD READING
HB-1487	04/14/83	81	FIRST READING
HB-1488	04/14/83	82	FIRST READING
HB-1489	04/14/83	82	FIRST READING
	05/18/83	75	SECOND READING

PROGRAM-LRTRNMST
08/20/85
LEGISLATIVE INFORMATION SYSTEM
HOUSE OF REPRESENTATIVES
PAGE 113

MASTER TRANSCRIPT INDEX

BILL NUMBER	DATE	PAGE	ACTION
HB-1489 (cont'd)	05/27/83	204	THIRD READING
HB-1490	04/14/83	82	FIRST READING
	05/18/83	37	SECOND READING
	05/24/83	135	THIRD READING
HB-1491	04/14/83	82	FIRST READING
HB-1492	04/14/83	82	FIRST READING
	05/18/83	10	SECOND READING
	05/23/83	154	THIRD READING
HB-1493	04/14/83	82	FIRST READING
HB-1494	04/14/83	82	FIRST READING
	05/19/83	205	SECOND READING
HB-1495	04/14/83	82	FIRST READING
	05/13/83	196	SECOND READING
	05/23/83	155	THIRD READING
	06/28/83	97	CONCURRENCE
	10/19/83	20	VETO MESSAGE
HB-1496	04/14/83	82	FIRST READING
	05/05/83	3	SECOND READING
	05/13/83	3	THIRD READING
HB-1497	04/14/83	82	FIRST READING
	05/18/83	76	SECOND READING
	05/18/83	78	OUT OF RECORD
	05/19/83	208	SECOND READING
	05/26/83	98	THIRD READING
HB-1498	04/14/83	82	FIRST READING
	05/13/83	196	SECOND READING
	05/13/83	196	HELD ON SECOND
	05/18/83	10	SECOND READING
	05/23/83	156	THIRD READING
HB-1499	04/14/83	82	FIRST READING
	04/15/83	12	TABLED
HB-1500	04/14/83	82	FIRST READING
	05/18/83	79	SECOND READING
	05/27/83	229	THIRD READING
	10/19/83	80	VETO MESSAGE
	10/20/83	157	VETO MESSAGE
	10/20/83	172	VETO MESSAGE
HB-1501	04/14/83	82	FIRST READING
	05/18/83	10	SECOND READING

PROGRAM-LRTRNMST
08/20/85
LEGISLATIVE INFORMATION SYSTEM
HOUSE OF REPRESENTATIVES
PAGE 114

MASTER TRANSCRIPT INDEX

BILL NUMBER	DATE	PAGE	ACTION
HB-1501 (cont'd)	05/23/83	157	THIRD READING
HB-1502	04/14/83	82	FIRST READING
	05/18/83	40	SECOND READING
	05/23/83	158	THIRD READING
HB-1503	04/14/83	83	FIRST READING
	05/18/83	39	SECOND READING
	05/23/83	158	THIRD READING
	10/18/83	129	VETO MESSAGE
HB-1504	04/14/83	83	FIRST READING
	05/18/83	40	SECOND READING
	05/23/83	159	THIRD READING
	06/28/83	98	CONCURRENCE
HB-1505	04/14/83	83	FIRST READING
	05/13/83	196	SECOND READING
	05/23/83	160	THIRD READING
HB-1506	04/14/83	83	FIRST READING
HB-1507	04/14/83	83	FIRST READING
	05/18/83	80	SECOND READING
	05/26/83	98	THIRD READING
HB-1508	04/14/83	83	FIRST READING
	05/18/83	80	SECOND READING
	05/25/83	102	RECALLED
	05/25/83	108	MOTION
	05/26/83	279	THIRD READING
HB-1509	04/14/83	83	FIRST READING
	05/13/83	197	SECOND READING
	05/23/83	167	THIRD READING
HB-1510	04/14/83	83	FIRST READING
	05/06/83	36	OTHER
HB-1511	04/14/83	83	FIRST READING
	05/06/83	36	OTHER
HB-1512	04/14/83	83	FIRST READING
	05/06/83	36	OTHER
HB-1513	04/14/83	83	FIRST READING
	05/06/83	36	OTHER
HB-1514	04/14/83	83	FIRST READING
	05/06/83	36	OTHER

PROGRAM-LRTRNMST
08/20/85

LEGISLATIVE INFORMATION SYSTEM
HOUSE OF REPRESENTATIVES

PAGE 115

MASTER TRANSCRIPT INDEX

BILL NUMBER	DATE	PAGE	ACTION
HB-1515	04/14/83	83	FIRST READING
	05/06/83	36	OTHER
HB-1516	04/14/83	83	FIRST READING
	05/18/83	80	SECOND READING
HB-1517	04/14/83	83	FIRST READING
	05/06/83	3	TABLED
HB-1518	04/14/83	83	FIRST READING
	05/06/83	3	TABLED
HB-1519	04/14/83	84	FIRST READING
	05/06/83	3	TABLED
HB-1520	04/14/83	84	FIRST READING
	05/18/83	81	SECOND READING
	05/26/83	243	THIRD READING
HB-1521	04/14/83	84	FIRST READING
	05/18/83	82	SECOND READING
	05/26/83	247	THIRD READING
	06/28/83	99	CONCURRENCE
HB-1522	04/14/83	84	FIRST READING
	05/01/84	44	SECOND READING
	05/22/84	112	THIRD READING
HB-1523	04/14/83	84	FIRST READING
HB-1524	04/14/83	84	FIRST READING
HB-1525	04/14/83	84	FIRST READING
	05/13/83	197	SECOND READING
	05/23/83	169	THIRD READING
HB-1526	04/14/83	84	FIRST READING
	05/18/83	82	SECOND READING
	05/26/83	252	THIRD READING
HB-1527	04/14/83	84	FIRST READING
	05/18/83	82	SECOND READING
	05/26/83	98	THIRD READING
HB-1528	04/14/83	84	FIRST READING
	05/09/84	2	SECOND READING
	05/16/84	45	SECOND READING
	05/16/84	47	HELD ON SECOND
	05/16/84	236	SECOND READING
	05/17/84	233	THIRD READING

PROGRAM-LRTRNMST
08/20/85

LEGISLATIVE INFORMATION SYSTEM
HOUSE OF REPRESENTATIVES

PAGE 116

MASTER TRANSCRIPT INDEX

BILL NUMBER	DATE	PAGE	ACTION
HB-1529	04/14/83	84	FIRST READING
HB-1530	04/14/83	84	FIRST READING
	05/18/83	82	SECOND READING
	05/18/83	128	OUT OF RECORD
	05/18/83	129	SECOND READING
	05/26/83	254	THIRD READING
	10/19/83	98	VETO MESSAGE
HB-1531	04/14/83	84	FIRST READING
HB-1532	04/14/83	85	FIRST READING
HB-1533	04/14/83	85	FIRST READING
	05/06/83	36	OTHER
HB-1534	04/14/83	85	FIRST READING
HB-1535	04/14/83	85	FIRST READING
	05/03/83	8	OTHER
	05/15/84	66	SECOND READING
	05/15/84	67	OUT OF RECORD
	05/15/84	140	SECOND READING
	05/15/84	145	HELD ON SECOND
	05/17/84	5	SECOND READING
	05/17/84	8	MOTION
	05/17/84	10	HELD ON SECOND
	05/18/84	135	SECOND READING
	05/23/84	120	THIRD READING
	05/24/84	301	MOTION
HB-1536	04/14/83	85	FIRST READING
HB-1537	04/14/83	85	FIRST READING
HB-1538	04/14/83	85	FIRST READING
	05/18/83	157	SECOND READING
HB-1539	04/14/83	85	FIRST READING
HB-1540	04/14/83	85	FIRST READING
HB-1541	04/14/83	85	FIRST READING
	05/06/83	36	OTHER
HB-1542	04/14/83	85	FIRST READING
HB-1543	04/14/83	85	FIRST READING
	05/06/83	36	OTHER
HB-1544	04/14/83	85	FIRST READING

PROGRAM-LRTRNMST
08/20/85
LEGISLATIVE INFORMATION SYSTEM
HOUSE OF REPRESENTATIVES
PAGE 117

MASTER TRANSCRIPT INDEX

BILL NUMBER	DATE	PAGE	ACTION
HB-1545	04/14/83	85	FIRST READING
HB-1546	04/14/83	86	FIRST READING
	05/18/84	151	SECOND READING
	05/22/84	59	RECALLED
	05/22/84	63	MOTION
	05/23/84	32	THIRD READING
HB-1547	04/14/83	86	FIRST READING
	05/18/83	158	SECOND READING
HB-1548	04/14/83	86	FIRST READING
HB-1549	04/14/83	86	FIRST READING
	05/18/83	158	SECOND READING
	05/25/83	213	THIRD READING
	10/19/83	105	VETO MESSAGE
HB-1550	04/14/83	86	FIRST READING
	05/10/83	3	SECOND READING
	05/13/83	3	THIRD READING
HB-1551	04/14/83	86	FIRST READING
	05/18/83	159	SECOND READING
HB-1552	04/14/83	86	FIRST READING
HB-1553	04/14/83	86	FIRST READING
	05/03/83	10	OTHER
HB-1554	04/14/83	86	FIRST READING
	05/03/83	12	OTHER
HB-1555	04/14/83	86	FIRST READING
HB-1556	04/14/83	86	FIRST READING
	05/15/84	67	OUT OF RECORD
	05/16/84	13	SECOND READING
	05/18/84	122	THIRD READING
HB-1557	04/14/83	86	FIRST READING
	05/13/83	198	SECOND READING
	05/23/83	179	THIRD READING
	10/18/83	130	VETO MESSAGE
HB-1558	04/14/83	86	FIRST READING
	05/18/83	159	SECOND READING
	05/27/83	117	THIRD READING
HB-1559	04/14/83	86	FIRST READING
	05/18/83	160	SECOND READING

PROGRAM-LRTRNMST
08/20/85
LEGISLATIVE INFORMATION SYSTEM
HOUSE OF REPRESENTATIVES
PAGE 118

MASTER TRANSCRIPT INDEX

BILL NUMBER	DATE	PAGE	ACTION
HB-1559 (cont'd)	05/18/83	160	HELD ON SECOND
	05/19/83	116	SECOND READING
HB-1560	04/14/83	87	FIRST READING
HB-1561	04/14/83	87	FIRST READING
	05/18/83	160	SECOND READING
	05/27/83	205	THIRD READING
	06/28/83	105	CONCURRENCE
HB-1562	04/14/83	87	FIRST READING
	05/18/83	160	SECOND READING
	05/27/83	206	THIRD READING
HB-1563	04/14/83	87	FIRST READING
	05/18/83	160	SECOND READING
	05/10/84	19	SECOND READING
	05/16/84	65	THIRD READING
	06/22/84	10	CONCURRENCE
	06/29/84	24	CONCURRENCE
HB-1564	04/14/83	87	FIRST READING
	05/18/83	161	SECOND READING
	05/26/83	98	THIRD READING
HB-1565	04/14/83	87	FIRST READING
	05/18/83	161	SECOND READING
	05/27/83	133	MOTION
	05/27/83	137	THIRD READING
HB-1566	04/14/83	87	FIRST READING
	05/18/83	161	SECOND READING
	05/27/83	133	MOTION
	05/27/83	137	THIRD READING
HB-1567	04/14/83	87	FIRST READING
	05/13/83	198	SECOND READING
	05/23/83	181	THIRD READING
HB-1568	04/14/83	87	FIRST READING
HB-1569	04/14/83	87	FIRST READING
	05/04/83	55	OTHER
HB-1570	04/14/83	87	FIRST READING
HB-1571	04/14/83	88	FIRST READING
	05/18/83	161	SECOND READING
HB-1572	04/14/83	88	FIRST READING

PROGRAM-LRTRNMST
08/20/85

LEGISLATIVE INFORMATION SYSTEM
HOUSE OF REPRESENTATIVES

PAGE 119

MASTER TRANSCRIPT INDEX

BILL NUMBER	DATE	PAGE	ACTION
HB-1573	04/14/83	88	FIRST READING
	05/18/83	165	SECOND READING
	05/10/84	19	SECOND READING
	05/16/84	50	RECALLED
	05/22/84	45	THIRD READING
HB-1574	04/14/83	88	FIRST READING
	05/03/83	-2	OTHER
HB-1575	04/14/83	88	FIRST READING
	05/06/83	6	OTHER
HB-1576	04/14/83	88	FIRST READING
HB-1577	04/14/83	88	FIRST READING
	05/13/83	198	SECOND READING
	05/23/83	182	THIRD READING
HB-1578	04/15/83	4	FIRST READING
HB-1579	04/15/83	4	FIRST READING
	05/18/83	166	SECOND READING
	05/26/83	98	THIRD READING
HB-1580	04/15/83	4	FIRST READING
HB-1581	04/15/83	4	FIRST READING
HB-1582	04/15/83	4	FIRST READING
	04/28/83	114	TABLED
HB-1583	04/15/83	4	FIRST READING
	05/18/83	166	SECOND READING
	05/27/83	63	RECALLED
	05/27/83	66	THIRD READING
HB-1584	04/15/83	4	FIRST READING
	05/11/83	13	SECOND READING
	05/13/83	3	THIRD READING
	06/28/83	209	CONCURRENCE
HB-1585	04/15/83	4	FIRST READING
HB-1586	04/15/83	4	FIRST READING
HB-1587	04/15/83	5	FIRST READING
	05/18/83	182	SECOND READING
	04/04/84	3	SECOND READING
	05/03/84	48	THIRD READING
HB-1588	04/15/83	5	FIRST READING

PROGRAM-LRTRNMST
08/20/85

LEGISLATIVE INFORMATION SYSTEM
HOUSE OF REPRESENTATIVES

PAGE 120

MASTER TRANSCRIPT INDEX

BILL NUMBER	DATE	PAGE	ACTION
HB-1588 (cont'd)	05/03/83	10	OTHER
HB-1589	04/15/83	5	FIRST READING
HB-1590	04/15/83	5	FIRST READING
	05/13/83	199	SECOND READING
	05/23/83	185	THIRD READING
HB-1591	04/15/83	5	FIRST READING
	05/03/83	5	OTHER
	05/08/84	10	SECOND READING
	05/23/84	190	THIRD READING
HB-1592	04/15/83	5	FIRST READING
HB-1593	04/15/83	5	FIRST READING
	05/18/83	10	SECOND READING
	05/23/83	185	THIRD READING
	06/28/83	210	CONCURRENCE
HB-1594	04/15/83	5	FIRST READING
	05/18/83	183	SECOND READING
	04/26/84	13	SECOND READING
	05/03/84	16	THIRD READING
HB-1595	04/15/83	5	FIRST READING
	05/11/83	13	SECOND READING
	05/13/83	3	THIRD READING
HB-1596	04/15/83	5	FIRST READING
	05/18/83	33	SECOND READING
	05/23/83	186	THIRD READING
HB-1597	04/15/83	5	FIRST READING
	05/18/83	186	SECOND READING
	05/26/83	98	THIRD READING
HB-1598	04/15/83	6	FIRST READING
	05/13/83	199	SECOND READING
	05/23/83	218	THIRD READING
HB-1599	04/15/83	6	FIRST READING
	05/13/83	199	SECOND READING
	05/23/83	219	THIRD READING
	10/18/83	60	VETO MESSAGE
HB-1600	04/15/83	6	FIRST READING
HB-1601	04/15/83	6	FIRST READING
	05/04/83	6	OTHER

MASTER TRANSCRIPT INDEX

BILL NUMBER	DATE	PAGE	ACTION
HB-1602	04/15/83	6	FIRST READING
	05/13/83	200	SECOND READING
	05/23/83	222	THIRD READING
	06/28/83	216	CONCURRENCE
HB-1603	04/15/83	6	FIRST READING
	05/18/83	183	SECOND READING
	05/25/83	215	THIRD READING
	06/28/83	217	CONCURRENCE
HB-1604	04/15/83	6	FIRST READING
HB-1605	04/15/83	6	FIRST READING
HB-1606	04/15/83	7	FIRST READING
HB-1607	04/15/83	7	FIRST READING
	05/18/83	184	SECOND READING
	05/26/83	266	THIRD READING
HB-1608	04/15/83	7	FIRST READING
	05/06/83	36	OTHER
HB-1609	04/15/83	7	FIRST READING
HB-1610	04/15/83	7	FIRST READING
	05/18/83	184	SECOND READING
	05/27/83	214	THIRD READING
	06/29/83	119	CONCURRENCE
HB-1611	04/15/83	7	FIRST READING
	05/26/83	104	SECOND READING
	05/27/83	10	THIRD READING
	05/27/83	180	THIRD READING
HB-1612	04/15/83	7	FIRST READING
	05/18/83	186	SECOND READING
	05/27/83	169	THIRD READING
HB-1613	04/15/83	7	FIRST READING
	05/13/83	200	SECOND READING
	10/18/83	68	MOTION
	10/19/83	199	RECALLED
	10/20/83	97	THIRD READING
	11/04/83	136	CONCURRENCE
HB-1614	04/15/83	7	FIRST READING
	05/18/83	12	SECOND READING
	05/23/83	223	THIRD READING
HB-1615	04/15/83	7	FIRST READING

MASTER TRANSCRIPT INDEX

BILL NUMBER	DATE	PAGE	ACTION
HB-1615(cont'd)	05/03/83	4	OTHER
HB-1616	04/15/83	7	FIRST READING
HB-1617	04/15/83	7	FIRST READING
HB-1618	04/15/83	8	FIRST READING
HB-1619	04/15/83	8	FIRST READING
HB-1620	04/15/83	8	FIRST READING
HB-1621	04/15/83	8	FIRST READING
HB-1622	04/15/83	8	FIRST READING
HB-1623	04/15/83	8	FIRST READING
HB-1624	04/15/83	8	FIRST READING
	05/25/83	307	SECOND READING
HB-1625	04/15/83	8	FIRST READING
HB-1626	04/15/83	8	FIRST READING
	05/03/83	9	OTHER
HB-1627	04/15/83	8	FIRST READING
HB-1628	04/15/83	8	FIRST READING
	05/03/83	6	OTHER
HB-1629	04/15/83	9	FIRST READING
	05/03/83	6	OTHER
HB-1630	04/15/83	9	FIRST READING
	05/03/83	6	OTHER
HB-1631	04/15/83	9	FIRST READING
	05/03/83	10	OTHER
HB-1632	04/15/83	9	FIRST READING
	05/18/83	191	SECOND READING
	04/24/84	6	SECOND READING
	05/09/84	4	THIRD READING
HB-1633	04/15/83	9	FIRST READING
HB-1634	04/15/83	9	FIRST READING
HB-1635	04/15/83	9	FIRST READING

BILL NUMBER	DATE	PAGE	ACTION
HB-1636	04/15/83	9	FIRST READING
HB-1637	04/15/83	9	FIRST READING
HB-1638	04/15/83	9	FIRST READING
	05/18/83	191	SECOND READING
	05/25/83	217	THIRD READING
HB-1639	04/15/83	9	FIRST READING
HB-1640	04/15/83	9	FIRST READING
	05/06/83	36	OTHER
HB-1641	04/15/83	10	FIRST READING
HB-1642	04/15/83	10	FIRST READING
HB-1643	04/15/83	10	FIRST READING
	05/03/83	8	OTHER
HB-1644	04/15/83	10	FIRST READING
	05/18/83	192	SECOND READING
	10/19/83	202	SECOND READING
	10/19/83	202	HELD ON SECOND
	10/20/83	150	SECOND READING
	10/20/83	153	THIRD READING
HB-1645	04/15/83	10	FIRST READING
	05/04/83	5	OTHER
HB-1646	04/15/83	10	FIRST READING
	05/04/83	5	OTHER
HB-1647	04/15/83	10	FIRST READING
	05/04/83	5	OTHER
HB-1648	04/15/83	10	FIRST READING
HB-1649	04/15/83	10	FIRST READING
	05/13/83	200	SECOND READING
	05/23/83	224	THIRD READING
HB-1650	04/15/83	10	FIRST READING
	05/11/83	13	SECOND READING
	05/13/83	3	THIRD READING
	06/28/83	218	CONCURRENCE
HB-1651	04/15/83	10	FIRST READING
	05/13/83	201	SECOND READING
	05/24/83	3	THIRD READING
	06/28/83	219	CONCURRENCE

BILL NUMBER	DATE	PAGE	ACTION
HB-1652	04/15/83	10	FIRST READING
	05/18/83	13	SECOND READING
	05/24/83	3	THIRD READING
HB-1653	04/15/83	11	FIRST READING
	05/18/83	193	SECOND READING
	05/26/83	267	THIRD READING
	06/28/83	219	CONCURRENCE
	06/28/83	222	OUT OF RECORD
	06/29/83	123	CONCURRENCE
HB-1654	04/15/83	11	FIRST READING
	05/03/83	4	OTHER
HB-1655	04/15/83	11	FIRST READING
	05/03/83	9	OTHER
HB-1656	04/15/83	11	FIRST READING
HB-1657	04/15/83	11	FIRST READING
	05/03/83	9	OTHER
HB-1658	04/15/83	11	FIRST READING
	05/16/84	242	SECOND READING
	05/25/84	108	THIRD READING
	06/28/84	6	CONCURRENCE
HB-1659	04/15/83	11	FIRST READING
HB-1660	04/15/83	11	FIRST READING
HB-1661	04/15/83	11	FIRST READING
	05/23/83	41	SECOND READING
	05/27/83	10	THIRD READING
	05/27/83	194	THIRD READING
HB-1662	04/15/83	11	FIRST READING
	05/18/83	194	SECOND READING
HB-1663	04/15/83	104	FIRST READING
	05/22/84	29	SECOND READING
	05/25/84	110	THIRD READING
HB-1664	04/15/83	104	FIRST READING
HB-1665	04/15/83	104	FIRST READING
	05/13/83	201	SECOND READING
	05/24/83	16	THIRD READING
	06/28/83	105	CONCURRENCE
HB-1666	04/15/83	105	FIRST READING

BILL NUMBER	DATE	PAGE	ACTION
HB-1666 (cont'd)	05/18/83	194	SECOND READING
	05/26/83	294	THIRD READING
HB-1667	04/15/83	105	FIRST READING
	05/18/83	13	SECOND READING
	05/24/83	5	THIRD READING
	10/19/83	21	VETO MESSAGE
HB-1668	04/15/83	105	FIRST READING
	05/26/83	51	MOTION
HB-1669	04/15/83	105	FIRST READING
	05/13/83	202	SECOND READING
	05/24/83	17	THIRD READING
HB-1670	04/15/83	105	FIRST READING
	05/10/83	3	SECOND READING
	05/13/83	4	THIRD READING
HB-1671	04/15/83	105	FIRST READING
	05/04/83	3	OTHER
HB-1672	04/15/83	105	FIRST READING
	05/04/83	3	OTHER
HB-1673	04/15/83	105	FIRST READING
	05/13/83	202	SECOND READING
	05/24/83	9	THIRD READING
HB-1674	04/15/83	105	FIRST READING
	05/13/83	203	SECOND READING
	05/24/83	10	THIRD READING
	10/19/83	23	VETO MESSAGE
HB-1675	04/15/83	105	FIRST READING
	05/03/83	54	OTHER
HB-1676	04/15/83	105	FIRST READING
HB-1677	04/15/83	105	FIRST READING
HB-1678	04/15/83	105	FIRST READING
HB-1679	04/15/83	106	FIRST READING
	05/19/83	214	SECOND READING
HB-1680	04/15/83	106	FIRST READING
	05/11/83	13	SECOND READING
	05/18/83	14	SECOND READING
	05/24/83	18	THIRD READING

BILL NUMBER	DATE	PAGE	ACTION
HB-1681	04/15/83	106	FIRST READING
HB-1682	04/15/83	106	FIRST READING
HB-1683	04/15/83	106	FIRST READING
	05/18/83	15	SECOND READING
	05/24/83	11	THIRD READING
	10/18/83	30	VETO MESSAGE
HB-1684	04/15/83	106	FIRST READING
HB-1685	04/15/83	106	FIRST READING
	05/18/83	197	SECOND READING
HB-1686	04/15/83	106	FIRST READING
HB-1687	04/15/83	106	FIRST READING
	05/18/83	198	SECOND READING
HB-1688	04/15/83	106	FIRST READING
	05/18/83	198	SECOND READING
HB-1689	04/15/83	106	FIRST READING
HB-1690	04/15/83	139	FIRST READING
	05/03/83	6	OTHER
HB-1691	04/15/83	107	FIRST READING
	05/18/83	198	SECOND READING
HB-1692	04/15/83	107	FIRST READING
	05/03/83	4	OTHER
HB-1693	04/15/83	107	FIRST READING
HB-1694	04/15/83	107	FIRST READING
HB-1695	04/15/83	107	FIRST READING
	05/18/83	198	SECOND READING
HB-1696	04/15/83	107	FIRST READING
	04/28/83	92	SECOND READING
	05/12/83	181	THIRD READING
HB-1697	04/15/83	107	FIRST READING
	05/06/83	36	OTHER
HB-1698	04/15/83	110	FIRST READING
HB-1699	04/15/83	110	FIRST READING

BILL NUMBER	DATE	PAGE	ACTION
HB-1700	04/15/83	107	FIRST READING
	05/06/83	36	OTHER
HB-1701	04/15/83	107	FIRST READING
HB-1702	04/15/83	107	FIRST READING
	05/19/83	215	SECOND READING
HB-1703	04/15/83	107	FIRST READING
	05/18/83	201	SECOND READING
	05/26/83	268	THIRD READING
	10/18/83	87	VETO MESSAGE
HB-1704	04/15/83	107	FIRST READING
	05/13/83	203	SECOND READING
	05/24/83	27	THIRD READING
	06/29/83	126	CONCURRENCE
	06/30/84	193	CONFERENCE
HB-1705	04/15/83	107	FIRST READING
HB-1706	04/15/83	107	FIRST READING
HB-1707	04/15/83	108	FIRST READING
	05/10/83	3	SECOND READING
	05/13/83	166	THIRD READING
	06/28/83	222	CONCURRENCE
	10/18/83	87	VETO MESSAGE
HB-1708	04/15/83	108	FIRST READING
	05/18/83	15	SECOND READING
	05/24/83	28	THIRD READING
HB-1709	04/15/83	108	FIRST READING
	05/18/83	15	SECOND READING
	05/24/83	30	THIRD READING
HB-1710	04/15/83	108	FIRST READING
	05/04/83	5	OTHER
HB-1711	04/15/83	108	FIRST READING
HB-1712	04/15/83	108	FIRST READING
	05/19/83	217	SECOND READING
HB-1713	04/15/83	108	FIRST READING
HB-1714	04/15/83	108	FIRST READING
	05/18/83	202	SECOND READING
HB-1715	04/15/83	108	FIRST READING

BILL NUMBER	DATE	PAGE	ACTION
HB-1716	04/15/83	108	FIRST READING
HB-1717	04/15/83	108	FIRST READING
HB-1718	04/15/83	108	FIRST READING
HB-1719	04/15/83	108	FIRST READING
HB-1720	04/15/83	109	FIRST READING
	05/06/83	36	OTHER
HB-1721	04/15/83	109	FIRST READING
HB-1722	04/15/83	109	FIRST READING
HB-1723	04/15/83	109	FIRST READING
	05/13/83	203	SECOND READING
	05/24/83	31	THIRD READING
	06/28/83	106	CONCURRENCE
HB-1724	04/15/83	109	FIRST READING
	05/13/83	204	SECOND READING
	05/24/83	32	THIRD READING
HB-1725	04/15/83	109	FIRST READING
	05/18/83	202	SECOND READING
	05/25/83	222	THIRD READING
HB-1726	04/15/83	109	FIRST READING
	05/22/84	23	SECOND READING
	05/24/84	119	THIRD READING
HB-1727	04/15/83	109	FIRST READING
	05/06/83	36	OTHER
HB-1728	04/15/83	109	FIRST READING
	05/06/83	36	OTHER
HB-1729	04/15/83	109	FIRST READING
	05/03/83	9	OTHER
HB-1730	04/15/83	109	FIRST READING
	05/03/83	9	OTHER
HB-1731	04/15/83	109	FIRST READING
	05/03/83	7	OTHER
HB-1732	04/15/83	109	FIRST READING
	05/06/83	36	OTHER
HB-1733	04/15/83	109	FIRST READING

PROGRAM-LRTRNMST
08/20/85

LEGISLATIVE INFORMATION SYSTEM
HOUSE OF REPRESENTATIVES

PAGE 129

MASTER TRANSCRIPT INDEX

BILL NUMBER	DATE	PAGE	ACTION
HB-1733(cont'd)	05/03/83,,	9	OTHER
HB-1734	04/15/83	110	FIRST READING
	04/26/84	14	SECOND READING
	05/03/84	16	THIRD READING
HB-1735	04/15/83	110	FIRST READING
HB-1736	04/15/83	110	FIRST READING
HB-1737	04/15/83	110	FIRST READING
HB-1738	04/15/83	110	FIRST READING
	05/19/83	223	SECOND READING
	05/24/83	44	THIRD READING
HB-1739	04/15/83	110	FIRST READING
HB-1740	04/15/83	110	FIRST READING
	05/18/83	203	SECOND READING
HB-1741	04/15/83	110	FIRST READING
	05/06/83	36	OTHER
HB-1742	04/15/83	110	FIRST READING
	05/06/83	36	OTHER
	05/16/84	38	SECOND READING
	05/22/84	48	THIRD READING
HB-1743	04/15/83	110	FIRST READING
	05/06/83	36	OTHER
HB-1744	04/15/83	110	FIRST READING
	05/06/83	36	OTHER
HB-1745	04/15/83	110	FIRST READING
HB-1746	04/15/83	111	FIRST READING
HB-1747	04/15/83	111	FIRST READING
HB-1748	04/15/83	111	FIRST READING
HB-1749	04/15/83	111	FIRST READING
	05/06/83	36	OTHER
HB-1750	04/15/83	111	FIRST READING
	05/18/83	16	SECOND READING
	05/18/83	17	OUT OF RECORD
	05/18/83	33	SECOND READING
	05/24/83	45	THIRD READING

PROGRAM-LRTRNMST
08/20/85

LEGISLATIVE INFORMATION SYSTEM
HOUSE OF REPRESENTATIVES

PAGE 130

MASTER TRANSCRIPT INDEX

BILL NUMBER	DATE	PAGE	ACTION
HB-1751	04/15/83	111	FIRST READING
	05/13/83	205	SECOND READING
	05/24/83	45	THIRD READING
	06/29/83	22	CONCURRENCE
HB-1752	04/15/83	111	FIRST READING
	05/06/83	36	OTHER
HB-1753	04/15/83	111	FIRST READING
	05/18/83	203	SECOND READING
	05/27/83	11	THIRD READING
	05/27/83	215	THIRD READING
	10/18/83	132	VETO MESSAGE
HB-1754	04/15/83	111	FIRST READING
HB-1755	04/15/83	111	FIRST READING
HB-1756	04/15/83	111	FIRST READING
HB-1757	04/15/83	111	FIRST READING
	04/10/84	5	SECOND READING
	04/26/84	38	THIRD READING
HB-1758	04/15/83	111	FIRST READING
HB-1759	04/15/83	111	FIRST READING
HB-1760	04/15/83	111	FIRST READING
	05/18/83	204	SECOND READING
	05/27/83	212	THIRD READING
HB-1761	04/15/83	112	FIRST READING
	05/18/83	204	SECOND READING
HB-1762	04/15/83	112	FIRST READING
	05/18/83	205	SECOND READING
	05/26/83	98	THIRD READING
HB-1763	04/15/83	112	FIRST READING
	05/03/83	35	OTHER
HB-1764	04/15/83	112	FIRST READING
	05/18/83	204	SECOND READING
HB-1765	04/15/83	112	FIRST READING
HB-1766	04/15/83	112	FIRST READING
HB-1767	04/15/83	112	FIRST READING

BILL NUMBER	DATE	PAGE	ACTION
HB-1768	04/15/83	112	FIRST READING
HB-1769	04/15/83	112	FIRST READING
HB-1770	04/15/83	112	FIRST READING
	05/04/83	6	OTHER
HB-1771	04/15/83	1 2	FIRST READING
	05/04/83	6	OTHER
HB-1772	04/15/83	1 2	FIRST READING
	05/18/83	2 5	SECOND READING
	05/27/83	2 0	RECALLED
	05/27/83	2 1 1	THIRD READING
	06/28/83	109	CONCURRENCE
HB-1773	04/15/83	112	FIRST READING
HB-1774	04/15/83	112	FIRST READING
	05/03/83	9	OTHER
HB-1775	04/15/83	112	FIRST READING
HB-1776	04/15/83	112	FIRST READING
	05/03/83	9	OTHER
HB-1777	04/15/83	113	FIRST READING
	05/10/83	3	SECOND READING
	05/13/83	4	THIRD READING
HB-1778	04/15/83	113	FIRST READING
	05/18/83	17	SECOND READING
	05/24/83	47	THIRD READING
	06/29/83	141	CONCURRENCE
HB-1779	04/15/83	113	FIRST READING
HB-1780	04/15/83	113	FIRST READING
	05/18/83	206	SECOND READING
	05/25/83	230	THIRD READING
	11/04/83	81	CONCURRENCE
HB-1781	04/15/83	113	FIRST READING
	05/18/83	206	SECOND READING
	05/25/83	232	THIRD READING
HB-1782	04/15/83	113	FIRST READING
HB-1783	04/15/83	113	FIRST READING
	05/06/83	36	OTHER

BILL NUMBER	DATE	PAGE	ACTION
HB-1784	04/15/83	113	FIRST READING
HB-1785	04/15/83	113	FIRST READING
	05/06/83	36	OTHER
HB-1786	04/15/83	113	FIRST READING
HB-1787	04/15/83	113	FIRST READING
HB-1788	04/15/83	113	FIRST READING
	05/13/83	205	SECOND READING
	05/24/83	48	THIRD READING
	10/18/83	88	VETO MESSAGE
HB-1789	04/15/83	113	FIRST READING
	04/28/83	92	SECOND READING
	05/12/83	182	THIRD READING
	06/29/83	45	CONCURRENCE
	07/01/83	38	CONFERENCE
HB-1790	04/15/83	113	FIRST READING
	05/19/83	115	SECOND READING
	05/26/83	270	THIRD READING
HB-1791	04/15/83	113	FIRST READING
HB-1792	04/15/83	114	FIRST READING
HB-1793	04/15/83	114	FIRST READING
	05/03/83	8	OTHER
HB-1794	04/15/83	114	FIRST READING
HB-1795	04/15/83	114	FIRST READING
HB-1796	04/15/83	114	FIRST READING
	05/13/83	206	SECOND READING
	05/25/83	239	THIRD READING
HB-1797	04/15/83	114	FIRST READING
HB-1798	04/15/83	114	FIRST READING
	05/18/83	206	SECOND READING
HB-1799	04/15/83	114	FIRST READING
HB-1800	04/15/83	114	FIRST READING
	05/16/84	14	SECOND READING
	05/23/84	144	THIRD READING
HB-1801	04/15/83	114	FIRST READING

BILL NUMBER	DATE	PAGE	ACTION
HB-1802	04/15/83	114	FIRST READING
	05/18/83	18	SECOND READING
	05/24/83	48	THIRD READING
HB-1803	04/15/83	114	FIRST READING
	05/18/83	207	SECOND READING
HB-1804	04/15/83	114	FIRST READING
HB-1805	04/15/83	114	FIRST READING
	05/19/83	251	SECOND READING
	05/27/83	11	THIRD READING
	05/27/83	180	THIRD READING
	06/29/83	178	CONCURRENCE
	06/30/83	168	MOTION
	06/30/83	169	CONFERENCE
HB-1806	04/15/83	114	FIRST READING
HB-1807	04/15/83	115	FIRST READING
HB-1808	04/15/83	115	FIRST READING
HB-1809	04/15/83	115	FIRST READING
	05/06/83	36	OTHER
HB-1810	04/15/83	115	FIRST READING
HB-1811	04/15/83	115	FIRST READING
HB-1812	04/15/83	115	FIRST READING
	05/27/83	133	SECOND READING
	05/27/83	137	MOTION
	06/29/83	24	THIRD READING
	07/01/83	273	CONCURRENCE
			CONFERENCE
HB-1813	04/15/83	115	FIRST READING
	05/18/83	208	SECOND READING
	05/24/83	234	THIRD READING
HB-1814	04/15/83	115	FIRST READING
	05/18/83	208	SECOND READING
	05/24/83	97	RECALLED
	05/24/83	237	THIRD READING
	10/19/83	82	VETO MESSAGE
	10/20/83	108	VETO MESSAGE
HB-1815	04/15/83	115	FIRST READING
HB-1816	04/15/83	115	FIRST READING

BILL NUMBER	DATE	PAGE	ACTION
HB-1816 (cont'd)	05/06/83	36	OTHER
HB-1817	04/15/83	115	FIRST READING
HB-1818	04/15/83	115	FIRST READING
	05/19/83	217	SECOND READING
	05/01/84	34	SECOND READING
	05/03/84	17	THIRD READING
HB-1819	04/15/83	115	FIRST READING
HB-1820	04/15/83	115	FIRST READING
HB-1821	04/15/83	115	FIRST READING
HB-1822	04/15/83	115	FIRST READING
HB-1823	04/15/83	116	FIRST READING
HB-1824	04/15/83	116	FIRST READING
HB-1825	04/15/83	116	FIRST READING
	05/18/83	213	SECOND READING
	05/26/83	98	THIRD READING
	10/19/83	90	VETO MESSAGE
HB-1826	04/15/83	116	FIRST READING
HB-1827	04/15/83	116	FIRST READING
HB-1828	04/15/83	116	FIRST READING
	05/18/83	214	SECOND READING
HB-1829	04/15/83	116	FIRST READING
	05/13/83	207	SECOND READING
	05/24/83	49	THIRD READING
HB-1830	04/15/83	116	FIRST READING
	05/13/83	208	SECOND READING
	05/25/83	242	THIRD READING
HB-1831	04/15/83	116	FIRST READING
	05/18/83	214	SECOND READING
	05/24/83	96	RECALLED
	05/25/83	246	THIRD READING
HB-1832	04/15/83	116	FIRST READING
HB-1833	04/15/83	116	FIRST READING
	05/03/83	6	OTHER
	05/06/83	36	OTHER

BILL NUMBER	DATE	PAGE	ACTION
HB-1834	04/15/83	116	FIRST READING
	05/18/83	18	SECOND READING
	05/24/83	51	THIRD READING
HB-1835	04/15/83	116	FIRST READING
	05/18/83	215	SECOND READING
	05/26/83	98	THIRD READING
	06/29/83	142	CONCURRENCE
	07/01/83	45	CONFERENCE
HB-1836	04/15/83	117	FIRST READING
HB-1837	04/15/83	117	FIRST READING
HB-1838	04/15/83	117	FIRST READING
	05/18/83	18	SECOND READING
	05/24/83	52	THIRD READING
	06/29/83	24	CONCURRENCE
	07/02/83	99	CONFERENCE
HB-1839	04/15/83	117	FIRST READING
	05/03/83	9	OTHER
	04/04/84	3	SECOND READING
	05/24/84	13	THIRD READING
HB-1840	04/15/83	117	FIRST READING
	05/06/83	36	OTHER
HB-1841	04/15/83	117	FIRST READING
	05/03/83	6	OTHER
HB-1842	04/15/83	117	FIRST READING
	05/18/83	19	SECOND READING
	05/24/83	53	THIRD READING
	06/28/83	110	CONCURRENCE
HB-1843	04/15/83	117	FIRST READING
HB-1844	04/15/83	117	FIRST READING
	05/10/83	3	SECOND READING
	05/13/83	4	THIRD READING
	06/29/83	142	CONCURRENCE
	06/29/83	144	OUT OF RECORD
	06/29/83	155	CONCURRENCE
HB-1845	04/15/83	117	FIRST READING
HB-1846	04/15/83	117	FIRST READING
HB-1847	04/15/83	117	FIRST READING
	05/18/83	215	SECOND READING

BILL NUMBER	DATE	PAGE	ACTION
HB-1847 (cont'd)	05/25/83	112	THIRD READING
	06/29/83	192	CONCURRENCE
	10/19/83	138	VETO MESSAGE
HB-1848	04/15/83	117	FIRST READING
	05/03/83	24	OTHER
HB-1849	04/15/83	118	FIRST READING
	05/18/83	215	SECOND READING
HB-1850	04/15/83	118	FIRST READING
HB-1851	04/15/83	118	FIRST READING
	05/18/83	217	SECOND READING
	05/25/83	115	THIRD READING
HB-1852	04/15/83	118	FIRST READING
HB-1853	04/15/83	118	FIRST READING
	05/18/83	218	SECOND READING
HB-1854	04/15/83	118	FIRST READING
	05/03/83	32	OTHER
HB-1855	04/15/83	118	FIRST READING
	05/18/83	218	SECOND READING
	04/11/84	8	SECOND READING
	04/24/84	15	THIRD READING
HB-1856	04/15/83	118	FIRST READING
	05/18/83	219	SECOND READING
HB-1857	04/15/83	118	FIRST READING
	05/13/83	208	SECOND READING
	05/24/83	53	THIRD READING
HB-1858	04/15/83	118	FIRST READING
HB-1859	04/15/83	118	FIRST READING
	05/23/83	42	SECOND READING
	05/10/84	20	SECOND READING
	05/23/84	58	THIRD READING
HB-1860	04/15/83	118	FIRST READING
HB-1861	04/15/83	118	FIRST READING
	05/18/83	219	SECOND READING
HB-1862	04/15/83	119	FIRST READING
	05/23/83	42	SECOND READING
	05/25/83	247	RECALLED

BILL NUMBER	DATE	PAGE	ACTION
HB-1862 (cont'd)	05/26/83	157	THIRD READING
HB-1863	04/15/83	119	FIRST READING
	05/03/83	12	OTHER
HB-1864	04/15/83	119	FIRST READING
	05/18/83	220	SECOND READING
	05/26/83	98	THIRD READING
	06/29/83	24	CONCURRENCE
	07/01/83	264	CONFERENCE
	07/01/83	266	OUT OF RECORD
HB-1865	04/15/83	119	FIRST READING
	05/03/83	6	OTHER
HB-1866	04/15/83	119	FIRST READING
	05/19/83	115	SECOND READING
HB-1867	04/15/83	119	FIRST READING
	05/06/83	36	OTHER
HB-1868	04/15/83	119	FIRST READING
HB-1869	04/15/83	119	FIRST READING
HB-1870	04/15/83	119	FIRST READING
	05/10/83	3	SECOND READING
	05/13/83	4	THIRD READING
HB-1871	04/15/83	119	FIRST READING
	05/13/83	208	SECOND READING
	05/24/83	55	THIRD READING
HB-1872	04/15/83	119	FIRST READING
	05/19/83	252	SECOND READING
	05/24/83	242	THIRD READING
HB-1873	04/15/83	119	FIRST READING
	05/18/83	220	SECOND READING
	05/25/83	253	THIRD READING
HB-1874	04/15/83	119	FIRST READING
	05/03/83	13	OTHER
	05/06/83	36	OTHER
HB-1875	04/15/83	119	FIRST READING
	05/06/83	36	OTHER
HB-1876	04/15/83	120	FIRST READING
HB-1877	04/15/83	120	FIRST READING

BILL NUMBER	DATE	PAGE	ACTION
HB-1877 (cont'd)	05/18/83	20	SECOND READING
	05/24/83	58	THIRD READING
	06/29/83	144	CONCURRENCE
HB-1878	04/15/83	120	FIRST READING
HB-1879	04/15/83	120	FIRST READING
	05/10/83	4	SECOND READING
	05/13/83	4	THIRD READING
HB-1880	04/15/83	120	FIRST READING
	05/18/83	221	SECOND READING
	05/26/83	98	THIRD READING
	06/29/83	146	CONCURRENCE
HB-1881	04/15/83	120	FIRST READING
	05/10/83	4	SECOND READING
	05/13/83	4	THIRD READING
	10/18/83	89	VETO MESSAGE
HB-1882	04/15/83	120	FIRST READING
	05/18/83	41	SECOND READING
	05/26/83	98	THIRD READING
HB-1883	04/15/83	120	FIRST READING
	05/18/83	221	SECOND READING
	05/26/83	98	THIRD READING
HB-1884	04/15/83	120	FIRST READING
HB-1885	04/15/83	120	FIRST READING
	05/13/83	209	SECOND READING
	05/24/83	58	THIRD READING
HB-1886	04/15/83	120	FIRST READING
	05/13/83	209	SECOND READING
	05/24/83	59	THIRD READING
HB-1887	04/15/83	120	FIRST READING
	05/13/83	209	SECOND READING
	05/25/83	253	THIRD READING
HB-1888	04/15/83	120	FIRST READING
	05/18/83	221	SECOND READING
	05/26/83	98	THIRD READING
HB-1889	04/15/83	120	FIRST READING
	05/18/83	222	SECOND READING
	05/26/83	98	THIRD READING
HB-1890	04/15/83	120	FIRST READING

BILL NUMBER	DATE	PAGE	ACTION
HB-1890 (cont'd)	05/10/83	4	SECOND READING
	05/13/83	4	THIRD READING
	06/29/83	146	CONCURRENCE
HB-1891	04/15/83	120	FIRST READING
HB-1892	04/15/83	121	FIRST READING
	05/03/83	4	OTHER
HB-1893	04/15/83	121	FIRST READING
	05/06/83	36	OTHER
HB-1894	04/15/83	121	FIRST READING
HB-1895	04/15/83	121	FIRST READING
	05/06/83	36	OTHER
HB-1896	04/15/83	121	FIRST READING
	05/06/83	36	OTHER
HB-1897	04/15/83	121	FIRST READING
	05/19/83	4	SECOND READING
HB-1898	04/15/83	121	FIRST READING
	05/19/83	114	SECOND READING
	05/27/83	133	MOTION
	05/27/83	137	THIRD READING
HB-1899	04/15/83	121	FIRST READING
HB-1900	04/15/83	121	FIRST READING
	05/06/83	36	OTHER
HB-1901	04/15/83	121	FIRST READING
HB-1902	04/15/83	121	FIRST READING
HB-1903	04/15/83	121	FIRST READING
HB-1904	04/15/83	121	FIRST READING
HB-1905	04/15/83	121	FIRST READING
HB-1906	04/15/83	121	FIRST READING
HB-1907	04/15/83	121	FIRST READING
HB-1908	04/15/83	122	FIRST READING
	05/06/83	30	MOTION
HB-1909	04/15/83	122	FIRST READING

BILL NUMBER	DATE	PAGE	ACTION
HB-1909 (cont'd)	05/06/83	36	OTHER
HB-1910	04/15/83	122	FIRST READING
	05/06/83	36	OTHER
HB-1911	04/15/83	122	FIRST READING
HB-1912	04/15/83	122	FIRST READING
HB-1913	04/15/83	122	FIRST READING
HB-1914	04/15/83	122	FIRST READING
	05/19/83	44	SECOND READING
	05/26/83	98	THIRD READING
HB-1915	04/15/83	122	FIRST READING
HB-1916	04/15/83	122	FIRST READING
HB-1917	04/15/83	122	FIRST READING
	05/18/83	20	SECOND READING
HB-1918	04/15/83	122	FIRST READING
	05/10/83	4	SECOND READING
	05/13/83	4	THIRD READING
HB-1919	04/15/83	122	FIRST READING
	05/03/83	10	OTHER
HB-1920	04/15/83	122	FIRST READING
	05/03/83	6	OTHER
HB-1921	04/15/83	122	FIRST READING
	05/18/83	41	SECOND READING
	05/26/83	99	THIRD READING
HB-1922	04/15/83	122	FIRST READING
	05/13/83	209	SECOND READING
	05/25/83	6	THIRD READING
	05/25/83	10	RECALLED
	05/25/83	10	THIRD READING
	06/28/83	111	CONCURRENCE
	06/28/83	113	OUT OF RECORD
	06/28/83	114	CONCURRENCE
HB-1923	04/15/83	123	FIRST READING
	05/19/83	4	SECOND READING
	05/26/83	99	THIRD READING
HB-1924	04/15/83	123	FIRST READING
	05/13/83	210	SECOND READING

MASTER TRANSCRIPT INDEX

BILL NUMBER	DATE	PAGE	ACTION
HB-1924 (cont'd)	05/25/83	11	THIRD READING
	11/04/83	12	CONCURRENCE
HB-1925	04/15/83	123	FIRST READING
	05/13/83	210	SECOND READING
	05/25/83	11	THIRD READING
	06/27/83	173	CONCURRENCE
	10/18/83	90	VETO MESSAGE
HB-1926	04/15/83	123	FIRST READING
	05/06/83	36	OTHER
HB-1927	04/15/83	123	FIRST READING
	05/10/83	4	SECOND READING
	05/13/83	4	THIRD READING
HB-1928	04/15/83	123	FIRST READING
	05/19/83	4	SECOND READING
	05/26/83	99	THIRD READING
HB-1929	04/15/83	123	FIRST READING
HB-1930	04/15/83	123	FIRST READING
HB-1931	04/15/83	123	FIRST READING
HB-1932	04/15/83	123	FIRST READING
HB-1933	04/15/83	123	FIRST READING
	05/13/83	211	SECOND READING
	05/25/83	12	RECALLED
	05/25/83	19	THIRD READING
HB-1934	04/15/83	123	FIRST READING
	05/13/83	211	SECOND READING
	05/25/83	20	THIRD READING
	06/28/83	113	CONCURRENCE
HB-1935	04/15/83	123	FIRST READING
	05/03/83	12	OTHER
	05/02/84	3	SECOND READING
	05/04/84	6	THIRD READING
HB-1936	04/15/83	123	FIRST READING
	05/19/83	5	SECOND READING
HB-1937	04/15/83	123	FIRST READING
HB-1938	04/15/83	123	FIRST READING
	05/19/83	12	SECOND READING
	05/19/83	12	HELD ON SECOND

MASTER TRANSCRIPT INDEX

BILL NUMBER	DATE	PAGE	ACTION
HB-1938 (cont'd)	05/19/83	116	SECOND READING
HB-1939	04/15/83	124	FIRST READING
	05/26/83	108	SECOND READING
	05/27/83	11	THIRD READING
	05/27/83	180	THIRD READING
	11/04/83	153	CONCURRENCE
	11/04/83	157	OUT OF RECORD
	11/04/83	201	CONCURRENCE
HB-1940	04/15/83	124	FIRST READING
HB-1941	04/15/83	124	FIRST READING
	05/11/83	13	SECOND READING
	05/13/83	166	THIRD READING
	06/29/83	25	CONCURRENCE
	07/01/83	268	CONFERENCE
HB-1942	04/15/83	124	FIRST READING
HB-1943	04/15/83	124	FIRST READING
	05/13/83	211	SECOND READING
	05/25/83	20	THIRD READING
HB-1944	04/15/83	124	FIRST READING
	05/10/83	4	SECOND READING
	05/13/83	4	THIRD READING
	06/29/83	147	CONCURRENCE
HB-1945	04/15/83	124	FIRST READING
HB-1946	04/15/83	124	FIRST READING
	05/06/83	36	MOTION
HB-1947	04/15/83	124	FIRST READING
HB-1948	04/15/83	124	FIRST READING
	05/19/83	113	SECOND READING
HB-1949	04/15/83	124	FIRST READING
	05/19/83	44	SECOND READING
HB-1950	04/15/83	124	FIRST READING
	05/19/83	11	SECOND READING
	05/26/83	99	THIRD READING
HB-1951	04/15/83	124	FIRST READING
HB-1952	04/15/83	124	FIRST READING
	05/10/83	4	SECOND READING
	05/13/83	4	THIRD READING

BILL NUMBER	DATE	PAGE	ACTION
HB-1953	04/15/83	124	FIRST READING
	05/10/83	4	SECOND READING
	05/13/83	4	THIRD READING
HB-1954	04/15/83	125	FIRST READING
HB-1955	04/15/83	1. 5	FIRST READING
	05/13/83	2 2	SECOND READING
	05/25/83	1	THIRD READING
	06/28/83	1 4	CONCURRENCE
	07/01/83	- 9	CONFERENCE
HB-1956	04/15/83	1. 5	FIRST READING
	05/03/83	10	OTHER
HB-1957	04/15/83	125	FIRST READING
HB-1958	04/15/83	125	FIRST READING
	05/10/83	4	SECOND READING
	05/13/83	4	THIRD READING
HB-1959	04/15/83	125	FIRST READING
HB-1960	04/15/83	125	FIRST READING
	05/18/83	20	SECOND READING
	05/25/83	22	THIRD READING
HB-1961	04/15/83	125	FIRST READING
	05/06/83	36	OTHER
HB-1962	04/15/83	125	FIRST READING
HB-1963	04/15/83	125	FIRST READING
	05/13/83	212	SECOND READING
	05/25/83	22	THIRD READING
HB-1964	04/15/83	125	FIRST READING
	05/06/83	36	OTHER
HB-1965	04/15/83	125	FIRST READING
HB-1966	04/15/83	126	FIRST READING
HB-1967	04/15/83	126	FIRST READING
HB-1968	04/15/83	126	FIRST READING
HB-1969	04/15/83	126	FIRST READING
HB-1970	04/15/83	126	FIRST READING

BILL NUMBER	DATE	PAGE	ACTION
HB-1971	04/15/83	126	FIRST READING
HB-1972	04/15/83	126	FIRST READING
	05/13/83	213	SECOND READING
	05/13/83	214	OUT OF RECORD
	05/17/83	3	SECOND READING
	05/25/83	23	THIRD READING
	06/29/83	151	CONCURRENCE
	10/18/83	90	VETO MESSAGE
HB-1973	04/15/83	126	FIRST READING
	05/19/83	12	SECOND READING
HB-1974	04/15/83	126	FIRST READING
HB-1975	04/15/83	126	FIRST READING
	05/04/83	4	OTHER
HB-1976	04/15/83	126	FIRST READING
HB-1977	04/15/83	126	FIRST READING
	05/03/83	5	OTHER
HB-1978	04/15/83	126	FIRST READING
	05/17/83	5	SECOND READING
	05/24/83	95	RECALLED
	05/26/83	99	THIRD READING
	06/29/83	212	CONCURRENCE
	10/19/83	221	MOTION
	10/20/83	118	CONFERENCE
HB-1979	04/15/83	126	FIRST READING
HB-1980	04/15/83	126	FIRST READING
HB-1981	04/15/83	126	FIRST READING
HB-1982	04/15/83	127	FIRST READING
	05/18/83	21	SECOND READING
	10/18/83	73	MOTION
	10/20/83	97	THIRD READING
HB-1983	04/15/83	127	FIRST READING
	05/23/83	44	SECOND READING
	05/27/83	133	MOTION
	05/27/83	137	THIRD READING
HB-1984	04/15/83	127	FIRST READING
	05/23/83	44	SECOND READING
	05/27/83	133	MOTION
	05/27/83	137	THIRD READING

BILL NUMBER	DATE	PAGE	ACTION
HB-1985	04/15/83	127	FIRST READING
	05/23/83	45	SECOND READING
	05/27/83	133	MOTION
	05/27/83	137	THIRD READING
HB-1986	04/15/83	127	FIRST READING
	05/23/83	48	SECOND READING
	05/27/83	133	MOTION
	05/27/83	137	THIRD READING
HB-1987	04/15/83	127	FIRST READING
	05/23/83	49	SECOND READING
	05/27/83	133	MOTION
	05/27/83	137	THIRD READING
HB-1988	04/15/83	127	FIRST READING
	05/23/83	50	SECOND READING
	05/27/83	133	MOTION
	05/27/83	137	THIRD READING
HB-1989	04/15/83	127	FIRST READING
	05/23/83	50	SECOND READING
	05/27/83	133	MOTION
	05/27/83	137	THIRD READING
HB-1990	04/15/83	127	FIRST READING
	05/23/83	52	SECOND READING
	05/27/83	133	MOTION
	05/27/83	137	THIRD READING
HB-1991	04/15/83	127	FIRST READING
	05/23/83	53	SECOND READING
	05/27/83	133	MOTION
	05/27/83	137	THIRD READING
HB-1992	04/15/83	127	FIRST READING
	05/23/83	55	SECOND READING
	05/27/83	133	MOTION
	05/27/83	137	THIRD READING
	06/29/83	153	CONCURRENCE
HB-1993	04/15/83	127	FIRST READING
	05/23/83	56	SECOND READING
HB-1994	04/15/83	127	FIRST READING
	05/23/83	56	SECOND READING
	05/27/83	133	MOTION
	05/27/83	137	THIRD READING
HB-1995	04/15/83	127	FIRST READING
	05/23/83	56	SECOND READING

BILL NUMBER	DATE	PAGE	ACTION
HB-1995 (cont'd)	05/27/83	133	MOTION
	05/27/83	137	THIRD READING
	10/20/83	34	VETO MESSAGE
HB-1996	04/15/83	127	FIRST READING
	05/23/83	57	SECOND READING
	05/27/83	132	RECALLED
	05/27/83	133	MOTION
	05/27/83	137	THIRD READING
HB-1997	04/15/83	127	FIRST READING
	05/23/83	57	SECOND READING
	05/27/83	133	MOTION
	05/27/83	137	THIRD READING
HB-1998	04/15/83	128	FIRST READING
	05/23/83	57	SECOND READING
HB-1999	04/15/83	128	FIRST READING
	05/03/83	7	OTHER
HB-2000	04/15/83	128	FIRST READING
	05/11/83	13	SECOND READING
	05/13/83	4	THIRD READING
	06/29/83	26	CONCURRENCE
	07/02/83	51	CONFERENCE
HB-2001	04/15/83	128	FIRST READING
HB-2002	04/15/83	128	FIRST READING
	05/19/83	13	SECOND READING
HB-2003	04/15/83	128	FIRST READING
	05/19/83	14	SECOND READING
	05/26/83	99	THIRD READING
	06/29/83	157	CONCURRENCE
HB-2004	04/15/83	128	FIRST READING
	05/17/83	5	SECOND READING
	05/27/83	12	THIRD READING
HB-2005	04/15/83	128	FIRST READING
	05/03/83	8	OTHER
HB-2006	04/15/83	128	FIRST READING
	05/19/83	20	SECOND READING
	05/26/83	99	THIRD READING
HB-2007	04/15/83	128	FIRST READING
HB-2008	04/15/83	128	FIRST READING

BILL NUMBER	DATE	PAGE	ACTION
HB-2008 (cont'd)	05/10/83	4	SECOND READING
	05/17/83	5	SECOND READING
	05/25/83	24	THIRD READING
	10/18/83	133	VETO MESSAGE
HB-2009	04/15/83	128	FIRST READING
	05/19/83	14	SECOND READING
HB-2010	04/15/83	128	FIRST READING
	05/23/83	42	SECOND READING
	05/25/83	305	RECALLED
	05/27/83	208	THIRD READING
	05/22/84	160	RECALLED
	05/25/84	2	THIRD READING
HB-2011	04/15/83	128	FIRST READING
	05/06/83	36	OTHER
HB-2012	04/15/83	128	FIRST READING
	05/23/83	58	SECOND READING
	05/23/83	59	OUT OF RECORD
	05/23/83	193	SECOND READING
	05/23/83	218	OUT OF RECORD
	05/25/83	136	SECOND READING
	05/27/83	139	THIRD READING
	06/29/83	209	CONCURRENCE
	10/20/83	35	VETO MESSAGE
HB-2013	04/15/83	128	FIRST READING
	05/19/83	15	SECOND READING
	05/27/83	122	THIRD READING
	06/29/83	160	CONCURRENCE
HB-2014	04/15/83	129	FIRST READING
	05/19/83	15	SECOND READING
	05/27/83	93	MOTION
	05/27/83	124	THIRD READING
	06/28/83	217	CONCURRENCE
	06/29/83	171	CONCURRENCE
	10/18/83	70	MOTION
HB-2015	04/15/83	129	FIRST READING
	05/17/83	6	SECOND READING
	05/25/83	24	THIRD READING
HB-2016	04/15/83	129	FIRST READING
	05/06/83	36	OTHER
HB-2017	04/15/83	129	FIRST READING
HB-2018	04/15/83	129	FIRST READING

BILL NUMBER	DATE	PAGE	ACTION
HB-2018 (cont'd)	05/06/83	36	OTHER
HB-2019	04/15/83	129	FIRST READING
	05/19/83	15	SECOND READING
	05/24/83	245	THIRD READING
	10/20/83	10	VETO MESSAGE
HB-2020	04/15/83	129	FIRST READING
	05/06/83	36	OTHER
HB-2021	04/15/83	129	FIRST READING
	05/03/83	4	OTHER
HB-2022	04/15/83	129	FIRST READING
HB-2023	04/15/83	129	FIRST READING
	05/19/83	20	SECOND READING
	05/19/83	270	MOTION
	05/20/83	182	RECALLED
	05/24/83	136	THIRD READING
	06/29/83	163	CONCURRENCE
	06/29/83	165	OUT OF RECORD
	06/29/83	198	CONCURRENCE
HB-2024	04/15/83	129	FIRST READING
HB-2025	04/15/83	129	FIRST READING
	05/25/83	313	SECOND READING
HB-2026	04/15/83	129	FIRST READING
	05/05/83	62	TABLED
HB-2027	04/15/83	129	FIRST READING
	05/03/83	9	OTHER
HB-2028	04/15/83	130	FIRST READING
HB-2029	04/15/83	130	FIRST READING
	05/11/83	14	SECOND READING
	05/13/83	4	THIRD READING
	06/28/83	115	CONCURRENCE
HB-2030	04/15/83	130	FIRST READING
	05/19/83	21	SECOND READING
HB-2031	04/15/83	130	FIRST READING
	05/19/83	21	SECOND READING
	05/25/83	259	THIRD READING
HB-2032	04/15/83	130	FIRST READING

BILL NUMBER	DATE	PAGE	ACTION
HB-2033	04/15/83	130	FIRST READING
	05/19/83	22	SECOND READING
	05/19/83	22	HELD ON SECOND
	05/23/83	60	SECOND READING
HB-2034	04/15/83	130	FIRST READING
	05/03/83	9	OTHER
HB-2035	04/15/83	130	FIRST READING
	05/19/83	22	SECOND READING
	05/26/83	275	THIRD READING
	06/29/83	206	CONCURRENCE
	10/19/83	107	VETO MESSAGE
HB-2036	04/15/83	130	FIRST READING
HB-2037	04/15/83	130	FIRST READING
HB-2038	04/15/83	130	FIRST READING
HB-2039	04/15/83	130	FIRST READING
HB-2040	04/15/83	131	FIRST READING
	05/25/83	271	SECOND READING
	05/25/83	271	OUT OF RECORD
	05/25/83	314	SECOND READING
	05/26/83	85	RECALLED
	05/26/83	90	MOTION
	05/27/83	210	THIRD READING
	05/15/84	67	SECOND READING
	05/22/84	163	RECALLED
	05/25/84	30	THIRD READING
	06/26/84	164	CONCURRENCE
	11/27/84	5	VETO MESSAGE
HB-2041	04/15/83	131	FIRST READING
	05/19/83	23	SECOND READING
HB-2042	04/15/83	131	FIRST READING
HB-2043	04/15/83	131	FIRST READING
HB-2044	04/15/83	131	FIRST READING
	05/03/83	33	OTHER
HB-2045	04/15/83	131	FIRST READING
HB-2046	04/15/83	131	FIRST READING
	05/18/83	21	SECOND READING
	05/27/83	13	THIRD READING

BILL NUMBER	DATE	PAGE	ACTION
HB-2047	04/15/83	131	FIRST READING
	05/19/83	112	SECOND READING
HB-2048	04/15/83	131	FIRST READING
HB-2049	04/15/83	131	FIRST READING
	05/06/83	36	OTHER
	06/29/84	90	OTHER
HB-2050	04/15/83	131	FIRST READING
	05/04/83	55	OTHER
HB-2051	04/15/83	131	FIRST READING
	05/06/83	36	OTHER
HB-2052	04/15/83	131	FIRST READING
HB-2053	04/15/83	131	FIRST READING
HB-2054	04/15/83	131	FIRST READING
HB-2055	04/15/83	131	FIRST READING
	05/19/83	44	SECOND READING
	05/26/83	99	THIRD READING
	06/28/83	116	CONCURRENCE
	07/02/83	173	CONFERENCE
HB-2056	04/15/83	131	FIRST READING
	05/19/83	45	SECOND READING
HB-2057	04/15/83	131	FIRST READING
HB-2058	04/15/83	132	FIRST READING
	05/10/83	4	SECOND READING
	05/13/83	4	THIRD READING
	06/29/83	45	CONCURRENCE
	07/01/83	53	CONFERENCE
	07/01/83	230	CONFERENCE
HB-2059	04/15/83	132	FIRST READING
	05/10/83	4	SECOND READING
	05/26/83	109	SECOND READING
HB-2060	04/15/83	132	FIRST READING
	05/11/83	14	SECOND READING
	05/13/83	5	THIRD READING
HB-2061	04/15/83	132	FIRST READING
HB-2062	04/15/83	132	FIRST READING
	05/17/83	7	SECOND READING

PROGRAM-LRTRNMST
08/20/85
LEGISLATIVE INFORMATION SYSTEM
HOUSE OF REPRESENTATIVES
PAGE 151

MASTER TRANSCRIPT INDEX

BILL NUMBER	DATE	PAGE	ACTION
HB-2062 (cont'd)	05/26/83	99	THIRD READING
HB-2063	04/15/83	132	FIRST READING
HB-2064	04/15/83	132	FIRST READING
	05/19/83	45	SECOND READING
HB-2065	04/15/83	132	FIRST READING
	05/17/83	8	SECOND READING
	05/25/83	25	THIRD READING
	10/18/83	91	VETO MESSAGE
HB-2066	04/15/83	132	FIRST READING
	05/03/83	10	TABLED
HB-2067	04/15/83	132	FIRST READING
HB-2068	04/15/83	132	FIRST READING
HB-2069	04/15/83	132	FIRST READING
HB-2070	04/15/83	132	FIRST READING
	05/10/83	4	SECOND READING
	05/13/83	5	THIRD READING
HB-2071	04/15/83	132	FIRST READING
	05/10/83	4	SECOND READING
	05/13/83	5	THIRD READING
	06/29/83	166	CONCURRENCE
HB-2072	04/15/83	132	FIRST READING
	05/19/83	25	SECOND READING
	05/26/83	99	THIRD READING
	06/29/83	266	CONCURRENCE
	10/19/83	222	MOTION
	10/20/83	155	CONFERENCE
HB-2073	04/15/83	133	FIRST READING
	05/17/83	8	SECOND READING
	05/25/83	26	THIRD READING
HB-2074	04/15/83	133	FIRST READING
	05/10/83	4	SECOND READING
	05/13/83	5	THIRD READING
HB-2075	04/15/83	133	FIRST READING
HB-2076	04/15/83	133	FIRST READING
	05/04/83	5	OTHER
HB-2077	04/15/83	133	FIRST READING

PROGRAM-LRTRNMST
08/20/85
LEGISLATIVE INFORMATION SYSTEM
HOUSE OF REPRESENTATIVES
PAGE 152

MASTER TRANSCRIPT INDEX

BILL NUMBER	DATE	PAGE	ACTION
HB-2077 (cont'd)	05/04/83	5	OTHER
HB-2078	04/15/83	133	FIRST READING
	05/17/83	9	SECOND READING
	05/25/83	27	THIRD READING
	06/28/83	5	CONCURRENCE
	07/01/83	142	CONFERENCE
	07/01/83	144	OUT OF RECORD
	07/01/83	250	CONFERENCE
HB-2079	04/15/83	133	FIRST READING
	05/17/83	10	SECOND READING
	05/27/83	214	THIRD READING
HB-2080	04/15/83	133	FIRST READING
	05/17/83	10	SECOND READING
	05/26/83	99	THIRD READING
HB-2081	04/15/83	133	FIRST READING
	05/19/83	25	SECOND READING
	05/26/83	99	THIRD READING
	06/29/83	166	CONCURRENCE
HB-2082	04/15/83	133	FIRST READING
	05/03/83	2	OTHER
HB-2083	04/15/83	133	FIRST READING
	05/19/83	26	SECOND READING
HB-2084	04/15/83	133	FIRST READING
	05/03/83	2	OTHER
HB-2085	04/15/83	133	FIRST READING
	05/18/83	22	SECOND READING
	05/24/83	140	THIRD READING
	06/29/83	168	CONCURRENCE
	10/18/83	92	VETO MESSAGE
HB-2086	04/15/83	133	FIRST READING
	05/03/83	2	OTHER
HB-2087	04/15/83	133	FIRST READING
	05/03/83	2	OTHER
HB-2088	04/15/83	133	FIRST READING
HB-2089	04/15/83	134	FIRST READING
	04/27/83	32	TABLED
HB-2090	04/15/83	134	FIRST READING
	05/04/83	6	OTHER

BILL NUMBER	DATE	PAGE	ACTION
HB-2091	04/15/83	134	FIRST READING
	05/13/83	56	MOTION
HB-2092	04/15/83	134	FIRST READING
	05/19/83	26	SECOND READING
	05/26/83	99	THIRD READING
HB-2093	04/15/83	134	FIRST READING
	05/10/83	5	SECOND READING
	05/13/83	5	THIRD READING
HB-2094	04/15/83	134	FIRST READING
	05/19/83	270	SECOND READING
	05/26/83	99	THIRD READING
HB-2095	04/15/83	134	FIRST READING
HB-2096	04/15/83	134	FIRST READING
HB-2097	04/15/83	134	FIRST READING
	05/17/83	10	SECOND READING
	05/26/83	99	THIRD READING
HB-2098	04/15/83	134	FIRST READING
HB-2099	04/15/83	134	FIRST READING
HB-2100	04/15/83	134	FIRST READING
	05/17/83	10	SECOND READING
	05/17/83	12	OUT OF RECORD
	05/18/83	23	SECOND READING
	11/01/83	96	THIRD READING
	11/01/83	96	MOTION
	11/04/83	139	CONCURRENCE
	11/04/83	140	OUT OF RECORD
	11/04/83	170	CONCURRENCE
HB-2101	04/15/83	134	FIRST READING
	05/05/83	6	OTHER
HB-2102	04/15/83	134	FIRST READING
	05/19/83	26	SECOND READING
	05/26/83	99	THIRD READING
HB-2103	04/15/83	134	FIRST READING
	05/19/83	26	SECOND READING
	05/27/83	206	THIRD READING
HB-2104	04/15/83	134	FIRST READING
HB-2105	04/15/83	135	FIRST READING

BILL NUMBER	DATE	PAGE	ACTION
HB-2105 (cont'd)	05/17/83	12	SECOND READING
	05/27/83	226	THIRD READING
HB-2106	04/15/83	135	FIRST READING
	05/19/83	32	SECOND READING
	05/27/83	180	THIRD READING
	11/04/83	56	CONCURRENCE
HB-2107	04/15/83	135	FIRST READING
	05/19/83	40	SECOND READING
HB-2108	04/15/83	135	FIRST READING
	05/17/83	12	SECOND READING
	05/26/83	99	THIRD READING
HB-2109	04/15/83	135	FIRST READING
	05/17/83	12	SECOND READING
	05/24/83	248	THIRD READING
	06/28/83	117	CONCURRENCE
HB-2110	04/15/83	135	FIRST READING
	05/17/83	12	SECOND READING
	05/26/83	100	THIRD READING
	10/18/83	93	VETO MESSAGE
HB-2111	04/15/83	135	FIRST READING
	05/17/83	13	SECOND READING
	05/26/83	100	THIRD READING
	10/18/83	93	VETO MESSAGE
HB-2112	04/15/83	135	FIRST READING
HB-2113	04/15/83	135	FIRST READING
HB-2114	04/15/83	135	FIRST READING
HB-2115	04/15/83	135	FIRST READING
	05/17/83	13	SECOND READING
	05/26/83	100	THIRD READING
HB-2116	04/15/83	135	FIRST READING
	05/18/83	24	SECOND READING
	05/26/83	100	THIRD READING
HB-2117	04/15/83	135	FIRST READING
	05/17/83	14	SECOND READING
	05/26/83	100	THIRD READING
HB-2118	04/15/83	135	FIRST READING
	05/17/83	14	SECOND READING

BILL NUMBER	DATE	PAGE	ACTION
HB-2119	04/15/83	135	FIRST READING
	05/06/83	36	OTHER
HB-2120	04/15/83	135	FIRST READING
HB-2121	04/15/83	136	FIRST READING
	05/04/83	5	OTHER
HB-2122	04/15/83	136	FIRST READING
	05/04/83	5	OTHER
HB-2123	04/15/83	136	FIRST READING
	05/17/83	14	SECOND READING
	05/26/83	100	THIRD READING
HB-2124	04/15/83	136	FIRST READING
HB-2125	04/15/83	136	FIRST READING
	05/03/83	9	OTHER
	05/04/83	4	OTHER
	05/06/83	36	OTHER
HB-2126	04/15/83	136	FIRST READING
	05/19/83	40	SECOND READING
HB-2127	04/15/83	136	FIRST READING
	05/03/83	24	OTHER
HB-2128	04/15/83	136	FIRST READING
HB-2129	04/15/83	136	FIRST READING
HB-2130	04/15/83	136	FIRST READING
HB-2131	04/15/83	136	FIRST READING
	05/03/83	6	OTHER
	05/24/83	295	RECALLED
HB-2132	04/15/83	136	FIRST READING
HB-2133	04/15/83	136	FIRST READING
HB-2134	04/15/83	136	FIRST READING
HB-2135	04/15/83	136	FIRST READING
	05/18/83	24	SECOND READING
	05/24/83	140	THIRD READING
	06/28/83	118	CONCURRENCE
HB-2136	04/15/83	137	FIRST READING
	05/19/83	40	SECOND READING

BILL NUMBER	DATE	PAGE	ACTION
HB-2137	04/15/83	137	FIRST READING
	05/03/83	31	OTHER
HB-2138	04/15/83	137	FIRST READING
HB-2139	04/15/83	137	FIRST READING
	05/03/83	11	TABLED
HB-2140	04/15/83	137	FIRST READING
	04/27/83	56	TABLED
HB-2141	04/15/83	137	FIRST READING
	05/08/84	27	SECOND READING
	05/16/84	72	THIRD READING
	05/23/84	201	THIRD READING
HB-2142	04/15/83	137	FIRST READING
	05/03/83	13	OTHER
HB-2143	04/15/83	137	FIRST READING
	05/03/83	13	OTHER
HB-2144	04/15/83	137	FIRST READING
	05/17/83	15	SECOND READING
	05/27/83	223	THIRD READING
HB-2145	04/15/83	137	FIRST READING
	05/03/83	13	OTHER
HB-2146	04/15/83	137	FIRST READING
HB-2147	04/15/83	137	FIRST READING
	05/10/83	5	SECOND READING
	05/13/83	5	THIRD READING
HB-2148	04/15/83	137	FIRST READING
HB-2149	04/15/83	137	FIRST READING
	05/19/83	41	SECOND READING
HB-2150	04/15/83	137	FIRST READING
HB-2151	04/15/83	137	FIRST READING
	05/04/83	4	OTHER
HB-2152	04/15/83	138	FIRST READING
	05/03/83	33	OTHER
HB-2153	04/15/83	138	FIRST READING
HB-2154	04/15/83	138	FIRST READING

PROGRAM-LRTRNMST
08/20/85

LEGISLATIVE INFORMATION SYSTEM
HOUSE OF REPRESENTATIVES

PAGE 157

MASTER TRANSCRIPT INDEX

BILL NUMBER	DATE	PAGE	ACTION
HB-2155	04/15/83	138	FIRST READING
HB-2156	04/15/83	138	FIRST READING
HB-2157	04/15/83	138	FIRST READING
HB-2158	04/15/83	138	FIRST READING
	05/03/83	35	OTHER
HB-2159	04/15/83	138	FIRST READING
HB-2160	04/15/83	138	FIRST READING
HB-2161	04/15/83	138	FIRST READING
HB-2162	04/15/83	138	FIRST READING
HB-2163	04/15/83	138	FIRST READING
HB-2164	04/15/83	139	FIRST READING
HB-2165	04/15/83	139	FIRST READING
HB-2166	04/15/83	139	FIRST READING
	05/19/83	41	SECOND READING
	04/11/84	4	SECOND READING
	05/09/84	64	THIRD READING
HB-2167	04/15/83	139	FIRST READING
HB-2168	04/15/83	139	FIRST READING
	05/03/83	31	OTHER
	05/06/83	36	OTHER
HB-2169	04/15/83	139	FIRST READING
	05/19/83	41	SECOND READING
HB-2170	04/15/83	139	FIRST READING
	05/17/83	15	SECOND READING
HB-2171	04/15/83	139	FIRST READING
	05/23/83	65	SECOND READING
	05/25/83	288	RECALLED
	05/26/83	90	THIRD READING
	06/29/83	168	CONCURRENCE
	10/19/83	170	VETO MESSAGE
HB-2172	04/15/83	139	FIRST READING
	05/19/83	41	SECOND READING
	05/19/83	42	HELD ON SECOND
	05/19/83	45	SECOND READING

PROGRAM-LRTRNMST
08/20/85

LEGISLATIVE INFORMATION SYSTEM
HOUSE OF REPRESENTATIVES

PAGE 158

MASTER TRANSCRIPT INDEX

BILL NUMBER	DATE	PAGE	ACTION
HB-2172 (cont'd)	05/19/83	80	HELD ON SECOND
	05/23/83	75	SECOND READING
HB-2173	04/15/83	139	FIRST READING
	05/03/83	4	OTHER
HB-2174	04/15/83	139	FIRST READING
	05/06/83	36	OTHER
HB-2175	04/15/83	140	FIRST READING
	05/06/83	36	OTHER
	05/02/84	10	SECOND READING
	05/25/84	25	THIRD READING
HB-2176	04/15/83	140	FIRST READING
	05/10/83	5	SECOND READING
	05/13/83	166	THIRD READING
	06/29/83	172	CONCURRENCE
HB-2177	04/15/83	140	FIRST READING
	05/06/83	31	MOTION
HB-2178	04/15/83	140	FIRST READING
	05/23/83	3	SECOND READING
	05/23/83	4	OUT OF RECORD
	05/23/83	9	SECOND READING
	05/23/83	10	OUT OF RECORD
HB-2179	04/15/83	140	FIRST READING
HB-2180	04/15/83	140	FIRST READING
HB-2181	04/15/83	140	FIRST READING
HB-2182	04/15/83	140	FIRST READING
	05/19/83	42	SECOND READING
	05/26/83	100	THIRD READING
	05/26/83	297	MOTION
	05/26/83	298	RECALLED
	05/26/83	298	THIRD READING
	06/29/83	174	CONCURRENCE
HB-2183	04/15/83	140	FIRST READING
HB-2184	04/15/83	140	FIRST READING
	05/19/83	81	SECOND READING
	05/24/83	294	RECALLED
	05/27/83	15	THIRD READING
HB-2185	04/15/83	140	FIRST READING

PROGRAM-LRTRNMST LEGISLATIVE INFORMATION SYSTEM PAGE 159
08/20/85 HOUSE OF REPRESENTATIVES

MASTER TRANSCRIPT INDEX

BILL NUMBER	DATE	PAGE	ACTION
HB-2186	04/15/83	140	FIRST READING
	05/03/83	35	OTHER
	05/02/84	10	SECOND READING
	05/23/84	38	THIRD READING
HB-2187	04/15/83	141	FIRST READING
HB-2188	04/15/83	141	FIRST READING
HB-2189	04/15/83	141	FIRST READING
HB-2190	04/15/83	141	FIRST READING
HB-2191	04/15/83	141	FIRST READING
HB-2192	04/15/83	141	FIRST READING
	05/03/83	33	OTHER
	05/10/84	20	SECOND READING
HB-2193	04/15/83	141	FIRST READING
HB-2194	04/15/83	141	FIRST READING
	05/17/83	21	RECALLED
	05/26/83	127	SECOND READING
	05/27/83	11	THIRD READING
HB-2195	04/15/83	141	FIRST READING
	05/06/83	36	OTHER
HB-2196	04/15/83	141	FIRST READING
	05/06/83	36	OTHER
HB-2197	04/15/83	141	FIRST READING
	05/19/83	81	SECOND READING
HB-2198	04/15/83	141	FIRST READING
HB-2199	04/15/83	141	FIRST READING
HB-2200	04/15/83	142	FIRST READING
	05/04/83	55	TABLED
HB-2201	04/15/83	142	FIRST READING
	05/17/83	15	SECOND READING
	05/26/83	100	THIRD READING
	06/29/83	144	CONCURRENCE
	07/01/83	222	CONFERENCE
HB-2202	04/15/83	142	FIRST READING
	05/19/83	82	SECOND READING
	05/27/83	22	THIRD READING

PROGRAM-LRTRNMST LEGISLATIVE INFORMATION SYSTEM PAGE 160
08/20/85 HOUSE OF REPRESENTATIVES

MASTER TRANSCRIPT INDEX

BILL NUMBER	DATE	PAGE	ACTION
HB-2203	04/15/83	142	FIRST READING
	05/19/83	83	SECOND READING
	05/26/83	100	THIRD READING
HB-2204	04/15/83	142	FIRST READING
HB-2205	04/15/83	142	FIRST READING
	05/03/83	7	OTHER
HB-2206	04/15/83	142	FIRST READING
	05/19/83	82	SECOND READING
HB-2207	04/15/83	142	FIRST READING
HB-2208	04/15/83	142	FIRST READING
	05/19/83	84	SECOND READING
	05/15/84	68	SECOND READING
	05/24/84	135	THIRD READING
HB-2209	04/15/83	142	FIRST READING
HB-2210	04/15/83	142	FIRST READING
	05/04/83	56	OTHER
HB-2211	04/15/83	142	FIRST READING
	05/06/83	36	OTHER
	05/22/84	25	SECOND READING
	05/24/84	107	THIRD READING
	05/24/84	108	RECALLED
	05/24/84	109	THIRD READING
	06/26/84	143	CONCURRENCE
HB-2212	04/15/83	143	FIRST READING
	05/10/83	5	SECOND READING
	05/13/83	5	THIRD READING
	05/17/83	16	SECOND READING
	05/26/83	100	THIRD READING
HB-2213	04/15/83	143	FIRST READING
	05/11/83	14	SECOND READING
	05/18/83	26	SECOND READING
	05/15/84	69	SECOND READING
	05/23/84	270	MOTION
HB-2214	04/15/83	143	FIRST READING
	05/03/83	33	OTHER
HB-2215	04/15/83	143	FIRST READING
HB-2216	04/15/83	143	FIRST READING

PROGRAM-LRTRNMST
08/20/85
LEGISLATIVE INFORMATION SYSTEM
HOUSE OF REPRESENTATIVES
PAGE 161

MASTER TRANSCRIPT INDEX

BILL NUMBER	DATE	PAGE	ACTION
HB-2217	04/15/83	143	FIRST READING
HB-2218	04/15/83	143	FIRST READING
	05/19/83	84	SECOND READING
	05/25/83	118	THIRD READING
	10/20/83	19	VETO MESSAGE
HB-2219	04/15/83	143	FIRST READING
	05/19/83	85	SECOND READING
	05/27/83	16	THIRD READING
HB-2220	04/15/83	143	FIRST READING
	05/19/83	85	SECOND READING
	05/26/83	100	THIRD READING
HB-2221	04/15/83	143	FIRST READING
	05/18/83	27	SECOND READING
	05/18/83	28	OUT OF RECORD
	05/18/83	30	SECOND READING
	05/27/83	228	THIRD READING
HB-2222	04/15/83	144	FIRST READING
HB-2223	04/15/83	144	FIRST READING
	05/05/83	6	OTHER
HB-2224	04/15/83	144	FIRST READING
	05/06/83	33	MOTION
HB-2225	04/15/83	144	FIRST READING
HB-2226	04/15/83	144	FIRST READING
HB-2227	04/15/83	144	FIRST READING
HB-2228	04/15/83	144	FIRST READING
	05/04/83	6	OTHER
	05/23/83	76	SECOND READING
	05/27/83	133	MOTION
	05/27/83	137	THIRD READING
HB-2229	04/15/83	144	FIRST READING
	05/03/83	6	OTHER
HB-2230	04/15/83	144	FIRST READING
	05/17/83	17	SECOND READING
	05/26/83	100	THIRD READING
	06/28/83	119	CONCURRENCE
HB-2231	04/15/83	144	FIRST READING
	05/19/83	86	SECOND READING

PROGRAM-LRTRNMST
08/20/85
LEGISLATIVE INFORMATION SYSTEM
HOUSE OF REPRESENTATIVES
PAGE 162

MASTER TRANSCRIPT INDEX

BILL NUMBER	DATE	PAGE	ACTION
HB-2232	04/15/83	144	FIRST READING
HB-2233	04/15/83	144	FIRST READING
	05/19/83	86	SECOND READING
HB-2234	04/15/83	144	FIRST READING
	05/25/83	272	SECOND READING
	05/27/83	11	THIRD READING
	05/27/83	193	THIRD READING
	11/04/83	80	CONCURRENCE
HB-2235	04/15/83	145	FIRST READING
	05/23/83	77	SECOND READING
HB-2236	04/15/83	145	FIRST READING
HB-2237	04/15/83	145	FIRST READING
HB-2238	04/15/83	145	FIRST READING
HB-2239	04/15/83	145	FIRST READING
HB-2240	04/15/83	145	FIRST READING
HB-2241	04/15/83	145	FIRST READING
HB-2242	04/15/83	145	FIRST READING
	05/19/83	101	SECOND READING
	05/27/83	212	THIRD READING
	06/28/83	120	CONCURRENCE
HB-2243	04/15/83	145	FIRST READING
	05/19/83	87	SECOND READING
HB-2244	04/15/83	145	FIRST READING
	05/17/83	17	SECOND READING
	05/27/83	11	THIRD READING
	05/27/83	180	THIRD READING
	06/29/83	175	CONCURRENCE
	10/19/83	150	VETO MESSAGE
HB-2245	04/15/83	145	FIRST READING
	05/03/83	33	OTHER
HB-2246	04/15/83	145	FIRST READING
HB-2247	04/15/83	145	FIRST READING
	05/06/83	36	OTHER
HB-2248	04/15/83	145	FIRST READING
	05/18/83	28	SECOND READING

PROGRAM-LRTRNMST
08/20/85
LEGISLATIVE INFORMATION SYSTEM
HOUSE OF REPRESENTATIVES
PAGE 163

MASTER TRANSCRIPT INDEX

BILL NUMBER	DATE	PAGE	ACTION
HB-2249	04/15/83	145	FIRST READING
	05/17/83	18	SECOND READING
HB-2250	04/15/83	146	FIRST READING
HB-2251	04/15/83	146	FIRST READING
	05/19/83	88	SECOND READING
	05/19/83	100	HELD ON SECOND
	05/23/83	87	SECOND READING
	05/26/83	100	THIRD READING
HB-2252	04/15/83	146	FIRST READING
HB-2253	04/15/83	146	FIRST READING
	05/03/83	31	OTHER
	05/02/84	10	SECOND READING
	05/09/84	9	THIRD READING
HB-2254	04/15/83	146	FIRST READING
	05/03/83	35	OTHER
HB-2255	04/15/83	146	FIRST READING
	05/06/83	36	OTHER
HB-2256	04/15/83	146	FIRST READING
HB-2257	04/15/83	146	FIRST READING
HB-2258	04/15/83	146	FIRST READING
HB-2259	04/15/83	146	FIRST READING
	05/06/83	36	OTHER
HB-2260	04/15/83	146	FIRST READING
HB-2261	04/15/83	146	FIRST READING
HB-2262	04/15/83	146	FIRST READING
HB-2263	04/15/83	146	FIRST READING
HB-2264	04/15/83	146	FIRST READING
	05/19/83	102	SECOND READING
HB-2265	04/15/83	146	FIRST READING
	05/19/83	103	SECOND READING
HB-2266	04/15/83	147	FIRST READING
	05/19/83	104	SECOND READING
	05/27/83	128	THIRD READING

PROGRAM-LRTRNMST
08/20/85
LEGISLATIVE INFORMATION SYSTEM
HOUSE OF REPRESENTATIVES
PAGE 164

MASTER TRANSCRIPT INDEX

BILL NUMBER	DATE	PAGE	ACTION
HB-2267	04/15/83	147	FIRST READING
	05/19/83	109	SECOND READING
	05/26/83	100	THIRD READING
HB-2268	04/15/83	147	FIRST READING
	05/19/83	110	SECOND READING
HB-2269	04/15/83	147	FIRST READING
	05/19/83	110	SECOND READING
HB-2270	04/15/83	147	FIRST READING
HB-2271	04/15/83	147	FIRST READING
HB-2272	04/15/83	147	FIRST READING
	04/28/83	113	TABLED
HB-2273	04/15/83	147	FIRST READING
	04/15/83	147	FIRST READING
HB-2274	04/15/83	147	FIRST READING
	05/19/83	111	SECOND READING
HB-2275	04/15/83	147	FIRST READING
	05/03/83	53	OTHER
HB-2276	04/15/83	147	FIRST READING
HB-2277	04/15/83	147	FIRST READING
	05/17/83	20	SECOND READING
	05/26/83	100	THIRD READING
HB-2278	04/19/83	5	FIRST READING
	05/17/84	10	SECOND READING
	05/24/84	183	RECALLED
	05/24/84	185	THIRD READING
HB-2279	04/19/83	5	FIRST READING
	05/23/84	265	SECOND READING
HB-2280	04/20/83	3	FIRST READING
HB-2281	04/20/83	3	FIRST READING
	10/19/83	180	SECOND READING
	10/20/83	69	RECALLED
	10/20/83	70	THIRD READING
	11/04/83	140	CONCURRENCE
HB-2282	04/21/83	5	FIRST READING
	05/19/83	111	SECOND READING
	05/25/83	123	THIRD READING

BILL NUMBER	DATE	PAGE	ACTION
HB-2283	04/21/83	5	FIRST READING
	05/17/83	21	SECOND READING
	05/26/83	100	THIRD READING
HB-2284	04/21/83	5	FIRST READING
	05/17/83	21	SECOND READING
	05/26/83	100	THIRD READING
	06/28/83	122	CONCURRENCE
HB-2285	04/21/83	5	FIRST READING
	05/19/83	111	SECOND READING
HB-2286	04/21/83	91	FIRST READING
	06/26/83	3	MOTION
HB-2287	04/26/83	1	FIRST READING
	05/19/83	111	SECOND READING
	05/25/83	295	RECALLED
	05/27/83	11	THIRD READING
	05/27/83	180	THIRD READING
	06/28/83	123	CONCURRENCE
HB-2288	04/26/83	1	FIRST READING
HB-2289	04/26/83	37	FIRST READING
HB-2290	04/26/83	37	FIRST READING
	05/23/83	91	SECOND READING
	05/23/83	92	OUT OF RECORD
	05/24/83	259	SECOND READING
	05/25/83	126	THIRD READING
	06/29/83	179	CONCURRENCE
	06/29/83	187	MOTION
HB-2291	05/04/83	58	FIRST READING
	05/02/84	4	SECOND READING
	05/03/84	21	THIRD READING
HB-2292	05/12/83	189	FIRST READING
HB-2293	05/19/83	2	FIRST READING
HB-2294	06/02/83	19	FIRST READING
HB-2295	06/02/83	20	FIRST READING
HB-2296	06/17/83	99	FIRST READING
	05/08/84	11	SECOND READING
	05/16/84	86	THIRD READING
	06/29/84	18	CONCURRENCE

BILL NUMBER	DATE	PAGE	ACTION
HB-2297	07/02/83	160	FIRST READING
HB-2298	07/02/83	160	FIRST READING
HB-2299	10/05/83	2	FIRST READING
HB-2300	10/05/83	2	FIRST READING
	10/19/83	61	SECOND READING
	10/20/83	73	THIRD READING
HB-2301	10/05/83	2	FIRST READING
HB-2302	10/05/83	2	FIRST READING
	10/19/83	62	SECOND READING
	10/20/83	73	THIRD READING
HB-2303	10/05/83	2	FIRST READING
HB-2304	10/05/83	2	FIRST READING
	10/19/83	222	MOTION
	10/19/83	224	SECOND READING
	10/19/83	224	HELD ON SECOND
	10/20/83	67	SECOND READING
	10/20/83	68	OUT OF RECORD
	10/20/83	71	SECOND READING
	10/20/83	72	HELD ON SECOND
	03/06/84	3	SECOND READING
	03/06/84	4	OUT OF RECORD
	04/04/84	9	SECOND READING
	04/10/84	9	TABLED
HB-2305	10/05/83	2	FIRST READING
	10/19/83	62	SECOND READING
	10/20/83	75	THIRD READING
	11/04/83	165	CONCURRENCE
HB-2306	10/05/83	3	FIRST READING
	10/19/83	67	SECOND READING
	10/20/83	76	THIRD READING
	11/04/83	200	CONCURRENCE
HB-2307	10/05/83	3	FIRST READING
	05/08/84	12	SECOND READING
	05/16/84	87	THIRD READING
HB-2308	10/05/83	3	FIRST READING
	10/19/83	63	SECOND READING
	10/20/83	77	THIRD READING
HB-2309	10/05/83	4	FIRST READING
	10/19/83	186	SECOND READING

BILL NUMBER	DATE	PAGE	ACTION
HB-2309 (cont'd)	10/20/83	78	THIRD READING
	11/04/83	141	CONCURRENCE
HB-2310	10/05/83	4	FIRST READING
	10/19/83	227	MOTION
	10/19/83	229	SECOND READING
	10/19/83	229	HELD ON SECOND
	10/20/83	68	SECOND READING
	10/20/83	68	THIRD READING
	05/15/84	139	CONCURRENCE
HB-2311	10/05/83	4	FIRST READING
	10/19/83	63	SECOND READING
	10/19/83	203	SECOND READING
	10/20/83	79	THIRD READING
	10/20/83	163	THIRD READING
HB-2312	10/05/83	4	FIRST READING
	10/19/83	67	SECOND READING
	10/20/83	80	THIRD READING
	12/12/84	36	MOTION
	12/12/84	102	CONCURRENCE
HB-2313	10/05/83	4	FIRST READING
	10/19/83	67	SECOND READING
	10/20/83	83	THIRD READING
	11/04/83	142	CONCURRENCE
HB-2314	10/05/83	4	FIRST READING
	10/19/83	67	SECOND READING
	10/20/83	84	THIRD READING
HB-2315	10/05/83	4	FIRST READING
	10/19/83	68	SECOND READING
	10/20/83	120	THIRD READING
	11/04/83	157	CONCURRENCE
HB-2316	10/05/83	4	FIRST READING
	10/19/83	194	SECOND READING
	10/20/83	92	THIRD READING
HB-2317	10/05/83	4	FIRST READING
	10/19/83	68	SECOND READING
	10/20/83	93	THIRD READING
	11/04/83	158	CONCURRENCE
HB-2318	10/05/83	4	FIRST READING
	10/19/83	68	SECOND READING
	10/20/83	94	THIRD READING
HB-2319	10/05/83	4	FIRST READING

BILL NUMBER	DATE	PAGE	ACTION
HB-2319 (cont'd)	10/19/83	69	SECOND READING
	10/19/83	70	OUT OF RECORD
	10/19/83	197	SECOND READING
	10/20/83	121	THIRD READING
	11/04/83	182	CONCURRENCE
HB-2320	10/05/83	4	FIRST READING
	10/19/83	70	SECOND READING
	10/20/83	116	THIRD READING
HB-2321	10/19/83	1	FIRST READING
	05/24/84	255	SECOND READING
	05/24/84	255	HELD ON SECOND
	05/24/84	257	SECOND READING
	05/25/84	112	RECALLED
	05/25/84	115	THIRD READING
HB-2322	10/19/83	2	FIRST READING
HB-2323	10/20/83	1	FIRST READING
	05/23/84	5	SECOND READING
	05/24/84	309	RECALLED
	05/25/84	124	THIRD READING
	05/25/84	132	OUT OF RECORD
HB-2324	10/20/83	1	FIRST READING
HB-2325	10/20/83	1	FIRST READING
	05/02/84	3	SECOND READING
	05/09/84	26	SECOND READING
	05/10/84	95	THIRD READING
	06/26/84	149	CONCURRENCE
HB-2326	10/20/83	2	FIRST READING
HB-2327	10/20/83	176	FIRST READING
	11/01/83	62	MOTION
	11/01/83	97	SECOND READING
	11/04/83	101	THIRD READING
	11/04/83	101	OUT OF RECORD
	04/04/84	25	THIRD READING
HB-2328	11/01/83	1	FIRST READING
	05/02/84	4	SECOND READING
	05/03/84	23	THIRD READING
HB-2329	11/01/83	1	FIRST READING
HB-2330	11/01/83	3	FIRST READING
HB-2331	11/02/83	4	FIRST READING

BILL NUMBER	DATE	PAGE	ACTION
HB-2332	11/03/83	39	FIRST READING
	04/03/84	3	SECOND READING
	05/16/84	94	RECALLED
	05/17/84	16	SECOND READING
	05/17/84	31	MOTION
	05/22/84	54	THIRD READING
	05/23/84	208	RECALLED
	05/23/84	209	THIRD READING
	06/21/84	81	CONCURRENCE
HB-2333	11/03/83	39	FIRST READING
HB-2334	11/03/83	42	FIRST READING
	05/22/84	30	SECOND READING
	05/22/84	32	OUT OF RECORD
	05/23/84	18	SECOND READING
	05/23/84	18	HELD ON SECOND
	05/23/84	211	SECOND READING
	05/24/84	144	SECOND READING
	05/24/84	148	THIRD READING
	06/26/84	155	CONCURRENCE
HB-2335	11/03/83	42	FIRST READING
HB-2336	11/04/83	5	FIRST READING
HB-2337	11/04/83	102	FIRST READING
	05/02/84	11	SECOND READING
HB-2338	11/04/83	102	FIRST READING
HB-2339	01/10/84	1	FIRST READING
	05/08/84	12	SECOND READING
	05/09/84	52	THIRD READING
	06/21/84	82	CONCURRENCE
	06/30/84	165	CONFERENCE
HB-2340	01/10/84	1	FIRST READING
HB-2341	01/10/84	1	FIRST READING
	05/08/84	13	SECOND READING
	05/08/84	13	HELD ON SECOND
	05/10/84	181	MOTION
HB-2342	01/10/84	1	FIRST READING
	05/10/84	181	MOTION
HB-2343	01/10/84	1	FIRST READING
HB-2344	01/10/84	2	FIRST READING

BILL NUMBER	DATE	PAGE	ACTION
HB-2345	01/10/84	2	FIRST READING
	04/10/84	6	SECOND READING
	05/09/84	49	THIRD READING
	06/21/84	83	CONCURRENCE
	11/27/84	9	VETO MESSAGE
HB-2346	01/11/84	1	FIRST READING
	04/04/84	22	SECOND READING
	04/11/84	30	THIRD READING
HB-2347	01/11/84	1	FIRST READING
	05/04/84	40	MOTION
	05/10/84	21	SECOND READING
	05/16/84	94	RECALLED
	05/16/84	95	THIRD READING
HB-2348	01/11/84	1	FIRST READING
	04/10/84	6	SECOND READING
	04/11/84	15	THIRD READING
HB-2349	01/11/84	1	FIRST READING
HB-2350	01/11/84	1	FIRST READING
	05/10/84	21	SECOND READING
	05/10/84	28	OUT OF RECORD
	06/22/84	152	MOTION
	06/22/84	153	SECOND READING
	06/28/84	2	THIRD READING
HB-2351	02/07/84	1	FIRST READING
HB-2352	02/07/84	1	FIRST READING
HB-2353	02/07/84	1	FIRST READING
	04/10/84	14	MOTION
	04/10/84	15	SECOND READING
	04/11/84	20	THIRD READING
HB-2354	02/07/84	2	FIRST READING
	05/04/84	11	MOTION
HB-2355	02/07/84	2	FIRST READING
	04/04/84	4	SECOND READING
	04/26/84	40	THIRD READING
	06/26/84	150	CONCURRENCE
HB-2356	02/07/84	2	FIRST READING
HB-2357	02/07/84	2	FIRST READING
HB-2358	02/07/84	2	FIRST READING

BILL NUMBER	DATE	PAGE	ACTION
HB-2359	02/07/84	2	FIRST READING
	05/02/84	5	SECOND READING
	05/03/84	24	THIRD READING
	06/26/84	153	CONCURRENCE
	11/28/84	68	VETO MESSAGE
HB-2360	02/07/84	2	FIRST READING
	04/11/84	8	SECOND READING
	04/26/84	43	RECALLED
	04/26/84	44	THIRD READING
HB-2361	02/07/84	2	FIRST READING
HB-2362	02/07/84	2	FIRST READING
HB-2363	02/07/84	2	FIRST READING
HB-2364	02/07/84	2	FIRST READING
	05/15/84	70	SECOND READING
	05/24/84	15	THIRD READING
HB-2365	02/07/84	2	FIRST READING
	04/24/84	7	SECOND READING
	04/26/84	29	THIRD READING
HB-2366	02/07/84	2	FIRST READING
	05/15/84	70	SECOND READING
HB-2367	02/07/84	3	FIRST READING
HB-2368	02/07/84	3	FIRST READING
	05/16/84	16	SECOND READING
	05/25/84	164	THIRD READING
	06/28/84	164	CONCURRENCE
	06/30/84	186	CONFERENCE
HB-2369	02/07/84	3	FIRST READING
	04/26/84	15	SECOND READING
	04/26/84	21	HELD ON SECOND
	05/02/84	11	SECOND READING
	05/03/84	9	SECOND READING
	05/10/84	146	THIRD READING
	05/22/84	66	THIRD READING
HB-2370	02/07/84	3	FIRST READING
HB-2371	02/07/84	3	FIRST READING
	05/01/84	38	SECOND READING
	05/04/84	58	TABLED
HB-2372	02/07/84	3	FIRST READING

BILL NUMBER	DATE	PAGE	ACTION
HB-2372 (cont'd)	05/08/84	7	SECOND READING
	05/29/84	10	RECALLED
	05/30/84	16	THIRD READING
HB-2373	02/07/84	3	FIRST READING
	05/08/84	13	SECOND READING
	05/24/84	66	THIRD READING
	06/30/84	149	CONCURRENCE
HB-2374	02/07/84	3	FIRST READING
	04/11/84	10	SECOND READING
	04/24/84	17	THIRD READING
HB-2375	02/07/84	3	FIRST READING
HB-2376	02/07/84	3	FIRST READING
	05/16/84	16	SECOND READING
	05/23/84	214	THIRD READING
HB-2377	02/07/84	4	FIRST READING
	04/03/84	4	SECOND READING
	04/04/84	33	THIRD READING
HB-2378	02/07/84	4	FIRST READING
HB-2379	02/08/84	37	FIRST READING
	05/01/84	39	SECOND READING
	05/09/84	74	THIRD READING
	05/09/84	75	OUT OF RECORD
	05/23/84	304	RECALLED
	05/25/84	132	THIRD READING
	11/28/84	74	VETO MESSAGE
HB-2380	02/08/84	37	FIRST READING
	04/11/84	10	SECOND READING
	05/09/84	75	THIRD READING
HB-2381	02/08/84	37	FIRST READING
	04/26/84	21	SECOND READING
	05/18/84	152	RECALLED
	05/18/84	156	HELD ON SECOND
	05/22/84	22	SECOND READING
	05/22/84	115	THIRD READING
	06/28/84	46	CONCURRENCE
	06/30/84	46	CONFERENCE
	06/30/84	230	CONFERENCE
HB-2382	02/08/84	37	FIRST READING
HB-2383	02/08/84	37	FIRST READING

BILL NUMBER	DATE	PAGE	ACTION
HB-2384	02/08/84	37	FIRST READING
	05/02/84	11	SECOND READING
	05/23/84	267	RECALLED
	05/24/84	149	THIRD READING
HB-2385	02/08/84	37	FIRST READING
HB-2386	02/08/84	37	FIRST READING
HB-2387	02/08/84	38	FIRST READING
	04/11/84	11	SECOND READING
	05/09/84	77	THIRD READING
HB-2388	02/08/84	38	FIRST READING
	04/26/84	22	SECOND READING
	04/26/84	26	HELD ON SECOND
	05/01/84	39	SECOND READING
	05/09/84	78	THIRD READING
	06/29/84	83	CONCURRENCE
HB-2389	02/08/84	38	FIRST READING
	04/25/84	6	SECOND READING
	04/26/84	45	THIRD READING
HB-2390	02/08/84	38	FIRST READING
HB-2391	02/08/84	38	FIRST READING
HB-2392	02/08/84	38	FIRST READING
HB-2393	02/08/84	38	FIRST READING
HB-2394	02/08/84	38	FIRST READING
	05/02/84	42	SECOND READING
	05/08/84	40	THIRD READING
HB-2395	02/08/84	38	FIRST READING
	04/11/84	30	SECOND READING
	04/26/84	10	THIRD READING
	06/28/84	154	CONCURRENCE
HB-2396	02/08/84	38	FIRST READING
	04/25/84	4	SECOND READING
	04/26/84	31	THIRD READING
HB-2397	02/08/84	38	FIRST READING
	06/06/84	8	MOTION
HB-2398	02/08/84	38	FIRST READING
	04/11/84	30	SECOND READING
	04/26/84	10	THIRD READING

BILL NUMBER	DATE	PAGE	ACTION
HB-2399	02/08/84	38	FIRST READING
HB-2400	02/08/84	38	FIRST READING
	05/08/84	14	SECOND READING
	05/16/84	102	THIRD READING
	06/26/84	94	CONCURRENCE
	06/30/84	106	OTHER
	07/01/84	75	CONFERENCE
HB-2401	02/08/84	38	FIRST READING
HB-2402	02/08/84	39	FIRST READING
HB-2403	02/08/84	39	FIRST READING
	05/01/84	40	SECOND READING
	05/09/84	87	THIRD READING
HB-2404	02/08/84	39	FIRST READING
HB-2405	02/08/84	39	FIRST READING
HB-2406	02/08/84	39	FIRST READING
HB-2407	02/08/84	39	FIRST READING
HB-2408	02/08/84	39	FIRST READING
HB-2409	02/08/84	39	FIRST READING
	05/10/84	29	SECOND READING
	05/16/84	114	THIRD READING
HB-2410	02/08/84	39	FIRST READING
	04/10/84	6	SECOND READING
	05/09/84	95	RECALLED
	05/09/84	97	THIRD READING
HB-2411	02/08/84	39	FIRST READING
	05/10/84	29	SECOND READING
HB-2412	02/08/84	39	FIRST READING
HB-2413	02/08/84	39	FIRST READING
HB-2414	02/08/84	42	FIRST READING
HB-2415	02/08/84	42	FIRST READING
HB-2416	03/06/84	5	FIRST READING
	05/10/84	30	SECOND READING
	05/10/84	30	HELD ON SECOND
	05/16/84	17	SECOND READING

PROGRAM-LRTRNMST
08/20/85
LEGISLATIVE INFORMATION SYSTEM
HOUSE OF REPRESENTATIVES
PAGE 175

MASTER TRANSCRIPT INDEX

BILL NUMBER	DATE	PAGE	ACTION
HB-2416 (cont'd)	05/25/84	138	THIRD READING
HB-2417	03/06/84	6	FIRST READING
	05/15/84	73	OUT OF RECORD
	05/16/84	17	SECOND READING
HB-2418	03/06/84	6	FIRST READING
	04/25/84	7	SECOND READING
	04/26/84	46	THIRD READING
HB-2419	03/06/84	6	FIRST READING
	05/15/84	74	SECOND READING
	05/16/84	117	THIRD READING
HB-2420	03/06/84	6	FIRST READING
	05/02/84	5	SECOND READING
	05/03/84	30	THIRD READING
HB-2421	03/06/84	6	FIRST READING
HB-2422	03/06/84	6	FIRST READING
HB-2423	03/06/84	6	FIRST READING
	05/10/84	30	SECOND READING
	05/10/84	32	HELD ON SECOND
	05/15/84	75	SECOND READING
	05/23/84	63	THIRD READING
	11/27/84	10	VETO MESSAGE
HB-2424	03/06/84	6	FIRST READING
	05/22/84	25	SECOND READING
	05/22/84	26	HELD ON SECOND
	05/22/84	167	SECOND READING
	05/24/84	194	THIRD READING
HB-2425	03/06/84	6	FIRST READING
	05/08/84	22	SECOND READING
	05/09/84	55	THIRD READING
HB-2426	03/06/84	6	FIRST READING
	05/15/84	76	OUT OF RECORD
	05/16/84	48	SECOND READING
	05/25/84	143	THIRD READING
HB-2427	03/06/84	6	FIRST READING
HB-2428	03/06/84	6	FIRST READING
	05/09/84	27	SECOND READING
	05/10/84	94	THIRD READING
	06/21/84	85	CONCURRENCE
	11/27/84	11	VETO MESSAGE

PROGRAM-LRTRNMST
08/20/85
LEGISLATIVE INFORMATION SYSTEM
HOUSE OF REPRESENTATIVES
PAGE 176

MASTER TRANSCRIPT INDEX

BILL NUMBER	DATE	PAGE	ACTION
HB-2429	03/06/84	6	FIRST READING
	05/01/84	40	SECOND READING
	05/09/84	98	THIRD READING
HB-2430	03/06/84	6	FIRST READING
	05/10/84	32	SECOND READING
	05/16/84	120	THIRD READING
	06/21/84	87	CONCURRENCE
HB-2431	03/06/84	6	FIRST READING
	04/25/84	7	SECOND READING
	04/25/84	8	OUT OF RECORD
	04/26/84	26	SECOND READING
	05/09/84	99	THIRD READING
HB-2432	03/06/84	6	FIRST READING
	05/10/84	180	MOTION
HB-2433	03/06/84	7	FIRST READING
HB-2434	03/06/84	7	FIRST READING
	05/10/84	33	SECOND READING
	05/16/84	125	THIRD READING
HB-2435	03/06/84	7	FIRST READING
HB-2436	03/06/84	7	FIRST READING
HB-2437	03/06/84	7	FIRST READING
	04/11/84	11	SECOND READING
	05/09/84	103	RECALLED
	05/09/84	104	THIRD READING
HB-2438	03/06/84	7	FIRST READING
	05/09/84	27	SECOND READING
	05/10/84	96	THIRD READING
HB-2439	03/06/84	7	FIRST READING
HB-2440	03/06/84	7	FIRST READING
	05/10/84	33	SECOND READING
	05/16/84	130	THIRD READING
HB-2441	03/06/84	7	FIRST READING
	05/08/84	22	SECOND READING
	05/08/84	23	OUT OF RECORD
	05/10/84	34	SECOND READING
	05/16/84	134	THIRD READING
HB-2442	03/06/84	7	FIRST READING

BILL NUMBER	DATE	PAGE	ACTION
HB-2443	03/06/84	7	FIRST READING
	05/10/84	37	SECOND READING
	05/10/84	38	HELD ON SECOND
	05/16/84	19	SECOND READING
	05/16/84	20	HELD ON SECOND
	05/17/84	32	SECOND READING
	05/17/84	33	HELD ON SECOND
	05/22/84	21	SECOND READING
HB-2444	03/06/84	7	FIRST READING
	05/10/84	38	SECOND READING
	05/16/84	138	THIRD READING
HB-2445	03/06/84	7	FIRST READING
	05/04/84	11	MOTION
HB-2446	03/06/84	7	FIRST READING
	05/04/84	13	MOTION
HB-2447	03/06/84	7	FIRST READING
HB-2448	03/06/84	7	FIRST READING
HB-2449	03/06/84	7	FIRST READING
	05/10/84	38	SECOND READING
HB-2450	03/06/84	8	FIRST READING
	04/25/84	14	SECOND READING
	05/24/84	299	RECALLED
	05/25/84	144	THIRD READING
HB-2451	03/06/84	8	FIRST READING
	05/08/84	24	SECOND READING
	05/09/84	106	THIRD READING
	12/12/84	36	MOTION
	12/12/84	105	CONCURRENCE
HB-2452	03/06/84	8	FIRST READING
	04/25/84	4	SECOND READING
	04/26/84	32	THIRD READING
HB-2453	03/06/84	8	FIRST READING
	04/25/84	8	SECOND READING
	05/09/84	107	THIRD READING
HB-2454	03/06/84	8	FIRST READING
	04/10/84	7	SECOND READING
	05/09/84	109	THIRD READING
	06/21/84	88	CONCURRENCE
	06/30/84	17	CONFERENCE

BILL NUMBER	DATE	PAGE	ACTION
HB-2455	03/06/84	8	FIRST READING
	05/10/84	41	SECOND READING
	05/16/84	143	THIRD READING
HB-2456	03/06/84	8	FIRST READING
HB-2457	03/06/84	8	FIRST READING
HB-2458	03/06/84	8	FIRST READING
	04/10/84	7	SECOND READING
	04/11/84	21	THIRD READING
	06/26/84	96	CONCURRENCE
	06/30/84	26	CONFERENCE
HB-2459	03/06/84	8	FIRST READING
	05/10/84	38	SECOND READING
	05/24/84	88	RECALLED
	05/24/84	89	HELD ON SECOND
	05/25/84	91	SECOND READING
	05/25/84	96	THIRD READING
HB-2460	03/06/84	8	FIRST READING
	05/02/84	5	SECOND READING
	05/03/84	30	THIRD READING
HB-2461	03/06/84	8	FIRST READING
	04/25/84	9	SECOND READING
	04/26/84	51	THIRD READING
HB-2462	03/06/84	8	FIRST READING
	04/26/84	27	SECOND READING
	05/09/84	109	THIRD READING
HB-2463	03/06/84	9	FIRST READING
	04/25/84	9	SECOND READING
	04/26/84	52	THIRD READING
HB-2464	03/06/84	9	FIRST READING
	05/02/84	16	SECOND READING
	05/16/84	144	RECALLED
	05/16/84	146	HELD ON SECOND
	05/16/84	269	SECOND READING
	05/24/84	81	THIRD READING
HB-2465	03/06/84	9	FIRST READING
HB-2466	03/06/84	9	FIRST READING
	04/11/84	4	SECOND READING
	04/24/84	8	THIRD READING
	06/21/84	88	CONCURRENCE

BILL NUMBER	DATE	PAGE	ACTION
HB-2467	03/06/84	9	FIRST READING
HB-2468	03/06/84	9	FIRST READING
	04/11/84	4	SECOND READING
	04/24/84	10	THIRD READING
HB-2469	03/06/84	9	FIRST READING
	04/11/84	11	SECOND READING
	04/26/84	53	THIRD READING
HB-2470	03/06/84	9	FIRST READING
	05/16/84	69	SECOND READING
	05/24/84	199	THIRD READING
HB-2471	03/06/84	9	FIRST READING
HB-2472	03/06/84	9	FIRST READING
HB-2473	03/06/84	9	FIRST READING
	05/08/84	25	SECOND READING
	05/16/84	146	THIRD READING
HB-2474	03/06/84	9	FIRST READING
HB-2475	03/06/84	9	FIRST READING
	05/02/84	3	SECOND READING
	05/04/84	6	THIRD READING
	06/26/84	165	CONCURRENCE
HB-2476	03/06/84	9	FIRST READING
	05/10/84	39	SECOND READING
	05/24/84	89	RECALLED
	05/24/84	91	HELD ON SECOND
	05/24/84	283	THIRD READING
HB-2477	03/06/84	9	FIRST READING
	05/08/84	2	SECOND READING
	05/30/84	17	THIRD READING
HB-2478	03/06/84	10	FIRST READING
HB-2479	03/06/84	10	FIRST READING
	05/10/84	39	SECOND READING
	05/16/84	278	RECALLED
	05/23/84	71	THIRD READING
	06/26/84	157	CONCURRENCE
HB-2480	03/06/84	10	FIRST READING
HB-2481	03/06/84	10	FIRST READING
	05/15/84	3	SECOND READING

BILL NUMBER	DATE	PAGE	ACTION
HB-2482	03/06/84	10	FIRST READING
HB-2483	03/06/84	10	FIRST READING
	05/02/84	16	SECOND READING
	05/09/84	110	THIRD READING
HB-2484	03/06/84	10	FIRST READING
HB-2485	03/06/84	10	FIRST READING
HB-2486	03/06/84	10	FIRST READING
	05/02/84	17	SECOND READING
	05/09/84	113	THIRD READING
HB-2487	03/06/84	10	FIRST READING
HB-2488	03/06/84	10	FIRST READING
	04/11/84	30	SECOND READING
	04/26/84	10	THIRD READING
HB-2489	03/06/84	10	FIRST READING
	04/10/84	7	SECOND READING
	04/26/84	54	THIRD READING
HB-2490	03/06/84	10	FIRST READING
HB-2491	03/06/84	12	FIRST READING
	04/25/84	15	SECOND READING
	04/26/84	33	THIRD READING
HB-2492	03/06/84	12	FIRST READING
	04/10/84	8	SECOND READING
	04/26/84	55	RECALLED
	04/26/84	56	THIRD READING
	04/26/84	61	OUT OF RECORD
	05/09/84	114	THIRD READING
HB-2493	03/06/84	12	FIRST READING
HB-2494	03/06/84	12	FIRST READING
HB-2495	03/07/84	26	FIRST READING
HB-2496	03/07/84	26	FIRST READING
	05/09/84	2	SECOND READING
	05/16/84	4	THIRD READING
HB-2497	03/07/84	26	FIRST READING
HB-2498	03/07/84	26	FIRST READING

BILL NUMBER	DATE	PAGE	ACTION
HB-2499	03/07/84	26	FIRST READING
	05/09/84	2	SECOND READING
	05/16/84	4	THIRD READING
HB-2500	03/07/84	26	FIRST READING
	05/09/84	2	SECOND READING
	05/16/84	5	THIRD READING
HB-2501	03/07/84	26	FIRST READING
HB-2502	03/07/84	26	FIRST READING
	04/25/84	10	SECOND READING
	04/26/84	61	THIRD READING
	11/27/84	14	VETO MESSAGE
HB-2503	03/07/84	26	FIRST READING
HB-2504	03/07/84	26	FIRST READING
	05/01/84	41	SECOND READING
	05/09/84	115	THIRD READING
HB-2505	03/07/84	27	FIRST READING
	04/10/84	8	SECOND READING
HB-2506	03/07/84	27	FIRST READING
HB-2507	03/07/84	27	FIRST READING
	05/01/84	35	SECOND READING
	05/03/84	32	THIRD READING
HB-2508	03/07/84	27	FIRST READING
HB-2509	03/07/84	27	FIRST READING
	04/10/84	9	SECOND READING
	04/11/84	21	THIRD READING
	06/27/84	2	CONCURRENCE
	06/27/84	3	OUT OF RECORD
	06/27/84	58	CONCURRENCE
	06/27/84	63	OUT OF RECORD
	06/28/84	153	CONCURRENCE
	07/01/84	25	CONFERENCE
	11/28/84	64	VETO MESSAGE
HB-2510	03/07/84	27	FIRST READING
	05/10/84	40	SECOND READING
	05/10/84	41	HELD ON SECOND
	05/15/84	85	SECOND READING
	05/16/84	150	THIRD READING
HB-2511	03/07/84	27	FIRST READING
	05/10/84	42	SECOND READING

BILL NUMBER	DATE	PAGE	ACTION
HB-2511 (cont'd)	05/16/84	159	RECALLED
	05/16/84	160	THIRD READING
HB-2512	03/07/84	27	FIRST READING
	05/15/84	77	SECOND READING
	05/16/84	161	THIRD READING
HB-2513	03/07/84	27	FIRST READING
	04/25/84	10	SECOND READING
	04/26/84	63	THIRD READING
	06/27/84	45	CONCURRENCE
HB-2514	03/07/84	27	FIRST READING
HB-2515	03/07/84	27	FIRST READING
	04/25/84	10	SECOND READING
	04/26/84	66	THIRD READING
HB-2516	03/07/84	27	FIRST READING
	05/08/84	25	SECOND READING
	05/16/84	169	RECALLED
	05/16/84	170	THIRD READING
	06/21/84	90	CONCURRENCE
	06/21/84	90	OUT OF RECORD
	06/26/84	161	CONCURRENCE
HB-2517	03/07/84	27	FIRST READING
HB-2518	03/07/84	28	FIRST READING
	05/01/84	41	SECOND READING
HB-2519	03/07/84	28	FIRST READING
	04/25/84	4	SECOND READING
	04/26/84	34	THIRD READING
HB-2520	03/07/84	28	FIRST READING
HB-2521	03/27/84	11	FIRST READING
	04/26/84	14	SECOND READING
	05/08/84	41	THIRD READING
HB-2522	03/27/84	11	FIRST READING
	04/26/84	27	SECOND READING
	05/09/84	120	THIRD READING
HB-2523	03/27/84	11	FIRST READING
	04/26/84	27	SECOND READING
	05/25/84	6	THIRD READING
HB-2524	03/27/84	11	FIRST READING
	05/02/84	3	SECOND READING

BILL NUMBER	DATE	PAGE	ACTION
HB-2524 (cont'd)	05/04/84	7	THIRD READING
HB-2525	03/27/84	11	FIRST READING
	05/02/84	4	SECOND READING
	05/04/84	7	THIRD READING
HB-2526	03/27/84	12	FIRST READING
HB-2527	03/27/84	12	FIRST READING
HB-2528	03/27/84	12	FIRST READING
	05/01/84	41	SECOND READING
	05/09/84	122	THIRD READING
HB-2529	03/27/84	12	FIRST READING
HB-2530	03/27/84	12	FIRST READING
	04/25/84	11	SECOND READING
	05/31/84	86	THIRD READING
	06/29/84	94	CONCURRENCE
HB-2531	03/27/84	12	FIRST READING
HB-2532	03/27/84	12	FIRST READING
HB-2533	03/27/84	12	FIRST READING
HB-2534	03/27/84	12	FIRST READING
	04/25/84	5	SECOND READING
	04/26/84	35	THIRD READING
	06/28/84	7	CONCURRENCE
HB-2535	03/27/84	12	FIRST READING
HB-2536	03/27/84	12	FIRST READING
HB-2537	03/27/84	12	FIRST READING
HB-2538	03/27/84	12	FIRST READING
HB-2539	03/27/84	12	FIRST READING
HB-2540	03/27/84	13	FIRST READING
	05/09/84	28	SECOND READING
	05/10/84	99	THIRD READING
HB-2541	03/27/84	13	FIRST READING
HB-2542	03/27/84	13	FIRST READING
	05/01/84	41	SECOND READING
	05/09/84	128	THIRD READING

BILL NUMBER	DATE	PAGE	ACTION
HB-2542 (cont'd)	06/27/84	40	CONCURRENCE
HB-2543	03/27/84	13	FIRST READING
HB-2544	03/27/84	13	FIRST READING
HB-2545	03/27/84	13	FIRST READING
	05/17/84	210	SECOND READING
	05/23/84	233	THIRD READING
HB-2546	03/27/84	13	FIRST READING
	05/08/84	3	SECOND READING
	05/29/84	3	RECALLED
	05/29/84	5	OUT OF RECORD
	05/29/84	28	SECOND READING
	05/31/84	40	THIRD READING
	06/29/84	93	CONCURRENCE
	07/01/84	117	CONFERENCE
HB-2547	03/27/84	13	FIRST READING
	05/08/84	3	SECOND READING
	05/31/84	64	THIRD READING
	06/29/84	93	CONCURRENCE
	07/01/84	123	CONFERENCE
HB-2548	03/27/84	13	FIRST READING
	05/09/84	28	TABLED
HB-2549	03/27/84	13	FIRST READING
	05/02/84	17	SECOND READING
	05/02/84	18	HELD ON SECOND
	05/08/84	3	SECOND READING
	05/08/84	3	HELD ON SECOND
	05/15/84	91	SECOND READING
	05/31/84	38	THIRD READING
HB-2550	03/27/84	13	FIRST READING
HB-2551	03/27/84	13	FIRST READING
HB-2552	03/27/84	14	FIRST READING
HB-2553	03/27/84	14	FIRST READING
	04/25/84	11	SECOND READING
	05/16/84	51	RECALLED
	05/22/84	119	RECALLED
	05/22/84	123	THIRD READING
HB-2554	03/27/84	14	FIRST READING
	05/09/84	28	SECOND READING
	05/10/84	102	THIRD READING

BILL NUMBER	DATE	PAGE	ACTION
HB-2555	03/27/84	14	FIRST READING
HB-2556	03/27/84	14	FIRST READING
	05/02/84	18	SECOND READING
	05/09/84	130	THIRD READING
	06/27/84	63	CONCURRENCE
	11/27/84	16	VETO MESSAGE
HB-2557	03/27/84	14	FIRST READING
HB-2558	03/27/84	14	FIRST READING
	05/16/84	22	SECOND READING
	05/22/84	79	THIRD READING
HB-2559	03/27/84	14	FIRST READING
	05/02/84	18	SECOND READING
	05/16/84	175	THIRD READING
	05/22/84	165	RECALLED
	05/23/84	216	THIRD READING
HB-2560	03/27/84	14	FIRST READING
	05/02/84	19	SECOND READING
	05/09/84	39	THIRD READING
	06/26/84	168	CONCURRENCE
	11/27/84	21	VETO MESSAGE
HB-2561	03/27/84	14	FIRST READING
HB-2562	03/27/84	14	FIRST READING
HB-2563	03/27/84	14	FIRST READING
HB-2564	03/27/84	14	FIRST READING
HB-2565	03/27/84	15	FIRST READING
	05/03/84	10	SECOND READING
HB-2566	03/27/84	15	FIRST READING
	05/16/84	252	SECOND READING
	05/24/84	256	RECALLED
	05/25/84	14	THIRD READING
	06/26/84	170	CONCURRENCE
HB-2567	03/27/84	15	FIRST READING
	05/03/84	6	SECOND READING
HB-2568	03/27/84	15	FIRST READING
	05/08/84	25	SECOND READING
	05/23/84	218	THIRD READING
HB-2569	03/27/84	15	FIRST READING

BILL NUMBER	DATE	PAGE	ACTION
HB-2569 (cont'd)	05/02/84	4	SECOND READING
	05/04/84	7	THIRD READING
	06/21/84	91	CONCURRENCE
HB-2570	03/27/84	15	FIRST READING
	05/01/84	42	SECOND READING
	05/09/84	139	THIRD READING
	06/21/84	93	CONCURRENCE
	06/30/84	10	CONFERENCE
HB-2571	03/27/84	15	FIRST READING
HB-2572	03/27/84	15	FIRST READING
HB-2573	03/27/84	15	FIRST READING
HB-2574	03/27/84	15	FIRST READING
	05/02/84	45	SECOND READING
	05/09/84	140	THIRD READING
	05/22/84	165	RECALLED
	05/24/84	20	THIRD READING
	06/26/84	172	CONCURRENCE
HB-2575	03/27/84	15	FIRST READING
	05/02/84	4	SECOND READING
	05/04/84	7	THIRD READING
HB-2576	03/27/84	15	FIRST READING
	05/09/84	29	SECOND READING
	05/10/84	103	THIRD READING
	06/26/84	96	CONCURRENCE
	06/30/84	228	CONFERENCE
HB-2577	03/27/84	15	FIRST READING
	05/04/84	14	MOTION
HB-2578	03/27/84	15	FIRST READING
	05/02/84	6	SECOND READING
	05/03/84	32	THIRD READING
HB-2579	03/27/84	15	FIRST READING
HB-2580	03/27/84	16	FIRST READING
	05/10/84	43	SECOND READING
	05/16/84	179	THIRD READING
HB-2581	03/27/84	16	FIRST READING
HB-2582	03/27/84	16	FIRST READING
	05/10/84	3	SECOND READING
	05/17/84	234	THIRD READING

BILL NUMBER	DATE	PAGE	ACTION
HB-2583	03/28/84	14	FIRST READING
HB-2584	03/28/84	14	FIRST READING
	05/02/84	4	SECOND READING
	05/04/84	7	THIRD READING
HB-2585	03/28/84	14	FIRST READING
HB-2586	03/28/84	14	FIRST READING
HB-2587	03/28/84	14	FIRST READING
HB-2588	03/28/84	14	FIRST READING
HB-2589	03/28/84	14	FIRST READING
HB-2590	03/28/84	14	FIRST READING
	05/02/84	4	SECOND READING
	05/04/84	7	THIRD READING
HB-2591	03/28/84	15	FIRST READING
	04/25/84	11	SECOND READING
	04/26/84	69	THIRD READING
HB-2592	03/28/84	15	FIRST READING
	05/08/84	25	SECOND READING
	05/16/84	180	THIRD READING
HB-2593	03/28/84	15	FIRST READING
HB-2594	03/28/84	15	FIRST READING
HB-2595	03/28/84	15	FIRST READING
	05/10/84	43	SECOND READING
	05/24/84	91	RECALLED
	05/24/84	92	HELD ON SECOND
	05/25/84	91	SECOND READING
	05/25/84	97	THIRD READING
HB-2596	03/28/84	15	FIRST READING
	05/02/84	6	SECOND READING
	05/03/84	33	THIRD READING
HB-2597	03/28/84	15	FIRST READING
	05/04/84	42	MOTION
	05/10/84	46	SECOND READING
	05/16/84	183	THIRD READING
	11/28/84	81	MOTION
	11/28/84	82	CONCURRENCE
	12/12/84	6	VETO MESSAGE

BILL NUMBER	DATE	PAGE	ACTION
HB-2598	03/28/84	15	FIRST READING
	05/10/84	46	SECOND READING
	05/16/84	185	THIRD READING
	06/26/84	174	CONCURRENCE
HB-2599	03/28/84	15	FIRST READING
HB-2600	03/28/84	15	FIRST READING
	04/25/84	12	SECOND READING
	04/26/84	72	THIRD READING
	06/30/84	36	CONCURRENCE
	06/30/84	37	OUT OF RECORD
	06/30/84	133	CONCURRENCE
HB-2601	03/28/84	15	FIRST READING
HB-2602	03/28/84	15	FIRST READING
HB-2603	03/28/84	15	FIRST READING
HB-2604	03/28/84	15	FIRST READING
HB-2605	03/28/84	16	FIRST READING
	04/25/84	12	SECOND READING
	04/26/84	73	THIRD READING
	06/30/84	145	CONCURRENCE
HB-2606	03/28/84	16	FIRST READING
	05/10/84	47	SECOND READING
	05/10/84	47	HELD ON SECOND
	05/15/84	86	SECOND READING
	05/23/84	134	RECALLED
	05/23/84	135	THIRD READING
HB-2607	03/28/84	16	FIRST READING
	05/04/84	18	MOTION
HB-2608	03/28/84	16	FIRST READING
	05/04/84	24	MOTION
HB-2609	03/28/84	16	FIRST READING
	04/25/84	15	SECOND READING
	05/10/84	144	THIRD READING
HB-2610	03/28/84	16	FIRST READING
	05/02/84	46	SECOND READING
	05/29/84	5	RECALLED
	05/31/84	21	THIRD READING
	06/29/84	95	CONCURRENCE
HB-2611	03/28/84	16	FIRST READING

BILL NUMBER	DATE	PAGE	ACTION
HB-2612	03/28/84	16	FIRST READING
HB-2613	03/28/84	16	FIRST READING
	05/16/84	49	SECOND READING
	05/25/84	133	THIRD READING
HB-2614	03/28/84	16	FIRST READING
HB-2615	03/28/84	16	FIRST READING
	05/03/84	11	SECOND READING
	05/10/84	153	THIRD READING
	11/27/84	23	VETO MESSAGE
HB-2616	03/28/84	16	FIRST READING
HB-2617	03/28/84	16	FIRST READING
	05/02/84	4	SECOND READING
	05/04/84	7	THIRD READING
HB-2618	03/28/84	16	FIRST READING
HB-2619	03/28/84	16	FIRST READING
	05/02/84	4	SECOND READING
	05/04/84	7	THIRD READING
HB-2620	03/28/84	17	FIRST READING
	05/10/84	47	SECOND READING
	05/10/84	47	HELD ON SECOND
	05/16/84	23	SECOND READING
HB-2621	03/28/84	17	FIRST READING
HB-2622	03/28/84	17	FIRST READING
	05/09/84	2	SECOND READING
	05/16/84	5	THIRD READING
HB-2623	03/28/84	17	FIRST READING
HB-2624	03/28/84	17	FIRST READING
	05/02/84	46	SECOND READING
	05/31/84	113	THIRD READING
	06/29/84	96	CONCURRENCE
HB-2625	03/28/84	17	FIRST READING
	05/02/84	46	SECOND READING
	05/31/84	115	THIRD READING
HB-2626	03/28/84	17	FIRST READING
	05/15/84	91	SECOND READING
	05/31/84	87	THIRD READING
	06/30/84	83	CONCURRENCE

BILL NUMBER	DATE	PAGE	ACTION
HB-2627	03/28/84	17	FIRST READING
	05/15/84	92	SECOND READING
	05/31/84	31	RECALLED
	05/31/84	35	THIRD READING
	06/30/84	84	CONCURRENCE
HB-2628	03/28/84	17	FIRST READING
HB-2629	03/28/84	19	FIRST READING
	05/08/84	26	SECOND READING
	05/08/84	26	HELD ON SECOND
	05/10/84	50	SECOND READING
	05/16/84	186	THIRD READING
HB-2630	03/28/84	19	FIRST READING
	05/10/84	48	SECOND READING
	05/16/84	187	RECALLED
	05/16/84	192	THIRD READING
HB-2631	03/28/84	19	FIRST READING
	05/02/84	47	SECOND READING
	05/31/84	67	THIRD READING
	06/29/84	98	CONCURRENCE
HB-2632	03/28/84	19	FIRST READING
	05/08/84	4	SECOND READING
	05/31/84	51	THIRD READING
HB-2633	03/28/84	19	FIRST READING
	04/25/84	12	SECOND READING
	04/26/84	73	THIRD READING
	06/29/84	99	CONCURRENCE
HB-2634	03/28/84	19	FIRST READING
	04/11/84	12	SECOND READING
	05/31/84	38	THIRD READING
HB-2635	03/28/84	19	FIRST READING
	04/26/84	74	THIRD READING
HB-2636	03/28/84	19	FIRST READING
	05/15/84	94	SECOND READING
	05/29/84	13	THIRD READING
	06/29/84	99	CONCURRENCE
HB-2637	03/28/84	20	FIRST READING
	05/15/84	95	SECOND READING
	05/29/84	14	THIRD READING
	06/29/84	93	CONCURRENCE
	07/01/84	48	CONFERENCE
	11/28/84	7	VETO MESSAGE

PROGRAM-LRTRNMST
08/20/85
LEGISLATIVE INFORMATION SYSTEM
HOUSE OF REPRESENTATIVES
PAGE 191

MASTER TRANSCRIPT INDEX

BILL NUMBER	DATE	PAGE	ACTION
HB-2638	03/28/84	20	FIRST READING
	05/02/84	47	SECOND READING
	05/30/84	49	THIRD READING
	06/29/84	93	CONCURRENCE
	07/01/84	49	CONFERENCE
	11/28/84	39	VETO MESSAGE
HB-2639	03/28/84	20	FIRST READING
	05/15/84	102	SECOND READING
	05/29/84	18	THIRD READING
	06/29/84	100	CONCURRENCE
HB-2640	03/28/84	20	FIRST READING
	05/15/84	102	SECOND READING
	05/31/84	88	THIRD READING
	06/29/84	93	CONCURRENCE
	07/01/84	50	CONFERENCE
HB-2641	03/28/84	20	FIRST READING
	05/15/84	106	SECOND READING
	05/31/84	30	THIRD READING
	06/30/84	85	CONCURRENCE
HB-2642	03/28/84	20	FIRST READING
	05/15/84	107	SECOND READING
	05/31/84	92	THIRD READING
	06/29/84	101	CONCURRENCE
HB-2643	03/28/84	20	FIRST READING
	05/15/84	109	SECOND READING
	05/29/84	19	THIRD READING
	06/29/84	102	CONCURRENCE
HB-2644	03/28/84	20	FIRST READING
	05/15/84	114	SECOND READING
	05/31/84	93	RECALLED
	05/31/84	94	THIRD READING
	06/29/84	103	CONCURRENCE
HB-2645	03/28/84	20	FIRST READING
	05/15/84	115	SECOND READING
	05/30/84	4	THIRD READING
	06/29/84	103	CONCURRENCE
HB-2646	03/28/84	20	FIRST READING
	05/15/84	115	SECOND READING
	05/30/84	6	THIRD READING
HB-2647	03/28/84	21	FIRST READING
	04/25/84	12	SECOND READING
	04/26/84	75	THIRD READING

PROGRAM-LRTRNMST
08/20/85
LEGISLATIVE INFORMATION SYSTEM
HOUSE OF REPRESENTATIVES
PAGE 192

MASTER TRANSCRIPT INDEX

BILL NUMBER	DATE	PAGE	ACTION
HB-2647 (cont'd)	06/29/84	104	CONCURRENCE
HB-2648	03/28/84	21	FIRST READING
	05/15/84	116	SECOND READING
	05/31/84	97	THIRD READING
	06/29/84	105	CONCURRENCE
HB-2649	03/28/84	21	FIRST READING
	05/02/84	49	SECOND READING
	05/30/84	51	THIRD READING
	07/01/84	6	CONCURRENCE
	07/01/84	136	CONFERENCE
	11/28/84	46	VETO MESSAGE
	11/28/84	60	VETO MESSAGE
HB-2650	03/28/84	21	FIRST READING
	04/25/84	13	SECOND READING
	04/26/84	75	THIRD READING
	06/29/84	105	CONCURRENCE
HB-2651	03/28/84	21	FIRST READING
	05/08/84	5	SECOND READING
	05/31/84	67	THIRD READING
	06/30/84	90	CONCURRENCE
HB-2652	03/28/84	21	FIRST READING
	05/15/84	118	SECOND READING
	05/29/84	20	THIRD READING
HB-2653	03/28/84	21	FIRST READING
	05/15/84	118	SECOND READING
	05/31/84	107	RECALLED
	05/31/84	111	THIRD READING
	06/30/84	91	CONCURRENCE
	11/28/84	57	VETO MESSAGE
	11/28/84	62	VETO MESSAGE
HB-2654	03/28/84	21	FIRST READING
	05/15/84	123	SECOND READING
	05/31/84	39	THIRD READING
	06/29/84	106	CONCURRENCE
HB-2655	03/28/84	21	FIRST READING
	05/15/84	123	SECOND READING
	05/31/84	97	THIRD READING
HB-2656	03/28/84	21	FIRST READING
HB-2657	03/28/84	21	FIRST READING
	05/09/84	29	SECOND READING
	05/10/84	104	THIRD READING

BILL NUMBER	DATE	PAGE	ACTION
HB-2657 (cont'd)	05/10/84	105	OUT OF RECORD
	05/15/84	150	THIRD READING
	05/15/84	151	OUT OF RECORD
	05/24/84	308	RECALLED
	05/25/84	121	THIRD READING
	06/26/84	175	CONCURRENCE
	12/12/84	54	MOTION
	12/12/84	124	CONFERENCE
HB-2658	03/28/84	22	FIRST READING
	05/02/84	7	SECOND READING
	05/03/84	34	THIRD READING
HB-2659	03/29/84	3	FIRST READING
	04/25/84	13	SECOND READING
	04/25/84	13	OUT OF RECORD
	04/26/84	28	SECOND READING
	05/31/84	98	RECALLED
	05/31/84	99	THIRD READING
	05/31/84	107	TABLED
HB-2660	03/29/84	3	FIRST READING
HB-2661	03/29/84	3	FIRST READING
HB-2662	03/29/84	3	FIRST READING
	05/02/84	49	SECOND READING
	05/10/84	157	THIRD READING
HB-2663	03/29/84	3	FIRST READING
	04/26/84	29	SECOND READING
	05/31/84	70	THIRD READING
	06/29/84	107	CONCURRENCE
HB-2664	03/29/84	3	FIRST READING
	04/26/84	29	SECOND READING
	05/31/84	70	THIRD READING
	06/29/84	93	CONCURRENCE
	07/01/84	53	CONFERENCE
HB-2665	03/29/84	3	FIRST READING
	04/25/84	14	SECOND READING
	04/26/84	76	THIRD READING
HB-2666	03/29/84	3	FIRST READING
	05/01/84	36	SECOND READING
	05/03/84	36	THIRD READING
	06/26/84	175	CONCURRENCE
HB-2667	03/29/84	3	FIRST READING

BILL NUMBER	DATE	PAGE	ACTION
HB-2668	03/29/84	3	FIRST READING
	05/02/84	4	SECOND READING
	05/03/84	7	SECOND READING
	05/08/84	43	THIRD READING
HB-2669	03/29/84	3	FIRST READING
	04/11/84	12	SECOND READING
	04/11/84	12	MOTION
	04/24/84	4	THIRD READING
HB-2670	03/29/84	3	FIRST READING
	05/10/84	48	SECOND READING
	05/10/84	50	HELD ON SECOND
	05/10/84	82	SECOND READING
	05/24/84	285	RECALLED
	05/24/84	296	SECOND READING
	05/25/84	116	THIRD READING
HB-2671	03/29/84	4	FIRST READING
	05/23/84	274	SECOND READING
	05/24/84	93	RECALLED
	05/24/84	268	THIRD READING
	05/25/84	92	RECALLED
	05/25/84	95	THIRD READING
HB-2672	03/29/84	4	FIRST READING
HB-2673	03/29/84	4	FIRST READING
HB-2674	03/29/84	4	FIRST READING
	05/23/84	275	SECOND READING
	05/25/84	100	THIRD READING
HB-2675	03/29/84	4	FIRST READING
HB-2676	03/29/84	4	FIRST READING
	05/01/84	49	TABLED
HB-2677	03/29/84	5	FIRST READING
HB-2678	03/29/84	5	FIRST READING
	05/09/84	29	SECOND READING
	05/15/84	148	THIRD READING
HB-2679	03/29/84	5	FIRST READING
HB-2680	03/29/84	5	FIRST READING
HB-2681	03/29/84	5	FIRST READING
	05/15/84	3	SECOND READING
	05/16/84	58	THIRD READING

BILL NUMBER	DATE	PAGE	ACTION
HB-2682	03/29/84	5	FIRST READING
HB-2683	03/29/84	9	FIRST READING
	04/11/84	36	TABLED
HB-2684	03/29/84	10	FIRST READING
	05/10/84	52	SECOND READING
	05/22/84	114	THIRD READING
	06/26/84	176	CONCURRENCE
HB-2685	04/03/84	2	FIRST READING
HB-2686	04/03/84	2	FIRST READING
HB-2687	04/03/84	2	FIRST READING
HB-2688	04/03/84	2	FIRST READING
HB-2689	04/03/84	2	FIRST READING
	04/25/84	14	SECOND READING
	04/25/84	15	OUT OF RECORD
	04/25/84	24	SECOND READING
	04/26/84	76	THIRD READING
	05/15/84	145	CONCURRENCE
HB-2690	04/03/84	2	FIRST READING
HB-2691	04/03/84	2	FIRST READING
HB-2692	04/03/84	2	FIRST READING
	05/09/84	30	SECOND READING
	05/10/84	105	THIRD READING
	06/26/84	178	CONCURRENCE
HB-2693	04/03/84	2	FIRST READING
	05/09/84	30	SECOND READING
	05/10/84	107	THIRD READING
	06/26/84	105	CONCURRENCE
HB-2694	04/03/84	2	FIRST READING
HB-2695	04/03/84	2	FIRST READING
HB-2696	04/03/84	3	FIRST READING
HB-2697	04/03/84	3	FIRST READING
HB-2698	04/03/84	3	FIRST READING
HB-2699	04/03/84	3	FIRST READING
	05/10/84	92	SECOND READING

BILL NUMBER	DATE	PAGE	ACTION
HB-2699 (cont'd)	05/16/84	195	THIRD READING
HB-2700	04/03/84	5	FIRST READING
HB-2701	04/03/84	6	FIRST READING
HB-2702	04/03/84	6	FIRST READING
	05/15/84	4	SECOND READING
	05/22/84	88	THIRD READING
HB-2703	04/03/84	6	FIRST READING
	05/10/84	180	MOTION
HB-2704	04/03/84	6	FIRST READING
HB-2705	04/03/84	6	FIRST READING
HB-2706	04/03/84	6	FIRST READING
	05/10/84	52	SECOND READING
	05/13/84	219	RECALLED
	05/23/84	220	THIRD READING
	06/27/84	4	CONCURRENCE
HB-2707	04/03/84	6	FIRST READING
	05/03/84	12	SECOND READING
	05/10/84	158	THIRD READING
HB-2708	04/03/84	8	FIRST READING
HB-2709	04/03/84	8	FIRST READING
HB-2710	04/04/84	39	FIRST READING
	05/10/84	52	SECOND READING
	05/23/84	228	THIRD READING
HB-2711	04/04/84	39	FIRST READING
	04/25/84	15	SECOND READING
	05/09/84	146	RECALLED
	05/09/84	150	THIRD READING
	06/14/84	88	CONCURRENCE
HB-2712	04/04/84	39	FIRST READING
HB-2713	04/04/84	39	FIRST READING
HB-2714	04/04/84	39	FIRST READING
	05/09/84	31	SECOND READING
	05/10/84	108	THIRD READING
	06/27/84	52	CONCURRENCE
HB-2715	04/04/84	39	FIRST READING

BILL NUMBER	DATE	PAGE	ACTION
HB-2715 (cont'd)	05/10/84	52	SECOND READING
	05/16/84	197	THIRD READING
HB-2716	04/04/84	39	FIRST READING
	05/15/84	87	SECOND READING
	05/16/84	198	THIRD READING
HB-2717	04/04/84	39	FIRST READING
	05/10/84	53	SECOND READING
	05/16/84	207	THIRD READING
	05/16/84	209	OUT OF RECORD
	05/24/84	200	THIRD READING
HB-2718	04/04/84	39	FIRST READING
HB-2719	04/04/84	40	FIRST READING
	05/10/84	53	OTHER
HB-2720	04/04/84	40	FIRST READING
HB-2721	04/04/84	40	FIRST READING
	05/02/84	50	SECOND READING
	05/15/84	36	THIRD READING
HB-2722	04/04/84	40	FIRST READING
HB-2723	04/04/84	40	FIRST READING
HB-2724	04/04/84	40	FIRST READING
HB-2725	04/04/84	40	FIRST READING
HB-2726	04/04/84	40	FIRST READING
	05/17/84	33	SECOND READING
	05/24/84	102	THIRD READING
HB-2727	04/04/84	40	FIRST READING
HB-2728	04/04/84	40	FIRST READING
HB-2729	04/04/84	40	FIRST READING
	05/15/84	124	SECOND READING
	05/31/84	16	RECALLED
	05/31/84	17	THIRD READING
	06/29/84	107	CONCURRENCE
HB-2730	04/04/84	40	FIRST READING
HB-2731	04/04/84	40	FIRST READING
	05/08/84	7	SECOND READING
	05/10/84	109	THIRD READING

BILL NUMBER	DATE	PAGE	ACTION
HB-2732	04/04/84	40	FIRST READING
	05/08/84	27	SECOND READING
	05/08/84	31	OUT OF RECORD
	05/08/84	32	SECOND READING
	05/10/84	162	RECALLED
	05/10/84	163	THIRD READING
	06/27/84	7	CONCURRENCE
HB-2733	04/04/84	41	FIRST READING
HB-2734	04/04/84	41	FIRST READING
	05/08/84	5	SECOND READING
	05/31/84	36	THIRD READING
HB-2735	04/04/84	41	FIRST READING
	05/09/84	30	SECOND READING
	05/17/84	236	RECALLED
	05/17/84	237	THIRD READING
HB-2736	04/04/84	41	FIRST READING
	05/10/84	53	SECOND READING
	05/16/84	209	THIRD READING
HB-2737	04/04/84	41	FIRST READING
HB-2738	04/04/84	41	FIRST READING
HB-2739	04/04/84	41	FIRST READING
	05/15/84	125	SECOND READING
	05/30/84	52	RECALLED
	05/31/84	72	THIRD READING
HB-2740	04/04/84	41	FIRST READING
	05/16/84	23	SECOND READING
	05/24/84	153	THIRD READING
	06/27/84	24	CONCURRENCE
	06/30/84	106	CONFERENCE
	07/01/84	86	CONFERENCE
HB-2741	04/04/84	41	FIRST READING
HB-2742	04/04/84	41	FIRST READING
	04/11/84	34	TABLED
HB-2743	04/04/84	41	FIRST READING
HB-2744	04/04/84	41	FIRST READING
HB-2745	04/04/84	41	FIRST READING
HB-2746	04/04/84	42	FIRST READING

MASTER TRANSCRIPT INDEX

BILL NUMBER	DATE	PAGE	ACTION
HB-2747	04/04/84	42	FIRST READING
	05/23/84	5	SECOND READING
	05/24/84	93	RECALLED
	05/24/84	95	HELD ON SECOND
	05/25/84	101	SECOND READING
	05/25/84	102	THIRD READING
HB-2748	04/04/84	42	FIRST READING
HB-2749	04/04/84	42	FIRST READING
HB-2750	04/04/84	42	FIRST READING
	05/01/84	43	SECOND READING
	05/10/84	165	THIRD READING
HB-2751	04/04/84	42	FIRST READING
	05/02/84	50	SECOND READING
	05/09/84	58	THIRD READING
	06/21/84	95	CONCURRENCE
HB-2752	04/04/84	42	FIRST READING
	05/02/84	4	SECOND READING
	05/04/84	7	THIRD READING
HB-2753	04/04/84	42	FIRST READING
	05/10/84	55	SECOND READING
	05/24/84	153	THIRD READING
HB-2754	04/04/84	42	FIRST READING
HB-2755	04/04/84	42	FIRST READING
HB-2756	04/04/84	42	FIRST READING
HB-2757	04/04/84	42	FIRST READING
HB-2758	04/04/84	42	FIRST READING
HB-2759	04/04/84	42	FIRST READING
HB-2760	04/04/84	43	FIRST READING
HB-2761	04/04/84	43	FIRST READING
	05/16/84	7	SECOND READING
	05/17/84	239	THIRD READING
HB-2762	04/04/84	43	FIRST READING
	05/23/84	304	SECOND READING
	05/24/84	292	RECALLED
	05/25/84	27	THIRD READING
	12/12/84	37	MOTION

MASTER TRANSCRIPT INDEX

BILL NUMBER	DATE	PAGE	ACTION
HB-2762 (cont'd)	12/12/84	106	CONCURRENCE
HB-2763	04/04/84	43	FIRST READING
	05/22/84	22	SECOND READING
HB-2764	04/04/84	43	FIRST READING
HB-2765	04/04/84	43	FIRST READING
	05/02/84	50	SECOND READING
	05/15/84	128	RECALLED
	05/29/84	9	RECALLED
	05/30/84	70	THIRD READING
	06/29/84	108	CONCURRENCE
HB-2766	04/04/84	43	FIRST READING
	05/02/84	51	SECOND READING
	05/10/84	165	THIRD READING
HB-2767	04/04/84	43	FIRST READING
HB-2768	04/04/84	43	FIRST READING
HB-2769	04/04/84	43	FIRST READING
	05/15/84	125	SECOND READING
	05/31/84	71	THIRD READING
	06/29/84	109	CONCURRENCE
HB-2770	04/04/84	43	FIRST READING
HB-2771	04/04/84	43	FIRST READING
HB-2772	04/04/84	43	FIRST READING
HB-2773	04/04/84	44	FIRST READING
	05/09/84	31	SECOND READING
	05/10/84	110	RECALLED
	05/10/84	111	THIRD READING
HB-2774	04/04/84	44	FIRST READING
HB-2775	04/04/84	44	FIRST READING
	05/16/84	24	SECOND READING
	05/23/84	46	THIRD READING
	06/29/84	4	CONCURRENCE
HB-2776	04/04/84	44	FIRST READING
	05/15/84	125	SECOND READING
	05/31/84	72	THIRD READING
	06/29/84	110	CONCURRENCE
HB-2777	04/04/84	44	FIRST READING

PROGRAM-LRTRNMST
08/20/85
LEGISLATIVE INFORMATION SYSTEM
HOUSE OF REPRESENTATIVES
PAGE 201

MASTER TRANSCRIPT INDEX

BILL NUMBER	DATE	PAGE	ACTION
HB-2778	04/04/84	44	FIRST READING
HB-2779	04/04/84	44	FIRST READING
HB-2780	04/04/84	44	FIRST READING
	05/10/84	56	SECOND READING
HB-2781	04/05/84	10	FIRST READING
	05/10/84	59	SECOND READING
	05/24/84	120	THIRD READING
HB-2782	04/05/84	10	FIRST READING
HB-2783	04/05/84	10	FIRST READING
	05/16/84	9	SECOND READING
	05/17/84	240	THIRD READING
	06/28/84	10	CONCURRENCE
HB-2784	04/05/84	10	FIRST READING
	05/09/84	2	SECOND READING
	05/16/84	5	THIRD READING
HB-2785	04/05/84	10	FIRST READING
	05/08/84	5	SECOND READING
	05/08/84	6	OUT OF RECORD
	05/08/84	54	SECOND READING
	05/30/84	9	RECALLED
	05/30/84	12	THIRD READING
	06/29/84	93	CONCURRENCE
	07/01/84	55	CONFERENCE
HB-2786	04/05/84	10	FIRST READING
	05/08/84	6	SECOND READING
	05/30/84	18	THIRD READING
HB-2787	04/05/84	10	FIRST READING
	05/03/84	12	SECOND READING
	05/10/84	176	RECALLED
	05/10/84	177	THIRD READING
	06/27/84	9	CONCURRENCE
HB-2788	04/05/84	11	FIRST READING
	05/15/84	126	SECOND READING
	05/30/84	38	THIRD READING
HB-2789	04/05/84	11	FIRST READING
	05/15/84	126	SECOND READING
	05/30/84	40	THIRD READING
HB-2790	04/05/84	11	FIRST READING

PROGRAM-LRTRNMST
08/20/85
LEGISLATIVE INFORMATION SYSTEM
HOUSE OF REPRESENTATIVES
PAGE 202

MASTER TRANSCRIPT INDEX

BILL NUMBER	DATE	PAGE	ACTION
HB-2791	04/05/84	11	FIRST READING
HB-2792	04/05/84	11	FIRST READING
	05/01/84	44	SECOND READING
	05/15/84	166	THIRD READING
HB-2793	04/05/84	11	FIRST READING
HB-2794	04/05/84	11	FIRST READING
HB-2795	04/05/84	11	FIRST READING
HB-2796	04/05/84	11	FIRST READING
HB-2797	04/05/84	11	FIRST READING
	05/02/84	7	SECOND READING
	05/08/84	43	THIRD READING
HB-2798	04/05/84	11	FIRST READING
	05/01/84	36	THIRD READING
	05/03/84	37	THIRD READING
HB-2799	04/05/84	11	FIRST READING
	05/02/84	51	SECOND READING
	05/15/84	172	THIRD READING
HB-2800	04/05/84	11	FIRST READING
	05/02/84	51	SECOND READING
	05/16/84	211	THIRD READING
HB-2801	04/05/84	12	FIRST READING
HB-2802	04/05/84	12	FIRST READING
HB-2803	04/05/84	12	FIRST READING
	05/01/84	36	SECOND READING
	05/03/84	39	THIRD READING
HB-2804	04/05/84	12	FIRST READING
	05/10/84	59	SECOND READING
	05/15/84	181	THIRD READING
	06/27/84	11	CONCURRENCE
HB-2805	04/05/84	12	FIRST READING
	05/02/84	52	SECOND READING
	05/15/84	187	RECALLED
	05/15/84	189	THIRD READING
	06/27/84	12	CONCURRENCE
HB-2806	04/05/84	12	FIRST READING

BILL NUMBER	DATE	PAGE	ACTION
HB-2807	04/05/84	12	FIRST READING
	05/03/84	7	SECOND READING
	05/08/84	44	THIRD READING
HB-2808	04/05/84	12	FIRST READING
HB-2809	04/05/84	12	FIRST READING
	05/10/84	60	SECOND READING
	05/16/84	228	THIRD READING
HB-2810	04/05/84	12	FIRST READING
	05/10/84	5	SECOND READING
	05/15/84	151	THIRD READING
	06/26/84	97	CONCURRENCE
HB-2811	04/05/84	12	FIRST READING
	05/10/84	7	SECOND READING
	05/15/84	153	THIRD READING
HB-2812	04/05/84	12	FIRST READING
	05/17/84	34	SECOND READING
	05/23/84	251	RECALLED
	05/23/84	258	THIRD READING
HB-2813	04/05/84	12	FIRST READING
	05/09/84	2	SECOND READING
	05/16/84	5	THIRD READING
HB-2814	04/05/84	13	FIRST READING
HB-2815	04/05/84	13	FIRST READING
	05/02/84	8	SECOND READING
	05/08/84	45	THIRD READING
HB-2816	04/05/84	13	FIRST READING
	05/01/84	37	SECOND READING
	05/03/84	40	THIRD READING
HB-2817	04/05/84	13	FIRST READING
HB-2818	04/05/84	13	FIRST READING
	05/08/84	34	SECOND READING
	05/17/84	44	THIRD READING
HB-2819	04/05/84	13	FIRST READING
HB-2820	04/05/84	13	FIRST READING
HB-2821	04/05/84	13	FIRST READING
	05/15/84	126	SECOND READING
	05/31/84	73	THIRD READING

BILL NUMBER	DATE	PAGE	ACTION
HB-2822	04/05/84	13	FIRST READING
HB-2823	04/05/84	13	FIRST READING
HB-2824	04/05/84	13	FIRST READING
HB-2825	04/05/84	13	FIRST READING
HB-2826	04/05/84	13	FIRST READING
HB-2827	04/05/84	14	FIRST READING
	05/10/84	60	SECOND READING
	05/17/84	45	THIRD READING
	06/27/84	15	CONCURRENCE
	06/27/84	19	OUT OF RECORD
	06/27/84	25	CONCURRENCE
HB-2828	04/05/84	14	FIRST READING
HB-2829	04/05/84	14	FIRST READING
	05/04/84	26	MOTION
HB-2830	04/05/84	14	FIRST READING
	05/08/84	8	SECOND READING
	05/09/84	65	THIRD READING
HB-2831	04/05/84	14	FIRST READING
HB-2832	04/05/84	14	FIRST READING
	05/02/84	52	SECOND READING
	05/17/84	52	RECALLED
	05/17/84	61	HELD ON SECOND
	05/18/84	136	SECOND READING
	05/23/84	259	THIRD READING
HB-2833	04/05/84	14	FIRST READING
	05/02/84	52	SECOND READING
	05/16/84	52	RECALLED
	05/17/84	61	THIRD READING
	05/17/84	64	OUT OF RECORD
	05/17/84	73	THIRD READING
HB-2834	04/05/84	14	FIRST READING
HB-2835	04/05/84	14	FIRST READING
	05/10/84	60	SECOND READING
	05/24/84	95	RECALLED
	05/24/84	98	HELD ON SECOND
	05/24/84	273	SECOND READING
	05/24/84	274	THIRD READING

BILL NUMBER	DATE	PAGE	ACTION
HB-2836	04/05/84	14	FIRST READING
	05/08/84	37	SECOND READING
	05/08/84	37	HELD ON SECOND
	05/10/84	60	SECOND READING
	05/23/84	76	THIRD READING
HB-2837	04/05/84	15	FIRST READING
	05/09/84	2	SECOND READING
	05/15/84	6	SECOND READING
	05/23/84	290	RECALLED
	05/24/84	3	THIRD READING
	06/26/84	100	CONCURRENCE
	07/01/84	114	CONFERENCE
HB-2838	04/05/84	15	FIRST READING
	05/10/84	61	SECOND READING
	05/17/84	64	RECALLED
	05/17/84	68	THIRD READING
HB-2839	04/05/84	15	FIRST READING
HB-2840	04/05/84	15	FIRST READING
HB-2841	04/05/84	15	FIRST READING
HB-2842	04/05/84	15	FIRST READING
HB-2843	04/05/84	15	FIRST READING
HB-2844	04/05/84	15	FIRST READING
HB-2845	04/05/84	15	FIRST READING
HB-2846	04/05/84	15	FIRST READING
HB-2847	04/05/84	15	FIRST READING
HB-2848	04/05/84	15	FIRST READING
HB-2849	04/05/84	16	FIRST READING
HB-2850	04/05/84	16	FIRST READING
HB-2851	04/05/84	16	FIRST READING
HB-2852	04/05/84	16	FIRST READING
HB-2853	04/10/84	2	FIRST READING
	05/02/84	53	SECOND READING
	05/02/84	53	HELD ON SECOND
	05/24/84	209	THIRD READING

BILL NUMBER	DATE	PAGE	ACTION
HB-2853 (cont'd)	06/27/84	19	CONCURRENCE
HB-2854	04/10/84	2	FIRST READING
HB-2855	04/10/84	2	FIRST READING
HB-2856	04/10/84	2	FIRST READING
	05/10/84	81	SECOND READING
	05/15/84	154	THIRD READING
	06/27/84	26	CONCURRENCE
HB-2857	04/10/84	2	FIRST READING
	05/08/84	34	SECOND READING
	05/17/84	72	THIRD READING
	06/27/84	28	CONCURRENCE
	06/27/84	35	OUT OF RECORD
	06/27/84	74	CONCURRENCE
	06/30/84	11	CONFERENCE
HB-2858	04/10/84	2	FIRST READING
HB-2859	04/10/84	2	FIRST READING
	05/08/84	35	SECOND READING
	05/17/84	73	RECALLED
	05/17/84	74	THIRD READING
HB-2860	04/10/84	2	FIRST READING
HB-2861	04/10/84	2	FIRST READING
HB-2862	04/10/84	3	FIRST READING
	05/10/84	62	SECOND READING
	05/17/84	80	THIRD READING
	05/17/84	83	OUT OF RECORD
	05/24/84	210	THIRD READING
HB-2863	04/10/84	3	FIRST READING
HB-2864	04/10/84	19	FIRST READING
	05/09/84	31	SECOND READING
	05/10/84	113	THIRD READING
HB-2865	04/10/84	19	FIRST READING
	05/10/84	62	SECOND READING
	05/17/84	83	THIRD READING
	11/27/84	24	VETO MESSAGE
HB-2866	04/10/84	19	FIRST READING
HB-2867	04/10/84	19	FIRST READING

BILL NUMBER	DATE	PAGE	ACTION
HB-2868	04/10/84	19	FIRST READING
HB-2869	04/10/84	19	FIRST READING
	05/15/84	88	SECOND READING
	05/17/84	88	THIRD READING
HB-2870	04/10/84	20	FIRST READING
HB-2871	04/10/84	20	FIRST READING
	05/16/84	255	SECOND READING
	05/17/84	92	THIRD READING
	06/27/84	35	CONCURRENCE
HB-2872	04/10/84	20	FIRST READING
HB-2873	04/10/84	20	FIRST READING
	05/10/84	62	SECOND READING
	05/10/84	63	OUT OF RECORD
	05/10/84	93	SECOND READING
	05/17/84	98	THIRD READING
HB-2874	04/10/84	20	FIRST READING
HB-2875	04/10/84	20	FIRST READING
	05/15/84	130	SECOND READING
	05/17/84	107	THIRD READING
	05/23/84	276	RECALLED
	05/24/84	22	THIRD READING
HB-2876	04/10/84	20	FIRST READING
	05/10/84	63	SECOND READING
	05/17/84	117	THIRD READING
	06/27/84	36	CONCURRENCE
	06/30/84	21	CONFERENCE
HB-2877	04/10/84	20	FIRST READING
	05/16/84	258	SECOND READING
	05/22/84	82	THIRD READING
HB-2878	04/10/84	20	FIRST READING
	05/10/84	63	SECOND READING
	05/10/84	64	HELD ON SECOND
	05/15/84	138	SECOND READING
	05/23/84	307	RECALLED
	05/24/84	154	THIRD READING
HB-2879	04/10/84	20	FIRST READING
HB-2880	04/10/84	20	FIRST READING
HB-2881	04/10/84	20	FIRST READING

BILL NUMBER	DATE	PAGE	ACTION
HB-2882	04/10/84	20	FIRST READING
HB-2883	04/10/84	20	FIRST READING
	05/09/84	32	SECOND READING
	05/10/84	114	THIRD READING
HB-2884	04/10/84	21	FIRST READING
	05/10/84	64	SECOND READING
	05/24/84	121	THIRD READING
HB-2885	04/10/84	21	FIRST READING
	05/10/84	64	SECOND READING
	05/17/84	121	THIRD READING
HB-2886	04/10/84	21	FIRST READING
HB-2887	04/10/84	21	FIRST READING
	05/02/84	8	SECOND READING
	05/03/84	41	THIRD READING
	06/27/84	37	CONCURRENCE
HB-2888	04/10/84	21	FIRST READING
	05/10/84	64	SECOND READING
	05/24/84	32	THIRD READING
HB-2889	04/10/84	21	FIRST READING
HB-2890	04/11/84	44	FIRST READING
HB-2891	04/11/84	44	FIRST READING
	05/10/84	65	SECOND READING
	05/24/84	101	RECALLED
	05/24/84	102	HELD ON SECOND
	05/25/84	103	SECOND READING
	05/25/84	103	THIRD READING
HB-2892	04/11/84	44	FIRST READING
	05/09/84	32	SECOND READING
	05/09/84	33	HELD ON SECOND
	05/16/84	235	SECOND READING
	05/17/84	241	THIRD READING
	05/17/84	244	OUT OF RECORD
	05/24/84	7	THIRD READING
	06/26/84	100	CONCURRENCE
	06/30/84	54	CONFERENCE
	06/30/84	60	OUT OF RECORD
	06/30/84	114	CONFERENCE
HB-2893	04/11/84	44	FIRST READING
HB-2894	04/11/84	44	FIRST READING

PROGRAM-LRTRNMST
08/20/85

LEGISLATIVE INFORMATION SYSTEM
HOUSE OF REPRESENTATIVES

PAGE 209

MASTER TRANSCRIPT INDEX

BILL NUMBER	DATE	PAGE	ACTION
HB-2894 (cont'd)	05/09/84	33	SECOND READING
	05/10/84	119	THIRD READING
HB-2895	04/11/84	45	FIRST READING
HB-2896	04/11/84	45	FIRST READING
	05/09/84	2	SECOND READING
	05/16/84	5	THIRD READING
	06/27/84	37	CONCURRENCE
HB-2897	04/11/84	45	FIRST READING
HB-2898	04/11/84	45	FIRST READING
	05/09/84	34	SECOND READING
	05/10/84	124	THIRD READING
HB-2899	04/11/84	45	FIRST READING
	05/10/84	94	SECOND READING
	05/17/84	122	THIRD READING
	05/17/84	123	OUT OF RECORD
	05/24/84	32	OTHER
HB-2900	04/11/84	45	FIRST READING
	05/09/84	34	SECOND READING
	05/15/84	155	THIRD READING
	05/15/84	156	OUT OF RECORD
	05/25/84	151	THIRD READING
	05/25/84	156	OTHER
HB-2901	04/11/84	45	FIRST READING
HB-2902	04/11/84	45	FIRST READING
HB-2903	04/11/84	45	FIRST READING
HB-2904	04/11/84	45	FIRST READING
HB-2905	04/11/84	45	FIRST READING
	05/10/84	94	SECOND READING
	05/15/84	156	THIRD READING
HB-2906	04/11/84	46	FIRST READING
	05/24/84	98	SECOND READING
	05/24/84	101	HELD ON SECOND
	05/25/84	104	SECOND READING
	05/25/84	105	THIRD READING
HB-2907	04/11/84	46	FIRST READING
HB-2908	04/11/84	46	FIRST READING
	05/10/84	65	SECOND READING

PROGRAM-LRTRNMST
08/20/85

LEGISLATIVE INFORMATION SYSTEM
HOUSE OF REPRESENTATIVES

PAGE 210

MASTER TRANSCRIPT INDEX

BILL NUMBER	DATE	PAGE	ACTION
HB-2908 (cont'd)	05/17/84	124	THIRD READING
HB-2909	04/11/84	46	FIRST READING
	05/10/84	66	SECOND READING
	05/17/84	125	THIRD READING
HB-2910	04/11/84	46	FIRST READING
	05/10/84	66	SECOND READING
	05/17/84	126	RECALLED
	05/17/84	132	MOTION
	05/17/84	134	THIRD READING
HB-2911	04/11/84	46	FIRST READING
	05/09/84	2	SECOND READING
	05/16/84	10	SECOND READING
HB-2912	04/11/84	46	FIRST READING
HB-2913	04/11/84	46	FIRST READING
	05/09/84	2	SECOND READING
	05/16/84	5	THIRD READING
	07/01/84	124	CONCURRENCE
HB-2914	04/11/84	46	FIRST READING
HB-2915	04/11/84	46	FIRST READING
HB-2916	04/11/84	46	FIRST READING
	05/10/84	66	SECOND READING
	05/17/84	141	THIRD READING
HB-2917	04/11/84	46	FIRST READING
	05/09/84	2	SECOND READING
	05/16/84	5	THIRD READING
	06/26/84	101	CONCURRENCE
	06/30/84	60	CONFERENCE
HB-2918	04/11/84	46	FIRST READING
HB-2919	04/11/84	46	FIRST READING
	05/09/84	34	SECOND READING
	05/10/84	125	THIRD READING
HB-2920	04/11/84	47	FIRST READING
HB-2921	04/11/84	47	FIRST READING
	05/10/84	67	SECOND READING
	05/17/84	146	THIRD READING
HB-2922	04/11/84	47	FIRST READING

BILL NUMBER	DATE	PAGE	ACTION
HB-2923	04/11/84	47	FIRST READING
	05/10/84	67	SECOND READING
	05/17/84	147	THIRD READING
HB-2924	04/11/84	47	FIRST READING
	05/09/84	34	SECOND READING
	05/09/84	36	HELD ON SECOND
	05/15/84	7	SECOND READING
	05/16/84	274	RECALLED
	05/17/84	244	THIRD READING
HB-2925	04/11/84	47	FIRST READING
HB-2926	04/11/84	47	FIRST READING
	05/15/84	131	SECOND READING
	05/17/84	152	THIRD READING
	06/27/84	74	CONCURRENCE
HB-2927	04/11/84	47	FIRST READING
	05/09/84	25	SECOND READING
	05/17/84	247	THIRD READING
HB-2928	04/11/84	47	FIRST READING
HB-2929	04/11/84	47	FIRST READING
	05/04/84	28	MOTION
HB-2930	04/11/84	47	FIRST READING
HB-2931	04/11/84	47	FIRST READING
	05/10/84	68	SECOND READING
HB-2932	04/11/84	47	FIRST READING
HB-2933	04/11/84	47	FIRST READING
	05/10/84	68	SECOND READING
HB-2934	04/11/84	48	FIRST READING
	05/15/84	132	SECOND READING
	05/17/84	153	THIRD READING
HB-2935	04/11/84	48	FIRST READING
HB-2936	04/11/84	48	FIRST READING
	05/09/84	3	SECOND READING
	05/16/84	5	THIRD READING
HB-2937	04/11/84	48	FIRST READING
	05/10/84	178	MOTION
	05/16/84	26	SECOND READING
	05/17/84	155	THIRD READING

BILL NUMBER	DATE	PAGE	ACTION
HB-2938	04/11/84	48	FIRST READING
HB-2939	04/11/84	48	FIRST READING
	05/10/84	68	SECOND READING
	05/23/84	146	THIRD READING
HB-2940	04/11/84	48	FIRST READING
HB-2941	04/11/84	48	FIRST READING
HB-2942	04/11/84	48	FIRST READING
HB-2943	04/11/84	48	FIRST READING
HB-2944	04/11/84	48	FIRST READING
HB-2945	04/11/84	49	FIRST READING
HB-2946	04/11/84	49	FIRST READING
	05/09/84	36	SECOND READING
	05/15/84	158	RECALLED
	05/15/84	159	THIRD READING
HB-2947	04/11/84	49	FIRST READING
HB-2948	04/11/84	49	FIRST READING
HB-2949	04/11/84	49	FIRST READING
HB-2950	04/11/84	49	FIRST READING
	05/10/84	69	SECOND READING
	05/17/84	156	THIRD READING
	06/27/84	76	CONCURRENCE
HB-2951	04/11/84	49	FIRST READING
HB-2952	04/11/84	49	FIRST READING
	05/09/84	36	SECOND READING
	05/10/84	126	THIRD READING
	06/27/84	77	CONCURRENCE
HB-2953	04/11/84	49	FIRST READING
	05/08/84	8	SECOND READING
	05/09/84	66	THIRD READING
	06/26/84	102	CONCURRENCE
	06/30/84	210	OTHER
	07/01/84	29	CONFERENCE
HB-2954	04/11/84	50	FIRST READING
HB-2955	04/11/84	50	FIRST READING

PROGRAM-LRTRNMST
08/20/85
LEGISLATIVE INFORMATION SYSTEM
HOUSE OF REPRESENTATIVES
PAGE 213

MASTER TRANSCRIPT INDEX

BILL NUMBER	DATE	PAGE	ACTION
HB-2956	04/11/84	50	FIRST READING
HB-2957	04/11/84	50	FIRST READING
HB-2958	04/12/84	1	FIRST READING
HB-2959	04/12/84	1	FIRST READING
HB-2960	04/12/84	1	FIRST READING
	05/10/84	69	SECOND READING
	05/23/84	82	THIRD READING
HB-2961	04/12/84	1	FIRST READING
	05/10/84	72	SECOND READING
	05/25/84	156	THIRD READING
	06/27/84	85	CONCURRENCE
	11/28/84	66	VETO MESSAGE
HB-2962	04/12/84	1	FIRST READING
	05/16/84	238	SECOND READING
	05/17/84	245	THIRD READING
HB-2963	04/12/84	1	FIRST READING
HB-2964	04/12/84	1	FIRST READING
HB-2965	04/12/84	1	FIRST READING
HB-2966	04/12/84	2	FIRST READING
HB-2967	04/12/84	2	FIRST READING
HB-2968	04/12/84	2	FIRST READING
HB-2969	04/12/84	2	FIRST READING
HB-2970	04/12/84	2	FIRST READING
HB-2971	04/12/84	2	FIRST READING
	05/10/84	72	SECOND READING
	05/17/84	157	THIRD READING
HB-2972	04/12/84	2	FIRST READING
	05/10/84	72	SECOND READING
	05/17/84	158	THIRD READING
HB-2973	04/12/84	2	FIRST READING
HB-2974	04/12/84	2	FIRST READING
HB-2975	04/12/84	2	FIRST READING

PROGRAM-LRTRNMST
08/20/85
LEGISLATIVE INFORMATION SYSTEM
HOUSE OF REPRESENTATIVES
PAGE 214

MASTER TRANSCRIPT INDEX

BILL NUMBER	DATE	PAGE	ACTION
HB-2976	04/12/84	2	FIRST READING
HB-2977	04/12/84	2	FIRST READING
HB-2978	04/12/84	2	FIRST READING
HB-2979	04/12/84	3	FIRST READING
HB-2980	04/12/84	3	FIRST READING
HB-2981	04/12/84	3	FIRST READING
HB-2982	04/12/84	3	FIRST READING
HB-2983	04/12/84	3	FIRST READING
HB-2984	04/12/84	3	FIRST READING
HB-2985	04/12/84	3	FIRST READING
HB-2986	04/12/84	3	FIRST READING
	05/10/84	72	SECOND READING
HB-2987	04/12/84	3	FIRST READING
	05/18/84	137	SECOND READING
	05/22/84	124	RECALLED
	05/22/84	126	THIRD READING
	06/26/84	106	CONCURRENCE
	06/30/84	231	CONFERENCE
	07/01/84	115	CONFERENCE
HB-2988	04/13/84	1	FIRST READING
HB-2989	04/13/84	1	FIRST READING
HB-2990	04/13/84	1	FIRST READING
HB-2991	04/13/84	1	FIRST READING
HB-2992	04/13/84	1	FIRST READING
	05/10/84	73	SECOND READING
	05/17/84	160	THIRD READING
	06/27/84	87	CONCURRENCE
	11/28/84	67	VETO MESSAGE
HB-2993	04/13/84	1	FIRST READING
HB-2994	04/13/84	2	FIRST READING
	05/10/84	73	SECOND READING
	05/17/84	162	THIRD READING

PROGRAM-LRTRNMST
08/20/85

LEGISLATIVE INFORMATION SYSTEM
HOUSE OF REPRESENTATIVES

PAGE 215

MASTER TRANSCRIPT INDEX

BILL NUMBER	DATE	PAGE	ACTION
HB-2995	04/13/84	2	FIRST READING
HB-2996	04/13/84	2	FIRST READING
HB-2997	04/13/84	2	FIRST READING
HB-2998	04/13/84	2	FIRST READING
HB-2999	04/13/84	2	FIRST READING
HB-3000	04/13/84	2	FIRST READING
HB-3001	04/13/84	2	FIRST READING
	05/15/84	132	SECOND READING
	05/23/84	149	THIRD READING
HB-3002	04/13/84	2	FIRST READING
HB-3003	04/13/84	2	FIRST READING
HB-3004	04/13/84	2	FIRST READING
HB-3005	04/13/84	2	FIRST READING
HB-3006	04/13/84	2	FIRST READING
HB-3007	04/13/84	3	FIRST READING
HB-3008	04/13/84	3	FIRST READING
HB-3009	04/13/84	3	FIRST READING
HB-3010	04/13/84	3	FIRST READING
HB-3011	04/13/84	3	FIRST READING
HB-3012	04/13/84	3	FIRST READING
HB-3013	04/13/84	3	FIRST READING
HB-3014	04/13/84	3	FIRST READING
HB-3015	04/13/84	3	FIRST READING
HB-3016	04/13/84	3	FIRST READING
HB-3017	04/13/84	3	FIRST READING
HB-3018	04/13/84	3	FIRST READING
HB-3019	04/13/84	3	FIRST READING

PROGRAM-LRTRNMST
08/20/85

LEGISLATIVE INFORMATION SYSTEM
HOUSE OF REPRESENTATIVES

PAGE 216

MASTER TRANSCRIPT INDEX

BILL NUMBER	DATE	PAGE	ACTION
HB-3020	04/13/84	3	FIRST READING
HB-3021	04/13/84	3	FIRST READING
HB-3022	04/13/84	4	FIRST READING
HB-3023	04/13/84	4	FIRST READING
HB-3024	04/13/84	4	FIRST READING
	05/10/84	73	SECOND READING
	05/24/84	113	THIRD READING
HB-3025	04/13/84	4	FIRST READING
	05/15/84	127	SECOND READING
	05/31/84	75	THIRD READING
HB-3026	04/13/84	4	FIRST READING
	05/10/84	5	SECOND READING
	05/18/84	2	THIRD READING
HB-3027	04/13/84	4	FIRST READING
	05/10/84	74	SECOND READING
	05/10/84	75	OUT OF RECORD
	05/15/84	133	SECOND READING
	05/17/84	165	THIRD READING
HB-3028	04/13/84	4	FIRST READING
HB-3029	04/13/84	4	FIRST READING
	05/09/84	37	SECOND READING
	05/25/84	147	THIRD READING
HB-3030	04/13/84	4	FIRST READING
HB-3031	04/13/84	4	FIRST READING
	05/08/84	35	SECOND READING
	05/16/84	55	RECALLED
	05/17/84	166	THIRD READING
	06/27/84	96	CONCURRENCE
HB-3032	04/13/84	4	FIRST READING
	05/10/84	75	SECOND READING
	05/17/84	170	THIRD READING
HB-3033	04/13/84	4	FIRST READING
	05/08/84	35	SECOND READING
	05/08/84	38	RECALLED
	05/08/84	53	SECOND READING
	05/24/84	216	RECALLED
	05/24/84	220	THIRD READING
	05/24/84	225	OUT OF RECORD

PROGRAM-LRTRNMST
08/20/85

LEGISLATIVE INFORMATION SYSTEM
HOUSE OF REPRESENTATIVES

PAGE 217

MASTER TRANSCRIPT INDEX

BILL NUMBER	DATE	PAGE	ACTION
HB-3033(cont'd)	05/24/84	242	OTHER
HB-3034	04/13/84	4	FIRST READING
	05/10/84	75	SECOND READING
	05/17/84	173	THIRD READING
HB-3035	04/13/84	4	FIRST READING
	05/08/84	36	SECOND READING
	05/17/84	173	THIRD READING
HB-3036	04/13/84	5	FIRST READING
	05/10/84	75	SECOND READING
	05/17/84	175	THIRD READING
	05/17/84	176	OUT OF RECORD
	05/23/84	188	RECALLED
	05/23/84	189	HELD ON SECOND
	05/24/84	243	SECOND READING
	05/25/84	36	THIRD READING
	06/27/84	108	CONCURRENCE
	06/27/84	113	OUT OF RECORD
	06/28/84	45	CONCURRENCE
	06/30/84	119	CONFERENCE
HB-3037	04/13/84	5	FIRST READING
	05/10/84	75	SECOND READING
	05/23/84	182	RECALLED
	05/24/84	245	RECALLED
	05/25/84	40	THIRD READING
HB-3038	04/13/84	5	FIRST READING
	05/23/84	7	SECOND READING
	05/24/84	245	RECALLED
	05/25/84	41	THIRD READING
HB-3039	04/13/84	5	FIRST READING
	05/10/84	76	SECOND READING
	05/23/84	187	RECALLED
	05/25/84	42	THIRD READING
HB-3040	04/13/84	5	FIRST READING
	05/10/84	76	SECOND READING
	05/23/84	185	RECALLED
	05/23/84	186	HELD ON SECOND
	05/23/84	286	RECALLED
	05/25/84	48	THIRD READING
HB-3041	04/13/84	5	FIRST READING
	05/10/84	76	SECOND READING
	05/10/84	77	HELD ON SECOND
	05/18/84	151	SECOND READING
	05/23/84	174	RECALLED

PROGRAM-LRTRNMST
08/20/85

LEGISLATIVE INFORMATION SYSTEM
HOUSE OF REPRESENTATIVES

PAGE 218

MASTER TRANSCRIPT INDEX

BILL NUMBER	DATE	PAGE	ACTION
HB-3041(cont'd)	05/25/84	49	THIRD READING
	06/28/84	12	CONCURRENCE
HB-3042	04/13/84	5	FIRST READING
	05/10/84	77	SECOND READING
	05/23/84	186	HELD ON SECOND
	05/23/84	186	RECALLED
	05/23/84	287	SECOND READING
	05/25/84	52	THIRD READING
	06/28/84	14	CONCURRENCE
HB-3043 .	04/13/84	5	FIRST READING
	05/10/84	77	SECOND READING
	05/23/84	186	RECALLED
	05/23/84	187	HELD ON SECOND
	05/23/84	287	SECOND READING
	05/25/84	52	THIRD READING
HB-3044	04/13/84	5	FIRST READING
	05/16/84	261	SECOND READING
	05/24/84	246	RECALLED
	05/25/84	54	THIRD READING
	05/25/84	54	OTHER
HB-3045	04/13/84	5	FIRST READING
	05/15/84	134	SECOND READING
	05/23/84	288	RECALLED
	05/25/84	54	THIRD READING
HB-3046	04/13/84	5	FIRST READING
	05/08/84	37	SECOND READING
HB-3047	04/13/84	6	FIRST READING
HB-3048	04/13/84	6	FIRST READING
HB-3049	04/13/84	6	FIRST READING
HB-3050	04/13/84	6	FIRST READING
	05/08/84	37	SECOND READING
	05/17/84	177	THIRD READING
HB-3051	04/13/84	6	FIRST READING
HB-3052	04/13/84	6	FIRST READING
	05/15/84	134	OUT OF RECORD
	05/16/84	26	SECOND READING
	05/17/84	180	THIRD READING
HB-3053	04/13/84	6	FIRST READING

BILL NUMBER	DATE	PAGE	ACTION
HB-3054	04/13/84	6	FIRST READING
HB-3055	04/13/84	6	FIRST READING
	05/10/84	78	SECOND READING
	05/17/84	183	THIRD READING
HB-3056	04/13/84	6	FIRST READING
	05/10/84	80	SECOND READING
	05/17/84	186	RECALLED
	05/17/84	186	THIRD READING
HB-3057	04/13/84	7	FIRST READING
	05/15/84	135	SECOND READING
	05/23/84	91	THIRD READING
	06/28/84	15	CONCURRENCE
HB-3058	04/13/84	7	FIRST READING
HB-3059	04/13/84	7	FIRST READING
	05/08/84	8	SECOND READING
	05/09/84	67	THIRD READING
	06/28/84	16	CONCURRENCE
HB-3060	04/13/84	7	FIRST READING
	05/22/84	23	SECOND READING
	05/25/84	77	THIRD READING
	06/28/84	17	CONCURRENCE
	06/30/84	120	CONFERENCE
HB-3061	04/13/84	7	FIRST READING
	05/09/84	3	SECOND READING
	05/16/84	5	THIRD READING
HB-3062	04/13/84	7	FIRST READING
	05/23/84	30	SECOND READING
	05/25/84	135	THIRD READING
HB-3063	04/13/84	7	FIRST READING
	05/15/84	138	SECOND READING
	05/17/84	192	THIRD READING
HB-3064	04/13/84	7	FIRST READING
HB-3065	04/13/84	7	FIRST READING
	05/09/84	37	SECOND READING
	05/10/84	130	THIRD READING
HB-3066	04/13/84	7	FIRST READING
	05/09/84	38	SECOND READING
	05/10/84	132	THIRD READING

BILL NUMBER	DATE	PAGE	ACTION
HB-3067	04/13/84	7	FIRST READING
	05/09/84	39	SECOND READING
	05/10/84	134	HELD ON SECOND
	05/10/84	134	RECALLED
	05/16/84	11	SECOND READING
	05/22/84	43	THIRD READING
	06/30/84	247	CONCURRENCE
HB-3068	04/13/84	8	FIRST READING
	05/10/84	94	SECOND READING
	05/17/84	193	THIRD READING
HB-3069	04/13/84	8	FIRST READING
	05/15/84	14	SECOND READING
	05/18/84	5	THIRD READING
	05/18/84	15	OUT OF RECORD
	05/22/84	171	RECALLED
	05/23/84	155	THIRD READING
	06/28/84	21	CONCURRENCE
HB-3070	04/13/84	8	FIRST READING
	05/08/84	38	SECOND READING
	05/18/84	15	THIRD READING
HB-3071	04/13/84	8	FIRST READING
	05/15/84	127	SECOND READING
	05/31/84	81	THIRD READING
HB-3072	04/13/84	8	FIRST READING
	05/15/84	15	SECOND READING
	05/16/84	282	RECALLED
	05/18/84	17	THIRD READING
	06/28/84	23	CONCURRENCE
HB-3073	04/13/84	8	FIRST READING
	05/22/84	32	SECOND READING
	05/22/84	37	MOTION
	05/22/84	40	HELD ON SECOND
	05/23/84	18	SECOND READING
	05/23/84	18	HELD ON SECOND
	05/23/84	28	SECOND READING
	05/23/84	105	THIRD READING
HB-3074	04/13/84	8	FIRST READING
	05/04/84	43	MOTION
	05/16/84	261	SECOND READING
	05/23/84	106	THIRD READING
HB-3075	04/13/84	8	FIRST READING
HB-3076	04/13/84	8	FIRST READING

PROGRAM-LRTRNMST
08/20/85
LEGISLATIVE INFORMATION SYSTEM
HOUSE OF REPRESENTATIVES
PAGE 221

MASTER TRANSCRIPT INDEX

BILL NUMBER	DATE	PAGE	ACTION
HB-3077	04/13/84	8	FIRST READING
HB-3078	04/13/84	8	FIRST READING
HB-3079	04/13/84	8	FIRST READING
HB-3080	04/13/84	8	FIRST READING
HB-3081	04/13/84	9	FIRST READING
HB-3082	04/13/84	9	FIRST READING
HB-3083	04/13/84	9	FIRST READING
	05/18/84	137	SECOND READING
	05/18/84	151	OUT OF RECORD
	05/23/84	7	SECOND READING
	05/23/84	7	HELD ON SECOND
	05/23/84	293	SECOND READING
	05/24/84	122	THIRD READING
HB-3084	04/13/84	9	FIRST READING
	05/23/84	7	SECOND READING
	05/23/84	7	HELD ON SECOND
	05/24/84	130	SECOND READING
	05/24/84	131	TABLED
HB-3085	04/13/84	9	FIRST READING
	05/23/84	7	SECOND READING
	05/23/84	7	HELD ON SECOND
	05/24/84	131	SECOND READING
HB-3086	04/13/84	9	FIRST READING
	05/09/84	39	SECOND READING
	05/15/84	162	THIRD READING
HB-3087	04/13/84	9	FIRST READING
	05/09/84	3	SECOND READING
	05/16/84	5	THIRD READING
HB-3088	04/13/84	9	FIRST READING
HB-3089	04/13/84	9	FIRST READING
	05/09/84	3	SECOND READING
	05/16/84	5	THIRD READING
	06/28/84	25	CONCURRENCE
HB-3090	04/13/84	9	FIRST READING
	05/09/84	3	SECOND READING
	05/16/84	5	THIRD READING
	06/30/84	7	CONCURRENCE
	12/11/84	27	MOTION

PROGRAM-LRTRNMST
08/20/85
LEGISLATIVE INFORMATION SYSTEM
HOUSE OF REPRESENTATIVES
PAGE 222

MASTER TRANSCRIPT INDEX

BILL NUMBER	DATE	PAGE	ACTION
HB-3090 (cont'd)	12/12/84	60	CONFERENCE
HB-3091	04/13/84	9	FIRST READING
	05/24/84	303	SECOND READING
	05/25/84	28	THIRD READING
	06/29/84	5	CONCURRENCE
HB-3092	04/13/84	10	FIRST READING
	05/09/84	59	SECOND READING
	05/24/84	132	THIRD READING
	06/28/84	26	CONCURRENCE
HB-3093	04/13/84	10	FIRST READING
	05/09/84	60	SECOND READING
	05/10/84	134	THIRD READING
	06/28/84	27	CONCURRENCE
	06/30/84	248	CONFERENCE
HB-3094	04/13/84	10	FIRST READING
	05/09/84	60	SECOND READING
	05/16/84	62	THIRD READING
HB-3095	04/13/84	10	FIRST READING
	05/09/84	60	SECOND READING
	05/10/84	135	THIRD READING
HB-3096	04/13/84	10	FIRST READING
	05/15/84	15	SECOND READING
	05/18/84	18	THIRD READING
HB-3097	04/13/84	10	FIRST READING
	05/15/84	16	SECOND READING
	05/15/84	22	HELD ON SECOND
	05/16/84	262	SECOND READING
	05/18/84	19	THIRD READING
HB-3098	04/13/84	10	FIRST READING
	05/15/84	22	SECOND READING
	05/18/84	36	THIRD READING
HB-3099	04/13/84	10	FIRST READING
	05/15/84	23	SECOND READING
	05/24/84	54	THIRD READING
	06/28/84	28	CONCURRENCE
HB-3100	04/13/84	10	FIRST READING
	05/23/84	45	OTHER
HB-3101	04/13/84	10	FIRST READING
	05/15/84	23	SECOND READING
	05/18/84	52	THIRD READING

BILL NUMBER	DATE	PAGE	ACTION
HB-3102	04/13/84	10	FIRST READING
	05/15/84	23	SECOND READING
	05/18/84	53	RECALLED
	05/18/84	56	THIRD READING
	05/18/84	61	OUT OF RECORD
	05/22/84	84	RECALLED
	05/22/84	86	THIRD READING
	06/28/84	29	CONCURRENCE
HB-3103	04/13/84	11	FIRST READING
HB-3104	04/13/84	11	FIRST READING
HB-3105	04/13/84	11	FIRST READING
	05/04/84	32	MOTION
HB-3106	04/13/84	11	FIRST READING
	05/15/84	10	SECOND READING
	05/23/84	276	RECALLED
HB-3107	04/13/84	11	FIRST READING
	05/04/84	32	MOTION
HB-3108	04/13/84	11	FIRST READING
	05/23/84	18	SECOND READING
	05/23/84	18	HELD ON SECOND
	05/23/84	278	SECOND READING
	05/24/84	68	THIRD READING
HB-3109	04/19/84	1	FIRST READING
HB-3110	04/19/84	1	FIRST READING
	05/09/84	60	SECOND READING
	05/18/84	3	RECALLED
	05/24/84	173	THIRD READING
	06/29/84	49	CONCURRENCE
HB-3111	04/19/84	1	FIRST READING
HB-3112	04/19/84	1	FIRST READING
HB-3113	04/19/84	1	FIRST READING
HB-3114	04/19/84	1	FIRST READING
HB-3115	04/19/84	1	FIRST READING
HB-3116	04/19/84	1	FIRST READING
	05/09/84	61	SECOND READING
	05/10/84	136	THIRD READING

BILL NUMBER	DATE	PAGE	ACTION
HB-3117	04/19/84	1	FIRST READING
	05/15/84	25	SECOND READING
	05/23/84	108	THIRD READING
HB-3118	04/19/84	1	FIRST READING
HB-3119	04/19/84	2	FIRST READING
	05/15/84	27	SECOND READING
	05/18/84	62	THIRD READING
HB-3120	04/19/84	2	FIRST READING
	05/09/84	3	SECOND READING
	05/16/84	5	THIRD READING
HB-3121	04/19/84	2	FIRST READING
HB-3122	04/19/84	2	FIRST READING
HB-3123	04/19/84	2	FIRST READING
	05/16/84	263	SECOND READING
	05/18/84	63	THIRD READING
	06/28/84	34	CONCURRENCE
HB-3124	04/19/84	2	FIRST READING
HB-3125	04/19/84	2	FIRST READING
	05/09/84	3	SECOND READING
	05/10/84	7	SECOND READING
	05/15/84	163	THIRD READING
HB-3126	04/19/84	2	FIRST READING
	05/09/84	61	SECOND READING
	05/10/84	137	THIRD READING
HB-3127	04/19/84	2	FIRST READING
	05/15/84	11	SECOND READING
	05/15/84	14	HELD ON SECOND
	05/16/84	238	SECOND READING
	05/24/84	225	THIRD READING
HB-3128	04/19/84	2	FIRST READING
	05/15/84	27	SECOND READING
	05/18/84	156	MOTION
	05/30/84	73	RECALLED
	05/31/84	52	THIRD READING
	06/28/84	48	CONCURRENCE
	06/30/84	218	CONFERENCE
HB-3129	04/19/84	2	FIRST READING
	05/15/84	27	SECOND READING
	05/22/84	127	RECALLED

MASTER TRANSCRIPT INDEX

BILL NUMBER	DATE	PAGE	ACTION
HB-3129 (cont'd)	05/22/84	132	THIRD READING
	05/24/84	302	RECALLED
HB-3130	04/19/84	2	FIRST READING
HB-3131	04/19/84	2	FIRST READING
HB-3132	04/19/84	2	FIRST READING
HB-3133	04/19/84	3	FIRST READING
HB-3134	04/19/84	3	FIRST READING
	05/15/84	135	SECOND READING
	05/24/84	235	THIRD READING
HB-3135	04/19/84	3	FIRST READING
	05/16/84	28	SECOND READING
	05/24/84	297	RECALLED
	05/25/84	165	THIRD READING
HB-3136	04/19/84	3	FIRST READING
	05/08/84	9	SECOND READING
	05/09/84	68	THIRD READING
	06/28/84	46	CONCURRENCE
	06/29/84	91	OTHER
	06/30/84	104	OTHER
HB-3137	04/19/84	3	FIRST READING
HB-3138	04/19/84	3	FIRST READING
HB-3139	04/19/84	3	FIRST READING
HB-3140	04/19/84	3	FIRST READING
	05/09/84	61	SECOND READING
	05/09/84	62	HELD ON SECOND
	05/10/84	7	SECOND READING
	05/15/84	164	THIRD READING
	11/27/84	31	VETO MESSAGE
HB-3141	04/19/84	3	FIRST READING
	05/09/84	3	SECOND READING
	05/23/84	280	SECOND READING
	05/25/84	10	THIRD READING
HB-3142	04/19/84	3	FIRST READING
HB-3143	04/19/84	3	FIRST READING
	05/15/84	29	SECOND READING
	05/18/84	65	THIRD READING
	06/28/84	128	CONCURRENCE

MASTER TRANSCRIPT INDEX

BILL NUMBER	DATE	PAGE	ACTION
HB-3143 (cont'd)	11/27/84	32	VETO MESSAGE
HB-3144	04/19/84	3	FIRST READING
	05/09/84	62	SECOND READING
	05/10/84	139	THIRD READING
HB-3145	04/19/84	4	FIRST READING
HB-3146	04/19/84	4	FIRST READING
HB-3147	04/19/84	4	FIRST READING
HB-3148	04/19/84	4	FIRST READING
	05/15/84	30	SECOND READING
	05/18/84	68	THIRD READING
	06/28/84	132	CONCURRENCE
	11/27/84	33	VETO MESSAGE
HB-3149	04/19/84	4	FIRST READING
HB-3150	04/19/84	4	FIRST READING
	05/08/84	9	SECOND READING
	05/09/84	71	THIRD READING
HB-3151	04/19/84	4	FIRST READING
	05/16/84	264	SECOND READING
HB-3152	04/19/84	4	FIRST READING
	05/15/84	43	SECOND READING
	05/18/84	70	THIRD READING
	05/23/84	138	RECALLED
	05/23/84	139	THIRD READING
HB-3153	04/19/84	4	FIRST READING
HB-3154	04/19/84	4	FIRST READING
HB-3155	04/19/84	4	FIRST READING
HB-3156	04/19/84	4	FIRST READING
	05/16/84	268	SECOND READING
HB-3157	04/19/84	5	FIRST READING
HB-3158	04/19/84	5	FIRST READING
HB-3159	04/19/84	5	FIRST READING
HB-3160	04/19/84	5	FIRST READING
HB-3161	04/19/84	5	FIRST READING

BILL NUMBER	DATE	PAGE	ACTION
HB-3161 (cont'd)	05/09/84	62	SECOND READING
	05/23/84	117	THIRD READING
	11/27/84	65	VETO MESSAGE
HB-3162	04/19/84	5	FIRST READING
	05/15/84	43	SECOND READING
	05/15/84	51	OUT OF RECORD
	05/17/84	36	SECOND READING
	05/17/84	43	HELD ON SECOND
	05/23/84	18	SECOND READING
	05/24/84	258	RECALLED
	05/25/84	118	THIRD READING
HB-3163	04/19/84	5	FIRST READING
HB-3164	04/19/84	5	FIRST READING
HB-3165	04/19/84	5	FIRST READING
	05/15/84	51	SECOND READING
	05/24/84	175	RECALLED
	05/24/84	182	THIRD READING
HB-3166	04/19/84	5	FIRST READING
HB-3167	04/19/84	5	FIRST READING
HB-3168	04/19/84	5	FIRST READING
HB-3169	04/19/84	5	FIRST READING
HB-3170	04/19/84	5	FIRST READING
HB-3171	04/19/84	6	FIRST READING
HB-3172	04/19/84	6	FIRST READING
	05/15/84	51	SECOND READING
	05/15/84	51	TABLED
HB-3173	04/19/84	6	FIRST READING
HB-3174	04/19/84	6	FIRST READING
	05/23/84	171	SECOND READING
	05/25/84	55	THIRD READING
HB-3175	04/19/84	6	FIRST READING
	05/15/84	51	SECOND READING
	05/25/84	54	OTHER
HB-3176	04/19/84	6	FIRST READING
	05/15/84	52	SECOND READING
	05/23/84	176	RECALLED

BILL NUMBER	DATE	PAGE	ACTION
HB-3176 (cont'd)	05/25/84	57	THIRD READING
HB-3177	04/19/84	6	FIRST READING
	05/15/84	52	SECOND READING
	05/15/84	52	OUT OF RECORD
	05/18/84	152	OUT OF RECORD
	05/22/84	28	SECOND READING
	05/23/84	179	RECALLED
	05/25/84	58	THIRD READING
	06/26/84	104	CONCURRENCE
	07/01/84	45	MOTION
HB-3178	04/19/84	6	FIRST READING
	05/15/84	52	SECOND READING
	05/23/84	281	RECALLED
	05/25/84	60	THIRD READING
	11/27/84	37	VETO MESSAGE
HB-3179	04/19/84	6	FIRST READING
	05/15/84	53	SECOND READING
	05/24/84	252	RECALLED
	05/25/84	65	THIRD READING
HB-3180	04/19/84	6	FIRST READING
	05/15/84	53	SECOND READING
	05/23/84	181	RECALLED
	05/25/84	71	THIRD READING
HB-3181	04/19/84	6	FIRST READING
	05/16/84	29	SECOND READING
	05/16/84	31	HELD ON SECOND
	05/16/84	265	SECOND READING
	05/24/84	236	THIRD READING
HB-3182	04/19/84	6	FIRST READING
HB-3183	04/19/84	7	FIRST READING
	05/15/84	53	SECOND READING
	05/24/84	239	THIRD READING
HB-3184	04/19/84	7	FIRST READING
HB-3185	04/19/84	7	FIRST READING
HB-3186	04/19/84	7	FIRST READING
HB-3187	04/19/84	7	FIRST READING
HB-3188	04/19/84	7	FIRST READING
HB-3189	04/19/84	7	FIRST READING

BILL NUMBER	DATE	PAGE	ACTION
HB-3189(cont'd)	05/16/84	31	SECOND READING
HB-3190	04/19/84	7	FIRST READING
HB-3191	04/19/84	7	FIRST READING
HB-3192	04/19/84	7	FIRST READING
	05/09/84	3	SECOND READING
	05/16/84	12	SECOND READING
HB-3193	04/19/84	7	FIRST READING
	05/23/84	24	SECOND READING
	05/25/84	72	THIRD READING
	06/28/84	135	CONCURRENCE
HB-3194	04/19/84	7	FIRST READING
	05/23/84	26	SECOND READING
	05/25/84	73	THIRD READING
HB-3195	04/19/84	7	FIRST READING
	05/23/84	27	SECOND READING
	05/25/84	75	THIRD READING
HB-3196	04/19/84	7	FIRST READING
HB-3197	04/19/84	7	FIRST READING
	05/10/84	9	SECOND READING
	05/15/84	165	THIRD READING
HB-3198	04/19/84	8	FIRST READING
HB-3199	04/19/84	8	FIRST READING
	05/09/84	62	SECOND READING
	05/10/84	140	THIRD READING
HB-3200	04/19/84	8	FIRST READING
HB-3201	04/19/84	8	FIRST READING
	05/15/84	54	SECOND READING
	05/18/84	79	THIRD READING
HB-3202	04/19/84	8	FIRST READING
	05/15/84	54	SECOND READING
	05/18/84	81	THIRD READING
HB-3203	04/19/84	8	FIRST READING
	05/15/84	54	SECOND READING
	05/25/84	21	THIRD READING
	05/25/84	84	MOTION
	05/25/84	85	THIRD READING

BILL NUMBER	DATE	PAGE	ACTION
HB-3204	04/19/84	8	FIRST READING
	05/15/84	54	SECOND READING
	05/18/84	85	THIRD READING
	06/28/84	139	CONCURRENCE
HB-3205	04/19/84	8	FIRST READING
	05/15/84	55	OUT OF RECORD
	05/16/84	31	SECOND READING
	05/18/84	87	RECALLED
	05/18/84	90	THIRD READING
	06/28/84	140	CONCURRENCE
HB-3206	04/19/84	8	FIRST READING
	05/15/84	56	OUT OF RECORD
	05/16/84	33	SECOND READING
	05/16/84	276	RECALLED
	05/18/84	90	THIRD READING
	06/28/84	142	CONCURRENCE
HB-3207	04/19/84	8	FIRST READING
HB-3208	04/19/84	8	FIRST READING
	05/15/84	56	SECOND READING
	05/18/84	93	THIRD READING
	06/28/84	143	CONCURRENCE
HB-3209	04/19/84	8	FIRST READING
	05/09/84	62	SECOND READING
	05/10/84	141	THIRD READING
HB-3210	04/19/84	9	FIRST READING
HB-3211	04/19/84	9	FIRST READING
	05/09/84	63	SECOND READING
	05/10/84	143	THIRD READING
HB-3212	04/19/84	9	FIRST READING
	05/09/84	3	SECOND READING
	05/16/84	239	SECOND READING
	05/24/84	55	THIRD READING
HB-3213	04/19/84	9	FIRST READING
	05/08/84	9	SECOND READING
	05/09/84	70	THIRD READING
HB-3214	04/19/84	9	FIRST READING
HB-3215	04/19/84	10	FIRST READING
HB-3216	04/19/84	10	FIRST READING
	05/15/84	57	SECOND READING

BILL NUMBER	DATE	PAGE	ACTION
HB-3216 (cont'd)	05/22/84	98	THIRD READING
HB-3217	04/19/84	10	FIRST READING
HB-3218	04/19/84	10	FIRST READING
	05/23/84	28	SECOND READING
	05/23/84	28	HELD ON SECOND
	05/23/84	284	SECOND READING
	05/24/84	56	THIRD READING
HB-3219	04/19/84	10	FIRST READING
	05/08/84	10	SECOND READING
	05/09/84	71	THIRD READING
HB-3220	04/19/84	11	FIRST READING
HB-3221	04/19/84	11	FIRST READING
	05/17/84	43	SECOND READING
	05/17/84	44	OUT OF RECORD
	05/22/84	169	SECOND READING
	05/23/84	119	THIRD READING
	06/28/84	143	CONCURRENCE
HB-3222	04/19/84	11	FIRST READING
HB-3223	04/19/84	11	FIRST READING
HB-3224	04/19/84	11	FIRST READING
HB-3225	04/19/84	11	FIRST READING
HB-3226	04/19/84	11	FIRST READING
HB-3227	04/19/84	11	FIRST READING
	05/16/84	268	SECOND READING
	05/25/84	158	RECALLED
HB-3228	04/19/84	11	FIRST READING
HB-3229	04/19/84	11	FIRST READING
	05/15/84	57	SECOND READING
	05/15/84	59	OUT OF RECORD
	05/24/84	81	OTHER
HB-3230	04/19/84	11	FIRST READING
	05/15/84	60	SECOND READING
	05/24/84	186	THIRD READING
HB-3231	04/19/84	11	FIRST READING
	05/04/84	33	MOTION
	05/23/84	31	SECOND READING

BILL NUMBER	DATE	PAGE	ACTION
HB-3231 (cont'd)	05/23/84	31	HELD ON SECOND
	05/23/84	285	SECOND READING
	05/25/84	164	THIRD READING
	06/28/84	144	CONCURRENCE
HB-3232	04/19/84	12	FIRST READING
	05/16/84	37	SECOND READING
	05/25/84	137	THIRD READING
HB-3233	04/19/84	12	FIRST READING
	05/15/84	64	SECOND READING
	05/24/84	297	RECALLED
	05/25/84	11	THIRD READING
HB-3234	04/19/84	12	FIRST READING
	05/15/84	64	SECOND READING
	05/18/84	96	THIRD READING
HB-3235	04/19/84	12	FIRST READING
	05/15/84	129	SECOND READING
	05/30/84	41	THIRD READING
HB-3236	04/19/84	12	FIRST READING
HB-3237	04/19/84	12	FIRST READING
HB-3238	04/19/84	12	FIRST READING
HB-3239	04/19/84	12	FIRST READING
	05/15/84	65	SECOND READING
	05/18/84	94	THIRD READING
HB-3240	04/19/84	12	FIRST READING
	05/15/84	66	SECOND READING
	05/18/84	97	THIRD READING
HB-3241	04/19/84	12	FIRST READING
HB-3242	04/19/84	12	FIRST READING
HB-3243	04/19/84	13	FIRST READING
	05/16/84	269	SECOND READING
	05/25/84	161	THIRD READING
	05/25/84	163	OTHER
HB-3244	04/19/84	13	FIRST READING
HB-3245	04/19/84	13	FIRST READING
HB-3246	04/19/84	13	FIRST READING
	05/15/84	66	SECOND READING

BILL NUMBER	DATE	PAGE	ACTION
HB-3246 (cont'd)	05/18/84	103	THIRD READING
HB-3247	04/19/84	13	FIRST READING
HB-3248	04/19/84	13	FIRST READING
HB-3249	04/19/84	13	FIRST READING
HB-3250	04/19/84	13	FIRST READING
HB-3251	04/19/84	13	FIRST READING
HB-3252	04/19/84	13	FIRST READING
HB-3253	04/19/84	13	FIRST READING
	05/04/84	50	MOTION
	05/23/84	31	SECOND READING
	05/23/84	32	HELD ON SECOND
HB-3254	04/19/84	13	FIRST READING
HB-3255	04/19/84	13	FIRST READING
	05/16/84	269	SECOND READING
	05/23/84	303	RECALLED
	05/25/84	13	THIRD READING
	06/28/84	46	CONCURRENCE
HB-3256	04/19/84	14	FIRST READING
HB-3257	04/19/84	14	FIRST READING
HB-3258	04/19/84	14	FIRST READING
HB-3259	04/19/84	14	FIRST READING
HB-3260	04/19/84	14	FIRST READING
HB-3261	04/19/84	14	FIRST READING
HB-3262	04/19/84	14	FIRST READING
HB-3263	04/19/84	14	FIRST READING
	05/09/84	3	SECOND READING
	05/16/84	5	THIRD READING
HB-3264	04/19/84	14	FIRST READING
HB-3265	04/19/84	14	FIRST READING
HB-3266	04/19/84	14	FIRST READING

BILL NUMBER	DATE	PAGE	ACTION
HB-3267	04/24/84	4	FIRST READING
HB-3268	04/24/84	24	FIRST READING
HB-3269	04/24/84	24	FIRST READING
HB-3270	04/24/84	24	FIRST READING
HB-3271	04/24/84	24	FIRST READING
HB-3272	04/25/84	27	FIRST READING
HB-3273	05/01/84	2	FIRST READING
HB-3274	05/02/84	62	FIRST READING
HB-3275	05/15/84	199	FIRST READING
HB-3276	05/16/84	286	FIRST READING
HB-3277	05/24/84	314	FIRST READING
	05/31/84	4	MOTION
	05/31/84	6	SECOND READING
	05/31/84	6	HELD ON SECOND
	06/05/84	14	SECOND READING
	06/05/84	15	THIRD READING
	06/05/84	16	OUT OF RECORD
	06/06/84	26	THIRD READING
HB-3278	05/30/84	90	FIRST READING
HB-3279	06/21/84	3	FIRST READING
HB-3280	06/22/84	157	FIRST READING
HB-3281	11/14/84	2	FIRST READING
HB-3282	11/14/84	2	FIRST READING
HB-3283	11/14/84	2	FIRST READING
HB-3284	11/14/84	2	FIRST READING
HB-3285	11/14/84	2	FIRST READING
HB-3286	11/14/84	2	FIRST READING
	11/27/84	5	MOTION
	11/27/84	51	MOTION
	11/27/84	62	MOTION
	11/27/84	63	SECOND READING
	11/28/84	70	THIRD READING

PROGRAM-LRTRNMST
08/20/85
LEGISLATIVE INFORMATION SYSTEM
HOUSE OF REPRESENTATIVES
PAGE 235

MASTER TRANSCRIPT INDEX

BILL NUMBER	DATE	PAGE	ACTION
HB-3287	11/14/84	2	FIRST READING
HB-3288	11/14/84	2	FIRST READING
HB-3289	11/28/84	5	FIRST READING
HB-3290	11/28/84	5	FIRST READING
HB-3291	11/28/84	73	FIRST READING
SB-0002	06/01/83	3	FIRST READING
	06/10/83	30	MOTION
	06/15/83	86	SECOND READING
	06/20/83	166	THIRD READING
SB-0003	05/23/83	1	FIRST READING
	06/08/83	8	SECOND READING
	06/20/83	169	THIRD READING
SB-0010	05/23/83	1	FIRST READING
	06/07/83	13	SECOND READING
	06/24/83	193	THIRD READING
	11/02/83	32	VETO MESSAGE
SB-0011	05/24/83	299	FIRST READING
	06/15/83	2	SECOND READING
	06/21/83	108	MOTION
	06/21/83	222	SECOND READING
	06/21/83	222	HELD ON SECOND
	06/22/83	275	SECOND READING
	06/24/83	44	THIRD READING
SB-0012	05/23/83	1	FIRST READING
	06/08/83	39	SECOND READING
	06/15/83	136	RECALLED
	06/17/83	140	MOTION
	06/17/83	10	THIRD READING
	06/17/83	35	THIRD READING
	06/28/83	225	NON-CONCURRENCE
SB-0013	05/20/83	2	FIRST READING
	06/08/83	3	SECOND READING
	06/14/83	28	THIRD READING
SB-0016	05/24/83	299	FIRST READING
	06/16/83	83	SECOND READING
	06/24/83	2	THIRD READING
	06/29/83	245	NON-CONCURRENCE
SB-0020	05/23/83	1	FIRST READING
	06/08/83	39	SECOND READING

PROGRAM-LRTRNMST
08/20/85
LEGISLATIVE INFORMATION SYSTEM
HOUSE OF REPRESENTATIVES
PAGE 236

MASTER TRANSCRIPT INDEX

BILL NUMBER	DATE	PAGE	ACTION
SB-0020 (cont'd)	06/15/83	128	THIRD READING
SB-0022	05/27/83	242	FIRST READING
	06/15/83	86	SECOND READING
	06/25/83	9	THIRD READING
	11/02/83	24	VETO MESSAGE
SB-0023	05/27/83	243	FIRST READING
	06/15/83	86	SECOND READING
SB-0024	05/24/83	299	FIRST READING
	06/08/83	3	SECOND READING
	06/14/83	28	THIRD READING
SB-0025	05/20/83	2	FIRST READING
	06/22/83	144	SECOND READING
	06/23/83	72	THIRD READING
	06/23/83	75	OUT OF RECORD
	06/25/83	11	THIRD READING
	06/30/83	11	NON-CONCURRENCE
	11/03/83	32	CONFERENCE
SB-0026	05/23/83	227	FIRST READING
	06/15/83	4	SECOND READING
	06/17/83	53	MOTION
	06/20/83	123	RECALLED
	06/20/83	130	MOTION
	06/25/83	12	THIRD READING
	06/28/83	226	NON-CONCURRENCE
	07/02/83	128	CONFERENCE
SB-0027	04/05/83	55	FIRST READING
	06/15/83	87	SECOND READING
	06/21/83	7	THIRD READING
SB-0029	05/27/83	243	FIRST READING
	06/15/83	87	SECOND READING
	06/21/83	8	RECALLED
	06/21/83	9	THIRD READING
SB-0030	06/01/83	3	FIRST READING
	06/16/83	139	SECOND READING
	06/21/83	14	THIRD READING
SB-0033	06/02/83	2	FIRST READING
	06/10/83	31	MOTION
SB-0037	05/27/83	243	FIRST READING
	06/15/83	88	SECOND READING
	06/21/83	19	THIRD READING

PROGRAM-LRTRNMST
08/20/85
LEGISLATIVE INFORMATION SYSTEM
HOUSE OF REPRESENTATIVES
PAGE 237

MASTER TRANSCRIPT INDEX

BILL NUMBER	DATE	PAGE	ACTION
SB-0039	05/26/83	303	FIRST READING
	06/14/83	3	SECOND READING
	06/21/83	2	THIRD READING
SB-0041	05/27/83	243	FIRST READING
	06/16/83	83	SECOND READING
SB-0042	05/27/83	233	FIRST READING
	06/14/83	9	SECOND READING
	06/15/83	126	THIRD READING
SB-0044	05/23/83	1	FIRST READING
	06/14/83	10	SECOND READING
	10/19/83	3	MOTION
	10/19/83	71	SECOND READING
	11/02/83	223	THIRD READING
SB-0046	05/23/83	1	FIRST READING
SB-0047	05/20/83	2	FIRST READING
	06/15/83	88	SECOND READING
	06/21/83	29	THIRD READING
SB-0049	05/25/83	228	FIRST READING
	06/14/83	3	SECOND READING
	06/21/83	2	THIRD READING
SB-0053	05/20/83	2	FIRST READING
	06/15/83	88	SECOND READING
	06/23/83	75	THIRD READING
SB-0054	05/23/83	1	FIRST READING
	06/09/83	4	SECOND READING
	06/25/83	18	THIRD READING
SB-0057	05/23/83	1	FIRST READING
	06/08/83	3	SECOND READING
	06/14/83	28	THIRD READING
SB-0058	05/27/83	243	FIRST READING
SB-0060	05/20/83	3	FIRST READING
	06/14/83	3	SECOND READING
	06/21/83	2	THIRD READING
SB-0061	05/23/83	1	FIRST READING
	06/08/83	8	SECOND READING
	06/21/83	35	RECALLED
	06/24/83	170	THIRD READING
	11/02/83	25	VETO MESSAGE
	11/02/83	26	OUT OF RECORD

PROGRAM-LRTRNMST
08/20/85
LEGISLATIVE INFORMATION SYSTEM
HOUSE OF REPRESENTATIVES
PAGE 238

MASTER TRANSCRIPT INDEX

BILL NUMBER	DATE	PAGE	ACTION
SB-0061 (cont'd)	11/02/83	81	VETO MESSAGE
SB-0062	05/26/83	305	FIRST READING
	06/14/83	3	SECOND READING
	06/21/83	2	THIRD READING
SB-0063	06/02/83	2	FIRST READING
	06/16/83	84	SECOND READING
	06/27/83	330	THIRD READING
SB-0066	05/23/83	2	FIRST READING
	06/15/83	88	SECOND READING
	06/24/83	51	THIRD READING
	11/02/83	4	VETO MESSAGE
SB-0069	04/05/83	55	FIRST READING
	06/08/83	4	SECOND READING
	06/14/83	28	THIRD READING
	11/02/83	144	VETO MESSAGE
SB-0070	05/24/83	299	FIRST READING
	06/16/83	104	SECOND READING
	06/27/83	4	THIRD READING
SB-0071	05/27/83	243	FIRST READING
	06/14/83	3	SECOND READING
	06/21/83	2	THIRD READING
	11/02/83	144	VETO MESSAGE
SB-0076	05/24/83	300	FIRST READING
	06/14/83	3	SECOND READING
	06/16/83	85	THIRD READING
	06/24/83	2	THIRD READING
SB-0077	05/23/83	2	FIRST READING
SB-0078	05/23/83	2	FIRST READING
	06/08/83	39	SECOND READING
	06/15/83	127	THIRD READING
SB-0080	06/02/83	7	FIRST READING
SB-0083	05/24/83	300	FIRST READING
	06/08/83	4	SECOND READING
	06/14/83	28	THIRD READING
	06/29/83	3	NON-CONCURRENCE
	07/01/83	233	CONFERENCE
	07/02/83	38	CONFERENCE
SB-0084	05/26/83	305	FIRST READING
	06/15/83	7	SECOND READING

PROGRAM-LRTRNMST
08/20/85
LEGISLATIVE INFORMATION SYSTEM
HOUSE OF REPRESENTATIVES
PAGE 239

MASTER TRANSCRIPT INDEX

BILL NUMBER	DATE	PAGE	ACTION
SB-0084 (cont'd)	06/17/83	56	THIRD READING
SB-0085	05/24/83	299	FIRST READING
	06/08/83	40	SECOND READING
	06/24/83	2	THIRD READING
SB-0086	05/23/83	2	FIRST READING
	06/15/83	9	SECOND READING
	06/20/83	96	RECALLED
	06/24/83	2	THIRD READING
SB-0089	06/01/83	3	FIRST READING
	06/15/83	105	SECOND READING
	06/15/83	112	HELD ON SECOND
	06/20/83	3	SECOND READING
	06/21/83	36	THIRD READING
	06/29/83	4	NON-CONCURRENCE
SB-0092	05/23/83	2	FIRST READING
SB-0097	05/26/83	305	FIRST READING
	06/09/83	4	SECOND READING
	06/09/83	5	HELD ON SECOND
	06/15/83	89	SECOND READING
	06/21/83	55	THIRD READING
	11/01/83	4	VETO MESSAGE
SB-0098	04/05/83	55	FIRST READING
	06/08/83	40	SECOND READING
	06/29/83	2	THIRD READING
	06/29/83	39	NON-CONCURRENCE
	07/01/83	270	CONFERENCE
	11/02/83	5	VETO MESSAGE
SB-0099	06/02/83	2	FIRST READING
	06/15/83	96	SECOND READING
	06/22/83	168	THIRD READING
SB-0100	05/24/83	299	FIRST READING
	06/08/83	4	SECOND READING
	06/14/83	28	THIRD READING
SB-0101	05/20/83	3	FIRST READING
	06/08/83	9	SECOND READING
	06/22/83	263	RECALLED
	06/23/83	139	THIRD READING
	06/28/83	227	NON-CONCURRENCE
	07/02/83	87	CONFERENCE
SB-0104	04/05/83	55	FIRST READING
	04/15/83	52	MOTION

PROGRAM-LRTRNMST
08/20/85
LEGISLATIVE INFORMATION SYSTEM
HOUSE OF REPRESENTATIVES
PAGE 240

MASTER TRANSCRIPT INDEX

BILL NUMBER	DATE	PAGE	ACTION
SB-0104 (cont'd)	04/15/83	53	SECOND READING
	04/20/83	10	THIRD READING
SB-0105	05/24/83	299	FIRST READING
	06/08/83	4	SECOND READING
	06/14/83	28	THIRD READING
SB-0107	05/20/83	3	FIRST READING
	06/15/83	91	SECOND READING
	06/22/83	181	THIRD READING
SB-0108	06/01/83	3	FIRST READING
SB-0112	05/20/83	3	FIRST READING
	06/08/83	9	SECOND READING
	06/21/83	59	THIRD READING
SB-0117	05/24/83	300	FIRST READING
	06/08/83	4	SECOND READING
	06/14/83	10	SECOND READING
	06/24/83	2	THIRD READING
SB-0122	05/24/83	299	FIRST READING
	06/08/83	4	SECOND READING
	06/14/83	28	THIRD READING
SB-0123	05/26/83	305	FIRST READING
	06/07/83	13	SECOND READING
	06/21/83	66	THIRD READING
SB-0124	06/01/83	4	FIRST READING
	06/15/83	91	SECOND READING
	06/21/83	68	THIRD READING
SB-0125	05/23/83	2	FIRST READING
	06/15/83	91	SECOND READING
	06/20/83	136	RECALLED
	06/21/83	69	THIRD READING
SB-0127	05/23/83	2	FIRST READING
SB-0128	05/23/83	2	FIRST READING
	06/08/83	4	SECOND READING
	06/16/83	86	SECOND READING
	06/24/83	2	RECALLED
	06/24/83	3	THIRD READING
	11/02/83	27	VETO MESSAGE
SB-0131	06/02/83	2	FIRST READING
	06/22/83	2	SECOND READING
	06/25/83	20	THIRD READING

BILL NUMBER	DATE	PAGE	ACTION
SB-0133	05/20/83	3	FIRST READING
	06/08/83	10	SECOND READING
	06/08/83	10	HELD ON SECOND
	06/09/83	25	SECOND READING
	06/23/83	76	THIRD READING
	11/02/83	121	VETO MESSAGE
SB-0134	05/23/83	2	FIRST READING
	06/14/83	3	SECOND READING
	06/21/83	3	THIRD READING
SB-0135	05/24/83	299	FIRST READING
	06/08/83	4	SECOND READING
	06/15/83	10	SECOND READING
	06/24/83	3	THIRD READING
SB-0136	05/20/83	3	FIRST READING
	06/08/83	40	SECOND READING
	06/24/83	3	THIRD READING
SB-0137	05/23/83	2	FIRST READING
	06/08/83	4	SECOND READING
	06/14/83	29	THIRD READING
SB-0139	06/01/83	4	FIRST READING
	06/15/83	113	SECOND READING
	06/24/83	182	THIRD READING
	11/04/83	37	VETO MESSAGE
SB-0141	05/24/83	300	FIRST READING
	06/08/83	10	SECOND READING
	06/21/83	77	THIRD READING
SB-0142	05/23/83	2	FIRST READING
	06/08/83	40	SECOND READING
	06/24/83	3	RECALLED
	06/24/83	5	THIRD READING
SB-0143	05/23/83	2	FIRST READING
	11/01/83	63	MOTION
	11/01/83	64	SECOND READING
	11/02/83	228	RECALLED
	11/02/83	229	OUT OF RECORD
	11/02/83	238	SECOND READING
	11/02/83	240	THIRD READING
SB-0146	05/23/83	227	FIRST READING
SB-0147	05/26/83	305	FIRST READING
	06/15/83	114	SECOND READING
	06/21/83	79	THIRD READING
SB-0147 (cont'd)	11/02/83	27	VETO MESSAGE
SB-0149	05/23/83	2	FIRST READING
	06/08/83	10	SECOND READING
	06/20/83	122	RECALLED
	06/21/83	82	THIRD READING
	11/01/83	17	VETO MESSAGE
SB-0150	05/23/83	227	FIRST READING
SB-0151	05/23/83	2	FIRST READING
	06/15/83	119	SECOND READING
	06/21/83	86	RECALLED
	06/21/83	87	THIRD READING
	11/01/83	6	VETO MESSAGE
	11/02/83	146	VETO MESSAGE
	11/02/83	147	OUT OF RECORD
SB-0152	05/23/83	227	FIRST READING
	06/14/83	3	SECOND READING
	06/20/83	67	SECOND READING
SB-0161	05/23/83	2	FIRST READING
	06/15/83	112	SECOND READING
	06/21/83	97	RECALLED
	06/25/83	22	RECALLED
	06/25/83	23	THIRD READING
SB-0162	05/23/83	3	FIRST READING
	06/15/83	13	SECOND READING
	06/24/83	5	THIRD READING
SB-0167	05/20/83	3	FIRST READING
	06/15/83	113	SECOND READING
	06/21/83	99	THIRD READING
SB-0168	06/02/83	2	FIRST READING
SB-0171	05/23/83	3	FIRST READING
	06/15/83	114	SECOND READING
	06/21/83	109	RECALLED
	06/23/83	208	THIRD READING
	06/23/83	209	OUT OF RECORD
	06/24/83	208	THIRD READING
	05/04/84	34	MOTION
SB-0172	05/23/83	227	FIRST READING
	06/14/83	11	SECOND READING
	06/27/83	383	THIRD READING
SB-0173	05/23/83	3	FIRST READING

PROGRAM-LRTRNMST
08/20/85
LEGISLATIVE INFORMATION SYSTEM
HOUSE OF REPRESENTATIVES
PAGE 243

MASTER TRANSCRIPT INDEX

BILL NUMBER	DATE	PAGE	ACTION
SB-0173 (cont'd)	06/15/83	114	SECOND READING
	06/21/83	112	THIRD READING
SB-0174	06/01/83	4	FIRST READING
	06/15/83	115	SECOND READING
	06/20/83	139	RECALLED
	06/21/83	113	THIRD READING
SB-0175	05/23/83	3	FIRST READING
	06/15/83	115	SECOND READING
	06/21/83	114	THIRD READING
SB-0176	05/23/83	3	FIRST READING
	06/16/83	141	SECOND READING
	06/21/83	117	THIRD READING
	11/01/83	13	VETO MESSAGE
SB-0177	04/07/83	5	FIRST READING
	04/07/83	5	MOTION
	04/13/83	41	SECOND READING
	04/13/83	59	OUT OF RECORD
	04/14/83	64	SECOND READING
	04/15/83	40	THIRD READING
SB-0178	06/01/83	4	FIRST READING
SB-0179	05/24/83	300	FIRST READING
	06/14/83	11	SECOND READING
	06/24/83	5	THIRD READING
SB-0182	05/26/83	303	FIRST READING
	06/08/83	4	SECOND READING
	06/14/83	29	THIRD READING
SB-0185	06/02/83	2	FIRST READING
	06/15/83	125	SECOND READING
	06/21/83	120	THIRD READING
	06/21/83	121	OUT OF RECORD
SB-0186	05/23/83	3	FIRST READING
	06/15/83	2	SECOND READING
	06/21/83	3	THIRD READING
	06/29/83	11	NON-CONCURRENCE
	06/29/83	12	OUT OF RECORD
	06/29/83	13	NON-CONCURRENCE
	07/02/83	16	CONFERENCE
	11/02/83	37	VETO MESSAGE
SB-0187	06/01/83	4	FIRST READING
	06/15/83	116	SECOND READING
	06/21/83	121	RECALLED

PROGRAM-LRTRNMST
08/20/85
LEGISLATIVE INFORMATION SYSTEM
HOUSE OF REPRESENTATIVES
PAGE 244

MASTER TRANSCRIPT INDEX

BILL NUMBER	DATE	PAGE	ACTION
SB-0187 (cont'd)	06/21/83	129	THIRD READING
	11/02/83	117	VETO MESSAGE
SB-0188	05/26/83	305	FIRST READING
	06/14/83	3	SECOND READING
	06/15/83	14	SECOND READING
	06/20/83	140	RECALLED
SB-0189	06/01/83	4	FIRST READING
	06/15/83	116	SECOND READING
	10/19/83	72	SECOND READING
	10/19/83	201	RECALLED
	10/20/83	98	THIRD READING
	11/04/83	14	NON-CONCURRENCE
SB-0191	05/24/83	2	FIRST READING
	06/08/83	11	SECOND READING
	06/21/83	133	THIRD READING
SB-0192	05/24/83	2	FIRST READING
	06/15/83	117	SECOND READING
	06/21/83	134	RECALLED
	06/23/83	85	THIRD READING
SB-0193	05/24/83	300	FIRST READING
	06/15/83	121	SECOND READING
	06/21/83	135	THIRD READING
SB-0195	05/24/83	298	FIRST READING
	06/15/83	117	SECOND READING
	06/21/83	139	THIRD READING
SB-0197	06/02/83	2	FIRST READING
	06/15/83	14	SECOND READING
	06/22/83	274	RECALLED
	06/24/83	5	THIRD READING
SB-0201	05/24/83	2	FIRST READING
	06/14/83	12	SECOND READING
	06/20/83	97	RECALLED
	06/23/83	144	THIRD READING
SB-0203	05/24/83	298	FIRST READING
SB-0204	05/24/83	2	FIRST READING
	06/15/83	117	SECOND READING
	06/21/83	141	THIRD READING
SB-0205	06/01/83	4	FIRST READING
	06/14/83	3	SECOND READING
	06/21/83	3	THIRD READING

PROGRAM-LRTRNMST
08/20/85
LEGISLATIVE INFORMATION SYSTEM
HOUSE OF REPRESENTATIVES
PAGE 245

MASTER TRANSCRIPT INDEX

BILL NUMBER	DATE	PAGE	ACTION
SB-0206	06/23/83	9	SECOND READING
	06/25/83	30	RECALLED
	06/25/83	31	THIRD READING
	06/25/83	33	RECALLED
	06/25/83	34	THIRD READING
SB-0208	05/24/83	298	FIRST READING
	06/14/83	12	SECOND READING
	06/20/83	99	RECALLED
	06/24/83	5	THIRD READING
	06/29/83	4	NON-CONCURRENCE
SB-0209	06/02/83	2	FIRST READING
	06/14/83	119	SECOND READING
	06/25/83	35	RECALLED
	06/25/83	37	THIRD READING
SB-0210	06/01/83	4	FIRST READING
	06/14/83	3	SECOND READING
	06/21/83	3	THIRD READING
SB-0211	05/24/83	2	FIRST READING
	06/08/83	14	SECOND READING
	06/21/83	142	RECALLED
	06/21/83	143	THIRD READING
SB-0212	05/26/83	303	FIRST READING
SB-0213	05/24/83	298	FIRST READING
	06/08/83	4	SECOND READING
	06/14/83	29	THIRD READING
SB-0214	05/26/83	303	FIRST READING
	06/08/83	4	SECOND READING
	06/14/83	29	THIRD READING
SB-0215	05/24/83	298	FIRST READING
	06/08/83	4	SECOND READING
	06/14/83	29	THIRD READING
SB-0216	05/26/83	1	FIRST READING
	05/26/83	303	FIRST READING
SB-0219	05/24/83	300	FIRST READING
	06/14/83	12	SECOND READING
	06/17/83	68	THIRD READING
	06/17/83	71	OUT OF RECORD
	06/23/83	34	RECALLED
	06/24/83	54	THIRD READING
	06/29/83	6	NON-CONCURRENCE
	07/01/83	60	CONFERENCE

PROGRAM-LRTRNMST
08/20/85
LEGISLATIVE INFORMATION SYSTEM
HOUSE OF REPRESENTATIVES
PAGE 246

MASTER TRANSCRIPT INDEX

BILL NUMBER	DATE	PAGE	ACTION
SB-0220	05/24/83	2	FIRST READING
	06/08/83	41	SECOND READING
	06/24/83	5	THIRD READING
SB-0222	05/24/83	2	FIRST READING
	06/14/83	14	SECOND READING
	06/24/83	5	THIRD READING
SB-0223	05/24/83	300	FIRST READING
	06/14/83	4	SECOND READING
	06/21/83	3	THIRD READING
SB-0225	05/24/83	298	FIRST READING
	06/08/83	11	SECOND READING
	06/21/83	145	THIRD READING
SB-0226	06/01/83	4	FIRST READING
SB-0228	06/01/83	4	FIRST READING
	06/15/83	119	SECOND READING
	06/22/83	252	RECALLED
	06/23/83	86	THIRD READING
	06/29/83	8	NON-CONCURRENCE
	07/01/83	144	CONFERENCE
	11/02/83	175	VETO MESSAGE
SB-0230	06/01/83	4	FIRST READING
	06/15/83	120	SECOND READING
	06/21/83	151	THIRD READING
SB-0233	05/24/83	298	FIRST READING
	06/09/83	5	SECOND READING
	06/09/83	6	HELD ON SECOND
	06/15/83	120	SECOND READING
	06/21/83	161	THIRD READING
SB-0235	04/05/83	56	FIRST READING
	06/14/83	14	SECOND READING
	06/24/83	5	THIRD READING
SB-0237	05/24/83	298	FIRST READING
	11/28/84	64	MOTION
	11/28/84	71	MOTION
SB-0239	05/25/83	228	FIRST READING
	06/08/83	11	SECOND READING
	06/21/83	168	THIRD READING
	06/23/83	138	THIRD READING
SB-0240	05/24/83	298	FIRST READING
	06/09/83	6	SECOND READING

PROGRAM-LRTRNMST
08/20/85
LEGISLATIVE INFORMATION SYSTEM
HOUSE OF REPRESENTATIVES
PAGE 247

MASTER TRANSCRIPT INDEX

BILL NUMBER	DATE	PAGE	ACTION
SB-0240 (cont'd)	06/21/83	165	THIRD READING
SB-0241	05/24/83	298	FIRST READING
	06/23/83	4	SECOND READING
SB-0242	05/24/83	298	FIRST READING
	06/15/83	121	SECOND READING
	06/21/83	179	THIRD READING
SB-0243	05/27/83	233	FIRST READING
	06/15/83	15	SECOND READING
	06/24/83	5	THIRD READING
SB-0244	05/24/83	298	FIRST READING
	06/08/83	41	SECOND READING
	06/20/83	100	RECALLED
	06/24/83	63	THIRD READING
	06/29/83	6	NON-CONCURRENCE
	07/01/83	61	CONFERENCE
SB-0245	05/24/83	300	FIRST READING
	06/15/83	121	SECOND READING
	06/21/83	166	THIRD READING
SB-0246	05/24/83	2	FIRST READING
	06/15/83	15	SECOND READING
SB-0247	05/24/83	298	FIRST READING
	06/16/83	142	SECOND READING
	06/21/83	175	THIRD READING
	11/02/83	28	VETO MESSAGE
SB-0249	05/24/83	299	FIRST READING
	06/08/83	42	SECOND READING
	06/20/83	103	RECALLED
	06/24/83	5	THIRD READING
	06/26/83	2	OTHER
SB-0252	05/24/83	2	FIRST READING
	06/15/83	122	SECOND READING
	06/21/83	177	THIRD READING
SB-0255	06/02/83	2	FIRST READING
	06/22/83	2	SECOND READING
	06/25/83	96	THIRD READING
SB-0256	06/02/83	2	FIRST READING
	06/22/83	3	SECOND READING
	06/25/83	99	THIRD READING
SB-0257	06/02/83	2	FIRST READING

PROGRAM-LRTRNMST
08/20/85
LEGISLATIVE INFORMATION SYSTEM
HOUSE OF REPRESENTATIVES
PAGE 248

MASTER TRANSCRIPT INDEX

BILL NUMBER	DATE	PAGE	ACTION
SB-0257 (cont'd)	06/22/83	3	SECOND READING
	06/25/83	100	THIRD READING
SB-0258	06/01/83	5	FIRST READING
	06/22/83	6	SECOND READING
	06/25/83	100	THIRD READING
SB-0259	06/02/83	2	FIRST READING
	06/22/83	6	SECOND READING
	06/25/83	101	THIRD READING
SB-0260	06/01/83	5	FIRST READING
	06/22/83	7	SECOND READING
	06/25/83	102	THIRD READING
SB-0261	06/01/83	5	FIRST READING
	06/15/83	122	SECOND READING
	06/21/83	178	THIRD READING
SB-0262	06/02/83	2	FIRST READING
	06/22/83	7	SECOND READING
	06/25/83	103	THIRD READING
SB-0263	06/01/83	5	FIRST READING
	06/15/83	122	SECOND READING
	06/21/83	180	RECALLED
	06/21/83	181	THIRD READING
	11/02/83	29	VETO MESSAGE
SB-0264	06/02/83	3	FIRST READING
	06/22/83	7	SECOND READING
	06/25/83	103	THIRD READING
SB-0266	05/24/83	299	FIRST READING
	06/08/83	14	SECOND READING
	06/21/83	187	THIRD READING
SB-0272	05/24/83	300	FIRST READING
	06/15/83	125	SECOND READING
	06/21/83	188	THIRD READING
	06/29/83	7	NON-CONCURRENCE
	07/01/83	222	CONFERENCE
SB-0275	06/02/83	3	FIRST READING
SB-0276	06/02/83	3	FIRST READING
SB-0277	06/02/83	3	FIRST READING
SB-0278	06/02/83	3	FIRST READING
	06/22/83	8	SECOND READING

PROGRAM-LRTRNMST
08/20/85

LEGISLATIVE INFORMATION SYSTEM
HOUSE OF REPRESENTATIVES

PAGE 249

MASTER TRANSCRIPT INDEX

BILL NUMBER	DATE	PAGE	ACTION
SB-0278 (cont'd)	06/23/83	185	RECALLED
	06/25/83	105	THIRD READING
SB-0279	06/02/83	3	FIRST READING
SB-0280	06/02/83	3	FIRST READING
	06/22/83	12	SECOND READING
	06/25/83	111	THIRD READING
SB-0284	05/24/83	2	FIRST READING
	06/15/83	125	SECOND READING
	06/23/83	87	THIRD READING
SB-0285	05/24/83	2	FIRST READING
	06/08/83	42	SECOND READING
	06/24/83	5	THIRD READING
SB-0286	05/24/83	299	FIRST READING
	06/14/83	15	SECOND READING
	06/17/83	72	THIRD READING
	06/20/83	160	THIRD READING
	11/01/83	18	VETO MESSAGE
SB-0288	06/02/83	3	FIRST READING
	06/14/83	15	SECOND READING
	06/24/83	6	THIRD READING
	11/01/83	147	VETO MESSAGE
SB-0289	05/25/83	228	FIRST READING
	06/14/83	4	SECOND READING
	06/21/83	3	THIRD READING
SB-0290	05/24/83	300	FIRST READING
	06/14/83	16	SECOND READING
	06/24/83	6	THIRD READING
SB-0292	05/24/83	299	FIRST READING
	06/08/83	4	SECOND READING
	06/14/83	29	THIRD READING
SB-0294	06/02/83	3	FIRST READING
	06/21/83	222	SECOND READING
	06/21/83	223	HELD ON SECOND
	06/25/83	166	SECOND READING
	04/11/84	30	SECOND READING
	05/31/84	6	THIRD READING
SB-0297	05/26/83	305	FIRST READING
	06/14/83	4	SECOND READING
	06/21/83	3	THIRD READING

PROGRAM-LRTRNMST
08/20/85

LEGISLATIVE INFORMATION SYSTEM
HOUSE OF REPRESENTATIVES

PAGE 250

MASTER TRANSCRIPT INDEX

BILL NUMBER	DATE	PAGE	ACTION
SB-0299	05/24/83	300	FIRST READING
	06/08/83	4	SECOND READING
	06/14/83	29	THIRD READING
SB-0300	05/24/83	297	FIRST READING
	06/22/83	15	SECOND READING
	06/22/83	17	OUT OF RECORD
	06/22/83	25	SECOND READING
	06/25/83	112	THIRD READING
SB-0301	05/25/83	228	FIRST READING
	06/22/83	14	SECOND READING
	06/25/83	117	THIRD READING
SB-0302	05/26/83	305	FIRST READING
	06/14/83	16	SECOND READING
	06/27/83	206	THIRD READING
	11/01/83	65	VETO MESSAGE
	11/01/83	67	OUT OF RECORD
SB-0303	06/02/83	3	FIRST READING
	06/14/83	16	SECOND READING
	06/24/83	6	THIRD READING
SB-0304	05/25/83	2	FIRST READING
	06/15/83	142	SECOND READING
	06/21/83	190	THIRD READING
	11/01/83	19	VETO MESSAGE
SB-0306	05/26/83	305	FIRST READING
	06/14/83	4	SECOND READING
	06/21/83	223	HELD ON SECOND
	06/22/83	275	SECOND READING
	06/24/83	6	THIRD READING
	11/01/83	20	VETO MESSAGE
SB-0309	06/02/83	7	FIRST READING
SB-0310	05/27/83	3	FIRST READING
	06/15/83	15	SECOND READING
	06/27/83	7	THIRD READING
	06/30/83	10	NON-CONCURRENCE
	07/02/83	3	CONFERENCE
	07/02/83	133	CONFERENCE
SB-0313	05/27/83	3	FIRST READING
	06/08/83	5	SECOND READING
	06/15/83	24	SECOND READING
	06/21/83	223	RECALLED
	06/24/83	43	THIRD READING

BILL NUMBER	DATE	PAGE	ACTION
SB-0313(cont'd)	06/29/83	213	NON-CONCURRENCE
	07/01/83	66	CONFERENCE
	07/02/83	102	CONFERENCE
SB-0314	05/25/83	228	FIRST READING
	06/08/83	4	SECOND READING
	06/14/83	17	SECOND READING
	06/27/83	333	THIRD READING
SB-0315	05/25/83	228	FIRST READING
	06/14/83	17	SECOND READING
	06/20/83	102	RECALLED
	06/22/83	186	THIRD READING
SB-0316	05/24/83	300	FIRST READING
	06/08/83	42	SECOND READING
	06/22/83	188	THIRD READING
	11/02/83	7	VETO MESSAGE
SB-0319	05/24/83	297	FIRST READING
	06/15/83	143	SECOND READING
	06/21/83	191	THIRD READING
	11/02/83	39	VETO MESSAGE
SB-0322	05/26/83	305	FIRST READING
	06/08/83	14	SECOND READING
	06/21/83	195	THIRD READING
SB-0323	05/25/83	2	FIRST READING
	06/16/83	142	SECOND READING
	06/21/83	205	RECALLED
	06/21/83	205	THIRD READING
	11/02/83	8	VETO MESSAGE
SB-0325	05/26/83	305	FIRST READING
	06/15/83	144	SECOND READING
	06/24/83	6	THIRD READING
SB-0327	05/26/83	306	FIRST READING
	06/16/83	144	SECOND READING
	06/21/83	208	THIRD READING
SB-0328	05/24/83	297	FIRST READING
	05/26/83	289	MOTION
	05/26/83	295	MOTION
	05/26/83	296	SECOND READING
	05/27/83	6	SECOND READING
	05/27/83	9	THIRD READING
	06/07/83	10	NON-CONCURRENCE
	06/10/83	39	CONFERENCE
	06/10/83	39	MOTION

BILL NUMBER	DATE	PAGE	ACTION
SB-0329	05/27/83	3	FIRST READING
	06/08/83	5	SECOND READING
	06/14/83	29	THIRD READING
SB-0330	05/24/83	300	FIRST READING
	06/14/83	18	SECOND READING
	06/24/83	6	THIRD READING
SB-0331	05/24/83	297	FIRST READING
	06/08/83	5	SECOND READING
	06/14/83	29	THIRD READING
SB-0332	05/24/83	300	FIRST READING
	06/14/83	4	SECOND READING
	06/20/83	68	SECOND READING
	06/24/83	6	THIRD READING
	06/29/83	215	NON-CONCURRENCE
	07/02/83	68	CONFERENCE
SB-0333	05/25/83	228	FIRST READING
	06/08/83	5	SECOND READING
	06/14/83	29	THIRD READING
SB-0335	05/24/83	301	FIRST READING
	06/07/83	11	SECOND READING
	06/24/83	6	THIRD READING
SB-0336	05/25/83	228	FIRST READING
	06/15/83	158	SECOND READING
SB-0337	05/24/83	297	FIRST READING
	06/10/83	31	MOTION
	06/15/83	145	SECOND READING
	06/23/83	258	RECALLED
	06/23/83	259	THIRD READING
	06/28/83	228	NON-CONCURRENCE
SB-0338	06/01/83	5	FIRST READING
	06/15/83	145	SECOND READING
	06/21/83	209	THIRD READING
SB-0340	05/25/83	228	FIRST READING
SB-0341	05/24/83	297	FIRST READING
	06/09/83	7	SECOND READING
	06/21/83	210	THIRD READING
SB-0342	06/01/83	5	FIRST READING
	06/15/83	25	SECOND READING
	06/27/83	357	THIRD READING

MASTER TRANSCRIPT INDEX

BILL NUMBER	DATE	PAGE	ACTION
SB-0345	05/24/83	301	FIRST READING
	06/14/83	4	SECOND READING
	06/21/83	3	THIRD READING
SB-0346	05/26/83	306	FIRST READING
	06/16/83	144	SECOND READING
	06/24/83	43	RECALLED
	06/24/83	43	THIRD READING
	06/28/83	239	NON-CONCURRENCE
SB-0348	05/27/83	4	FIRST READING
SB-0349	05/25/83	2	FIRST READING
SB-0350	05/25/83	2	FIRST READING
	06/07/83	14	SECOND READING
	06/21/83	210	THIRD READING
SB-0353	05/26/83	306	FIRST READING
	06/14/83	18	SECOND READING
	06/24/83	6	THIRD READING
SB-0354	05/24/83	301	FIRST READING
	06/15/83	28	SECOND READING
SB-0355	05/24/83	297	FIRST READING
	06/15/83	145	SECOND READING
	06/21/83	216	THIRD READING
SB-0356	05/26/83	306	FIRST READING
	06/08/83	15	SECOND READING
	06/20/83	141	RECALLED
	06/21/83	219	THIRD READING
SB-0357	05/24/83	301	FIRST READING
	06/15/83	146	SECOND READING
	06/21/83	219	RECALLED
	06/21/83	220	THIRD READING
	06/30/83	5	NON-CONCURRENCE
	07/02/83	164	CONFERENCE
SB-0358	05/25/83	228	FIRST READING
	06/07/83	11	SECOND READING
	06/24/83	6	THIRD READING
SB-0359	05/25/83	5	FIRST READING
	06/15/83	28	SECOND READING
	06/22/83	358	THIRD READING
SB-0363	05/26/83	306	FIRST READING
	06/14/83	4	SECOND READING

MASTER TRANSCRIPT INDEX

BILL NUMBER	DATE	PAGE	ACTION
SB-0363(cont'd)	06/21/83	3	THIRD READING
SB-0364	05/25/83	228	FIRST READING
	06/08/83	5	SECOND READING
	06/14/83	29	THIRD READING
SB-0365	05/24/83	301	FIRST READING
	06/08/83	15	SECOND READING
	06/21/83	221	THIRD READING
SB-0370	05/25/83	229	FIRST READING
SB-0372	05/26/83	306	FIRST READING
	06/16/83	145	SECOND READING
SB-0373	05/25/83	2	FIRST READING
	06/22/83	17	SECOND READING
	06/23/83	186	RECALLED
	06/25/83	118	THIRD READING
SB-0374	05/25/83	2	FIRST READING
	06/22/83	23	SECOND READING
	06/25/83	119	THIRD READING
	07/02/83	22	CONFERENCE
	11/02/83	115	VETO MESSAGE
SB-0375	05/25/83	3	FIRST READING
	06/22/83	24	SECOND READING
	06/25/83	119	THIRD READING
	11/04/83	202	CONFERENCE
SB-0376	05/25/83	3	FIRST READING
	06/22/83	31	SECOND READING
	06/25/83	120	THIRD READING
SB-0377	05/25/83	3	FIRST READING
	06/22/83	31	SECOND READING
	06/22/83	37	OUT OF RECORD
	06/22/83	133	SECOND READING
	06/25/83	122	THIRD READING
SB-0378	05/25/83	3	FIRST READING
	06/22/83	37	SECOND READING
	06/25/83	130	THIRD READING
	07/02/83	97	CONFERENCE
	11/01/83	88	VETO MESSAGE
	11/02/83	103	VETO MESSAGE
	11/04/83	33	VETO MESSAGE
SB-0379	05/25/83	3	FIRST READING
	06/22/83	38	SECOND READING

BILL NUMBER	DATE	PAGE	ACTION
SB-0379 (cont'd)	06/25/83	131	THIRD READING
SB-0380	05/25/83	3	FIRST READING
	06/22/83	39	SECOND READING
	06/25/83	134	THIRD READING
SB-0381	05/25/83	3	FIRST READING
	06/22/83	39	SECOND READING
	06/22/83	137	THIRD READING
SB-0382	05/24/83	297	FIRST READING
	06/22/83	42	SECOND READING
	06/25/83	142	THIRD READING
SB-0383	05/25/83	3	FIRST READING
	06/22/83	43	SECOND READING
	06/25/83	145	THIRD READING
SB-0384	05/25/83	3	FIRST READING
	06/22/83	43	SECOND READING
	06/22/83	154	THIRD READING
	07/02/83	95	CONFERENCE
SB-0385	05/25/83	3	FIRST READING
	06/22/83	44	SECOND READING
	06/25/83	155	THIRD READING
SB-0386	05/25/83	4	FIRST READING
	06/22/83	44	SECOND READING
	06/25/83	156	THIRD READING
SB-0387	05/25/83	4	FIRST READING
	06/22/83	44	SECOND READING
	06/25/83	160	THIRD READING
SB-0388	05/25/83	4	FIRST READING
	06/25/83	46	SECOND READING
	06/25/83	161	THIRD READING
	04/11/84	40	CONFERENCE
	04/11/84	40	MOTION
SB-0389	06/01/83	5	FIRST READING
	06/22/83	47	SECOND READING
	06/26/83	4	THIRD READING
SB-0390	06/01/83	5	FIRST READING
	06/22/83	47	SECOND READING
	06/26/83	17	THIRD READING
	07/02/83	85	CONFERENCE
SB-0391	05/25/83	4	FIRST READING

BILL NUMBER	DATE	PAGE	ACTION
SB-0391 (cont'd)	06/22/83	48	SECOND READING
	06/26/83	87	THIRD READING
SB-0392	05/25/83	4	FIRST READING
	06/22/83	49	SECOND READING
	06/26/83	87	THIRD READING
SB-0393	06/01/83	5	FIRST READING
	06/22/83	54	SECOND READING
	06/26/83	88	THIRD READING
SB-0394	05/25/83	4	FIRST READING
	06/22/83	109	SECOND READING
	06/26/83	89	THIRD READING
	07/02/83	13	CONFERENCE
	11/01/83	98	VETO MESSAGE
SB-0395	05/25/83	4	FIRST READING
	06/22/83	110	SECOND READING
	06/26/83	89	THIRD READING
SB-0397	05/25/83	4	FIRST READING
SB-0398	05/25/83	4	FIRST READING
	06/22/83	110	SECOND READING
	06/26/83	90	THIRD READING
SB-0399	05/25/83	4	FIRST READING
	06/22/83	115	SECOND READING
	06/26/83	91	THIRD READING
SB-0400	05/24/83	301	FIRST READING
	06/15/83	28	SECOND READING
	06/05/84	5	SECOND READING
	06/12/84	4	THIRD READING
SB-0401	05/25/83	4	FIRST READING
	06/22/83	115	SECOND READING
	06/26/83	92	THIRD READING
SB-0402	05/25/83	229	FIRST READING
	06/14/83	5	SECOND READING
	06/21/83	3	THIRD READING
SB-0403	05/26/83	306	FIRST READING
	05/27/83	233	FIRST READING
	06/08/83	43	SECOND READING
	06/14/83	4	SECOND READING
	06/24/83	6	THIRD READING
	11/01/83	21	VETO MESSAGE
	11/01/83	22	OUT OF RECORD

BILL NUMBER	DATE	PAGE	ACTION
SB-0403 (cont'd)	11/01/83	25	VETO MESSAGE
SB-0404	06/15/83	32	SECOND READING
	06/24/83	6	THIRD READING
SB-0406	04/15/83	104	FIRST READING
	04/27/83	52	MOTION
SB-0407	05/25/83	5	FIRST READING
	06/22/83	116	SECOND READING
	06/26/83	93	THIRD READING
SB-0409	05/26/83	306	FIRST READING
	06/07/83	18	SECOND READING
	06/24/83	6	THIRD READING
SB-0411	05/26/83	306	FIRST READING
	06/15/83	29	SECOND READING
SB-0412	05/26/83	306	FIRST READING
	06/07/83	13	SECOND READING
	06/25/83	38	THIRD READING
SB-0413	05/24/83	301	FIRST READING
	06/14/83	4	SECOND READING
	06/21/83	3	THIRD READING
SB-0415	05/26/83	303	FIRST READING
SB-0416	05/26/83	303	FIRST READING
	06/15/83	147	SECOND READING
	06/15/83	147	HELD ON SECOND
			SECOND READING
	06/23/83	90	THIRD READING
	06/23/83	91	MOTION
SB-0417	05/24/83	301	FIRST READING
	06/15/83	30	SECOND READING
	06/24/83	6	THIRD READING
SB-0418	06/01/83	5	FIRST READING
	06/15/83	30	SECOND READING
	06/26/83	94	RECALLED
SB-0419	05/24/83	301	FIRST READING
	06/08/83	5	SECOND READING
	06/14/83	29	THIRD READING
SB-0428	05/26/83	306	FIRST READING
	06/14/83	19	SECOND READING
	06/24/83	6	RECALLED

BILL NUMBER	DATE	PAGE	ACTION
SB-0428 (cont'd)	06/24/83	7	THIRD READING
SB-0431	05/27/83	233	FIRST READING
	06/14/83	4	SECOND READING
	06/21/83	3	THIRD READING
SB-0432	06/01/83	5	FIRST READING
	06/15/83	31	SECOND READING
SB-0433	05/26/83	306	FIRST READING
	06/16/83	88	SECOND READING
	06/24/83	7	THIRD READING
SB-0434	06/15/83	31	SECOND READING
	06/17/83	75	THIRD READING
	06/20/83	162	THIRD READING
	06/28/83	229	NON-CONCURRENCE
	07/02/83	4	CONFERENCE
SB-0435	05/26/83	306	FIRST READING
	06/15/83	2	SECOND READING
	06/21/83	3	THIRD READING
SB-0436	06/15/83	32	SECOND READING
SB-0437	05/24/83	297	FIRST READING
	05/26/83	306	FIRST READING
	06/15/83	150	SECOND READING
	06/26/83	18	THIRD READING
	06/29/83	7	NON-CONCURRENCE
	07/01/83	71	CONFERENCE
	07/01/83	282	CONFERENCE
SB-0440	05/26/83	307	FIRST READING
	05/26/83	307	FIRST READING
	06/14/83	4	SECOND READING
	06/20/83	68	SECOND READING
	06/24/83	7	THIRD READING
	06/29/83	7	NON-CONCURRENCE
	06/30/83	118	CONFERENCE
SB-0447	06/14/83	4	SECOND READING
SB-0448	05/27/83	233	FIRST READING
	06/08/83	15	SECOND READING
	06/23/83	209	THIRD READING
	11/01/83	50	VETO MESSAGE
	11/02/83	92	VETO MESSAGE
SB-0450	05/24/83	297	FIRST READING
	06/10/83	7	MOTION

MASTER TRANSCRIPT INDEX

BILL NUMBER	DATE	PAGE	ACTION
SB-0450 (cont'd)	06/06/84	41	MOTION
	06/06/84	52	SECOND READING
	06/19/84	14	RECALLED
	06/20/84	15	RECALLED
	06/20/84	26	THIRD READING
SB-0451	05/25/83	5	FIRST READING
	06/08/83	43	SECOND READING
	06/27/83	371	THIRD READING
SB-0453	05/25/83	5	FIRST READING
	06/08/83	5	SECOND READING
	06/14/83	20	SECOND READING
SB-0454	05/24/83	301	FIRST READING
	06/16/83	88	SECOND READING
	06/27/83	190	THIRD READING
SB-0455	05/24/83	301	FIRST READING
	06/08/83	5	SECOND READING
	06/14/83	29	THIRD READING
SB-0457	05/26/83	307	FIRST READING
	06/07/83	12	SECOND READING
	06/15/83	131	RECALLED
	06/27/83	317	THIRD READING
	06/30/83	7	NON-CONCURRENCE
	07/02/83	161	CONFERENCE
SB-0459	05/26/83	307	FIRST READING
	06/15/83	148	SECOND READING
	06/15/83	148	HELD ON SECOND
	06/26/83	28	THIRD READING
	06/29/83	40	NON-CONCURRENCE
	07/01/83	288	CONFERENCE
SB-0463	05/24/83	297	FIRST READING
	06/07/83	14	SECOND READING
	06/26/83	29	THIRD READING
SB-0467	05/26/83	307	FIRST READING
	06/08/83	43	SECOND READING
	06/20/83	181	RECALLED
	06/24/83	7	RECALLED
	06/24/83	8	THIRD READING
SB-0468	05/26/83	307	FIRST READING
	06/15/83	150	SECOND READING
SB-0469	05/25/83	5	FIRST READING
	06/08/83	43	SECOND READING

MASTER TRANSCRIPT INDEX

BILL NUMBER	DATE	PAGE	ACTION
SB-0469 (cont'd)	06/22/83	57	THIRD READING
SB-0471	05/24/83	301	FIRST READING
	06/08/83	5	SECOND READING
	06/14/83	29	THIRD READING
SB-0472	05/24/83	301	FIRST READING
	06/08/83	5	SECOND READING
	06/14/83	29	THIRD READING
SB-0473	05/24/83	301	FIRST READING
	06/08/83	5	SECOND READING
	06/14/83	29	THIRD READING
SB-0474	05/25/83	5	FIRST READING
	06/16/83	145	SECOND READING
SB-0476	05/25/83	229	FIRST READING
	06/08/83	5	SECOND READING
	06/14/83	29	THIRD READING
	11/02/83	9	VETO MESSAGE
	11/02/83	10	OUT OF RECORD
	11/02/83	31	VETO MESSAGE
SB-0477	05/27/83	233	FIRST READING
	06/26/83	83	SECOND READING
SB-0478	05/27/83	233	FIRST READING
	06/14/83	4	SECOND READING
	06/21/83	3	THIRD READING
SB-0479	05/27/83	233	FIRST READING
	06/14/83	20	SECOND READING
	06/24/83	8	THIRD READING
SB-0481	06/01/83	5	FIRST READING
	06/22/83	119	SECOND READING
	06/26/83	44	THIRD READING
	07/02/83	15	CONFERENCE
SB-0482	05/26/83	307	FIRST READING
	06/14/83	20	SECOND READING
	06/27/83	191	THIRD READING
	11/01/83	22	VETO MESSAGE
SB-0485	06/02/83	3	FIRST READING
	06/15/83	150	SECOND READING
	06/24/83	8	RECALLED
	06/24/83	9	THIRD READING
SB-0487	05/27/83	3	FIRST READING

PROGRAM-LRTRNMST
08/20/85

LEGISLATIVE INFORMATION SYSTEM
HOUSE OF REPRESENTATIVES

PAGE 261

MASTER TRANSCRIPT INDEX

BILL NUMBER	DATE	PAGE	ACTION
SB-0487 (cont'd)	06/14/83	4	SECOND READING
	06/21/83	3	THIRD READING
SB-0488	05/26/83	307	FIRST READING
SB-0489	05/25/83	229	FIRST READING
SB-0490	05/24/83	298	FIRST READING
	06/16/83	91	SECOND READING
	06/17/83	87	THIRD READING
	06/20/83	163	THIRD READING
SB-0492	05/24/83	301	FIRST READING
	06/15/83	151	SECOND READING
	06/24/83	10	RECALLED
	06/25/83	48	THIRD READING
	06/29/83	216	NON-CONCURRENCE
	07/01/83	80	CONFERENCE
	07/01/83	174	CONFERENCE
SB-0495	05/25/84	189	FIRST READING
	06/22/84	117	SECOND READING
	06/25/84	205	RECALLED
	06/25/84	210	THIRD READING
SB-0496	05/26/83	307	FIRST READING
	06/16/83	93	SECOND READING
	06/27/83	12	THIRD READING
	06/30/83	5	NON-CONCURRENCE
	11/02/83	152	VETO MESSAGE
SB-0498	05/27/83	3	FIRST READING
	06/22/83	121	SECOND READING
	06/26/83	47	THIRD READING
	06/29/83	213	NON-CONCURRENCE
	06/29/83	215	NON-CONCURRENCE
SB-0500	05/24/83	301	FIRST READING
	06/14/83	21	SECOND READING
	06/24/83	68	THIRD READING
SB-0501	05/24/83	301	FIRST READING
	06/08/83	16	SECOND READING
	06/24/83	10	THIRD READING
	11/02/83	148	VETO MESSAGE
SB-0502	06/01/83	5	FIRST READING
	06/08/83	32	SECOND READING
	06/24/83	11	THIRD READING
	11/02/83	42	VETO MESSAGE
	11/04/83	42	VETO MESSAGE

PROGRAM-LRTRNMST
08/20/85

LEGISLATIVE INFORMATION SYSTEM
HOUSE OF REPRESENTATIVES

PAGE 262

MASTER TRANSCRIPT INDEX

BILL NUMBER	DATE	PAGE	ACTION
SB-0503	05/25/83	229	FIRST READING
	06/08/83	44	SECOND READING
SB-0504	05/24/83	302	FIRST READING
	06/15/83	152	SECOND READING
	06/20/83	141	RECALLED
	06/24/83	11	THIRD READING
SB-0506	05/27/83	233	FIRST READING
	06/08/83	44	SECOND READING
	06/24/83	11	THIRD READING
SB-0507	05/26/83	303	FIRST READING
	06/08/83	5	SECOND READING
	06/15/83	33	SECOND READING
SB-0508	05/23/84	3	FIRST READING
SB-0509	05/23/84	310	FIRST READING
SB-0510	05/23/84	310	FIRST READING
SB-0511	05/26/83	307	FIRST READING
	06/15/83	37	SECOND READING
	06/27/83	359	THIRD READING
SB-0512	05/27/83	3	FIRST READING
	06/14/83	32	SECOND READING
	06/24/83	11	THIRD READING
	11/01/83	23	VETO MESSAGE
SB-0513	05/24/83	302	FIRST READING
	06/15/83	33	SECOND READING
	06/15/83	37	OUT OF RECORD
	06/15/83	57	SECOND READING
	06/27/83	355	THIRD READING
	06/29/83	216	NON-CONCURRENCE
	07/02/83	92	CONFERENCE
	07/02/83	95	OUT OF RECORD
	07/02/83	103	CONFERENCE
SB-0514	05/26/83	303	FIRST READING
	06/14/83	5	SECOND READING
	06/21/83	3	THIRD READING
SB-0515	05/27/83	233	FIRST READING
	06/21/83	227	SECOND READING
	06/21/83	227	HELD ON SECOND
	06/22/83	276	SECOND READING
	06/24/83	11	THIRD READING

PROGRAM-LRTRNMST
08/20/85
LEGISLATIVE INFORMATION SYSTEM
HOUSE OF REPRESENTATIVES
PAGE 263

MASTER TRANSCRIPT INDEX

BILL NUMBER	DATE	PAGE	ACTION
SB-0516	05/27/83	233	FIRST READING
	06/07/83	14	SECOND READING
	06/23/83	99	THIRD READING
SB-0517	05/25/83	229	FIRST READING
	06/15/83	37	SECOND READING
	06/20/83	105	RECALLED
SB-0518	05/25/83	229	FIRST READING
	06/07/83	14	SECOND READING
	06/23/83	263	THIRD READING
SB-0520	05/25/83	229	FIRST READING
	06/10/83	15	MOTION
	06/15/83	156	SECOND READING
	06/23/83	266	RECALLED
	06/23/83	273	THIRD READING
	11/02/83	48	VETO MESSAGE
SB-0521	05/25/83	229	FIRST READING
	06/16/83	149	SECOND READING
	06/24/83	174	RECALLED
	06/24/83	176	THIRD READING
	06/28/83	230	NON-CONCURRENCE
	07/01/83	81	CONFERENCE
	11/02/83	67	VETO MESSAGE
SB-0522	06/02/83	3	FIRST READING
	06/15/83	37	SECOND READING
	06/15/83	38	HELD ON SECOND
	06/20/83	69	SECOND READING
	06/27/83	13	THIRD READING
SB-0523	05/26/83	307	FIRST READING
	06/15/83	38	SECOND READING
SB-0524	05/27/83	233	FIRST READING
SB-0526	05/27/83	233	FIRST READING
	06/23/83	5	SECOND READING
	06/27/83	13	THIRD READING
	06/28/83	234	NON-CONCURRENCE
	06/28/83	238	TABLED
	06/28/83	244	NON-CONCURRENCE
	06/23/83	155	CONFERENCE
SB-0527	06/02/83	3	FIRST READING
	06/23/83	11	SECOND READING
SB-0529	05/24/83	302	FIRST READING
	06/15/83	39	SECOND READING

PROGRAM-LRTRNMST
08/20/85
LEGISLATIVE INFORMATION SYSTEM
HOUSE OF REPRESENTATIVES
PAGE 264

MASTER TRANSCRIPT INDEX

BILL NUMBER	DATE	PAGE	ACTION
SB-0529 (cont'd)	06/24/83	11	THIRD READING
SB-0530	05/24/83	302	FIRST READING
	06/15/83	39	SECOND READING
	06/24/83	11	THIRD READING
	06/28/83	231	NON-CONCURRENCE
	06/30/83	152	CONFERENCE
SB-0531	05/25/83	229	FIRST READING
	06/08/83	16	SECOND READING
	06/22/83	256	RECALLED
	06/23/83	100	THIRD READING
SB-0532	05/25/83	5	FIRST READING
	06/20/83	4	SECOND READING
SB-0536	06/01/83	5	FIRST READING
	06/22/83	146	SECOND READING
	06/22/83	160	HELD ON SECOND
	06/23/83	279	SECOND READING
	06/23/83	307	OUT OF RECORD
	06/23/83	313	HELD ON SECOND
	06/24/83	235	SECOND READING
	06/24/83	290	THIRD READING
	11/02/83	179	VETO MESSAGE
SB-0537	05/25/83	229	FIRST READING
	06/15/83	157	SECOND READING
SB-0541	05/24/83	302	FIRST READING
	06/15/83	158	SECOND READING
	06/05/84	8	SECOND READING
	06/12/84	37	THIRD READING
SB-0542	07/02/83	19	CONFERENCE
SB-0543	05/24/83	298	FIRST READING
SB-0544	05/26/83	307	FIRST READING
	06/14/83	5	SECOND READING
	06/21/83	4	THIRD READING
SB-0545	05/26/83	307	FIRST READING
	06/14/83	5	SECOND READING
	06/21/83	4	THIRD READING
SB-0546	05/26/83	308	FIRST READING
	06/15/83	158	SECOND READING
	10/18/83	74	MOTION
	10/19/83	72	SECOND READING
	10/19/83	72	HELD ON SECOND

PROGRAM-LRTRNMST
08/20/85

LEGISLATIVE INFORMATION SYSTEM
HOUSE OF REPRESENTATIVES

PAGE 265

MASTER TRANSCRIPT INDEX

BILL NUMBER	DATE	PAGE	ACTION
SB-0546 (cont'd)	11/01/83	85	SECOND READING
	11/01/83	86	HELD ON SECOND
	11/04/83	108	SECOND READING
	11/04/83	132	THIRD READING
SB-0547	05/26/83	308	FIRST READING
	06/20/83	26	SECOND READING
	06/22/83	191	THIRD READING
SB-0550	05/27/83	233	FIRST READING
	06/15/83	40	SECOND READING
SB-0551	05/25/83	229	FIRST READING
	06/15/83	2	SECOND READING
	06/21/83	4	THIRD READING
SB-0552	06/02/83	7	FIRST READING
SB-0557	05/26/83	308	FIRST READING
	06/14/83	33	SECOND READING
	06/24/83	11	THIRD READING
	06/25/83	57	THIRD READING
	06/28/83	232	NON-CONCURRENCE
	07/02/83	123	CONFERENCE
	07/02/83	162	CONFERENCE
SB-0559	05/24/83	302	FIRST READING
	06/07/83	15	SECOND READING
	06/20/83	142	RECALLED
	06/24/83	11	THIRD READING
	06/24/83	41	RECALLED
	06/24/83	41	THIRD READING
SB-0561	05/24/83	302	FIRST READING
	06/14/83	5	SECOND READING
	06/21/83	4	THIRD READING
SB-0563	06/01/83	6	FIRST READING
	06/10/83	20	MOTION
SB-0564	05/27/83	2	FIRST READING
SB-0565	05/27/83	234	FIRST READING
	06/23/83	12	SECOND READING
SB-0568	05/26/83	303	FIRST READING
	06/15/83	40	SECOND READING
	06/27/83	371	RECALLED
	06/27/83	372	THIRD READING
SB-0569	05/26/83	303	FIRST READING

PROGRAM-LRTRNMST
08/20/85

LEGISLATIVE INFORMATION SYSTEM
HOUSE OF REPRESENTATIVES

PAGE 266

MASTER TRANSCRIPT INDEX

BILL NUMBER	DATE	PAGE	ACTION
SB-0569 (cont'd)	06/08/83	16	SECOND READING
SB-0570	06/01/83	6	FIRST READING
	06/15/83	159	SECOND READING
	06/27/83	360	THIRD READING
SB-0571	05/26/83	308	FIRST READING
	06/08/83	5	SECOND READING
	06/15/83	40	SECOND READING
	06/22/83	193	THIRD READING
	11/02/83	149	VETO MESSAGE
SB-0572	05/24/83	302	FIRST READING
	06/08/83	16	SECOND READING
SB-0573	05/25/83	229	FIRST READING
	06/08/83	17	SECOND READING
SB-0574	05/25/83	229	FIRST READING
	06/08/83	17	SECOND READING
	06/24/83	184	THIRD READING
SB-0576	05/25/83	229	FIRST READING
	06/16/83	95	SECOND READING
	06/24/83	11	THIRD READING
	11/01/83	24	VETO MESSAGE
SB-0578	05/25/83	230	FIRST READING
	06/15/83	159	SECOND READING
	06/22/83	257	RECALLED
	06/23/83	216	THIRD READING
	06/28/83	233	NON-CONCURRENCE
	07/01/83	291	CONFERENCE
SB-0581	05/26/83	308	FIRST READING
	06/15/83	160	SECOND READING
	06/26/83	93	RECALLED
	06/27/83	293	THIRD READING
	11/01/83	26	VETO MESSAGE
SB-0582	05/24/83	298	FIRST READING
	06/08/83	44	SECOND READING
	06/24/83	11	THIRD READING
	11/01/83	30	VETO MESSAGE
SB-0583	05/24/83	302	FIRST READING
	06/08/83	5	SECOND READING
	06/14/83	30	THIRD READING
	11/02/83	73	VETO MESSAGE
SB-0586	05/27/83	234	FIRST READING

BILL NUMBER	DATE	PAGE	ACTION
SB-0586 (cont'd)	06/14/83	5	SECOND READING
	06/21/83	4	THIRD READING
SB-0587	05/26/83	308	FIRST READING
SB-0588	05/25/83	230	FIRST READING
	06/07/83	15	SECOND READING
	06/20/83	143	RECALLED
	06/23/83	13	SECOND READING
SB-0589	05/25/83	230	FIRST READING
	06/16/83	96	SECOND READING
	06/27/83	326	THIRD READING
	06/29/83	218	NON-CONCURRENCE
	07/01/83	248	CONFERENCE
	11/04/83	82	CONFERENCE
SB-0590	05/24/83	305	FIRST READING
	06/08/83	5	SECOND READING
	06/14/83	49	SECOND READING
	06/24/83	11	THIRD READING
SB-0591	05/27/83	234	FIRST READING
	06/15/83	159	SECOND READING
	06/23/83	147	THIRD READING
	11/02/83	120	VETO MESSAGE
SB-0593	05/24/83	302	FIRST READING
	06/08/83	5	SECOND READING
	06/14/83	30	THIRD READING
SB-0594	05/24/83	302	FIRST READING
	06/08/83	5	SECOND READING
	06/14/83	30	THIRD READING
SB-0595	05/24/83	304	FIRST READING
	06/08/83	6	SECOND READING
	06/14/83	30	THIRD READING
SB-0597	05/26/83	308	FIRST READING
	06/15/83	2	SECOND READING
	06/21/83	4	THIRD READING
SB-0598	05/26/83	308	FIRST READING
	06/15/83	2	SECOND READING
	06/20/83	69	SECOND READING
	06/24/83	11	THIRD READING
	11/02/83	10	VETO MESSAGE
SB-0599	05/25/83	319	FIRST READING
	06/07/83	15	SECOND READING

BILL NUMBER	DATE	PAGE	ACTION
SB-0599 (cont'd)	06/27/83	335	RECALLED
	06/27/83	337	THIRD READING
	06/29/83	221	NON-CONCURRENCE
	07/02/83	6	CONFERENCE
SB-0600	05/26/83	308	FIRST READING
	06/08/83	18	SECOND READING
	06/24/83	11	THIRD READING
SB-0603	05/27/83	3	FIRST READING
	06/08/83	46	SECOND READING
	06/24/83	11	THIRD READING
SB-0604	05/24/83	304	FIRST READING
SB-0607	05/25/83	230	FIRST READING
	06/08/83	6	SECOND READING
	06/16/83	97	SECOND READING
	06/27/83	338	THIRD READING
	11/02/83	11	VETO MESSAGE
SB-0608	05/25/83	230	FIRST READING
	06/08/83	6	SECOND READING
	06/14/83	30	THIRD READING
SB-0613	05/26/83	308	FIRST READING
	06/16/83	157	SECOND READING
	06/26/83	66	RECALLED
	06/27/83	15	THIRD READING
SB-0616	05/26/83	1	FIRST READING
	06/14/83	5	SECOND READING
	06/21/83	4	THIRD READING
SB-0618	05/26/83	303	FIRST READING
	06/15/83	161	SECOND READING
SB-0619	05/26/83	304	FIRST READING
	06/15/83	161	SECOND READING
	06/24/83	12	RECALLED
	06/25/83	67	THIRD READING
	11/01/83	36	VETO MESSAGE
SB-0620	06/01/83	6	FIRST READING
	06/16/83	161	SECOND READING
	06/26/83	67	RECALLED
	06/26/83	74	RECALLED
	06/27/83	339	THIRD READING
	06/29/83	217	NON-CONCURRENCE
SB-0621	05/24/83	302	FIRST READING

MASTER TRANSCRIPT INDEX

BILL NUMBER	DATE	PAGE	ACTION
SB-0621 (cont'd)	06/20/83	70	SECOND READING
	06/24/83	12	RECALLED
	06/24/83	14	THIRD READING
	06/29/83	222	NON-CONCURRENCE
SB-0623	05/26/83	308	FIRST READING
	06/08/83	6	SECOND READING
	06/14/83	30	THIRD READING
SB-0624	05/27/83	234	FIRST READING
	06/15/83	41	SECOND READING
	06/24/83	14	THIRD READING
SB-0626	06/01/83	6	FIRST READING
	06/15/83	42	SECOND READING
	06/15/83	42	HELD ON SECOND
	06/22/84	111	SECOND READING
SB-0628	05/27/83	234	FIRST READING
	06/08/83	46	SECOND READING
	06/27/83	382	THIRD READING
SB-0631	05/25/83	319	FIRST READING
	06/09/83	7	SECOND READING
SB-0632	05/25/83	319	FIRST READING
	06/15/83	42	SECOND READING
	06/15/83	42	HELD ON SECOND
	06/16/83	98	SECOND READING
	06/16/83	99	HELD ON SECOND
	06/20/83	72	SECOND READING
	06/27/83	384	THIRD READING
SB-0637	05/26/83	304	FIRST READING
	06/15/83	42	SECOND READING
SB-0638	05/26/83	308	FIRST READING
	06/15/83	43	SECOND READING
	06/15/83	44	OUT OF RECORD
	06/16/83	99	SECOND READING
	06/27/83	327	THIRD READING
SB-0643	05/27/83	4	FIRST READING
	06/16/83	162	SECOND READING
	06/22/83	194	THIRD READING
	11/02/83	74	VETO MESSAGE
SB-0644	05/26/83	1	FIRST READING
	06/16/83	162	SECOND READING
	06/24/83	14	THIRD READING

MASTER TRANSCRIPT INDEX

BILL NUMBER	DATE	PAGE	ACTION
SB-0645	05/26/83	2	FIRST READING
	06/16/83	163	SECOND READING
	06/24/83	14	THIRD READING
SB-0648	05/26/83	308	FIRST READING
	06/14/83	5	SECOND READING
	06/21/83	4	THIRD READING
SB-0649	05/27/83	234	FIRST READING
SB-0652	05/27/83	4	FIRST READING
	06/08/83	6	SECOND READING
	06/14/83	30	THIRD READING
SB-0653	05/27/83	2	FIRST READING
	06/08/83	46	SECOND READING
	06/17/83	91	THIRD READING
SB-0655	05/26/83	308	FIRST READING
	06/08/83	6	SECOND READING
	06/14/83	30	THIRD READING
SB-0656	05/26/83	309	FIRST READING
SB-0659	05/24/83	302	FIRST READING
	06/14/83	5	SECOND READING
	06/15/83	44	SECOND READING
	06/24/83	14	THIRD READING
SB-0665	06/01/83	6	FIRST READING
SB-0668	05/26/83	304	FIRST READING
	06/15/83	162	SECOND READING
	06/26/83	69	RECALLED
	06/27/83	361	RECALLED
	06/27/83	361	THIRD READING
	06/29/83	222	NON-CONCURRENCE
	10/18/83	75	MOTION
	10/20/83	119	CONFERENCE
	11/03/83	27	CONFERENCE
	11/04/83	43	VETO MESSAGE
SB-0669	05/26/83	304	FIRST READING
	06/15/83	163	SECOND READING
	06/15/83	165	HELD ON SECOND
	06/16/83	164	SECOND READING
	06/27/83	362	THIRD READING
SB-0671	05/26/83	309	FIRST READING
	06/15/83	44	SECOND READING
	06/05/84	7	SECOND READING

BILL NUMBER	DATE	PAGE	ACTION
SB-0671 (cont'd)	06/05/84	8	HELD ON SECOND
	06/06/84	13	SECOND READING
	06/12/84	6	THIRD READING
SB-0673	05/26/83	304	FIRST READING
	06/08/83	47	SECOND READING
	06/27/83	192	THIRD READING
SB-0674	05/26/83	2	FIRST READING
SB-0675	05/26/83	309	FIRST READING
	06/14/83	5	SECOND READING
	06/21/83	4	THIRD READING
SB-0676	05/26/83	304	FIRST READING
	06/08/83	6	SECOND READING
	06/14/83	30	THIRD READING
SB-0677	05/26/83	2	FIRST READING
	06/15/83	165	SECOND READING
	06/20/83	65	RECALLED
	06/27/83	262	THIRD READING
SB-0678	05/26/83	304	FIRST READING
	06/09/83	8	SECOND READING
	06/24/83	68	THIRD READING
SB-0680	05/26/83	304	FIRST READING
	06/22/83	122	SECOND READING
	06/26/83	49	THIRD READING
	06/29/83	213	NON-CONCURRENCE
SB-0681	05/26/83	304	FIRST READING
	06/15/83	44	SECOND READING
	06/17/83	97	THIRD READING
SB-0682	05/26/83	304	FIRST READING
	06/08/83	19	SECOND READING
	06/24/83	71	THIRD READING
SB-0688	05/24/83	302	FIRST READING
	06/08/83	6	SECOND READING
	06/14/83	30	THIRD READING
	11/01/83	67	VETO MESSAGE
SB-0690	05/27/83	234	FIRST READING
	06/14/83	5	SECOND READING
	06/20/83	72	SECOND READING
	06/20/83	80	OUT OF RECORD
	06/21/83	227	SECOND READING
	06/21/83	227	HELD ON SECOND

BILL NUMBER	DATE	PAGE	ACTION
SB-0690 (cont'd)	06/22/83	276	SECOND READING
	06/24/83	15	RECALLED
	06/24/83	16	THIRD READING
	06/28/83	238	NON-CONCURRENCE
	07/01/83	145	CONFERENCE
	07/02/83	105	CONFERENCE
SB-0695	05/24/83	302	FIRST READING
	06/15/83	44	SECOND READING
	06/24/83	16	THIRD READING
	11/02/83	12	VETO MESSAGE
	11/02/83	13	OUT OF RECORD
	11/02/83	84	VETO MESSAGE
SB-0696	05/26/83	309	FIRST READING
	06/15/83	167	SECOND READING
	06/24/83	16	THIRD READING
SB-0697	05/27/83	234	FIRST READING
	06/08/83	6	SECOND READING
	06/14/83	30	THIRD READING
	11/02/83	13	VETO MESSAGE
SB-0699	05/27/83	3	FIRST READING
	06/14/83	5	SECOND READING
	06/21/83	4	THIRD READING
SB-0700	05/24/83	302	FIRST READING
	06/15/83	45	SECOND READING
	06/22/83	57	THIRD READING
SB-0702	05/24/83	303	FIRST READING
	06/08/83	48	SECOND READING
	06/15/83	141	RECALLED
	06/24/83	16	THIRD READING
	06/28/83	239	NON-CONCURRENCE
	06/30/83	122	CONFERENCE
	07/02/83	65	CONFERENCE
SB-0703	05/24/83	303	FIRST READING
	06/15/83	3	SECOND READING
	06/21/83	4	THIRD READING
SB-0705	05/26/83	304	FIRST READING
	06/08/83	6	SECOND READING
	06/14/83	30	THIRD READING
SB-0706	05/26/83	309	FIRST READING
	06/08/83	6	SECOND READING
	06/14/83	30	THIRD READING

PROGRAM-LRTRNMST
08/20/85
LEGISLATIVE INFORMATION SYSTEM
HOUSE OF REPRESENTATIVES
PAGE 273

MASTER TRANSCRIPT INDEX

BILL NUMBER	DATE	PAGE	ACTION
SB-0709	05/26/83	309	FIRST READING
	06/08/83	6	SECOND READING
	06/14/83	35	SECOND READING
	06/24/83	16	THIRD READING
SB-0712	05/24/83	303	FIRST READING
	06/08/83	6	SECOND READING
	06/14/83	30	THIRD READING
SB-0713	05/26/83	304	FIRST READING
	06/08/83	19	SECOND READING
	06/27/83	341	THIRD READING
	11/01/83	30	VETO MESSAGE
SB-0714	05/26/83	304	FIRST READING
	06/22/83	123	SECOND READING
	06/26/83	51	THIRD READING
	06/29/83	213	NON-CONCURRENCE
	07/02/83	36	CONFERENCE
	07/02/83	38	OUT OF RECORD
	07/02/83	57	CONFERENCE
SB-0715	05/26/83	304	FIRST READING
	06/22/83	130	SECOND READING
	06/26/83	55	THIRD READING
	06/29/83	213	NON-CONCURRENCE
SB-0716	05/26/83	309	FIRST READING
	06/08/83	6	SECOND READING
	06/14/83	30	THIRD READING
SB-0717	05/27/83	234	FIRST READING
	06/08/83	48	SECOND READING
	06/27/83	383	THIRD READING
SB-0719	05/26/83	305	FIRST READING
	06/15/83	45	SECOND READING
	06/27/83	378	THIRD READING
SB-0721	05/26/83	309	FIRST READING
	06/08/83	6	SECOND READING
	06/15/83	46	SECOND READING
	06/24/83	16	RECALLED
	06/24/83	16	THIRD READING
SB-0725	05/24/83	303	FIRST READING
	06/14/83	5	SECOND READING
	06/21/83	4	THIRD READING
SB-0726	05/26/83	2	FIRST READING
	06/15/83	47	SECOND READING

PROGRAM-LRTRNMST
08/20/85
LEGISLATIVE INFORMATION SYSTEM
HOUSE OF REPRESENTATIVES
PAGE 274

MASTER TRANSCRIPT INDEX

BILL NUMBER	DATE	PAGE	ACTION
SB-0726 (cont'd)	06/26/83	71	RECALLED
	06/27/83	16	THIRD READING
	06/30/83	10	NON-CONCURRENCE
	07/01/83	85	CONFERENCE
	11/01/83	70	VETO MESSAGE
SB-0727	05/27/83	234	FIRST READING
	06/16/83	108	SECOND READING
	06/24/83	165	THIRD READING
SB-0728	05/27/83	234	FIRST READING
	06/14/83	36	SECOND READING
	06/27/83	367	RECALLED
	06/27/83	367	THIRD READING
	06/29/83	217	NON-CONCURRENCE
SB-0729	05/26/83	305	FIRST READING
SB-0731	05/24/83	303	FIRST READING
	06/14/83	36	SECOND READING
	06/24/83	17	THIRD READING
	11/02/83	76	VETO MESSAGE
SB-0733	05/26/83	309	FIRST READING
	06/14/83	37	SECOND READING
SB-0736	05/26/83	2	FIRST READING
	06/09/83	9	SECOND READING
	06/27/83	266	RECALLED
	06/27/83	268	THIRD READING
	11/01/83	31	VETO MESSAGE
SB-0738	05/26/83	309	FIRST READING
	06/15/83	49	SECOND READING
	06/15/83	51	OUT OF RECORD
	06/16/83	115	SECOND READING
	06/24/83	17	THIRD READING
SB-0739	05/27/83	234	FIRST READING
	06/15/83	51	SECOND READING
	06/24/83	17	THIRD READING
SB-0740	05/27/83	234	FIRST READING
	06/15/83	168	SECOND READING
	06/27/83	257	THIRD READING
	11/02/83	14	VETO MESSAGE
SB-0743	05/24/83	303	FIRST READING
	06/08/83	6	SECOND READING
	06/14/83	31	THIRD READING

PROGRAM-LRTRNMST
08/20/85
LEGISLATIVE INFORMATION SYSTEM
HOUSE OF REPRESENTATIVES
PAGE 275

MASTER TRANSCRIPT INDEX

BILL NUMBER	DATE	PAGE	ACTION
SB-0745	05/27/83	234	FIRST READING
	06/08/83	32	SECOND READING
SB-0749	05/26/83	2	FIRST READING
	06/03/83	7	SECOND READING
	06/20/83	153	RECALLED
	06/22/83	276	SECOND READING
	06/27/83	354	THIRD READING
	06/29/83	217	NON-CONCURRENCE
SB-0751	05/27/83	3	FIRST READING
	06/15/83	168	SECOND READING
	04/03/84	4	SECOND READING
	04/04/84	19	RECALLED
	04/10/84	10	THIRD READING
SB-0757	05/26/83	309	FIRST READING
	06/08/83	35	SECOND READING
	06/23/83	217	THIRD READING
SB-0761	05/26/83	309	FIRST READING
SB-0762	05/27/83	244	FIRST READING
	06/08/83	6	SECOND READING
	06/14/83	31	THIRD READING
SB-0766	05/26/83	309	FIRST READING
	06/22/83	132	SECOND READING
	06/26/83	57	THIRD READING
	06/29/83	213	NON-CONCURRENCE
SB-0768	05/27/83	234	FIRST READING
	06/16/83	117	SECOND READING
	06/24/83	17	THIRD READING
	06/24/83	155	RECALLED
SB-0772	05/27/83	235	FIRST READING
	06/14/83	5	SECOND READING
	06/21/83	4	THIRD READING
SB-0773	05/26/83	310	FIRST READING
SB-0774	06/01/83	6	FIRST READING
	06/15/83	171	SECOND READING
	06/15/83	171	HELD ON SECOND
	06/17/83	12	MOTION
	06/20/83	27	SECOND READING
	06/20/83	37	HELD ON SECOND
	06/23/83	15	SECOND READING
	06/23/83	29	MOTION
	06/23/83	67	MOTION

PROGRAM-LRTRNMST
08/20/85
LEGISLATIVE INFORMATION SYSTEM
HOUSE OF REPRESENTATIVES
PAGE 276

MASTER TRANSCRIPT INDEX

BILL NUMBER	DATE	PAGE	ACTION
SB-0774 (cont'd)	06/27/83	94	MOTION
SB-0775	05/26/83	310	FIRST READING
	06/15/83	168	SECOND READING
	06/26/83	63	RECALLED
	06/27/83	207	THIRD READING
SB-0776	05/26/83	309	FIRST READING
	06/15/83	171	SECOND READING
	06/22/83	60	THIRD READING
	11/02/83	153	VETO MESSAGE
SB-0779	05/26/83	310	FIRST READING
	06/15/83	52	SECOND READING
	06/24/83	72	THIRD READING
SB-0780	05/26/83	305	FIRST READING
	06/14/83	5	SECOND READING
	06/21/83	4	THIRD READING
SB-0786	05/26/83	310	FIRST READING
	06/17/83	2	SECOND READING
	06/17/83	10	OUT OF RECORD
	06/20/83	37	SECOND READING
	06/20/83	37	HELD ON SECOND
	06/22/83	146	SECOND READING
	06/22/83	269	RECALLED
	06/23/83	218	MOTION
	06/23/83	222	THIRD READING
SB-0787	05/26/83	310	FIRST READING
	06/23/83	162	SECOND READING
	06/24/83	17	THIRD READING
SB-0788	05/26/83	310	FIRST READING
	06/14/83	5	SECOND READING
	06/20/83	81	SECOND READING
SB-0789	05/27/83	235	FIRST READING
	06/08/83	35	SECOND READING
	06/23/83	230	THIRD READING
SB-0790	05/24/83	303	FIRST READING
	06/15/83	171	SECOND READING
	06/24/83	17	THIRD READING
SB-0791	05/27/83	4	FIRST READING
	06/15/83	172	SECOND READING
	06/27/83	292	THIRD READING
SB-0792	05/26/83	310	FIRST READING

BILL NUMBER	DATE	PAGE	ACTION
SB-0792 (cont'd)	06/15/83	52	SECOND READING
	06/26/83	81	RECALLED
	06/27/83	294	THIRD READING
	06/27/83	299	RECALLED
	06/27/83	299	THIRD READING
SB-0794	05/26/83	310	FIRST READING
	06/15/83	67	SECOND READING
	06/24/83	17	THIRD READING
	11/02/83	15	VETO MESSAGE
SB-0795	05/26/83	310	FIRST READING
	06/14/83	6	SECOND READING
	06/16/83	118	SECOND READING
	06/27/83	23	THIRD READING
SB-0796	05/26/83	310	FIRST READING
	06/15/83	172	SECOND READING
	06/24/83	17	THIRD READING
SB-0797	05/26/83	310	FIRST READING
	06/15/83	63	SECOND READING
	06/24/83	17	THIRD READING
SB-0799	05/24/83	303	FIRST READING
	06/15/83	63	SECOND READING
	06/27/83	212	THIRD READING
SB-0800	05/26/83	310	FIRST READING
	06/26/83	82	SECOND READING
	06/27/83	271	RECALLED
	06/27/83	272	OUT OF RECORD
	06/27/83	304	SECOND READING
	06/27/83	308	THIRD READING
SB-0803	05/27/83	4	FIRST READING
	06/08/83	7	SECOND READING
	06/14/83	31	THIRD READING
SB-0805	05/27/83	4	FIRST READING
	06/08/83	7	SECOND READING
	06/14/83	31	THIRD READING
SB-0806	05/26/83	311	FIRST READING
	06/14/83	6	SECOND READING
	06/21/83	4	THIRD READING
SB-0807	05/27/83	235	FIRST READING
	06/08/83	7	SECOND READING
	06/14/83	31	THIRD READING

BILL NUMBER	DATE	PAGE	ACTION
SB-0808	05/27/83	235	FIRST READING
	06/09/83	22	SECOND READING
	06/24/83	17	THIRD READING
SB-0809	05/27/83	235	FIRST READING
	06/15/83	3	SECOND READING
	06/21/83	4	THIRD READING
SB-0811	05/27/83	235	FIRST READING
	06/14/83	37	SECOND READING
	06/24/83	17	THIRD READING
	06/28/83	240	NON-CONCURRENCE
	06/30/83	144	CONFERENCE
	11/02/83	161	VETO MESSAGE
SB-0812	05/27/83	235	FIRST READING
	06/14/83	6	SECOND READING
	06/21/83	4	THIRD READING
SB-0814	05/27/83	235	FIRST READING
	06/14/83	6	SECOND READING
	06/21/83	4	THIRD READING
SB-0815	05/27/83	235	FIRST READING
	06/15/83	64	SECOND READING
	06/23/83	235	THIRD READING
SB-0816	05/27/83	4	FIRST READING
	06/08/83	7	SECOND READING
	06/14/83	31	THIRD READING
SB-0817	05/27/83	235	FIRST READING
	06/08/83	7	SECOND READING
	06/14/83	31	THIRD READING
SB-0819	06/14/83	31	THIRD READING
SB-0820	05/26/83	311	FIRST READING
	06/15/83	173	SECOND READING
	06/22/83	66	THIRD READING
SB-0821	05/27/83	235	FIRST READING
SB-0822	05/27/83	235	FIRST READING
	06/14/83	40	SECOND READING
	06/24/83	17	THIRD READING
SB-0824	05/26/83	310	FIRST READING
	06/14/83	6	SECOND READING
	06/15/83	64	SECOND READING
	06/27/83	213	RECALLED

PROGRAM-LRTRNMST
08/20/85
LEGISLATIVE INFORMATION SYSTEM
HOUSE OF REPRESENTATIVES
PAGE 279

MASTER TRANSCRIPT INDEX

BILL NUMBER	DATE	PAGE	ACTION
SB-0824 (cont'd)	06/27/83	214	THIRD READING
	06/29/83	219	NON-CONCURRENCE
	07/01/83	292	CONFERENCE
	11/02/83	89	VETO MESSAGE
SB-0826	05/25/83	230	FIRST READING
	06/15/83	173	SECOND READING
	06/27/83	369	THIRD READING
	11/02/83	79	VETO MESSAGE
SB-0827	05/27/83	235	FIRST READING
	06/14/83	6	SECOND READING
	06/21/83	5	THIRD READING
SB-0831	05/26/83	310	FIRST READING
	06/08/83	7	SECOND READING
	06/15/83	64	SECOND READING
	06/24/83	17	THIRD READING
SB-0832	05/27/83	235	FIRST READING
	06/15/83	173	SECOND READING
SB-0833	05/26/83	311	FIRST READING
	06/14/83	6	SECOND READING
	06/20/83	83	SECOND READING
	06/06/84	10	SECOND READING
	06/12/84	10	THIRD READING
	06/29/84	21	NON-CONCURRENCE
	06/30/84	227	CONFERENCE
	12/11/84	4	VETO MESSAGE
SB-0834	05/26/83	311	FIRST READING
	06/15/83	6	SECOND READING
	06/15/83	64	SECOND READING
	06/24/83	17	THIRD READING
SB-0835	05/26/83	311	FIRST READING
	06/15/83	65	SECOND READING
	06/06/84	10	SECOND READING
	06/06/84	11	OUT OF RECORD
	06/13/84	8	SECOND READING
	06/14/84	53	THIRD READING
SB-0836	05/26/83	311	FIRST READING
	06/14/83	6	SECOND READING
	06/15/83	66	SECOND READING
	06/24/83	18	THIRD READING
SB-0838	05/26/83	311	FIRST READING
	06/15/83	174	SECOND READING
	06/20/83	145	RECALLED

PROGRAM-LRTRNMST
08/20/85
LEGISLATIVE INFORMATION SYSTEM
HOUSE OF REPRESENTATIVES
PAGE 280

MASTER TRANSCRIPT INDEX

BILL NUMBER	DATE	PAGE	ACTION
SB-0838 (cont'd)	06/23/83	151	THIRD READING
SB-0840	05/26/83	312	FIRST READING
	05/27/83	236	FIRST READING
	06/14/83	6	SECOND READING
	06/21/83	5	THIRD READING
SB-0847	05/27/83	236	FIRST READING
	06/14/83	62	SECOND READING
	06/24/83	18	RECALLED
	06/24/83	18	THIRD READING
SB-0849	05/26/83	311	FIRST READING
	06/15/83	174	SECOND READING
	06/23/83	149	THIRD READING
	06/29/83	41	NON-CONCURRENCE
	07/01/83	151	CONFERENCE
	11/02/83	18	VETO MESSAGE
SB-0850	05/26/83	311	FIRST READING
	06/09/83	22	SECOND READING
	06/24/83	18	THIRD READING
SB-0851	05/27/83	236	FIRST READING
	06/10/83	33	MOTION
SB-0852	05/27/83	236	FIRST READING
	06/15/83	176	SECOND READING
	06/24/83	18	THIRD READING
SB-0854	05/26/83	311	FIRST READING
	06/08/83	7	SECOND READING
	06/14/83	31	THIRD READING
SB-0858	05/24/83	305	FIRST READING
	06/15/83	67	SECOND READING
	06/24/83	18	THIRD READING
SB-0859	05/26/83	311	FIRST READING
	06/14/83	6	SECOND READING
	06/21/83	221	SECOND READING
	06/21/83	222	HELD ON SECOND
	06/22/83	67	SECOND READING
	06/22/83	68	THIRD READING
SB-0860	05/26/83	311	FIRST READING
	06/15/83	177	SECOND READING
	06/24/83	18	RECALLED
	06/24/83	19	THIRD READING
SB-0862	05/27/83	236	FIRST READING

BILL NUMBER	DATE	PAGE	ACTION
SB-0862 (cont'd)	06/14/83	6	SECOND READING
	06/16/83	118	SECOND READING
SB-0863	05/26/83	311	FIRST READING
	06/15/83	67	SECOND READING
	06/24/83	19	THIRD READING
SB-0864	05/26/83	311	FIRST READING
	06/14/83	40	SECOND READING
	06/24/83	19	RECALLED
	06/24/83	20	THIRD READING
	11/02/83	162	VETO MESSAGE
SB-0866	05/27/83	236	FIRST READING
	06/14/83	42	SECOND READING
	06/24/83	20	THIRD READING
SB-0873	05/27/83	236	FIRST READING
SB-0876	05/27/83	236	FIRST READING
SB-0879	05/27/83	236	FIRST READING
	06/16/83	118	SECOND READING
	06/27/83	29	RECALLED
	06/27/83	32	THIRD READING
	06/28/83	244	NON-CONCURRENCE
	07/02/83	40	CONFERENCE
SB-0881	05/26/83	311	FIRST READING
	06/07/83	12	SECOND READING
	06/24/83	20	THIRD READING
SB-0882	05/26/83	313	FIRST READING
	06/07/83	12	SECOND READING
	06/24/83	20	RECALLED
	06/24/83	21	THIRD READING
SB-0883	05/26/83	313	FIRST READING
	06/14/83	40	SECOND READING
	06/22/83	195	THIRD READING
SB-0886	05/27/83	236	FIRST READING
SB-0887	05/27/83	236	FIRST READING
	06/15/83	67	SECOND READING
	06/24/83	21	THIRD READING
SB-0891	05/27/83	236	FIRST READING
	06/21/83	222	SECOND READING
	06/21/83	222	HELD ON SECOND
	06/22/83	161	SECOND READING

BILL NUMBER	DATE	PAGE	ACTION
SB-0891 (cont'd)	06/24/83	181	THIRD READING
	11/02/83	16	VETO MESSAGE
SB-0895	05/27/83	236	FIRST READING
	06/15/83	68	SECOND READING
	06/24/83	21	THIRD READING
SB-0896	05/26/83	313	FIRST READING
	05/27/83	236	FIRST READING
	06/15/83	68	SECOND READING
	06/24/83	21	THIRD READING
SB-0899	05/26/83	313	FIRST READING
	06/15/83	3	SECOND READING
	06/21/83	5	THIRD READING
SB-0902	05/26/83	310	FIRST READING
	05/27/83	244	FIRST READING
SB-0903	05/27/83	236	FIRST READING
	06/15/83	68	SECOND READING
	06/24/83	21	THIRD READING
	06/28/83	241	NON-CONCURRENCE
	06/29/83	38	MOTION
	06/29/83	39	NON-CONCURRENCE
SB-0904	05/27/83	236	FIRST READING
	06/14/83	42	SECOND READING
	06/27/83	373	THIRD READING
SB-0906	06/02/83	7	FIRST READING
	06/15/83	3	SECOND READING
	06/21/83	5	THIRD READING
	11/02/83	19	VETO MESSAGE
SB-0907	06/15/83	3	SECOND READING
SB-0909	05/24/83	303	FIRST READING
SB-0910	05/26/83	313	FIRST READING
	06/15/83	69	SECOND READING
	06/24/83	21	THIRD READING
SB-0911	05/24/83	303	FIRST READING
	06/08/83	7	SECOND READING
SB-0912	05/26/83	313	FIRST READING
	06/07/83	12	SECOND READING
	06/24/83	21	THIRD READING
SB-0913	05/27/83	237	FIRST READING

BILL NUMBER	DATE	PAGE	ACTION
SB-0913(cont'd)	06/14/83	6	SECOND READING
	06/21/83	5	THIRD READING
SB-0915	05/27/83	237	FIRST READING
	06/08/83	7	SECOND READING
	06/14/83	31	THIRD READING
SB-0917	05/27/83	237	FIRST READING
	06/08/83	7	SECOND READING
	06/14/83	31	THIRD READING
SB-0919	05/26/83	313	FIRST READING
	06/14/83	6	SECOND READING
	06/15/83	70	SECOND READING
	06/20/83	105	RECALLED
	06/27/83	34	THIRD READING
	06/29/83	219	NON-CONCURRENCE
	07/01/83	294	CONFERENCE
	11/01/83	39	VETO MESSAGE
SB-0923	05/26/83	313	FIRST READING
	06/10/83	25	MOTION
	06/15/83	177	SECOND READING
	06/24/83	21	RECALLED
	06/24/83	22	OUT OF RECORD
	06/24/83	42	SECOND READING
	06/24/83	42	THIRD READING
	06/28/83	242	NON-CONCURRENCE
	06/28/83	243	OUT OF RECORD
	06/29/83	9	NON-CONCURRENCE
	07/01/83	86	CONFERENCE
SB-0924	05/26/83	313	FIRST READING
	06/15/83	71	SECOND READING
	06/24/83	23	THIRD READING
SB-0926	05/26/83	312	FIRST READING
	05/27/83	237	FIRST READING
	06/14/83	43	SECOND READING
	06/27/83	328	THIRD READING
SB-0927	05/26/83	313	FIRST READING
SB-0928	05/26/83	313	FIRST READING
SB-0929	05/26/83	313	FIRST READING
SB-0931	05/27/83	237	FIRST READING
	06/15/83	178	SECOND READING
	06/22/83	258	RECALLED
	06/24/83	23	THIRD READING

BILL NUMBER	DATE	PAGE	ACTION
SB-0932	05/27/83	237	FIRST READING
SB-0933	05/27/83	237	FIRST READING
	06/14/83	6	SECOND READING
	06/15/83	71	SECOND READING
	06/24/83	23	RECALLED
	06/24/83	24	THIRD READING
SB-0934	05/27/83	2	FIRST READING
	06/14/83	43	SECOND READING
	06/22/83	196	THIRD READING
SB-0936	06/02/83	7	FIRST READING
SB-0937	05/27/83	237	FIRST READING
	06/15/83	3	SECOND READING
	06/21/83	5	THIRD READING
SB-0938	05/26/83	312	FIRST READING
	05/27/83	237	FIRST READING
	06/20/83	39	SECOND READING
	06/23/83	31	RECALLED
	06/24/83	73	THIRD READING
SB-0941	05/27/83	237	FIRST READING
	06/08/83	7	SECOND READING
	06/14/83	31	THIRD READING
SB-0942	05/26/83	312	FIRST READING
	05/27/83	237	FIRST READING
	06/07/83	16	SECOND READING
	06/09/83	23	SECOND READING
	06/09/83	24	HELD ON SECOND
	06/15/83	178	SECOND READING
	06/24/83	24	THIRD READING
SB-0943	05/27/83	237	FIRST READING
	06/20/83	39	SECOND READING
	06/22/83	198	THIRD READING
SB-0945	05/27/83	237	FIRST READING
	06/14/83	44	SECOND READING
	06/27/83	215	THIRD READING
SB-0946	05/27/83	237	FIRST READING
	06/14/83	6	SECOND READING
	06/21/83	5	THIRD READING
SB-0947	05/27/83	238	FIRST READING
	06/14/83	7	SECOND READING
	06/21/83	5	THIRD READING

PROGRAM-LRTRNMST
08/20/85

LEGISLATIVE INFORMATION SYSTEM
HOUSE OF REPRESENTATIVES

PAGE 285

MASTER TRANSCRIPT INDEX

BILL NUMBER	DATE	PAGE	ACTION
SB-0948	05/27/83	238	FIRST READING
	06/14/83	7	SECOND READING
	06/21/83	5	THIRD READING
SB-0949	05/27/83	238	FIRST READING
	06/08/83	7	SECOND READING
	06/14/83	31	THIRD READING
	06/29/83	245	NON-CONCURRENCE
	07/02/83	55	CONFERENCE
SB-0950	05/27/83	238	FIRST READING
	06/16/83	121	SECOND READING
	06/24/83	24	THIRD READING
SB-0951	05/27/83	238	FIRST READING
	06/20/83	40	SECOND READING
	06/27/83	352	THIRD READING
SB-0952	05/27/83	238	FIRST READING
	06/14/83	7	SECOND READING
	06/21/83	5	THIRD READING
SB-0953	05/27/83	3	FIRST READING
	06/15/83	71	SECOND READING
	06/27/83	309	THIRD READING
	06/27/83	311	RECALLED
	06/27/83	312	MOTION
	06/27/83	320	RECALLED
	06/27/83	321	THIRD READING
SB-0954	06/14/83	7	SECOND READING
SB-0955	05/27/83	238	FIRST READING
	06/08/83	36	SECOND READING
	06/23/83	112	THIRD READING
SB-0958	05/26/83	313	FIRST READING
	06/23/83	162	SECOND READING
	06/27/83	35	THIRD READING
SB-0961	05/26/83	313	FIRST READING
	06/14/83	7	SECOND READING
	06/21/83	5	THIRD READING
SB-0962	05/25/83	230	FIRST READING
	06/14/83	7	SECOND READING
	06/21/83	5	THIRD READING
SB-0963	05/24/83	303	FIRST READING
	06/08/83	7	SECOND READING
	06/14/83	31	THIRD READING

PROGRAM-LRTRNMST
08/20/85

LEGISLATIVE INFORMATION SYSTEM
HOUSE OF REPRESENTATIVES

PAGE 286

MASTER TRANSCRIPT INDEX

BILL NUMBER	DATE	PAGE	ACTION
SB-0966	06/02/83	3	FIRST READING
	06/15/83	71	SECOND READING
	06/15/83	72	HELD ON SECOND
	06/16/83	125	SECOND READING
	06/27/83	216	THIRD READING
SB-0970	05/24/83	303	FIRST READING
	06/14/83	44	SECOND READING
	06/24/83	24	THIRD READING
SB-0971	05/24/83	304	FIRST READING
	06/15/83	179	SECOND READING
SB-0972	06/02/83	4	FIRST READING
	06/15/83	179	SECOND READING
	06/22/83	73	THIRD READING
	06/29/83	10	NON-CONCURRENCE
	07/01/83	87	CONFERENCE
	07/01/83	262	CONFERENCE
SB-0973	05/26/83	312	FIRST READING
	05/27/83	3	FIRST READING
	06/14/83	44	SECOND READING
SB-0974	05/26/83	313	FIRST READING
	06/07/83	16	SECOND READING
	06/24/83	24	THIRD READING
SB-0975	05/26/83	314	FIRST READING
	06/14/83	7	SECOND READING
	06/21/83	5	THIRD READING
SB-0981	05/26/83	314	FIRST READING
	06/16/83	19	SECOND READING
	06/23/83	236	THIRD READING
	06/27/83	386	RECALLED
	06/27/83	387	THIRD READING
SB-0982	05/26/83	312	FIRST READING
	05/27/83	3	FIRST READING
	06/16/83	7	SECOND READING
	06/16/83	11	HELD ON SECOND
	06/22/83	164	SECOND READING
	06/23/83	113	THIRD READING
SB-0983	05/26/83	312	FIRST READING
	05/27/83	3	FIRST READING
	06/14/83	45	SECOND READING
	06/24/83	24	RECALLED
	06/24/83	25	THIRD READING

BILL NUMBER	DATE	PAGE	ACTION
SB-0986	05/26/83	314	FIRST READING
SB-0987	05/26/83	314	FIRST READING
SB-0990	05/26/83	314	FIRST READING
	06/14/83	46	SECOND READING
SB-0991	05/27/83	2	FIRST READING
	06/16/83	14	SECOND READING
	06/27/83	313	THIRD READING
	06/29/83	233	NON-CONCURRENCE
	07/01/83	236	CONFERENCE
SB-0995	05/27/83	2	FIRST READING
	06/16/83	15	SECOND READING
	06/27/83	314	THIRD READING
	11/01/83	40	VETO MESSAGE
SB-0996	05/26/83	312	FIRST READING
	05/27/83	2	FIRST READING
	06/16/83	12	SECOND READING
	06/27/83	315	THIRD READING
	11/01/83	42	VETO MESSAGE
SB-0999	05/27/83	2	FIRST READING
	06/10/83	26	MOTION
SB-1000	05/26/83	312	FIRST READING
	05/27/83	4	FIRST READING
	06/22/83	166	HELD ON SECOND
	06/23/83	163	SECOND READING
	06/27/83	96	THIRD READING
SB-1001	05/26/83	312	FIRST READING
	05/27/83	4	FIRST READING
	06/16/83	18	SECOND READING
	06/23/83	191	RECALLED
	06/27/83	112	THIRD READING
	06/29/83	228	NON-CONCURRENCE
	07/01/83	238	CONFERENCE
	07/02/83	100	CONFERENCE
	11/02/83	131	VETO MESSAGE
SB-1002	05/27/83	238	FIRST READING
	06/20/83	52	SECOND READING
	06/23/83	156	RECALLED
	06/23/83	160	HELD ON SECOND
	06/23/83	196	RECALLED
	06/27/83	121	THIRD READING
	06/29/83	235	NON-CONCURRENCE
	07/02/83	67	CONFERENCE

BILL NUMBER	DATE	PAGE	ACTION
SB-1002 (cont'd)	11/04/83	30	CONFERENCE
SB-1003	05/27/83	238	FIRST READING
SB-1004	05/27/83	238	FIRST READING
	06/16/83	13	SECOND READING
	06/27/83	124	THIRD READING
SB-1005	05/27/83	238	FIRST READING
SB-1006	05/27/83	238	FIRST READING
	06/16/83	12	SECOND READING
	06/27/83	125	THIRD READING
SB-1008	05/27/83	2	FIRST READING
	06/15/83	3	SECOND READING
	06/21/83	5	THIRD READING
SB-1009	05/26/83	314	FIRST READING
	06/15/83	72	SECOND READING
	06/24/83	25	THIRD READING
SB-1010	05/27/83	238	FIRST READING
	06/15/83	72	SECOND READING
SB-1011	05/27/83	238	FIRST READING
	06/16/83	13	SECOND READING
	06/20/83	13	HELD ON SECOND
	06/20/83	42	SECOND READING
	06/20/83	43	HELD ON SECOND
	06/22/83	167	SECOND READING
	06/27/83	127	THIRD READING
SB-1012	05/24/83	303	FIRST READING
	06/15/83	76	SECOND READING
	06/24/83	25	THIRD READING
SB-1013	05/26/83	314	FIRST READING
	06/15/83	72	SECOND READING
	06/24/83	25	THIRD READING
SB-1014	05/27/83	239	FIRST READING
SB-1015	05/27/83	239	FIRST READING
	06/15/83	73	SECOND READING
	06/27/83	128	THIRD READING
SB-1016	05/27/83	239	FIRST READING
SB-1017	05/27/83	2	FIRST READING
	06/16/83	16	SECOND READING

PROGRAM-LRTRNMST
08/20/85
LEGISLATIVE INFORMATION SYSTEM
HOUSE OF REPRESENTATIVES
PAGE 289

MASTER TRANSCRIPT INDEX

BILL NUMBER	DATE	PAGE	ACTION
SB-1017 (cont'd)	06/16/83	17	HELD ON SECOND
	06/20/83	43	SECOND READING
	06/27/83	134	THIRD READING
SB-1018	05/27/83	239	FIRST READING
SB-1019	05/26/83	312	FIRST READING
	05/27/83	239	FIRST READING
SB-1020	05/26/83	312	FIRST READING
	05/27/83	4	FIRST READING
	06/14/83	46	SECOND READING
	06/24/83	25	THIRD READING
	11/01/83	79	VETO MESSAGE
SB-1021	05/27/83	239	FIRST READING
	06/10/83	27	MOTION
SB-1022	05/27/83	239	FIRST READING
	06/10/83	34	MOTION
	06/16/83	17	SECOND READING
	06/27/83	143	THIRD READING
	06/29/83	230	NON-CONCURRENCE
SB-1023	05/27/83	239	FIRST READING
SB-1024	05/27/83	239	FIRST READING
	06/16/83	168	HELD ON SECOND
	06/22/83	227	SECOND READING
	06/23/83	47	THIRD READING
	06/28/83	245	NON-CONCURRENCE
	12/12/84	33	MOTION
	12/12/84	47	MOTION
	12/12/84	148	CONFERENCE
SB-1025	05/27/83	239	FIRST READING
	06/16/83	20	SECOND READING
	06/24/83	25	THIRD READING
	11/02/83	133	VETO MESSAGE
SB-1026	05/27/83	239	FIRST READING
	06/15/83	73	SECOND READING
	06/23/83	160	RECALLED
	06/23/83	161	HELD ON SECOND
	06/23/83	197	SECOND READING
	06/23/83	204	MOTION
	06/27/83	149	THIRD READING
	06/29/83	230	NON-CONCURRENCE
	07/01/83	153	CONFERENCE
	07/02/83	136	CONFERENCE

PROGRAM-LRTRNMST
08/20/85
LEGISLATIVE INFORMATION SYSTEM
HOUSE OF REPRESENTATIVES
PAGE 290

MASTER TRANSCRIPT INDEX

BILL NUMBER	DATE	PAGE	ACTION
SB-1027	05/27/83	239	FIRST READING
	06/16/83	20	SECOND READING
	06/20/83	146	RECALLED
	06/21/83	5	THIRD READING
	06/22/83	147	SECOND READING
	06/27/83	151	THIRD READING
SB-1028	05/27/83	239	FIRST READING
	06/15/83	3	SECOND READING
	06/21/83	6	THIRD READING
SB-1029	05/27/83	239	FIRST READING
SB-1030	05/27/83	240	FIRST READING
	06/15/83	73	SECOND READING
	06/15/83	74	HELD ON SECOND
	06/24/83	46	SECOND READING
	06/24/83	47	THIRD READING
	06/28/83	246	NON-CONCURRENCE
	06/30/83	129	CONFERENCE
	06/30/83	131	OUT OF RECORD
	07/01/83	104	CONFERENCE
SB-1031	05/27/83	4	FIRST READING
	06/15/83	74	SECOND READING
	06/15/83	75	HELD ON SECOND
	06/16/83	125	SECOND READING
	06/16/83	126	HELD ON SECOND
	06/20/83	84	SECOND READING
	06/20/83	86	HELD ON SECOND
	06/23/83	33	SECOND READING
SB-1032	05/27/83	4	FIRST READING
SB-1033	05/27/83	240	FIRST READING
	06/16/83	20	SECOND READING
	06/16/83	21	HELD ON SECOND
	06/22/83	149	SECOND READING
	06/27/83	153	THIRD READING
	11/02/83	135	VETO MESSAGE
SB-1034	05/27/83	240	FIRST READING
	06/14/83	47	SECOND READING
	06/27/83	159	THIRD READING
SB-1035	05/27/83	240	FIRST READING
	06/20/83	46	SECOND READING
	06/27/83	161	THIRD READING
SB-1036	05/26/83	314	FIRST READING
	06/16/83	21	SECOND READING

PROGRAM-LRTRNMST
08/20/85

LEGISLATIVE INFORMATION SYSTEM
HOUSE OF REPRESENTATIVES

PAGE 291

MASTER TRANSCRIPT INDEX

BILL NUMBER	DATE	PAGE	ACTION
SB-1036 (cont'd)	06/24/83	25	THIRD READING
SB-1037	05/27/83	240	FIRST READING
	06/14/83	7	SECOND READING
	06/21/83	6	THIRD READING
SB-1038	05/27/83	240	FIRST READING
SB-1039	05/26/83	314	FIRST READING
	06/14/83	47	SECOND READING
SB-1040	06/02/83	4	FIRST READING
	06/14/83	47	SECOND READING
	06/14/83	49	OUT OF RECORD
	06/15/83	75	SECOND READING
	06/27/83	39	THIRD READING
SB-1045	05/27/83	240	FIRST READING
	06/07/83	16	SECOND READING
	06/27/83	195	THIRD READING
SB-1047	05/27/83	240	FIRST READING
	06/14/83	50	SECOND READING
	06/24/83	25	THIRD READING
SB-1048	05/27/83	240	FIRST READING
	06/16/83	21	SECOND READING
	06/24/83	25	THIRD READING
SB-1049	05/27/83	240	FIRST READING
SB-1052	05/26/83	314	FIRST READING
	06/07/83	12	SECOND READING
	06/20/83	184	RECALLED
	06/24/83	25	THIRD READING
SB-1054	05/27/83	240	FIRST READING
	06/16/83	21	SECOND READING
	06/26/83	70	RECALLED
	06/27/83	45	THIRD READING
SB-1056	05/27/83	4	FIRST READING
	06/09/83	24	SECOND READING
	06/24/83	25	THIRD READING
	11/02/83	19	VETO MESSAGE
SB-1057	05/26/83	314	FIRST READING
	06/20/83	47	SECOND READING
	06/20/83	52	HELD ON SECOND
	06/22/83	148	SECOND READING
	06/23/83	152	THIRD READING

PROGRAM-LRTRNMST
08/20/85

LEGISLATIVE INFORMATION SYSTEM
HOUSE OF REPRESENTATIVES

PAGE 292

MASTER TRANSCRIPT INDEX

BILL NUMBER	DATE	PAGE	ACTION
SB-1057 (cont'd)	06/29/83	231	NON-CONCURRENCE
SB-1058	05/26/83	314	FIRST READING
	06/14/83	7	SECOND READING
	06/21/83	6	THIRD READING
SB-1059	05/27/83	240	FIRST READING
	06/07/83	17	SECOND READING
	06/27/83	349	THIRD READING
SB-1061	05/27/83	240	FIRST READING
	06/07/83	17	SECOND READING
	06/26/83	76	RECALLED
	06/27/83	351	THIRD READING
	06/29/83	232	NON-CONCURRENCE
	07/01/83	105	CONFERENCE
SB-1062	05/27/83	5	FIRST READING
	06/14/83	7	SECOND READING
	06/20/83	86	SECOND READING
	06/24/83	25	THIRD READING
SB-1063	05/25/83	230	FIRST READING
	06/08/83	7	SECOND READING
	06/14/83	31	THIRD READING
SB-1064	05/27/83	240	FIRST READING
	06/14/83	7	SECOND READING
	06/21/83	6	THIRD READING
	06/29/83	54	NON-CONCURRENCE
	07/01/83	257	OUT OF RECORD
	07/01/83	257	CONFERENCE
	07/01/83	261	CONFERENCE
SB-1067	05/24/83	303	FIRST READING
	06/15/83	3	SECOND READING
	06/21/83	6	THIRD READING
	12/12/84	5	MOTION
	12/12/84	48	MOTION
	12/12/84	67	NON-CONCURRENCE
	12/12/84	125	CONFERENCE
SB-1069	05/27/83	241	FIRST READING
	06/14/83	7	SECOND READING
	06/21/83	6	THIRD READING
SB-1070	05/27/83	3	FIRST READING
	06/16/83	27	SECOND READING
	06/16/83	36	HELD ON SECOND
	06/22/83	148	SECOND READING
	06/23/83	123	RECALLED

PROGRAM-LRTRNMST
08/20/85

LEGISLATIVE INFORMATION SYSTEM
HOUSE OF REPRESENTATIVES

MASTER TRANSCRIPT INDEX

PAGE 293

BILL NUMBER	DATE	PAGE	ACTION
SB-1070 (cont'd)	06/25/83	85	RECALLED
	06/27/83	178	THIRD READING
	06/29/83	234	NON-CONCURRENCE
	07/01/83	241	CONFERENCE
	11/02/83	211	VETO MESSAGE
SB-1072	05/26/83	314	FIRST READING
	06/15/83	77	SECOND READING
	06/24/83	25	THIRD READING
SB-1073	05/26/83	314	FIRST READING
	06/16/83	36	SECOND READING
	06/24/83	25	RECALLED
	06/24/83	72	THIRD READING
	06/29/83	233	NON-CONCURRENCE
SB-1074	05/26/83	314	FIRST READING
SB-1075	06/01/83	6	FIRST READING
	06/20/83	86	SECOND READING
	06/20/83	89	OUT OF RECORD
	06/21/83	228	SECOND READING
	06/21/83	228	HELD ON SECOND
SB-1078	05/27/83	241	FIRST READING
	06/14/83	7	SECOND READING
	06/21/83	6	THIRD READING
SB-1079	05/27/83	241	FIRST READING
	06/08/83	7	SECOND READING
	06/14/83	32	THIRD READING
SB-1083	06/01/83	6	FIRST READING
	06/14/83	7	SECOND READING
	06/21/83	228	SECOND READING
	06/21/83	228	HELD ON SECOND
	06/27/83	343	SECOND READING
	06/27/83	344	THIRD READING
SB-1084	06/01/83	6	FIRST READING
SB-1088	05/27/83	241	FIRST READING
	06/20/83	53	SECOND READING
SB-1091	05/26/83	314	FIRST READING
	06/16/83	36	SECOND READING
	06/21/83	199	THIRD READING
SB-1093	05/27/83	241	FIRST READING
	06/16/83	36	SECOND READING
	06/24/83	36	THIRD READING

PROGRAM-LRTRNMST
08/20/85

LEGISLATIVE INFORMATION SYSTEM
HOUSE OF REPRESENTATIVES

MASTER TRANSCRIPT INDEX

PAGE 294

BILL NUMBER	DATE	PAGE	ACTION
SB-1093 (cont'd)	06/28/83	246	NON-CONCURRENCE
	10/20/83	157	CONFERENCE
SB-1095	05/24/83	303	FIRST READING
	06/15/83	3	SECOND READING
	06/21/83	6	THIRD READING
SB-1096	05/27/83	241	FIRST READING
SB-1097	05/26/83	315	FIRST READING
	06/07/83	17	SECOND READING
	06/27/83	370	THIRD READING
SB-1098	05/24/83	304	FIRST READING
	06/15/83	3	SECOND READING
	06/21/83	6	THIRD READING
SB-1104	05/26/83	315	FIRST READING
	06/14/83	50	SECOND READING
	06/20/83	182	RECALLED
	06/24/83	36	RECALLED
	06/24/83	36	THIRD READING
	11/01/83	43	VETO MESSAGE
SB-1106	05/27/83	241	FIRST READING
	06/16/83	37	SECOND READING
	06/16/83	42	HELD ON SECOND
	06/20/83	53	SECOND READING
SB-1107	05/27/83	241	FIRST READING
	06/16/83	42	SECOND READING
	06/16/83	43	HELD ON SECOND
	06/20/83	54	SECOND READING
	06/27/83	223	THIRD READING
SB-1109	05/26/83	315	FIRST READING
	06/14/83	7	SECOND READING
	06/15/83	77	SECOND READING
	06/25/83	77	THIRD READING
SB-1111	05/27/83	4	FIRST READING
	06/15/83	78	SECOND READING
	06/24/83	36	THIRD READING
	11/01/83	46	VETO MESSAGE
SB-1113	11/29/84	2	FIRST READING
	12/12/84	5	MOTION
	12/12/84	50	MOTION
	12/12/84	122	SECOND READING
	01/09/85	3	THIRD READING

BILL NUMBER	DATE	PAGE	ACTION
SB-1114	05/26/83	315	FIRST READING
	06/16/83	43	SECOND READING
	06/24/83	36	THIRD READING
SB-1115	05/24/83	304	FIRST READING
	06/14/83	51	SECOND READING
	06/27/83	228	THIRD READING
SB-1116	05/27/83	241	FIRST READING
	06/16/83	43	SECOND READING
	06/16/83	44	OUT OF RECORD
	06/20/83	54	SECOND READING
	06/23/83	247	THIRD READING
	11/01/83	47	VETO MESSAGE
SB-1117	06/02/83	8	FIRST READING
	06/16/83	44	SECOND READING
	06/24/83	36	THIRD READING
SB-1118	05/26/83	315	FIRST READING
	10/19/83	224	MOTION
	10/19/83	225	SECOND READING
	10/19/83	225	HELD ON SECOND
	10/20/83	134	SECOND READING
	10/20/83	139	THIRD READING
SB-1119	06/01/83	6	FIRST READING
	06/16/83	44	SECOND READING
	06/26/83	85	RECALLED
	06/27/83	48	THIRD READING
SB-1120	05/24/83	304	FIRST READING
	06/14/83	8	SECOND READING
	06/16/83	126	SECOND READING
	06/24/83	36	RECALLED
	06/24/83	37	THIRD READING
SB-1121	05/26/83	315	FIRST READING
	06/15/83	3	SECOND READING
	06/20/83	89	SECOND READING
	06/24/83	37	THIRD READING
SB-1122	06/02/83	4	FIRST READING
	06/16/83	45	SECOND READING
	06/27/83	56	RECALLED
	06/27/83	57	THIRD READING
	11/01/83	77	VETO MESSAGE
SB-1123	05/27/83	241	FIRST READING
	06/15/83	3	SECOND READING
	06/20/83	91	SECOND READING

BILL NUMBER	DATE	PAGE	ACTION
SB-1123 (cont'd)	06/24/83	37	THIRD READING
	11/02/83	164	VETO MESSAGE
SB-1124	05/27/83	241	FIRST READING
	06/14/83	8	SECOND READING
	06/21/83	6	THIRD READING
SB-1127	06/01/83	6	FIRST READING
	06/15/83	78	SECOND READING
	06/23/83	248	THIRD READING
	11/02/83	173	VETO MESSAGE
SB-1132	05/27/83	241	FIRST READING
	06/16/83	51	SECOND READING
	06/27/83	201	THIRD READING
SB-1133	05/27/83	241	FIRST READING
	06/14/83	8	SECOND READING
	06/21/83	6	THIRD READING
SB-1134	05/27/83	241	FIRST READING
	06/08/83	8	SECOND READING
	06/14/83	32	THIRD READING
SB-1135	05/25/83	230	FIRST READING
	06/14/83	51	SECOND READING
	06/24/83	37	THIRD READING
	06/30/83	139	NON-CONCURRENCE
	07/02/83	50	CONFERENCE
SB-1136	05/27/83	241	FIRST READING
	06/16/83	46	SECOND READING
	06/24/83	37	THIRD READING
SB-1143	05/26/83	315	FIRST READING
	06/15/83	3	SECOND READING
	06/21/83	6	THIRD READING
SB-1144	05/27/83	242	FIRST READING
	06/22/83	142	SECOND READING
	06/26/83	58	THIRD READING
	06/29/83	213	NON-CONCURRENCE
SB-1145	05/26/83	315	FIRST READING
	06/14/83	8	SECOND READING
	06/21/83	6	THIRD READING
SB-1146	05/27/83	242	FIRST READING
	06/16/83	46	SECOND READING
	06/27/83	346	THIRD READING
	06/29/83	220	NON-CONCURRENCE

PROGRAM-LRTRNMST
08/20/85

LEGISLATIVE INFORMATION SYSTEM
HOUSE OF REPRESENTATIVES

PAGE 297

MASTER TRANSCRIPT INDEX

BILL NUMBER	DATE	PAGE	ACTION
SB-1147	05/24/83	304	FIRST READING
	06/14/83	52	SECOND READING
	06/20/83	184	RECALLED
	06/24/83	37	RECALLED
	06/24/83	38	THIRD READING
SB-1150	05/27/83	2	FIRST READING
	06/14/83	52	SECOND READING
	06/24/83	38	THIRD READING
SB-1153	05/26/83	315	FIRST READING
	06/23/83	166	SECOND READING
	06/26/83	60	RECALLED
	06/27/83	61	THIRD READING
	07/01/83	199	NON-CONCURRENCE
	10/18/83	77	MOTION
	10/20/83	119	CONFERENCE
	10/20/83	123	MOTION
	10/20/83	149	CONFERENCE
SB-1156	05/27/83	242	FIRST READING
	06/16/83	129	SECOND READING
	06/22/83	200	RECALLED
	06/22/83	202	THIRD READING
	11/02/83	98	VETO MESSAGE
SB-1157	05/24/83	304	FIRST READING
	06/15/83	3	SECOND READING
	06/21/83	6	THIRD READING
	11/01/83	48	VETO MESSAGE
SB-1158	06/02/83	8	FIRST READING
SB-1160	06/02/83	4	FIRST READING
	06/15/83	79	SECOND READING
SB-1166	05/24/83	304	FIRST READING
	06/14/83	54	SECOND READING
	06/24/83	38	THIRD READING
SB-1173	05/26/83	315	FIRST READING
	06/16/83	47	SECOND READING
	06/16/83	51	OUT OF RECORD
	06/20/83	55	SECOND READING
	06/27/83	272	THIRD READING
SB-1174	06/02/83	8	FIRST READING
	06/16/83	52	SECOND READING
	06/16/83	52	HELD ON SECOND
	06/20/83	57	SECOND READING
	06/22/83	259	RECALLED

PROGRAM-LRTRNMST
08/20/85

LEGISLATIVE INFORMATION SYSTEM
HOUSE OF REPRESENTATIVES

PAGE 298

MASTER TRANSCRIPT INDEX

BILL NUMBER	DATE	PAGE	ACTION
SB-1174 (cont'd)	06/22/83	263	HELD ON SECOND
	06/23/83	129	THIRD READING
	07/01/83	199	NON-CONCURRENCE
	11/02/83	20	VETO MESSAGE
SB-1175	06/01/83	6	FIRST READING
	06/14/83	54	SECOND READING
	06/24/83	38	THIRD READING
SB-1176	05/27/83	242	FIRST READING
	06/15/83	79	SECOND READING
	06/23/83	255	THIRD READING
	06/30/83	14	NON-CONCURRENCE
	07/02/83	107	CONFERENCE
SB-1179	05/25/84	188	FIRST READING
	06/20/84	42	SECOND READING
	06/21/84	47	THIRD READING
	06/28/84	157	NON-CONCURRENCE
	06/30/84	210	CONFERENCE
SB-1185	06/02/83	4	FIRST READING
	06/15/83	80	SECOND READING
	06/20/83	113	RECALLED
	06/22/83	236	THIRD READING
SB-1187	06/01/83	6	FIRST READING
	06/15/83	80	SECOND READING
	06/24/83	38	THIRD READING
SB-1188	05/26/83	315	FIRST READING
	06/14/83	55	SECOND READING
	06/27/83	261	THIRD READING
SB-1191	06/01/83	6	FIRST READING
	06/14/83	55	SECOND READING
	06/14/83	55	HELD ON SECOND
	06/24/83	62	SECOND READING
	06/24/83	187	RECALLED
	06/25/83	82	THIRD READING
SB-1192	05/26/83	315	FIRST READING
SB-1195	06/01/83	7	FIRST READING
	06/14/83	8	SECOND READING
	06/16/83	136	SECOND READING
	06/24/83	38	THIRD READING
	11/01/83	58	VETO MESSAGE
SB-1196	05/26/83	315	FIRST READING
	06/15/83	82	SECOND READING

MASTER TRANSCRIPT INDEX

BILL NUMBER	DATE	PAGE	ACTION
SB-1196(cont'd)	06/24/83	38	THIRD READING
SB-1197	05/26/83	315	FIRST READING
	06/14/83	8	SECOND READING
	06/21/83	6	THIRD READING
SB-1199	05/27/83	243	FIRST READING
	06/14/83	8	SECOND READING
	06/20/83	89	SECOND READING
	06/20/83	90	OUT OF RECORD
	06/20/83	91	SECOND READING
	06/27/83	63	THIRD READING
	06/28/83	247	NON-CONCURRENCE
	06/30/83	153	CONFERENCE
SB-1200	05/24/83	304	FIRST READING
	06/14/83	8	SECOND READING
	06/21/83	6	THIRD READING
SB-1201	05/27/83	243	FIRST READING
SB-1203	06/01/83	7	FIRST READING
	06/15/83	81	SECOND READING
	06/24/83	38	THIRD READING
	06/28/83	248	NON-CONCURRENCE
	07/01/83	106	CONFERENCE
SB-1206	06/01/83	7	FIRST READING
	06/16/83	53	SECOND READING
	10/18/83	73	MOTION
	10/20/83	101	THIRD READING
	10/20/83	102	OUT OF RECORD
	10/20/83	109	THIRD READING
	11/04/83	21	NON-CONCURRENCE
	11/04/83	21	OUT OF RECORD
	11/04/83	32	NON-CONCURRENCE
SB-1211	06/01/83	7	FIRST READING
	06/20/83	57	SECOND READING
	06/20/83	57	HELD ON SECOND
	06/21/83	228	SECOND READING
	06/21/83	228	HELD ON SECOND
	06/23/83	171	SECOND READING
	06/27/83	108	THIRD READING
	06/29/83	12	NON-CONCURRENCE
SB-1217	05/25/84	188	FIRST READING
	06/13/84	39	SECOND READING
	06/13/84	41	OUT OF RECORD
	06/13/84	50	SECOND READING
	06/19/84	17	RECALLED

MASTER TRANSCRIPT INDEX

BILL NUMBER	DATE	PAGE	ACTION
SB-1217(cont'd)	06/19/84	18	THIRD READING
	06/29/84	82	NON-CONCURRENCE
SB-1218	05/26/83	316	FIRST READING
	06/15/83	81	SECOND READING
	06/24/83	91	RECALLED
	06/24/83	95	HELD ON SECOND
	06/24/83	130	SECOND READING
	06/24/83	132	THIRD READING
	06/28/83	248	NON-CONCURRENCE
	06/30/83	156	CONFERENCE
	11/01/83	56	VETO MESSAGE
SB-1220	05/24/83	304	FIRST READING
	06/08/83	37	SECOND READING
	06/24/83	38	RECALLED
	06/24/83	40	THIRD READING
SB-1222	06/01/83	7	FIRST READING
	06/23/83	183	SECOND READING
	06/26/83	61	RECALLED
	06/26/83	62	HELD ON SECOND
	06/26/83	65	SECOND READING
	06/27/83	65	THIRD READING
	06/29/83	13	NON-CONCURRENCE
	07/02/83	108	CONFERENCE
SB-1223	05/23/84	310	FIRST READING
	06/07/84	21	MOTION
	06/13/84	49	SECOND READING
	06/25/84	215	THIRD READING
SB-1226	05/26/83	316	FIRST READING
	06/07/83	17	SECOND READING
	06/27/83	66	THIRD READING
	06/28/83	249	NON-CONCURRENCE
	07/02/83	17	CONFERENCE
SB-1228	05/27/83	243	FIRST READING
	06/07/83	18	SECOND READING
	06/27/83	317	THIRD READING
SB-1232	05/27/83	242	FIRST READING
	06/16/83	53	SECOND READING
	06/20/83	154	RECALLED
	06/24/83	40	THIRD READING
SB-1233	05/27/83	242	FIRST READING
	06/14/83	8	SECOND READING
	06/21/83	7	THIRD READING

PROGRAM-LRTRNMST
08/20/85
LEGISLATIVE INFORMATION SYSTEM
HOUSE OF REPRESENTATIVES
PAGE 301

MASTER TRANSCRIPT INDEX

BILL NUMBER	DATE	PAGE	ACTION
SB-1234	06/02/83	4	FIRST READING
	06/10/83	35	MOTION
	06/20/83	62	SECOND READING
	06/24/83	96	RECALLED
	06/24/83	97	THIRD READING
	06/24/83	101	OUT OF RECORD
	06/24/83	140	THIRD READING
SB-1236	06/14/84	138	FIRST READING
	06/19/84	89	MOTION
	06/21/84	21	MOTION
	06/22/84	112	SECOND READING
	06/25/84	71	THIRD READING
SB-1237	05/27/83	243	FIRST READING
	06/10/83	41	MOTION
	06/16/83	90	SECOND READING
	06/16/83	91	HELD ON SECOND
	06/20/83	58	SECOND READING
	06/27/83	201	THIRD READING
SB-1238	06/01/83	7	FIRST READING
	06/22/83	160	HELD ON SECOND
SB-1239	05/26/83	316	FIRST READING
	06/15/83	81	SECOND READING
	06/20/83	189	RECALLED
	06/27/83	316	THIRD READING
	11/02/83	21	VETO MESSAGE
SB-1241	05/26/83	316	FIRST READING
	06/14/83	56	SECOND READING
	06/22/83	81	RECALLED
	06/22/83	92	HELD ON SECOND
	06/23/83	35	SECOND READING
	06/23/83	35	THIRD READING
SB-1244	05/26/83	316	FIRST READING
	06/14/83	57	SECOND READING
	06/23/83	2	MOTION
	06/23/83	61	THIRD READING
SB-1251	05/27/83	243	FIRST READING
SB-1254	05/27/83	2	FIRST READING
	05/27/83	242	FIRST READING
	06/15/83	82	SECOND READING
	06/24/83	40	THIRD READING
SB-1256	06/01/83	7	FIRST READING
	06/16/83	54	SECOND READING

PROGRAM-LRTRNMST
08/20/85
LEGISLATIVE INFORMATION SYSTEM
HOUSE OF REPRESENTATIVES
PAGE 302

MASTER TRANSCRIPT INDEX

BILL NUMBER	DATE	PAGE	ACTION
SB-1256 (cont'd)	06/16/83	70	HELD ON SECOND
	06/20/83	59	SECOND READING
	06/27/83	352	THIRD READING
	11/02/83	120	VETO MESSAGE
SB-1257	05/27/83	243	FIRST READING
	06/16/83	70	SECOND READING
	06/16/83	71	HELD ON SECOND
	06/20/83	59	SECOND READING
	06/20/83	59	HELD ON SECOND
	06/22/83	149	SECOND READING
SB-1258	05/27/83	243	FIRST READING
	06/16/83	71	SECOND READING
	06/24/83	157	THIRD READING
SB-1260	05/27/83	243	FIRST READING
	06/22/83	149	SECOND READING
	06/22/83	151	HELD ON SECOND
	06/22/83	275	SECOND READING
	06/24/83	202	THIRD READING
	11/02/83	23	VETO MESSAGE
SB-1262	05/27/83	244	FIRST READING
SB-1263	06/01/83	7	FIRST READING
	06/14/83	58	SECOND READING
	06/14/83	60	OUT OF RECORD
	06/22/83	222	SECOND READING
	06/24/83	48	THIRD READING
	06/29/83	278	NON-CONCURRENCE
	07/02/83	158	CONFERENCE
	07/02/83	166	CONFERENCE
SB-1264	06/01/83	7	FIRST READING
	06/16/83	71	SECOND READING
	06/26/83	62	RECALLED
	06/27/83	69	THIRD READING
SB-1266	05/27/83	244	FIRST READING
SB-1268	05/27/83	242	FIRST READING
	06/15/83	82	SECOND READING
	06/27/83	234	RECALLED
	06/27/83	235	THIRD READING
	06/29/83	246	NON-CONCURRENCE
SB-1269	05/26/83	316	FIRST READING
	06/14/83	8	SECOND READING
	06/20/83	90	SECOND READING
	06/22/83	92	THIRD READING

PROGRAM-LRTRNMST
08/20/85

LEGISLATIVE INFORMATION SYSTEM
HOUSE OF REPRESENTATIVES

PAGE 303

MASTER TRANSCRIPT INDEX

BILL NUMBER	DATE	PAGE	ACTION
SB-1269 (cont'd)	06/28/83	249	NON-CONCURRENCE
	06/30/83	131	CONFERENCE
	11/01/83	49	VETO MESSAGE
SB-1270	05/26/83	316	FIRST READING
	06/14/83	8	SECOND READING
	06/21/83	228	SECOND READING
	06/21/83	228	HELD ON SECOND
	06/22/83	99	SECOND READING
	06/22/83	100	THIRD READING
SB-1272	05/26/83	316	FIRST READING
	06/16/83	72	SECOND READING
	06/27/83	71	THIRD READING
SB-1274	05/26/83	316	FIRST READING
	06/16/83	72	SECOND READING
	06/27/83	73	THIRD READING
SB-1276	05/26/83	316	FIRST READING
	06/16/83	72	SECOND READING
SB-1277	06/01/83	7	FIRST READING
	06/15/83	83	SECOND READING
	06/24/83	101	THIRD READING
SB-1278	06/01/83	8	FIRST READING
	06/14/83	60	SECOND READING
	06/24/83	40	THIRD READING
SB-1279	05/26/83	316	FIRST READING
	06/16/83	73	SECOND READING
	06/27/83	281	RECALLED
	06/24/83	282	MOTION
	06/27/83	286	RECALLED
	06/27/83	287	THIRD READING
SB-1298	06/01/83	7	FIRST READING
SB-1300	05/27/83	244	FIRST READING
SB-1301	06/01/83	7	FIRST READING
	06/22/83	151	SECOND READING
	06/24/83	111	THIRD READING
	11/02/83	142	VETO MESSAGE
	11/02/83	144	OUT OF RECORD
	11/03/83	28	VETO MESSAGE
SB-1306	05/26/83	316	FIRST READING
	06/14/83	8	SECOND READING
	06/21/83	7	THIRD READING

PROGRAM-LRTRNMST
08/20/85

LEGISLATIVE INFORMATION SYSTEM
HOUSE OF REPRESENTATIVES

PAGE 304

MASTER TRANSCRIPT INDEX

BILL NUMBER	DATE	PAGE	ACTION
SB-1307	06/01/83	7	FIRST READING
	06/15/83	4	SECOND READING
	06/27/83	203	SECOND READING
	06/27/83	205	THIRD READING
	06/29/83	248	NON-CONCURRENCE
	07/02/83	156	CONFERENCE
	11/02/83	140	VETO MESSAGE
SB-1308	05/27/83	244	FIRST READING
	06/16/83	79	SECOND READING
	06/24/83	40	THIRD READING
SB-1309	10/20/83	177	FIRST READING
	11/01/83	64	SECOND READING
	11/01/83	64	MOTION
	11/02/83	229	THIRD READING
SB-1310	05/27/83	2	FIRST READING
	06/15/83	83	SECOND READING
	06/24/83	40	THIRD READING
SB-1311	05/27/83	244	FIRST READING
	06/16/83	79	SECOND READING
	06/27/83	74	THIRD READING
	06/27/83	162	MOTION
	06/27/83	164	THIRD READING
SB-1312	05/27/83	244	FIRST READING
	06/16/83	79	SECOND READING
	06/20/83	164	RECALLED
	06/27/83	240	THIRD READING
SB-1313	05/27/83	242	FIRST READING
	06/16/83	136	SECOND READING
	06/27/83	88	THIRD READING
	06/29/83	40	NON-CONCURRENCE
	07/01/83	129	CONFERENCE
	07/02/83	38	CONFERENCE
SB-1315	05/24/83	304	FIRST READING
	06/16/83	137	SECOND READING
	06/24/83	40	THIRD READING
	06/30/83	12	NON-CONCURRENCE
	07/02/83	17	CONFERENCE
SB-1316	06/01/83	7	FIRST READING
	06/23/83	184	SECOND READING
	06/27/83	288	THIRD READING
SB-1317	05/27/83	242	FIRST READING
	06/09/83	32	TABLED

MASTER TRANSCRIPT INDEX

BILL NUMBER	DATE	PAGE	ACTION
SB-1318	05/26/83	316	FIRST READING
	06/20/83	92	SECOND READING
	06/24/83	40	THIRD READING
SB-1319	06/01/83	7	FIRST READING
	06/14/83	61	SECOND READING
	06/20/83	117	RECALLED
	06/27/83	247	THIRD READING
SB-1320	05/27/83	244	FIRST READING
SB-1324	05/24/83	304	FIRST READING
	06/16/83	79	SECOND READING
	06/27/83	249	THIRD READING
SB-1325	06/02/83	8	FIRST READING
	06/14/83	8	SECOND READING
	06/24/83	48	SECOND READING
	06/24/83	49	THIRD READING
SB-1328	05/27/83	4	FIRST READING
	06/16/83	81	SECOND READING
	06/24/83	40	THIRD READING
SB-1332	05/27/83	244	FIRST READING
	06/20/83	60	SECOND READING
	06/20/83	61	HELD ON SECOND
	06/21/83	222	SECOND READING
	06/22/83	211	THIRD READING
SB-1333	05/26/83	316	FIRST READING
	06/16/83	82	SECOND READING
	06/20/83	159	RECALLED
	06/22/83	212	THIRD READING
SB-1334	06/01/83	8	FIRST READING
	06/15/83	4	SECOND READING
	06/21/83	7	THIRD READING
SB-1336	06/02/83	4	FIRST READING
	06/16/83	82	SECOND READING
	06/20/83	157	RECALLED
	06/27/83	380	RECALLED
	06/27/83	381	THIRD READING
	06/29/83	266	NON-CONCURRENCE
	07/02/83	8	CONFERENCE
	07/02/83	157	CONFERENCE
SB-1343	05/27/83	244	FIRST READING
	06/16/83	82	SECOND READING
	06/22/83	101	THIRD READING

MASTER TRANSCRIPT INDEX

BILL NUMBER	DATE	PAGE	ACTION
SB-1344	05/24/83	304	FIRST READING
	06/10/83	37	MOTION
	06/16/83	82	SECOND READING
SB-1347	05/27/83	244	FIRST READING
	06/16/83	83	SECOND READING
	06/24/83	41	THIRD READING
SB-1348	05/24/83	304	FIRST READING
	06/14/83	8	SECOND READING
	06/20/83	94	SECOND READING
	06/24/83	41	THIRD READING
SB-1349	05/27/83	244	FIRST READING
	06/15/83	84	SECOND READING
	06/27/83	88	THIRD READING
SB-1354	05/27/83	242	FIRST READING
	06/15/83	85	SECOND READING
	06/22/83	101	THIRD READING
SB-1363	05/23/84	310	FIRST READING
SB-1371	05/16/84	286	FIRST READING
	06/06/84	53	MOTION
	06/06/84	54	SECOND READING
	06/13/84	37	THIRD READING
SB-1374	05/23/84	4	FIRST READING
	06/19/84	40	SECOND READING
	06/20/84	5	THIRD READING
SB-1375	05/23/84	310	FIRST READING
	06/14/84	35	SECOND READING
	06/19/84	47	HELD ON SECOND
	06/19/84	21	SECOND READING
	06/22/84	142	RECALLED
	06/25/84	3	THIRD READING
	06/28/84	47	NON-CONCURRENCE
SB-1381	05/29/84	2	FIRST READING
	06/13/84	5	SECOND READING
	06/20/84	77	THIRD READING
SB-1382	05/25/84	188	FIRST READING
	06/13/84	42	SECOND READING
	06/13/84	42	MOTION
	06/19/84	23	THIRD READING
	06/25/84	151	THIRD READING
SB-1384	05/23/84	3	FIRST READING

MASTER TRANSCRIPT INDEX

BILL NUMBER	DATE	PAGE	ACTION
SB-1384 (cont'd)	06/14/84	23	SECOND READING
	06/14/84	25	OUT OF RECORD
	06/21/84	5	SECOND READING
	06/25/84	218	RECALLED
	06/25/84	221	THIRD READING
SB-1385	05/23/84	3	FIRST READING
	06/07/84	5	SECOND READING
	06/07/84	6	OUT OF RECORD
	06/13/84	13	SECOND READING
	06/14/84	2	THIRD READING
	12/12/84	61	VETO MESSAGE
SB-1386	06/05/84	2	FIRST READING
	06/26/84	8	SECOND READING
	06/27/84	194	THIRD READING
SB-1395	05/24/84	253	FIRST READING
	06/21/84	14	SECOND READING
	06/25/84	5	THIRD READING
SB-1399	05/23/84	3	FIRST READING
	06/06/84	11	SECOND READING
	06/06/84	13	HELD ON SECOND
	06/07/84	13	SECOND READING
	06/07/84	17	OUT OF RECORD
	06/13/84	19	SECOND READING
	06/14/84	3	THIRD READING
SB-1401	05/23/84	2	FIRST READING
	06/13/84	20	SECOND READING
	06/14/84	4	THIRD READING
SB-1420	05/23/84	2	FIRST READING
	06/13/84	56	SECOND READING
	06/21/84	68	RECALLED
	06/25/84	9	THIRD READING
SB-1424	05/29/84	2	FIRST READING
	06/07/84	9	SECOND READING
	06/14/84	59	THIRD READING
SB-1425	05/23/84	2	FIRST READING
	06/20/84	36	SECOND READING
	06/22/84	3	RECALLED
	06/22/84	4	THIRD READING
SB-1429	05/23/84	3	FIRST READING
SB-1430	05/23/84	2	FIRST READING
	06/06/84	18	SECOND READING

MASTER TRANSCRIPT INDEX

BILL NUMBER	DATE	PAGE	ACTION
SB-1430 (cont'd)	06/12/84	12	THIRD READING
	06/28/84	158	NON-CONCURRENCE
	12/11/84	8	VETO MESSAGE
SB-1435	05/23/84	2	FIRST READING
SB-1441	05/18/84	2	FIRST READING
	05/25/84	167	SECOND READING
	05/25/84	167	MOTION
	05/29/84	12	THIRD READING
SB-1448	05/23/84	4	FIRST READING
	06/06/84	18	SECOND READING
	06/14/84	5	THIRD READING
SB-1450	06/05/84	21	FIRST READING
	06/19/84	44	SECOND READING
	06/19/84	47	OUT OF RECORD
	06/26/84	8	SECOND READING
	06/27/84	197	MOTION
	11/27/84	44	RECALLED
	11/27/84	48	THIRD READING
SB-1456	05/25/84	188	FIRST READING
	06/13/84	5	SECOND READING
	06/20/84	77	THIRD READING
SB-1457	05/25/84	188	FIRST READING
	06/13/84	5	SECOND READING
	06/20/84	41	SECOND READING
	06/21/84	73	THIRD READING
	06/21/84	77	OUT OF RECORD
	06/22/84	6	THIRD READING
SB-1459	05/23/84	310	FIRST READING
	06/07/84	17	SECOND READING
	06/13/84	30	THIRD READING
SB-1460	05/16/84	286	FIRST READING
	06/19/84	48	SECOND READING
	06/27/84	195	THIRD READING
SB-1462	05/23/84	4	FIRST READING
	06/13/84	20	SECOND READING
	06/14/84	7	THIRD READING
SB-1470	05/29/84	2	FIRST READING
	06/13/84	56	SECOND READING
	06/14/84	64	THIRD READING

BILL NUMBER	DATE	PAGE	ACTION
SB-1474	05/22/84	8	FIRST READING
	06/19/84	48	SECOND READING
	06/27/84	193	THIRD READING
SB-1478	05/25/84	189	FIRST READING
	06/21/84	17	SECOND READING
	06/25/84	23	THIRD READING
SB-1481	05/23/84	3	FIRST READING
	06/06/84	17	SECOND READING
	06/19/84	35	RECALLED
	06/19/84	36	MOTION
	06/21/84	66	THIRD READING
SB-1484	05/23/84	2	FIRST READING
	06/13/84	56	SECOND READING
	06/22/84	89	RECALLED
	06/22/84	104	MOTION
	06/25/84	23	THIRD READING
	06/25/84	43	MOTION
	06/25/84	45	THIRD READING
	07/01/84	73	NON-CONCURRENCE
SB-1491	05/23/84	310	FIRST READING
	06/13/84	58	SECOND READING
	06/19/84	36	THIRD READING
	12/11/84	21	VETO MESSAGE
SB-1509	05/23/84	2	FIRST READING
	06/13/84	64	SECOND READING
	06/14/84	74	THIRD READING
SB-1510	05/30/84	3	FIRST READING
	06/19/84	48	SECOND READING
	06/27/84	152	THIRD READING
SB-1513	05/30/84	3	FIRST READING
	06/19/84	49	SECOND READING
	06/26/84	107	RECALLED
	06/27/84	153	THIRD READING
SB-1518	05/24/84	2	FIRST READING
	06/13/84	6	SECOND READING
	06/20/84	77	THIRD READING
SB-1519	05/24/84	2	FIRST READING
	06/13/84	21	SECOND READING
	06/14/84	10	THIRD READING
SB-1522	05/23/84	2	FIRST READING
	06/21/84	18	SECOND READING

BILL NUMBER	DATE	PAGE	ACTION
SB-1522 (cont'd)	06/25/84	42	THIRD READING
	06/29/84	87	NON-CONCURRENCE
	06/30/84	67	CONFERENCE
SB-1524	05/25/84	188	FIRST READING
	06/21/84	41	SECOND READING
	06/25/84	45	THIRD READING
	06/29/84	15	NON-CONCURRENCE
	12/12/84	52	MOTION
	12/12/84	136	CONFERENCE
SB-1534	05/31/84	2	FIRST READING
	06/19/84	49	SECOND READING
	06/26/84	109	RECALLED
	06/27/84	154	THIRD READING
SB-1538	05/23/84	3	FIRST READING
	06/13/84	64	SECOND READING
	06/20/84	32	RECALLED
	06/25/84	47	RECALLED
	06/25/84	48	HELD ON SECOND
	06/25/84	96	THIRD READING
	06/28/84	159	NON-CONCURRENCE
	07/01/84	1	MOTION
	12/12/84	65	MOTION
	12/12/84	92	CONFERENCE
SB-1541	06/05/84	2	FIRST READING
	06/26/84	19	SECOND READING
	06/27/84	113	THIRD READING
	06/29/84	111	NON-CONCURRENCE
	07/01/84	58	CONFERENCE
SB-1546	05/31/84	2	FIRST READING
	06/26/84	74	SECOND READING
	06/27/84	145	RECALLED
	06/27/84	147	THIRD READING
	06/30/84	161	MOTION
	07/01/84	85	CONFERENCE
	07/01/84	131	OTHER
	07/01/84	148	CONFERENCE
SB-T547	06/05/84	2	FIRST READING
	06/19/84	50	SECOND READING
	06/27/84	155	THIRD READING
	06/29/84	111	NON-CONCURRENCE
	07/01/84	85	CONFERENCE
SB-1548	06/05/84	2	FIRST READING
	06/19/84	50	SECOND READING
	06/27/84	155	THIRD READING

PROGRAM-LRTRNMST
08/20/85

LEGISLATIVE INFORMATION SYSTEM
HOUSE OF REPRESENTATIVES

PAGE 311

MASTER TRANSCRIPT INDEX

BILL NUMBER	DATE	PAGE	ACTION
SB-1548 (cont'd)	06/29/84	112	NON-CONCURRENCE
	07/01/84	56	CONFERENCE
SB-1549	06/05/84	2	FIRST READING
	06/26/84	20	SECOND READING
	06/26/84	129	RECALLED
	06/27/84	159	RECALLED
	06/27/84	160	THIRD READING
	06/30/84	161	MOTION
	07/01/84	101	CONFERENCE
SB-1550	06/05/84	2	FIRST READING
	06/19/84	54	SECOND READING
	06/26/84	110	RECALLED
	06/27/84	176	THIRD READING
SB-1551	05/30/84	89	FIRST READING
	06/19/84	52	SECOND READING
	06/26/84	111	RECALLED
	06/27/84	169	THIRD READING
SB-1552	06/05/84	21	FIRST READING
	06/19/84	52	SECOND READING
	06/27/84	115	RECALLED
	06/27/84	129	THIRD READING
SB-1553	05/31/84	2	FIRST READING
	06/19/84	56	SECOND READING
	06/26/84	113	RECALLED
	06/27/84	185	THIRD READING
SB-1554	06/05/84	21	FIRST READING
	06/19/84	57	SECOND READING
	06/27/84	130	RECALLED
	06/27/84	142	THIRD READING
	06/30/84	161	MOTION
	07/01/84	109	CONFERENCE
SB-1555	05/31/84	2	FIRST READING
	06/26/84	22	SECOND READING
	06/27/84	147	THIRD READING
	06/30/84	161	MOTION
	06/30/84	165	MOTION
	07/01/84	46	NON-CONCURRENCE
SB-1556	05/31/84	2	FIRST READING
	06/19/84	65	SECOND READING
	06/26/84	113	RECALLED
	06/27/84	148	THIRD READING
SB-1557	05/31/84	2	FIRST READING

PROGRAM-LRTRNMST
08/20/85

LEGISLATIVE INFORMATION SYSTEM
HOUSE OF REPRESENTATIVES

PAGE 312

MASTER TRANSCRIPT INDEX

BILL NUMBER	DATE	PAGE	ACTION
SB-1557 (cont'd)	06/26/84	29	SECOND READING
	06/27/84	190	THIRD READING
	07/01/84	47	NON-CONCURRENCE
SB-1558	06/05/84	2	FIRST READING
	06/19/84	66	SECOND READING
	06/27/84	163	RECALLED
	06/27/84	168	THIRD READING
	06/30/84	161	MOTION
	07/01/84	112	CONFERENCE
SB-1559	05/30/84	3	FIRST READING
	06/19/84	69	SECOND READING
	06/26/84	115	RECALLED
	06/27/84	170	THIRD READING
SB-1560	05/30/84	89	FIRST READING
	06/13/84	81	SECOND READING
	06/14/84	68	THIRD READING
SB-1561	05/31/84	2	FIRST READING
	06/13/84	82	SECOND READING
	06/14/84	68	THIRD READING
SB-1562	06/05/84	16	FIRST READING
	06/19/84	70	SECOND READING
	06/26/84	118	RECALLED
	06/27/84	198	MOTION
	06/28/84	166	MOTION
	06/29/84	119	MOTION
	06/30/84	242	MOTION
	06/30/84	243	RECALLED
	06/30/84	245	THIRD READING
SB-1563	05/31/84	2	FIRST READING
	06/13/84	82	SECOND READING
	06/14/84	69	THIRD READING
SB-1564	05/31/84	3	FIRST READING
	06/19/84	70	SECOND READING
	06/27/84	149	THIRD READING
SB-1565	06/05/84	2	FIRST READING
	06/26/84	25	SECOND READING
	06/27/84	191	THIRD READING
SB-1566	05/31/84	3	FIRST READING
	06/19/84	71	SECOND READING
	06/27/84	156	RECALLED
	06/27/84	157	THIRD READING

BILL NUMBER	DATE	PAGE	ACTION
SB-1567	05/30/84	89	FIRST READING
	06/19/84	72	SECOND READING
	06/27/84	186	THIRD READING
SB-1568	05/31/84	3	FIRST READING
	06/26/84	32	SECOND READING
	06/27/84	176	RECALLED
	06/27/84	182	THIRD READING
SB-1569	05/30/84	89	FIRST READING
	06/12/84	15	SECOND READING
	06/14/84	70	THIRD READING
SB-1570	06/05/84	16	FIRST READING
	06/14/84	82	RECALLED
	06/14/84	83	THIRD READING
	07/01/84	71	NON-CONCURRENCE
SB-1571	05/31/84	3	FIRST READING
	06/26/84	33	SECOND READING
	06/27/84	169	THIRD READING
SB-1572	05/30/84	3	FIRST READING
	06/19/84	72	SECOND READING
	06/27/84	142	THIRD READING
SB-1573	05/31/84	3	FIRST READING
	06/19/84	72	SECOND READING
	06/26/84	121	RECALLED
	06/27/84	150	THIRD READING
SB-1574	06/05/84	16	FIRST READING
	06/26/84	34	SECOND READING
	06/27/84	183	THIRD READING
	06/30/84	161	MOTION
	07/01/84	113	CONFERENCE
SB-1575	05/31/84	3	FIRST READING
	06/19/84	74	SECOND READING
	06/26/84	122	RECALLED
	06/27/84	184	THIRD READING
SB-1576	05/31/84	3	FIRST READING
	06/19/84	74	SECOND READING
	06/27/84	143	THIRD READING
SB-1577	05/30/84	89	FIRST READING
	06/26/84	46	SECOND READING
	06/27/84	170	THIRD READING
SB-1578	05/31/84	3	FIRST READING

BILL NUMBER	DATE	PAGE	ACTION
SB-1578 (cont'd)	06/13/84	83	SECOND READING
	06/14/84	87	THIRD READING
SB-1579	05/30/84	89	FIRST READING
	06/19/84	75	SECOND READING
	06/27/84	187	THIRD READING
SB-1581	05/31/84	3	FIRST READING
	06/19/84	75	SECOND READING
	06/27/84	188	THIRD READING
SB-1582	05/31/84	4	FIRST READING
	06/19/84	75	SECOND READING
	06/27/84	189	THIRD READING
SB-1583	06/05/84	2	FIRST READING
	06/26/84	48	SECOND READING
	06/26/84	54	OUT OF RECORD
	06/26/84	86	SECOND READING
	06/27/84	185	THIRD READING
	07/01/84	48	NON-CONCURRENCE
SB-1584	06/05/84	16	FIRST READING
SB-1585	05/03/84	54	FIRST READING
	05/17/84	230	MOTION
	05/23/84	306	SECOND READING
	05/24/84	18	THIRD READING
SB-1586	05/31/84	4	FIRST READING
	06/19/84	75	SECOND READING
	06/27/84	196	THIRD READING
	12/12/84	5	MOTION
	12/12/84	50	MOTION
	12/12/84	51	NON-CONCURRENCE
	12/12/84	55	NON-CONCURRENCE
	12/12/84	135	CONFERENCE
SB-1587	05/30/84	90	FIRST READING
	06/26/84	54	SECOND READING
	06/27/84	144	THIRD READING
SB-1589	05/23/84	310	FIRST READING
	06/13/84	67	SECOND READING
	06/14/84	76	THIRD READING
SB-1590	05/30/84	3	FIRST READING
	06/19/84	78	SECOND READING
	06/26/84	123	THIRD READING
SB-1591	05/30/84	3	FIRST READING

BILL NUMBER	DATE	PAGE	ACTION
SB-1591 (cont'd)	06/19/84	84	SECOND READING
	06/26/84	123	THIRD READING
SB-1592	05/30/84	90	FIRST READING
	06/19/84	84	SECOND READING
	06/26/84	124	THIRD READING
SB-1593	05/30/84	3	FIRST READING
	06/19/84	85	SECOND READING
	06/26/84	125	THIRD READING
SB-1594	05/30/84	90	FIRST READING
	06/19/84	85	SECOND READING
	06/26/84	125	THIRD READING
SB-1595	05/30/84	3	FIRST READING
	06/26/84	54	SECOND READING
	06/26/84	59	OUT OF RECORD
	06/26/84	131	SECOND READING
	06/27/84	171	THIRD READING
SB-1596	05/23/84	4	FIRST READING
	06/06/84	16	SECOND READING
	06/12/84	33	THIRD READING
SB-1597	05/30/84	3	FIRST READING
	06/26/84	59	SECOND READING
	06/27/84	172	THIRD READING
SB-1598	05/23/84	4	FIRST READING
	06/06/84	17	SECOND READING
	06/12/84	34	THIRD READING
SB-1599	06/05/84	21	FIRST READING
	06/26/84	61	SECOND READING
	06/30/84	174	THIRD READING
	06/30/84	161	MOTION
	07/01/84	69	CONFERENCE
SB-1600	06/05/84	21	FIRST READING
	06/26/84	68	SECOND READING
	06/27/84	175	THIRD READING
SB-1602	05/23/84	2	FIRST READING
	06/13/84	6	SECOND READING
	06/14/84	25	SECOND READING
	06/19/84	2	THIRD READING
SB-1607	05/23/84	2	FIRST READING
	12/12/84	62	MOTION
	12/12/84	64	SECOND READING

BILL NUMBER	DATE	PAGE	ACTION
SB-1607 (cont'd)	01/09/85	2	RECALLED
	01/09/85	3	OUT OF RECORD
	01/09/85	5	SECOND READING
	01/09/85	10	THIRD READING
SB-1609	06/05/84	16	FIRST READING
	06/26/84	68	SECOND READING
	06/27/84	197	MOTION
	07/01/84	132	RECALLED
	07/01/84	135	THIRD READING
SB-1610	05/31/84	3	FIRST READING
	06/26/84	70	SECOND READING
	06/27/84	197	MOTION
	12/12/84	64	MOTION
	12/12/84	109	RECALLED
	12/12/84	121	THIRD READING
SB-1611	05/31/84	3	FIRST READING
SB-1612	05/25/84	187	FIRST READING
	06/21/84	22	SECOND READING
	06/21/84	23	OUT OF RECORD
	06/22/84	45	SECOND READING
	06/25/84	69	THIRD READING
	06/29/84	112	NON-CONCURRENCE
	07/01/84	129	CONFERENCE
SB-1618	05/23/84	2	FIRST READING
	06/13/84	21	SECOND READING
	06/14/84	11	THIRD READING
SB-1621	05/30/84	3	FIRST READING
	06/06/84	53	MOTION
	06/06/84	54	SECOND READING
	06/26/84	126	THIRD READING
SB-1625	05/25/84	188	FIRST READING
	06/21/84	23	SECOND READING
	06/22/84	135	RECALLED
	06/25/84	48	THIRD READING
SB-1629	05/23/84	310	FIRST READING
	06/13/84	69	SECOND READING
	06/22/84	48	SECOND READING
	06/25/84	54	THIRD READING
	06/29/84	20	NON-CONCURRENCE
	06/30/84	83	MOTION
	06/30/84	162	CONFERENCE
SB-1631	05/23/84	2	FIRST READING

PROGRAM-LRTRNMST
08/20/85
LEGISLATIVE INFORMATION SYSTEM
HOUSE OF REPRESENTATIVES
PAGE 317

MASTER TRANSCRIPT INDEX

BILL NUMBER	DATE	PAGE	ACTION
SB-1631 (cont'd)	06/20/84	48	SECOND READING
	06/25/84	64	THIRD READING
SB-1639	05/30/84	90	FIRST READING
SB-1644	05/23/84	2	FIRST READING
	06/20/84	65	SECOND READING
	06/22/84	125	RECALLED
	06/25/84	85	THIRD READING
	06/28/84	159	NON-CONCURRENCE
SB-1645	05/29/84	35	FIRST READING
SB-1649	06/05/84	2	FIRST READING
	06/26/84	72	SECOND READING
	06/27/84	151	THIRD READING
SB-1650	05/23/84	310	FIRST READING
	06/05/84	8	SECOND READING
	06/13/84	32	THIRD READING
	06/13/84	37	OUT OF RECORD
	06/14/84	91	THIRD READING
SB-1654	06/05/84	2	FIRST READING
	06/22/84	58	SECOND READING
	06/26/84	128	THIRD READING
SB-1655	05/29/84	2	FIRST READING
	06/13/84	6	SECOND READING
	06/20/84	77	THIRD READING
SB-1656	06/05/84	16	FIRST READING
	06/26/84	73	SECOND READING
	06/27/84	192	THIRD READING
SB-1657	05/15/84	199	FIRST READING
	05/29/84	33	MOTION
	05/30/84	37	SECOND READING
	05/30/84	37	MOTION
	05/31/84	13	THIRD READING
SB-1659	05/25/84	188	FIRST READING
	06/13/84	6	SECOND READING
	06/22/84	110	SECOND READING
	06/25/84	112	THIRD READING
SB-1664	05/23/84	3	FIRST READING
	06/22/84	58	SECOND READING
	06/25/84	98	THIRD READING
	12/12/84	7	VETO MESSAGE

PROGRAM-LRTRNMST
08/20/85
LEGISLATIVE INFORMATION SYSTEM
HOUSE OF REPRESENTATIVES
PAGE 318

MASTER TRANSCRIPT INDEX

BILL NUMBER	DATE	PAGE	ACTION
SB-1685	05/23/84	310	FIRST READING
	06/07/84	22	MOTION
SB-1691	05/23/84	310	FIRST READING
	06/13/84	70	SECOND READING
	06/14/84	91	THIRD READING
SB-1692	05/24/84	253	FIRST READING
	06/14/84	49	SECOND READING
	06/25/84	222	RECALLED
	06/25/84	223	THIRD READING
SB-1705	05/23/84	310	FIRST READING
	06/05/84	4	SECOND READING
	06/07/84	19	THIRD READING
SB-1707	05/23/84	311	FIRST READING
	06/13/84	80	SECOND READING
	06/14/84	92	THIRD READING
SB-1708	05/23/84	311	FIRST READING
	06/05/84	9	SECOND READING
	06/05/84	9	HELD ON SECOND
	06/07/84	10	SECOND READING
	06/12/84	38	THIRD READING
SB-1714	05/23/84	311	FIRST READING
	06/05/84	4	SECOND READING
	06/07/84	7	SECOND READING
	06/12/84	35	THIRD READING
SB-1725	05/29/84	35	FIRST READING
	06/13/84	71	SECOND READING
	06/19/84	37	RECALLED
	06/19/84	39	HELD ON SECOND
	06/21/84	24	SECOND READING
	06/22/84	136	RECALLED
	06/25/84	109	THIRD READING
SB-1727	05/24/84	2	FIRST READING
	06/22/84	59	SECOND READING
	06/25/84	123	THIRD READING
	12/12/84	28	VETO MESSAGE
SB-1728	05/24/84	253	FIRST READING
	06/05/84	4	SECOND READING
	06/07/84	19	THIRD READING
SB-1732	05/29/84	2	FIRST READING
SB-1733	05/29/84	3	FIRST READING

MASTER TRANSCRIPT INDEX

BILL NUMBER	DATE	PAGE	ACTION
SB-1733 (cont'd)	06/22/84	60	SECOND READING
	06/25/84	235	MOTION
	06/27/84	201	MOTION
	06/28/84	165	MOTION
	06/29/84	84	THIRD READING
	06/29/84	117	NON-CONCURRENCE
	06/30/84	182	CONFERENCE
SB-1734	05/23/84	311	FIRST READING
SB-1735	05/23/84	311	FIRST READING
	06/19/84	40	SECOND READING
	06/19/84	41	OUT OF RECORD
	06/20/84	45	SECOND READING
	06/22/84	134	RECALLED
	06/25/84	112	THIRD READING
	06/28/84	44	NON-CONCURRENCE
	06/30/84	8	CONFERENCE
SB-1740	05/23/84	311	FIRST READING
SB-1743	05/25/84	188	FIRST READING
	06/13/84	71	SECOND READING
	06/14/84	94	THIRD READING
	06/29/84	81	NON-CONCURRENCE
	06/30/84	166	CONFERENCE
SB-1746	05/23/84	311	FIRST READING
	06/22/84	107	SECOND READING
	06/25/84	130	THIRD READING
	06/29/84	82	NON-CONCURRENCE
	07/01/84	41	CONFERENCE
SB-1747	05/23/84	311	FIRST READING
	06/21/84	27	SECOND READING
	06/25/84	131	THIRD READING
SB-1750	06/13/84	83	SECOND READING
SB-1752	05/23/84	311	FIRST READING
SB-1754	05/30/84	4	FIRST READING
SB-1755	05/23/84	311	FIRST READING
	06/06/84	23	SECOND READING
	06/14/84	95	THIRD READING
SB-1756	05/24/84	253	FIRST READING
SB-1767	05/23/84	311	FIRST READING
	06/06/84	3	SECOND READING

MASTER TRANSCRIPT INDEX

BILL NUMBER	DATE	PAGE	ACTION
SB-1767 (cont'd)	06/14/84	135	THIRD READING
SB-1781	05/23/84	311	FIRST READING
	06/14/84	27	SECOND READING
	06/19/84	4	THIRD READING
SB-1790	05/25/84	188	FIRST READING
	06/22/84	68	SECOND READING
	06/25/84	235	MOTION
	06/27/84	201	MOTION
	06/28/84	128	OTHER
SB-1791	05/23/84	311	FIRST READING
	06/13/84	22	SECOND READING
	06/14/84	11	THIRD READING
SB-1793	05/24/84	253	FIRST READING
	06/21/84	30	SECOND READING
	06/25/84	132	THIRD READING
SB-1794	05/23/84	311	FIRST READING
	06/14/84	50	OUT OF RECORD
	06/21/84	33	SECOND READING
	06/21/84	36	OUT OF RECORD
	06/22/84	88	SECOND READING
	06/25/84	136	THIRD READING
	06/29/84	16	NON-CONCURRENCE
	06/30/84	249	CONFERENCE
SB-1797	05/23/84	312	FIRST READING
	06/06/84	3	SECOND READING
	06/14/84	27	SECOND READING
	06/22/84	118	RECALLED
	06/25/84	113	RECALLED
	06/25/84	122	THIRD READING
SB-1798	05/24/84	253	FIRST READING
	06/05/84	10	SECOND READING
	06/14/84	98	THIRD READING
SB-1801	05/23/84	312	FIRST READING
	06/13/84	6	SECOND READING
	06/20/84	77	THIRD READING
SB-1802	05/23/84	312	FIRST READING
SB-1803	05/25/84	188	FIRST READING
	06/21/84	36	SECOND READING
	06/25/84	137	THIRD READING
SB-1811	05/23/84	312	FIRST READING

MASTER TRANSCRIPT INDEX

BILL NUMBER	DATE	PAGE	ACTION
SB-1811 (cont'd)	06/06/84	23	SECOND READING
	06/06/84	25	OUT OF RECORD
	06/13/84	72	SECOND READING
	06/14/84	114	THIRD READING
SB-1812	05/23/84	312	FIRST READING
	06/06/84	25	SECOND READING
	06/14/84	115	THIRD READING
SB-1824	05/23/84	312	FIRST READING
	06/05/84	4	SECOND READING
	06/07/84	19	THIRD READING
SB-1839	05/23/84	312	FIRST READING
SB-1840	05/24/84	253	FIRST READING
	06/06/84	3	SECOND READING
	06/14/84	136	THIRD READING
SB-1841	05/23/84	312	FIRST READING
	06/07/84	11	SECOND READING
	06/14/84	116	RECALLED
	06/22/84	139	RECALLED
	06/25/84	157	THIRD READING
	06/29/84	81	NON-CONCURRENCE
	06/30/84	123	CONFERENCE
SB-1844	05/24/84	2	FIRST READING
	06/05/84	10	SECOND READING
	06/14/84	122	THIRD READING
	06/30/84	17	NON-CONCURRENCE
SB-1845	05/24/84	253	FIRST READING
	06/21/84	40	SECOND READING
	06/25/84	164	RECALLED
	06/25/84	165	THIRD READING
SB-1848	05/24/84	2	FIRST READING
SB-1850	05/29/84	3	FIRST READING
	06/14/84	51	SECOND READING
	06/25/84	235	MOTION
	06/27/84	201	MOTION
	06/28/84	165	MOTION
	06/29/84	119	MOTION
SB-1853	05/24/84	253	FIRST READING
	06/14/84	52	SECOND READING
	06/14/84	52	HELD ON SECOND
	06/21/84	37	SECOND READING
	06/25/84	166	THIRD READING

MASTER TRANSCRIPT INDEX

BILL NUMBER	DATE	PAGE	ACTION
SB-1853 (cont'd)	06/30/84	3	NON-CONCURRENCE
	06/30/84	247	CONFERENCE
SB-1855	05/24/84	2	FIRST READING
	06/21/84	44	SECOND READING
	06/25/84	168	THIRD READING
SB-1857	05/24/84	253	FIRST READING
	06/22/84	149	SECOND READING
	06/25/84	169	THIRD READING
SB-1859	05/24/84	2	FIRST READING
	06/05/84	14	SECOND READING
	06/25/84	172	RECALLED
	06/25/84	178	THIRD READING
SB-1861	05/24/84	253	FIRST READING
	06/06/84	3	SECOND READING
	06/14/84	136	THIRD READING
SB-1862	05/24/84	253	FIRST READING
	06/13/84	6	SECOND READING
	06/20/84	77	THIRD READING
SB-1864	05/29/84	3	FIRST READING
	06/14/84	52	SECOND READING
	06/22/84	144	RECALLED
	06/25/84	180	RECALLED
	06/25/84	184	THIRD READING
	06/30/84	6	NON-CONCURRENCE
	11/28/84	79	MOTION
	11/28/84	80	CONFERENCE
SB-1865	05/24/84	2	FIRST READING
	06/30/84	226	MOTION
SB-1866	05/24/84	311	FIRST READING
	06/12/84	4	SECOND READING
	06/14/84	20	MOTION
	06/14/84	21	RECALLED
	06/14/84	22	MOTION
	06/14/84	136	THIRD READING
SB-1870	05/24/84	312	FIRST READING
	06/13/84	22	SECOND READING
	06/14/84	13	THIRD READING
	06/29/84	8	NON-CONCURRENCE
	07/01/84	125	CONFERENCE
	12/11/84	10	VETO MESSAGE
	12/11/84	14	OUT OF RECORD
	12/11/84	18	VETO MESSAGE

PROGRAM-LRTRNMST
08/20/85
LEGISLATIVE INFORMATION SYSTEM
HOUSE OF REPRESENTATIVES
PAGE 323

MASTER TRANSCRIPT INDEX

BILL NUMBER	DATE	PAGE	ACTION
SB-1873	05/24/84	314	FIRST READING
SB-1875	05/24/84	312	FIRST READING
	06/07/84	33	MOTION
	06/13/84	74	SECOND READING
	06/14/84	117	THIRD READING
SB-1876	05/24/84	312	FIRST READING
	06/14/84	28	SECOND READING
	06/14/84	28	OUT OF RECORD
	06/22/84	144	RECALLED
	06/25/84	188	THIRD READING
SB-1878	05/25/84	187	FIRST READING
	06/13/84	29	SECOND READING
	06/14/84	13	THIRD READING
SB-1879	05/24/84	312	FIRST READING
	06/07/84	8	SECOND READING
	06/21/84	78	THIRD READING
SB-1880	05/29/84	35	FIRST READING
	06/06/84	4	SECOND READING
	06/14/84	136	THIRD READING
SB-1881	05/24/84	312	FIRST READING
	06/14/84	28	SECOND READING
	06/14/84	29	OUT OF RECORD
	06/19/84	41	SECOND READING
	06/20/84	6	THIRD READING
	06/29/84	8	NON-CONCURRENCE
SB-1882	05/29/84	35	FIRST READING
	06/12/84	4	SECOND READING
	06/14/84	136	THIRD READING
SB-1883	05/25/84	187	FIRST READING
	06/13/84	75	SECOND READING
	06/13/84	75	HELD ON SECOND
	06/13/84	80	SECOND READING
	06/25/84	194	THIRD READING
SB-1887	05/24/84	312	FIRST READING
	06/14/84	29	OUT OF RECORD
	06/19/84	43	SECOND READING
	06/21/84	79	THIRD READING
SB-1888	05/24/84	312	FIRST READING
	06/13/84	85	SECOND READING
	06/14/84	126	THIRD READING
	12/11/84	15	VETO MESSAGE

PROGRAM-LRTRNMST
08/20/85
LEGISLATIVE INFORMATION SYSTEM
HOUSE OF REPRESENTATIVES
PAGE 324

MASTER TRANSCRIPT INDEX

BILL NUMBER	DATE	PAGE	ACTION
SB-1889	05/25/84	188	FIRST READING
	06/14/84	58	SECOND READING
	06/25/84	194	THIRD READING
	06/25/84	236	MOTION
	06/27/84	201	MOTION
	06/28/84	165	MOTION
	06/29/84	119	MOTION
SB-1893	06/19/84	21	FIRST READING
	06/19/84	91	MOTION
	06/22/84	154	MOTION
	06/26/84	116	MOTION
	06/27/84	201	MOTION
	06/28/84	37	SECOND READING
	06/28/84	40	MOTION
	06/28/84	48	MOTION
	06/28/84	60	OTHER
	06/28/84	127	HELD ON SECOND
	06/28/84	165	MOTION
	06/29/84	64	SECOND READING
	06/29/84	76	MOTION
	06/29/84	77	THIRD READING
	06/29/84	118	NON-CONCURRENCE
	06/30/84	176	CONFERENCE
SB-1896	05/24/84	312	FIRST READING
	06/12/84	4	SECOND READING
	06/14/84	136	THIRD READING
SB-1905	05/24/84	312	FIRST READING
	06/06/84	4	SECOND READING
	06/14/84	136	THIRD READING
SB-1911	05/25/84	187	FIRST READING
	06/14/84	29	SECOND READING
	06/19/84	6	THIRD READING
	06/29/84	9	NON-CONCURRENCE
	06/30/84	153	CONFERENCE
SB-1920	05/24/84	312	FIRST READING
SB-1924	05/29/84	35	FIRST READING
	06/14/84	136	MOTION
	06/21/84	46	SECOND READING
	06/25/84	198	THIRD READING
	06/28/84	47	NON-CONCURRENCE
	12/11/84	19	MOTION
	12/12/84	56	CONFERENCE
SB-1925	05/25/84	187	FIRST READING
	06/13/84	76	SECOND READING

BILL NUMBER	DATE	PAGE	ACTION
SB-1925 (cont'd)	06/14/84	127	THIRD READING
	12/11/84	14	VETO MESSAGE
SB-1927	05/24/84	312	FIRST READING
SB-1928	05/24/84	312	FIRST READING
	06/13/84	23	SECOND READING
	06/14/84	14	THIRD READING
	06/29/84	10	NON-CONCURRENCE
	07/01/84	30	CONFERENCE
SB-1929	05/24/84	312	FIRST READING
	06/13/84	24	SECOND READING
	06/14/84	17	THIRD READING
SB-1930	05/24/84	313	FIRST READING
	06/12/84	4	SECOND READING
	06/14/84	30	SECOND READING
	06/19/84	7	THIRD READING
SB-1933	05/24/84	313	FIRST READING
	06/19/84	91	MOTION
	06/21/84	64	MOTION
	06/22/84	40	SECOND READING
	06/25/84	199	THIRD READING
	06/25/84	202	OUT OF RECORD
	06/25/84	204	THIRD READING
	06/28/84	45	NON-CONCURRENCE
	07/01/84	94	CONFERENCE
SB-1935	05/24/84	313	FIRST READING
	06/13/84	78	SECOND READING
	06/25/84	202	RECALLED
	06/25/84	233	THIRD READING
	12/11/84	16	VETO MESSAGE
SB-1936	05/24/84	313	FIRST READING
	06/13/84	26	SECOND READING
	06/19/84	8	THIRD READING
SB-1938	05/24/84	313	FIRST READING
	06/13/84	6	SECOND READING
	06/20/84	77	THIRD READING
SB-1939	05/24/84	313	FIRST READING
	06/13/84	78	SECOND READING
	06/21/84	70	RECALLED
	06/21/84	72	THIRD READING
	06/29/84	14	NON-CONCURRENCE
	06/30/84	155	CONFERENCE

BILL NUMBER	DATE	PAGE	ACTION
SB-1940	05/24/84	313	FIRST READING
	06/13/84	79	SECOND READING
	06/14/84	131	THIRD READING
SB-1941	05/30/84	89	FIRST READING
	06/13/84	79	SECOND READING
	06/14/84	132	THIRD READING
	06/14/84	134	OUT OF RECORD
	06/20/84	34	THIRD READING
SB-1943	05/25/84	187	FIRST READING
	06/14/84	30	OUT OF RECORD
	06/21/84	13	SECOND READING
	06/21/84	140	OTHER
	06/22/84	8	RECALLED
	06/22/84	9	THIRD READING
	06/30/84	3	NON-CONCURRENCE
SB-1944	05/24/84	313	FIRST READING
	06/13/84	6	SECOND READING
	06/20/84	78	THIRD READING
SB-1945	05/30/84	89	FIRST READING
	06/14/84	31	SECOND READING
	06/19/84	13	THIRD READING
	12/11/84	5	VETO MESSAGE
SB-1946	05/24/84	313	FIRST READING
	06/13/84	79	SECOND READING
	06/14/84	134	THIRD READING
SB-1947	05/30/84	89	FIRST READING
SB-1949	05/24/84	313	FIRST READING
	06/13/84	27	SECOND READING
	06/14/84	18	THIRD READING
SB-1950	05/25/84	187	FIRST READING
	06/14/84	33	SECOND READING
	06/19/84	13	THIRD READING
SB-1951	05/24/84	313	FIRST READING
	06/13/84	27	SECOND READING
	06/14/84	19	THIRD READING
SB-1953	05/24/84	313	FIRST READING
	06/13/84	6	SECOND READING
	06/20/84	78	THIRD READING
SB-1954	05/24/84	313	FIRST READING
	06/13/84	6	SECOND READING

BILL NUMBER	DATE	PAGE	ACTION
SB-1954 (cont'd)	06/20/84	78	THIRD READING
SB-1957	05/24/84	243	MOTION
	05/24/84	313	FIRST READING
	06/05/84	4	SECOND READING
	06/13/84	27	SECOND READING
	06/20/84	10	THIRD READING
SB-1958	11/29/84	2	FIRST READING
	12/12/84	5	MOTION
	12/12/84	53	MOTION
	12/12/84	123	SECOND READING
	01/09/85	23	RECALLED
	01/09/85	23	THIRD READING
SB-1959	11/29/84	2	FIRST READING
	12/11/84	29	MOTION
	12/12/84	5	MOTION
	12/12/84	53	MOTION
SB-1967	05/24/84	312	FIRST READING
HR-0001	01/12/83	39	ADOPTED
HR-0002	01/12/83	39	ADOPTED
HR-0003	01/12/83	40	ADOPTED
HR-0004	01/12/83	40	ADOPTED
	01/13/83	13	MOTION
HR-0014	01/26/83	7	RESOLUTION OFFERED
	01/26/83	114	ADOPTED
HR-0046	02/17/83	26	ADOPTED
HR-0047	06/07/83	20	ADOPTED
HR-0048	02/17/83	4	MOTION
HR-0055	02/23/83	3	RESOLUTION OFFERED
	02/23/83	4	MOTION
HR-0060	02/23/83	14	MOTION
	02/23/83	15	ADOPTED
HR-0062	02/24/83	8	ADOPTED
HR-0063	03/15/83	53	ADOPTED
HR-0079	03/03/83	7	ADOPTED

BILL NUMBER	DATE	PAGE	ACTION
HR-0081	06/07/83	21	ADOPTED
HR-0084	04/07/83	68	ADOPTED
HR-0088	03/09/83	31	MOTION
	03/09/83	59	ADOPTED
HR-0104	03/22/83	36	OTHER
HR-0115	03/16/83	43	MOTION
	03/16/83	45	ADOPTED
HR-0125	05/27/83	17	ADOPTED
HR-0127	04/13/83	7	TABLED
HR-0142	04/13/83	3	RESOLUTION OFFERED
HR-0155	06/07/83	21	ADOPTED
HR-0157	04/07/83	71	MOTION
	06/07/83	22	ADOPTED
HR-0159	06/21/84	97	ADOPTED
HR-0162	06/28/83	3	ADOPTED
HR-0176	04/15/83	102	ADOPTED
HR-0178	04/19/83	2	ADOPTED
HR-0204	04/27/83	31	ADOPTED
HR-0205	04/28/83	66	ADOPTED
HR-0210	04/28/83	64	ADOPTED
HR-0216	05/03/83	52	ADOPTED
HR-0224	06/21/84	98	ADOPTED
HR-0241	06/28/83	3	ADOPTED
HR-0244	07/01/83	191	ADOPTED
HR-0245	06/29/83	238	RESOLUTION OFFERED
	06/29/83	239	ADOPTED
HR-0252	05/20/83	201	ADOPTED
HR-0258	06/29/83	239	RESOLUTION OFFERED

BILL NUMBER	DATE	PAGE	ACTION
HR-0258 (cont'd)	06/29/83	243	ADOPTED
HR-0262	06/29/83	248	RESOLUTION OFFERED
	06/29/83	258	ADOPTED
HR-0264	06/28/83	3	ADOPTED
HR-0266	06/23/83	154	ADOPTED
HR-0271	05/17/83	182	MOTION
	05/17/83	194	RESOLUTION OFFERED
HR-0278	05/18/83	36	MOTION
	05/20/83	80	RESOLUTION OFFERED
	05/20/83	87	ADOPTED
HR-0279	05/18/83	36	MOTION
	05/20/83	81	RESOLUTION OFFERED
	05/20/83	87	ADOPTED
HR-0280	05/18/83	36	MOTION
	05/20/83	81	RESOLUTION OFFERED
	05/20/83	87	ADOPTED
HR-0281	05/18/83	102	RESOLUTION OFFERED
	05/18/83	104	ADOPTED
HR-0284	06/29/83	258	RESOLUTION OFFERED
	06/29/83	262	ADOPTED
HR-0314	06/28/83	3	ADOPTED
HR-0326	06/28/83	3	ADOPTED
HR-0327	06/28/83	3	ADOPTED
HR-0328	06/28/83	3	ADOPTED
HR-0329	06/28/83	3	ADOPTED
HR-0348	06/28/83	3	ADOPTED
HR-0349	06/28/83	3	ADOPTED
HR-0350	06/21/84	107	ADOPTED
HR-0357	06/09/83	3	ADOPTED
HR-0364	07/01/84	21	ADOPTED
HR-0369	06/21/83	230	ADOPTED

BILL NUMBER	DATE	PAGE	ACTION
HR-0372	06/15/83	181	ADOPTED
HR-0390	10/18/83	82	MOTION
	10/18/83	86	ADOPTED
HR-0391	03/28/84	10	TABLED
HR-0413	06/28/83	137	ADOPTED
	06/30/83	12	MOTION
	06/30/83	14	ADOPTED
HR-0420	06/25/83	4	ADOPTED
HR-0435	07/01/83	195	ADOPTED
HR-0457	06/30/83	175	ADOPTED
HR-0476	11/04/83	99	RESOLUTION OFFERED
HR-0493	10/19/83	231	RESOLUTION OFFERED
	10/19/83	235	ADOPTED
HR-0503	10/18/83	144	RESOLUTION OFFERED
	10/18/83	146	ADOPTED
HR-0508	10/20/83	175	RESOLUTION OFFERED
	10/20/83	176	ADOPTED
HR-0513	10/19/83	225	MOTION
	10/19/83	226	RESOLUTION OFFERED
HR-0529	11/04/83	49	MOTION
	11/04/83	51	RESOLUTION OFFERED
HR-0564	06/21/84	99	MOTION
	06/21/84	104	ADOPTED
HR-0567	11/02/83	241	RESOLUTION OFFERED
	11/02/83	242	ADOPTED
HR-0582	11/04/83	97	RESOLUTION OFFERED
	11/04/83	99	ADOPTED
HR-0597	03/28/84	6	RESOLUTION OFFERED
	03/28/84	8	ADOPTED
HR-0598	11/04/83	105	RESOLUTION OFFERED
	11/04/83	107	ADOPTED
HR-0601	11/04/83	204	ADOPTED

PROGRAM-LRTRNMST
08/20/85

LEGISLATIVE INFORMATION SYSTEM
HOUSE OF REPRESENTATIVES

PAGE 331

MASTER TRANSCRIPT INDEX

BILL NUMBER	DATE	PAGE	ACTION
HR-0620	02/08/84	34	ADOPTED
HR-0628	06/21/84	110	ADOPTED
HR-0640	02/08/84	2	ADOPTED
HR-0643	06/21/84	116	ADOPTED
HR-0717	03/07/84	2	RESOLUTION OFFERED
	03/07/84	4	ADOPTED
HR-0736	04/25/84	2	OTHER
HR-0748	03/27/84	6	ADOPTED
HR-0808	04/11/84	36	MOTION
	04/11/84	36	ADOPTED
HR-0809	04/11/84	36	MOTION
	04/11/84	36	ADOPTED
HR-0820	04/11/84	42	ADOPTED
HR-0822	04/11/84	37	ADOPTED
HR-0823	04/13/84	5	FIRST READING
	06/21/84	120	ADOPTED
HR-0837	07/01/84	1	ADOPTED
HR-0848	06/21/84	123	ADOPTED
HR-0872	05/03/84	2	RESOLUTION OFFERED
HR-0883	05/02/84	60	ADOPTED
HR-0929	05/15/84	195	ADOPTED
HR-0952	06/20/84	4	ADOPTED
HR-0961	07/01/84	3	ADOPTED
HR-0982	06/21/84	125	ADOPTED
HR-1013	06/21/84	127	ADOPTED
HR-1039	06/20/84	11	RESOLUTION OFFERED
HR-1043	06/13/84	84	ADOPTED
HR-1051	06/21/84	179	ADOPTED

PROGRAM-LRTRNMST
08/20/85

LEGISLATIVE INFORMATION SYSTEM
HOUSE OF REPRESENTATIVES

PAGE 332

MASTER TRANSCRIPT INDEX

BILL NUMBER	DATE	PAGE	ACTION
HR-1058	06/20/84	74	RESOLUTION OFFERED
HR-1095	06/30/84	39	MOTION
HR-1104	07/01/84	83	MOTION
	07/01/84	84	ADOPTED
HR-1105	06/26/84	3	ADOPTED
HR-1127	06/29/84	2	ADOPTED
HR-1141	06/29/84	113	MOTION
	06/29/84	114	ADOPTED
HR-1153	07/01/84	43	MOTION
	07/01/84	43	ADOPTED
HR-1159	06/30/84	18	MOTION
	06/30/84	19	RESOLUTION OFFERED
	07/01/84	6	TABLED
HR-1176	07/01/84	5	ADOPTED
	07/01/84	6	OUT OF RECORD
	07/01/84	21	ADOPTED
HR-1180	07/01/84	138	MOTION
	07/01/84	139	ADOPTED
HR-1264	11/27/84	70	ADOPTED
HR-1267	11/27/84	54	MOTION
	11/27/84	56	RESOLUTION OFFERED
	11/27/84	62	ADOPTED
	11/27/84	63	MOTION
HR-1273	11/27/84	25	ADOPTED
HR-1335	12/12/84	163	ADOPTED
HR-1384	01/09/85	50	RESOLUTION OFFERED
	01/09/85	62	ADOPTED
SR-0096	03/28/84	9	ADOPTED
HJR-0001	01/13/83	19	RESOLUTION OFFERED
HJR-0002	02/08/83	1	ADOPTED
HJR-0006	02/08/83	8	ADOPTED
HJR-0008	03/15/83	56	ADOPTED

PROGRAM-LRTRNMST
08/20/85
LEGISLATIVE INFORMATION SYSTEM
HOUSE OF REPRESENTATIVES
PAGE 333

MASTER TRANSCRIPT INDEX

BILL NUMBER	DATE	PAGE	ACTION
HJR-0012	02/17/83	11	MOTION
	02/17/83	16	ADOPTED
HJR-0013	06/28/83	124	CONCURRENCE
HJR-0014	03/02/83	3	ADOPTED
HJR-0020	03/22/83	28	ADOPTED
HJR-0022	04/05/83	51	MOTION
	04/05/83	52	ADOPTED
HJR-0026	04/26/83	7	ADOPTED
HJR-0030	04/19/83	64	ADOPTED
HJR-0033	06/29/83	188	RESOLUTION OFFERED
	06/29/83	191	ADOPTED
HJR-0035	06/28/83	124	CONCURRENCE
HJR-0036	04/28/83	116	ADOPTED
HJR-0048	05/27/83	230	ADOPTED
HJR-0050	05/27/83	230	ADOPTED
HJR-0062	06/20/83	17	ADOPTED
HJR-0064	06/23/83	307	MOTION
	06/23/83	311	ADOPTED
HJR-0068	10/18/83	80	MOTION
	10/18/83	81	ADOPTED
HJR-0072	07/02/83	154	ADOPTED
HJR-0105	11/04/83	92	MOTION
	11/04/83	93	RESOLUTION OFFERED
	11/04/83	95	OUT OF RECORD
	11/04/83	167	MOTION
	11/04/83	167	RESOLUTION OFFERED
HJR-0106	11/04/83	95	RESOLUTION OFFERED
	11/04/83	96	ADOPTED
HJR-0107	05/01/84	3	ADOPTED
HJR-0108	02/07/84	1	RESOLUTION OFFERED
HJR-0114	03/27/84	4	ADOPTED

PROGRAM-LRTRNMST
08/20/85
LEGISLATIVE INFORMATION SYSTEM
HOUSE OF REPRESENTATIVES
PAGE 334

MASTER TRANSCRIPT INDEX

BILL NUMBER	DATE	PAGE	ACTION
HJR-0120	03/06/84	2	ADOPTED
HJR-0123	05/09/84	10	RESOLUTION OFFERED
	05/16/84	206	ADOPTED
HJR-0124	06/21/84	128	ADOPTED
HJR-0137	04/11/84	34	ADOPTED
HJR-0138	04/12/84	3	FIRST READING
	06/21/84	128	ADOPTED
HJR-0142	05/03/84	49	OTHER
HJR-0146	05/10/84	2	ADOPTED
HJR-0147	06/29/84	6	CONCURRENCE
HJR-0151	06/20/84	71	RESOLUTION OFFERED
	06/20/84	73	OUT OF RECORD
	06/21/84	129	RESOLUTION OFFERED
HJR-0157	05/31/84	118	ADOPTED
HJR-0158	06/07/84	30	MOTION
	06/07/84	32	ADOPTED
HJR-0162	06/14/84	75	ADOPTED
HJR-0170	06/25/84	129	MOTION
	06/25/84	130	ADOPTED
HJR-0171	06/30/84	246	MOTION
	07/01/84	147	ADOPTED
	07/01/84	149	OTHER
HJR-0172	06/27/84	199	MOTION
HJR-0174	06/27/84	200	MOTION
	06/27/84	201	ADOPTED
HJR-0180	07/01/84	131	ADOPTED
HJR-0190	11/27/84	67	MOTION
	11/27/84	68	ADOPTED
	12/12/84	151	CONCURRENCE
HJR-0193	11/28/84	73	ADOPTED
HJR-0196	12/11/84	1	ADOPTED

MASTER TRANSCRIPT INDEX

BILL NUMBER	DATE	PAGE	ACTION
*HJR-0001	01/25/83	1	FIRST READING
	04/05/84	2	SECOND READING
	04/26/84	5	SECOND READING
	04/26/84	94	THIRD READING
	04/27/84	1	THIRD READING
	04/30/84	1	THIRD READING
	05/01/84	4	THIRD READING
*HJR-0002	01/27/83	7	FIRST READING
	04/26/83	38	SECOND READING
	11/03/83	14	SECOND READING
	11/03/83	14	THIRD READING
*HJR-0003	02/16/83	7	FIRST READING
	05/12/83	21	TABLED
*HJR-0004	02/16/83	8	FIRST READING
*HJR-0005	02/17/83	30	FIRST READING
	04/05/83	68	SECOND READING
	04/30/84	4	THIRD READING
	05/01/84	10	THIRD READING
*HJR-0006	02/23/83	19	FIRST READING
	03/22/83	34	SECOND READING
	11/03/83	10	SECOND READING
	04/26/84	95	THIRD READING
	04/27/84	2	THIRD READING
	04/30/84	2	THIRD READING
*HJR-0007	03/01/83	24	FIRST READING
*HJR-0008	03/02/83	49	FIRST READING
	11/03/83	39	SECOND READING
	04/26/84	7	SECOND READING
	05/02/84	20	THIRD READING
*HJR-0009	03/08/83	29	FIRST READING
*HJR-0010	03/14/83	45	FIRST READING
*HJR-0011	03/15/83	65	FIRST READING
	05/06/83	36	OTHER
*HJR-0012	03/15/83	69	FIRST READING
*HJR-0013	04/05/83	66	FIRST READING
	04/26/83	38	SECOND READING
	05/02/84	35	SECOND READING
	05/02/84	36	THIRD READING

MASTER TRANSCRIPT INDEX

BILL NUMBER	DATE	PAGE	ACTION
*HJR-0014	04/06/83	66	FIRST READING
	04/05/84	3	SECOND READING
	04/26/84	5	SECOND READING
	04/26/84	97	THIRD READING
	04/27/84	4	THIRD READING
	04/30/84	6	THIRD READING
	05/01/84	11	THIRD READING
*HJR-0015	04/26/83	40	FIRST READING
*HJR-0016	06/03/83	11	FIRST READING
*HJR-0017	11/03/83	40	FIRST READING
*HJR-0018	02/08/84	40	FIRST READING
*HJR-0019	03/06/84	10	FIRST READING
*HJR-0020	03/06/84	11	FIRST READING
	04/26/84	4	SECOND READING
	04/26/84	10	SECOND READING
	04/30/84	5	THIRD READING
	05/01/84	22	THIRD READING
*HJR-0021	03/07/84	28	FIRST READING
*HJR-0022	03/28/84	18	FIRST READING
*HJR-0023	04/10/84	21	FIRST READING
*HJR-0024	04/11/84	50	FIRST READING
*HJR-0025	04/19/84	9	FIRST READING
*HJR-0026	04/26/84	97	FIRST READING
*HJR-0042	03/28/84	11	TABLED
SJR-0001	01/13/83	16	ADOPTED
SJR-0005	02/24/83	6	ADOPTED
SJR-0007	03/03/83	18	ADOPTED
SJR-0011	03/10/83	27	ADOPTED
SJR-0012	03/09/83	30	ADOPTED
SJR-0013	07/01/84	7	RESOLUTION OFFERED
SJR-0014	03/16/83	6	ADOPTED

PROGRAM-LRTRNMST
08/20/85
LEGISLATIVE INFORMATION SYSTEM
HOUSE OF REPRESENTATIVES
PAGE 337

MASTER TRANSCRIPT INDEX

BILL NUMBER	DATE	PAGE	ACTION
SJR-0018	03/24/83	65	ADOPTED
SJR-0021	04/07/83	78	ADOPTED
SJR-0022	04/15/83	39	ADOPTED
SJR-0026	04/15/83	103	ADOPTED
SJR-0029	04/11/84	36	TABLED
SJR-0030	04/21/83	87	ADOPTED
SJR-0033	05/03/83	41	MOTION
	05/03/83	45	ADOPTED
SJR-0034	10/18/83	136	ADOPTED
SJR-0035	10/18/83	137	ADOPTED
	10/18/83	140	OUT OF RECORD
	10/20/83	123	ADOPTED
SJR-0036	06/29/83	191	ADOPTED
SJR-0038	07/02/83	167	ADOPTED
SJR-0039	05/06/83	2	ADOPTED
SJR-0042	05/13/83	215	ADOPTED
SJR-0045	05/20/83	202	ADOPTED
SJR-0050	06/03/83	8	ADOPTED
SJR-0052	06/29/83	152	ADOPTED
SJR-0053	06/10/83	41	ADOPTED
SJR-0056	06/17/83	100	ADOPTED
SJR-0060	07/01/83	226	MOTION
	07/01/83	228	ADOPTED
SJR-0061	07/01/83	107	ADOPTED
SJR-0063	10/05/83	5	ADOPTED
SJR-0070	10/20/83	174	ADOPTED
SJR-0074	11/04/83	204	ADOPTED
SJR-0075	01/11/84	2	ADOPTED

PROGRAM-LRTRNMST
08/20/85
LEGISLATIVE INFORMATION SYSTEM
HOUSE OF REPRESENTATIVES
PAGE 338

MASTER TRANSCRIPT INDEX

BILL NUMBER	DATE	PAGE	ACTION
SJR-0082	05/22/84	2	MOTION
	06/30/84	187	RESOLUTION OFFERED
	06/30/84	189	ADOPTED
SJR-0083	05/09/84	47	ADOPTED
SJR-0085	02/08/84	2	ADOPTED
SJR-0090	03/07/84	5	ADOPTED
SJR-0097	04/05/84	7	ADOPTED
SJR-0098	05/03/84	56	FIRST READING
SJR-0101	04/11/84	31	RESOLUTION OFFERED
	04/11/84	34	ADOPTED
SJR-0104	07/01/84	45	MOTION
	07/01/84	45	ADOPTED
SJR-0107	04/26/84	86	ADOPTED
SJR-0109	05/04/84	54	ADOPTED
SJR-0113	07/01/84	65	MOTION
	07/01/84	68	ADOPTED
SJR-0114	05/17/84	247	ADOPTED
SJR-0117	05/25/84	185	ADOPTED
SJR-0118	06/30/84	104	MOTION
	06/30/84	105	ADOPTED
SJR-0120	06/07/84	19	ADOPTED
SJR-0121	06/25/84	238	ADOPTED
SJR-0122	07/01/84	141	ADOPTED
SJR-0127	06/22/84	155	ADOPTED
SJR-0128	07/01/84	11	ADOPTED
SJR-0130	07/01/84	11	ADOPTED
SJR-0131	07/01/84	12	RESOLUTION OFFERED
SJR-0134	11/14/84	3	ADOPTED
SJR-0136	12/12/84	13	OTHER

MASTER TRANSCRIPT INDEX

DATE	PAGE	ACTION
12/12/84	153	MOTION
12/12/84	154	ADOPTED
12/12/84	67	RESOLUTION OFFERED
12/12/84	160	ADOPTED
01/09/85	29	ADOPTED
01/09/85	62	ADOPTED
12/11/84	49	MOTION
02/08/83	12	ADOPTED
03/02/83	9	ADOPTED
02/08/84	6	ADOPTED
03/07/84	6	ADOPTED
12/12/84	11	ADOPTED
05/17/84	229	MOTION

MASTER TRANSCRIPT INDEX

DATE	PAGE	SUBJECT
01/12/83	1	HOUSE TO ORDER - SECRETARY JIM EDGAR
	1	PRAYER - REVEREND CORNEAL DAVIS
	2	PRAYER - RABBI MORDECI SIMON
	3	PRAYER - BISHOP JOSEPH M. MCNICHOLAS
	5	PLEDGE OF ALLEGIANCE - SENATOR ALAN DIXON
	5	ROLL CALL FOR ATTENDANCE
	7	OATH OF OFFICE - MEMBERS
	9	NOMINATIONS FOR SPEAKER OF HOUSE
	27	OATH OF OFFICE - SPEAKER
	27	SPEAKER MADIGAN IN CHAIR
	43	APPOINTMENTS - MINORITY LEADERSHIP
	44	ADJOURNMENT
01/13/83	1	HOUSE TO ORDER - SPEAKER MADIGAN
	1	PRAYER - REVEREND BILL PECKHAM
	1	PLEDGE OF ALLEGIANCE
	2	ROLL CALL FOR ATTENDANCE
	4	RECESS
	4	PERFUNCTORY SESSION
	8	PERFUNCTORY SESSION - ADJOURNMENT
	8	HOUSE RECONVENES - SPEAKER MADIGAN IN CHAIR
	10	DEMOCRATIC LEADERSHIP
	12	REPRESENTATIVE GREIMAN IN CHAIR
	12	MESSAGE FROM SENATE
	18	AGREED RESOLUTIONS
	21	ADJOURNMENT
01/25/83	1	PERFUNCTORY SESSION - REP GREIMAN IN CHAIR
	1	PRAYER - CLERK O'BRIEN
	1	PLEDGE OF ALLEGIANCE
	1	COMMITTEE REPORT
	2	PERFUNCTORY SESSION - ADJOURNMENT
01/26/83	1	HOUSE TO ORDER - SPEAKER MADIGAN
	1	PRAYER - REVEREND WILLIAM PECKHAM
	1	PLEDGE OF ALLEGIANCE
	1	ROLL CALL FOR ATTENDANCE
	7	RECESS
	7	HOUSE RECONVENES - SPEAKER MADIGAN IN CHAIR
	114	AGREED RESOLUTIONS
	115	DEATH RESOLUTION
	116	GENERAL RESOLUTIONS
	119	DEATH RESOLUTION
	122	ADJOURNMENT
01/27/83	1	PERFUNCTORY SESSION
	1	HOUSE TO ORDER - SPEAKER GREIMAN
	1	PRAYER - REVEREND LUCCO
	1	PLEDGE OF ALLEGIANCE
	8	PERFUNCTORY SESSION - ADJOURNMENT

DATE	PAGE	SUBJECT
02/02/83	1	PERFUNCTORY SESSION
	1	HOUSE TO ORDER - SPEAKER O'BRIEN
	1	PRAYER - CLERK O'BRIEN
	1	PLEDGE OF ALLEGIANCE
	3	PERFUNCTORY SESSION - ADJOURNMENT
02/03/83	1	PERFUNCTORY SESSION
	1	HOUSE TO ORDER - SPEAKER BOWMAN
	1	PRAYER - CLERK O'BRIEN
	1	PLEDGE OF ALLEGIANCE
	1	PERFUNCTORY SESSION - ADJOURNMENT
02/08/83	1	HOUSE TO ORDER - SPEAKER GREIMAN
	1	PRAYER - REVEREND WILLIAM PECKHAM
	1	PLEDGE OF ALLEGIANCE
	7	RECESS
	7	HOUSE RECONVENES - SPEAKER MADIGAN IN CHAIR
	7	ROLL CALL FOR ATTENDANCE
	12	RECESS
	12	JOINT SESSION CONVENED
	14	STATE OF THE STATE MESSAGE - GOVERNOR THOMPSON
	27	JOINT SESSION ADJOURNED
	27	HOUSE RECONVENES - SPEAKER MADIGAN IN CHAIR
	27	ADJOURNMENT
02/09/83	1	HOUSE TO ORDER - SPEAKER MADIGAN
	1	PRAYER - REVEREND WILLIAM PECKHAM
	1	PLEDGE OF ALLEGIANCE
	1	ROLL CALL FOR ATTENDANCE
	2	COMMITTEE REPORT
	4	AGREED RESOLUTIONS
	5	GENERAL RESOLUTION
	5	DEATH RESOLUTIONS
	6	ADJOURNMENT
	6	PERFUNCTORY SESSION
	7	PERFUNCTORY SESSION - ADJOURNMENT
02/16/83	1	HOUSE TO ORDER - SPEAKER MADIGAN
	1	PRAYER - REVEREND EUGENE GIBSON
	1	PLEDGE OF ALLEGIANCE
	1	ROLL CALL FOR ATTENDANCE
	5	AGREED RESOLUTIONS
	7	ADJOURNMENT
	7	PERFUNCTORY SESSION
	11	PERFUNCTORY SESSION - ADJOURNMENT
02/17/83	1	HOUSE TO ORDER - SPEAKER MADIGAN
	1	PRAYER - PASTOR SAMMY HOOKS
	1	PLEDGE OF ALLEGIANCE
	1	ROLL CALL FOR ATTENDANCE
	2	COMMITTEE REPORTS

DATE	PAGE	SUBJECT
02/17/83 (cont'd)	24	AGREED RESOLUTIONS
	25	GENERAL RESOLUTIONS
	25	DEATH RESOLUTIONS
	28	ADJOURNMENT
	28	PERFUNCTORY SESSION
	28	COMMITTEE REPORT
	31	PERFUNCTORY SESSION - ADJOURNMENT
02/23/83	1	HOUSE TO ORDER - SPEAKER MADIGAN
	1	PRAYER - FATHER DANIEL J. COLLINS
	1	PLEDGE OF ALLEGIANCE
	1	ROLL CALL FOR ATTENDANCE
	2	COMMITTEE REPORT
	15	AGREED RESOLUTIONS
	15	GENERAL RESOLUTION
	17	ADJOURNMENT
	17	PERFUNCTORY SESSION
	21	PERFUNCTORY SESSION - ADJOURNMENT
02/24/83	1	HOUSE TO ORDER - SPEAKER MADIGAN
	1	PRAYER - FATHER DONALD MEIHLING
	2	PLEDGE OF ALLEGIANCE
	2	ROLL CALL FOR ATTENDANCE
	7	COMMITTEE REPORTS
	7	AGREED RESOLUTIONS
	10	ADJOURNMENT
	11	PERFUNCTORY SESSION
	11	COMMITTEE REPORT
	14	COMMITTEE REPORT
	15	PERFUNCTORY SESSION - ADJOURNMENT
03/01/83	1	HOUSE TO ORDER - SPEAKER MADIGAN
	1	PRAYER - REVEREND PAUL SIMMS
	1	PLEDGE OF ALLEGIANCE
	1	ROLL CALL FOR ATTENDANCE
	2	APPROVAL OF JOURNALS
	22	AGREED RESOLUTIONS
	22	GENERAL RESOLUTION
	23	ADJOURNMENT
	23	PERFUNCTORY SESSION
	25	PERFUNCTORY SESSION - ADJOURNMENT
03/02/83	1	HOUSE TO ORDER - SPEAKER MADIGAN
	1	PRAYER - FATHER PETER MASCARI
	2	PLEDGE OF ALLEGIANCE
	2	ROLL CALL FOR ATTENDANCE
	4	COMMITTEE REPORTS
	9	JOINT SESSION - CONVENE
	10	BUDGET MESSAGE - GOVERNOR THOMPSON
	26	JOINT SESSION - ADJOURNMENT
	26	HOUSE RECONVENES - SPEAKER MADIGAN IN CHAIR

ST

PROGRAM-LRTRNMST
08/20/85

LEGISLATIVE INFORMATION SYSTEM   PAGE 343
HOUSE OF REPRESENTATIVES

LEGISLATIVE INFORMATION SYSTEM   PAGE 344
HOUSE OF REPRESENTATIVES

MASTER TRANSCRIPT INDEX

MASTER TRANSCRIPT INDEX

PAGE	SUBJECT	DATE	PAGE	SUBJECT
d)				
28	REPRESENTATIVE GREIMAN IN CHAIR	03/09/83 (cont'd)	68	PERFUNCTORY SESSION - ADJOURNMENT
41	SPEAKER MADIGAN IN CHAIR			
46	AGREED RESOLUTIONS	03/10/83	1	HOUSE TO ORDER - SPEAKER MADIGAN
46	GENERAL RESOLUTION		1	PRAYER - FATHER RAYMOND RICK
46	DEATH RESOLUTION		1	PLEDGE OF ALLEGIANCE
47	ADJOURNMENT		1	ROLL CALL FOR ATTENDANCE
47	PERFUNCTORY SESSION		2	COMMITTEE REPORTS
49	COMMITTEE REPORT		26	AGREED RESOLUTIONS
50	MESSAGE FROM SENATE		26	DEATH RESOLUTION
50	PERFUNCTORY SESSION - ADJOURNMENT		28	ADJOURNMENT
			28	PERFUNCTORY SESSION
1	HOUSE TO ORDER - SPEAKER MADIGAN		30	PERFUNCTORY SESSION - ADJOURNMENT
1	PRAYER - REVEREND KENNETH COX			
1	PLEDGE OF ALLEGIANCE	03/14/83	1	HOUSE TO ORDER - SPEAKER MADIGAN
1	ROLL CALL FOR ATTENDANCE		1	PRAYER - REVEREND DONALD A. BORLAUG
3	COMMITTEE REPORTS		3	PLEDGE OF ALLEGIANCE
7	REPRESENTATIVE GREIMAN IN CHAIR		3	ROLL CALL FOR ATTENDANCE
18	AGREED RESOLUTION		37	AGREED RESOLUTIONS
19	DEATH RESOLUTION		43	ADJOURNMENT
20	ADJOURNMENT		43	PERFUNCTORY SESSION
20	PERFUNCTORY SESSION		46	PERFUNCTORY SESSION - ADJOURNMENT
22	COMMITTEE REPORT			
22	PERFUNCTORY SESSION - ADJOURNMENT	03/15/83	1	HOUSE TO ORDER - SPEAKER MADIGAN
			1	PRAYER - REVEREND MICHAEL SAILOR
1	HOUSE TO ORDER - SPEAKER MADIGAN		1	PLEDGE OF ALLEGIANCE
1	PRAYER - REVEREND EUGENE WINKLER		1	ROLL CALL FOR ATTENDANCE
1	PLEDGE OF ALLEGIANCE		2	COMMITTEE REPORTS
2	ROLL CALL FOR ATTENDANCE		60	AGREED RESOLUTIONS
3	APPROVAL OF THE JOURNALS		60	DEATH RESOLUTIONS
23	AGREED RESOLUTIONS		61	ADJOURNMENT
24	GENERAL RESOLUTIONS		62	PERFUNCTORY SESSION
25	DEATH RESOLUTION		70	PERFUNCTORY SESSION - ADJOURNMENT
26	ADJOURNMENT			
27	PERFUNCTORY SESSION	03/16/83	1	HOUSE TO ORDER - SPEAKER MADIGAN
27	MESSAGE FROM SENATE		1	PRAYER - REVEREND WAYNE VAN GELDEREN
30	PERFUNCTORY SESSION - ADJOURNMENT		1	PLEDGE OF ALLEGIANCE
			3	ROLL CALL FOR ATTENDANCE
1	HOUSE TO ORDER - SPEAKER MADIGAN		4	COMMITTEE REPORTS
1	PRAYER - FATHER HUGH CASSIDY		49	AGREED RESOLUTIONS
1	PLEDGE OF ALLEGIANCE		49	GENERAL RESOLUTIONS
1	ROLL CALL FOR ATTENDANCE		49	DEATH RESOLUTION
2	MESSAGE FROM SENATE		51	ADJOURNMENT
2	COMMITTEE REPORTS		51	PERFUNCTORY SESSION
3	APPROVAL OF JOURNALS		51	COMMITTEE REPORT
7	RECESS		52	PERFUNCTORY SESSION - ADJOURNMENT
8	HOUSE RECONVENES - SPEAKER MADIGAN IN CHAIR			
62	AGREED RESOLUTIONS	03/22/83	1	HOUSE TO ORDER - SPEAKER MADIGAN
62	GENERAL RESOLUTION		1	PRAYER - REVEREND BROOKS MARTIN
62	DEATH RESOLUTION		3	PLEDGE OF ALLEGIANCE
64	ADJOURNMENT		3	ROLL CALL FOR ATTENDANCE
64	PERFUNCTORY SESSION		3	COMMITTEE REPORT

DATE	PAGE	SUBJECT
03/22/83 (cont'd)	3	APPROVAL OF JOURNALS
	29	DEATH RESOLUTION
	33	ADJOURNMENT
	34	PERFUNCTORY SESSION
	43	PERFUNCTORY SESSION - ADJOURNMENT
03/23/83	1	HOUSE TO ORDER - SPEAKER MADIGAN
	1	PRAYER - RABBI ISRAEL ZOBERMAN
	1	PLEDGE OF ALLEGIANCE
	1	ROLL CALL FOR ATTENDANCE
	1	COMMITTEE REPORTS
	3	INTRODUCTION - STATE BASKETBALL CHAMPIONS
	7	RECONSIDERATION OF APPROVED JOURNALS
	15	COUNSEL GENERAL OF IRELAND - LIAM CANNIFFE
	32	ELECTION CONTEST REPORTS
	33	REPRESENTATIVE MCPIKE IN CHAIR
	82	AGREED RESOLUTIONS
	85	ADJOURNMENT
	85	PERFUNCTORY SESSION
	85	MESSAGES FROM SENATE
	88	COMMITTEE REPORT
	88	PERFUNCTORY SESSION - ADJOURNMENT
03/24/83	1	HOUSE TO ORDER - SPEAKER MADIGAN
	1	PRAYER - REVEREND DALE JIROUSEK
	1	PLEDGE OF ALLEGIANCE
	2	ROLL CALL FOR ATTENDANCE
	2	COMMITTEE REPORTS
	8	RECESS
	8	HOUSE RECONVENES - SPEAKER MADIGAN IN CHAIR
	24	REPRESENTATIVE MATIJEVICH IN CHAIR
	24	MESSAGE FROM SENATE
	31	SPEAKER MADIGAN IN CHAIR
	46	REPRESENTATIVE MCPIKE IN CHAIR
	65	AGREED RESOLUTIONS
	66	DEATH RESOLUTIONS
	66	GENERAL RESOLUTIONS
	66	ADJOURNMENT
	66	PERFUNCTORY SESSION
	66	MESSAGES FROM SENATE
	67	COMMITTEE REPORTS
	70	PERFUNCTORY SESSION - ADJOURNMENT
04/05/83	1	HOUSE TO ORDER - SPEAKER MADIGAN
	1	PRAYER - DR. RUDOLPH SCHULTZ
	1	PLEDGE OF ALLEGIANCE
	1	ROLL CALL FOR ATTENDANCE
	25	REPRESENTATIVE MCPIKE IN CHAIR
	45	REPRESENTATIVE GREIMAN IN CHAIR
	56	AGREED RESOLUTIONS
	57	DEATH RESOLUTIONS

DATE	PAGE	SUBJECT
04/05/83 (cont'd)	57	GENERAL RESOLUTIONS
	58	ADJOURNMENT
	58	PERFUNCTORY SESSION
	69	PERFUNCTORY SESSION - ADJOURNMENT
04/06/83	1	HOUSE TO ORDER - SPEAKER MADIGAN
	1	PRAYER - REVEREND THEODORE ROSE
	1	PLEDGE OF ALLEGIANCE
	2	ROLL CALL FOR ATTENDANCE
	2	COMMITTEE REPORTS
	46	REPRESENTATIVE MCPIKE IN CHAIR
	59	AGREED RESOLUTIONS
	63	ADJOURNMENT
	63	PERFUNCTORY SESSION
	63	COMMITTEE REPORTS
	67	PERFUNCTORY SESSION - ADJOURNMENT
04/07/83	1	HOUSE TO ORDER - SPEAKER MADIGAN
	1	PRAYER - REVEREND ERIC STUMPF
	1	PLEDGE OF ALLEGIANCE
	1	ROLL CALL FOR ATTENDANCE
	2	REPRESENTATIVE MCPIKE IN CHAIR
	4	COMMITTEE REPORTS
	77	AGREED RESOLUTIONS
	78	GENERAL RESOLUTIONS
	78	DEATH RESOLUTION
	81	ADJOURNMENT
	81	PERFUNCTORY SESSION
	81	MESSAGES FROM SENATE
	81	COMMITTEE REPORTS
	88	PERFUNCTORY SESSION - ADJOURNMENT
04/13/83	1	HOUSE TO ORDER - SPEAKER MADIGAN
	1	PRAYER - REVEREND PAUL FLESNER
	1	PLEDGE OF ALLEGIANCE
	1	ROLL CALL FOR ATTENDANCE
	37	RECESS
	38	HOUSE RECONVENES - SPEAKER MADIGAN IN CHAIR
	60	ADJOURNMENT
	60	PERFUNCTORY SESSION
	61	MESSAGE FROM SENATE
	70	PERFUNCTORY SESSION - ADJOURNMENT
04/14/83	1	HOUSE TO ORDER - SPEAKER MADIGAN
	1	PRAYER - FATHER ANTHONY TZORTZIS
	1	PLEDGE OF ALLEGIANCE
	1	ROLL CALL FOR ATTENDANCE
	2	COMMITTEE REPORTS
	5	REPRESENTATIVE GREIMAN IN CHAIR
	72	AGREED RESOLUTIONS
	74	GENERAL RESOLUTION

DATE	PAGE	SUBJECT
04/14/83 (cont'd)	74	ADJOURNMENT
	74	PERFUNCTORY SESSION
	74	MESSAGES FROM SENATE
	74	COMMITTEE REPORT
	87	COMMITTEE REPORTS
	88	PERFUNCTORY SESSION - ADJOURNMENT
04/15/83	1	HOUSE TO ORDER - SPEAKER MADIGAN
	1	PRAYER - REVEREND DON GLENN
	1	PLEDGE OF ALLEGIANCE
	2	ROLL CALL FOR ATTENDANCE
	2	COMMITTEE REPORTS
	5	RECESS
	6	PERFUNCTORY SESSION
	12	HOUSE RECONVENES - SPEAKER MADIGAN IN CHAIR
	15	REPRESENTATIVE MCPIKE IN CHAIR
	53	REPRESENTATIVE CAPPARELLI IN CHAIR
	103	AGREED RESOLUTIONS
	104	ADJOURNMENT
	104	PERFUNCTORY SESSION
	125	COMMITTEE REPORT
	147	PERFUNCTORY SESSION - ADJOURNED
04/19/83	1	HOUSE TO ORDER - SPEAKER MADIGAN
	1	PRAYER - REVEREND WILLIAM T. RUCKER
	2	PLEDGE OF ALLEGIANCE
	2	ROLL CALL FOR ATTENDANCE
	13	REPRESENTATIVE MCPIKE IN CHAIR
	68	AGREED RESOLUTIONS
	73	ADJOURNMENT
	73	PERFUNCTORY SESSION
	73	COMMITTEE REPORT
	74	PERFUNCTORY SESSION - ADJOURNMENT
04/20/83	1	HOUSE TO ORDER - SPEAKER MCPIKE
	1	PRAYER - REVEREND HAROLD CHIOLERO
	1	PLEDGE OF ALLEGIANCE
	1	ROLL CALL FOR ATTENDANCE
	2	COMMITTEE REPORTS
	38	SPEAKER MADIGAN IN CHAIR
	44	ADJOURNMENT
	44	PERFUNCTORY SESSION
	44	COMMITTEE REPORT
	44	PERFUNCTORY SESSION - ADJOURNMENT
04/21/83	1	HOUSE TO ORDER - SPEAKER MADIGAN
	1	PRAYER - REVEREND RICHARD CHRISMAN
	1	PLEDGE OF ALLEGIANCE
	2	ROLL CALL FOR ATTENDANCE
	2	COMMITTEE REPORTS
	21	REPRESENTATIVE YOURELL IN CHAIR

DATE	PAGE	SUBJECT
04/21/83 (cont'd)	85	AGREED RESOLUTIONS
	86	DEATH RESOLUTIONS
	86	GENERAL RESOLUTIONS
	91	ADJOURNMENT
	91	PERFUNCTORY SESSION
	91	COMMITTEE REPORT
	91	PERFUNCTORY SESSION - ADJOURNMENT
04/26/83	1	HOUSE TO ORDER - SPEAKER MCPIKE
	1	PRAYER - REPRESENTATIVE MCGANN
	1	PLEDGE OF ALLEGIANCE
	1	ROLL CALL FOR ATTENDANCE
	2	COMMITTEE REPORT
	2	RECESS
	2	HOUSE RECONVENES - REPRESENTATIVE MCPIKE IN CHAIR
	23	REPRESENTATIVE GREIMAN IN CHAIR
	38	ADJOURNMENT
	38	PERFUNCTORY SESSION
	45	PERFUNCTORY SESSION - ADJOURNMENT
04/27/83	1	HOUSE TO ORDER - SPEAKER MCPIKE
	1	PRAYER - REVEREND RICHARD MAYE
	2	PLEDGE OF ALLEGIANCE
	2	ROLL CALL FOR ATTENDANCE
	2	COMMITTEE REPORTS
	33	REPRESENTATIVE BRAUN IN CHAIR
	33	TURNER SWORN IN
	35	SPEAKER MCPIKE IN CHAIR
	57	AGREED RESOLUTIONS
	58	DEATH RESOLUTIONS
	59	ADJOURNMENT
04/28/83	1	HOUSE TO ORDER - SPEAKER MADIGAN
	1	PRAYER - FATHER ANTHONY TZORTZIS
	1	PLEDGE OF ALLEGIANCE
	1	ROLL CALL FOR ATTENDANCE
	2	COMMITTEE REPORTS
	40	REPRESENTATIVE GREIMAN IN CHAIR
	116	AGREED RESOLUTIONS
	117	PERFUNCTORY SESSION
	117	COMMITTEE REPORTS
	118	MESSAGES FROM SENATE
	118	PERFUNCTORY SESSION - ADJOURNMENT
05/03/83	1	HOUSE TO ORDER - SPEAKER MADIGAN
	1	PRAYER - REVEREND GEORGE WADDLES
	2	PLEDGE OF ALLEGIANCE
	2	ROLL CALL FOR ATTENDANCE
	3	COMMITTEE REPORTS
	3	MESSAGE FROM SENATE
	9	REPRESENTATIVE MCPIKE IN CHAIR

DATE	PAGE	SUBJECT
05/03/83 (cont'd)	56	ADJOURNMENT
	56	PERFUNCTORY SESSION
	56	MESSAGE FROM SENATE
	56	COMMITTEE REPORTS
	57	PERFUNCTORY SESSION - ADJOURNMENT
05/04/83	1	HOUSE TO ORDER - SPEAKER MADIGAN
	1	PRAYER - REVEREND R. MARK BIDDLE
	2	PLEDGE OF ALLEGIANCE
	2	ROLL CALL FOR ATTENDANCE
	7	COMMITTEE REPORTS
	8	REPRESENTATIVE BRESLIN IN CHAIR
	57	ADJOURNMENT
	57	PERFUNCTORY SESSION
	57	COMMITTEE REPORTS
	58	PERFUNCTORY SESSION - ADJOURNMENT
05/05/83	1	HOUSE TO ORDER - SPEAKER MCPIKE
	1	PRAYER - RABBI ISRAEL ZOBERMAN
	1	PLEDGE OF ALLEGIANCE
	1	ROLL CALL FOR ATTENDANCE
	1	COMMITTEE REPORTS
	21	REPRESENTATIVE GREIMAN IN CHAIR
	56	AGREED RESOLUTIONS
	58	DEATH RESOLUTIONS
	58	GENERAL RESOLUTIONS
	63	ADJOURNMENT
	63	PERFUNCTORY SESSION
	63	COMMITTEE REPORT
	64	PERFUNCTORY SESSION - ADJOURNMENT
05/06/83	1	HOUSE TO ORDER - SPEAKER MADIGAN
	1	PRAYER - REVEREND TERRY REBERT
	1	PLEDGE OF ALLEGIANCE
	2	ROLL CALL FOR ATTENDANCE
	37	AGREED RESOLUTIONS
	39	DEATH RESOLUTIONS
	39	GENERAL RESOLUTIONS
	40	ADJOURNMENT
	40	PERFUNCTORY SESSION
	40	COMMITTEE REPORTS
	46	PERFUNCTORY SESSION - ADJOURNMENT
05/10/83	1	HOUSE TO ORDER - SPEAKER MCPIKE
	1	PRAYER - REVEREND JERRY MOE
	2	PLEDGE OF ALLEGIANCE
	2	ROLL CALL FOR ATTENDANCE
	2	COMMITTEE REPORTS
	5	RECESS
	6	HOUSE RECONVENES - REPRESENTATIVE MCPIKE IN CHAIR
	21	REPRESENTATIVE GREIMAN IN CHAIR

DATE	PAGE	SUBJECT
05/10/83 (cont'd)	101	REPRESENTATIVE MATIJEVICH IN CHAIR
	141	REPRESENTATIVE CAPPARELLI IN CHAIR
	171	REPRESENTATIVE YOURELL IN CHAIR
	182	ADJOURNMENT
	182	PERFUNCTORY SESSION
	182	COMMITTEE REPORTS
	183	PERFUNCTORY SESSION - ADJOURNMENT
05/11/83	1	HOUSE TO ORDER - SPEAKER MCPIKE
	1	PRAYER - REVEREND WILLIAM J. PECKHAM
	1	PLEDGE OF ALLEGIANCE
	1	ROLL CALL FOR ATTENDANCE
	19	MESSAGE FROM SENATE
	47	REPRESENTATIVE GREIMAN IN CHAIR
	118	REPRESENTATIVE BRESLIN IN CHAIR
	179	REPRESENTATIVE MCPIKE IN CHAIR
	196	AGREED RESOLUTIONS
	197	DEATH RESOLUTION
	197	GENERAL RESOLUTIONS
	197	ADJOURNMENT
05/12/83	1	HOUSE TO ORDER - SPEAKER MADIGAN
	1	PRAYER - FATHER ANTHONY TZORTIZ
	1	PLEDGE OF ALLEGIANCE
	1	ROLL CALL FOR ATTENDANCE
	2	COMMITTEE REPORT
	55	REPRESENTATIVE CAPPARELLI IN CHAIR
	85	RECESS
	86	HOUSE RECONVENES - REP. CAPPARELLI IN CHAIR
	112	REPRESENTATIVE GREIMAN IN CHAIR
	179	SPEAKER MADIGAN IN CHAIR
	188	AGREED RESOLUTIONS
	189	GENERAL RESOLUTIONS
	189	ADJOURNMENT
05/13/83	1	HOUSE TO ORDER - SPEAKER MCPIKE
	1	PRAYER - REVEREND JOSEPH MILLER
	1	PLEDGE OF ALLEGIANCE
	1	ROLL CALL FOR ATTENDANCE
	31	SPEAKER MADIGAN IN CHAIR
	102	REPRESENTATIVE MATIJEVICH IN CHAIR
	204	SPEAKER MADIGAN IN CHAIR
	216	ADJOURNMENT
05/17/83	1	HOUSE TO ORDER - SPEAKER MADIGAN
	1	PRAYER - RABBI ISRAEL ZOBERMAN
	1	PLEDGE OF ALLEGIANCE
	1	ROLL CALL FOR ATTENDANCE
	42	RECESS
	43	HOUSE TO ORDER - SPEAKER MADIGAN IN CHAIR
	98	REPRESENTATIVE YOURELL IN CHAIR

MASTER TRANSCRIPT INDEX

MASTER TRANSCRIPT INDEX

PAGE	SUBJECT
160	GENERAL RESOLUTIONS
180	SPEAKER MADIGAN IN CHAIR
194	AGREED RESOLUTIONS
195	COMMITTEE REPORTS
195	ADJOURNMENT
1	HOUSE TO ORDER - SPEAKER MADIGAN
1	PLEDGE OF ALLEGIANCE
1	ROLL CALL FOR ATTENDANCE
37	REPRESENTATIVE MATIJEVICH IN CHAIR
96	PRAYER - MOST REVEREND INNOCENT LOTOCKY
172	SPEAKER MADIGAN IN CHAIR
193	REPRESENTATIVE BRAUN IN CHAIR
208	SPEAKER MADIGAN IN CHAIR
213	REPRESENTATIVE BRAUN IN CHAIR
290	COMMITTEE REPORT
291	ADJOURNMENT
1	HOUSE TO ORDER - SPEAKER MCPIKE
1	PRAYER - REVEREND JAMES NEWMAN
1	PLEDGE OF ALLEGIANCE
1	ROLL CALL FOR ATTENDANCE
36	REPRESENTATIVE MATIJEVICH IN CHAIR
81	REPRESENTATIVE GREIMAN IN CHAIR
85	REPRESENTATIVE CAPPARELLI IN CHAIR
102	REPRESENTATIVE GREIMAN IN CHAIR
219	MESSAGE FROM SENATE
219	COMMITTEE REPORT
248	SPEAKER MADIGAN IN CHAIR
255	REPRESENTATIVE CAPPARELLI IN CHAIR
272	AGREED RESOLUTIONS
272	GENERAL RESOLUTIONS
272	DEATH RESOLUTION
273	MESSAGE FROM SENATE
273	ADJOURNMENT
1	HOUSE TO ORDER - SPEAKER MADIGAN
1	PRAYER - REVEREND JOE HARROD
2	PLEDGE OF ALLEGIANCE
2	ROLL CALL FOR ATTENDANCE
30	REPRESENTATIVE YOURELL IN CHAIR
55	REPRESENTATIVE GREIMAN IN CHAIR
100	REPRESENTATIVE YOURELL IN CHAIR
203	ADJOURNMENT
1	REPRESENTATIVE MCPIKE IN CHAIR
1	ROLL CALL FOR ATTENDANCE
44	REPRESENTATIVE GREIMAN IN CHAIR
220	REPRESENTATIVE YOURELL IN CHAIR
226	AGREED RESOLUTIONS
227	DEATH RESOLUTIONS

DATE	PAGE	SUBJECT
05/23/83 (cont'd)	227	ADJOURNMENT
	227	PERFUNCTORY SESSION
	228	MESSAGES FROM SENATE
	228	PERFUNCTORY SESSION - ADJOURNMENT
05/24/83	1	HOUSE TO ORDER - SPEAKER MADIGAN
	1	PRAYER - REVEREND JOHN A. RENKEN
	1	PLEDGE OF ALLEGIANCE
	1	ROLL CALL FOR ATTENDANCE
	26	REPRESENTATIVE MATIJEVICH IN CHAIR
	78	REPRESENTATIVE YOURELL IN CHAIR
	185	REPRESENTATIVE BRESLIN IN CHAIR
	296	ADJOURNMENT
	296	PERFUNCTORY SESSION
	296	MESSAGE FROM SENATE
	305	PERFUNCTORY SESSION - ADJOURNMENT
05/25/83	1	HOUSE TO ORDER - SPEAKER MADIGAN
	1	PRAYER - REVEREND W. P. WITKOP
	1	PLEDGE OF ALLEGIANCE
	1	ROLL CALL FOR ATTENDANCE
	108	REPRESENTATIVE GREIMAN IN CHAIR
	230	REPRESENTATIVE GREIMAN IN CHAIR
	242	MESSAGE FROM SENATE
	317	REPRESENTATIVE BRAUN IN CHAIR
	318	AGREED RESOLUTIONS
	319	DEATH RESOLUTIONS
	319	ADJOURNMENT
	319	PERFUNCTORY SESSION
	319	MESSAGE FROM SENATE
	319	CONSENT CALENDAR 2ND READING 2ND DAY
	320	PERFUNCTORY SESSION - ADJOURNMENT
05/26/83	1	HOUSE TO ORDER - REPRESENTATIVE MCPIKE
	1	PRAYER - FATHER ANTHONY TZORTZIS
	1	PLEDGE OF ALLEGIANCE
	1	ROLL CALL FOR ATTENDANCE
	23	REPRESENTATIVE MATIJEVICH IN CHAIR
	105	REPRESENTATIVE YOURELL IN CHAIR
	128	REPRESENTATIVE CAPPARELLI IN CHAIR
	129	REPRESENTATIVE YOURELL IN CHAIR
	218	REPRESENTATIVE BRESLIN IN CHAIR
	237	REPRESENTATIVE MATIJEVICH IN CHAIR
	242	REPRESENTATIVE BRESLIN IN CHAIR
	296	CONSENT CALENDAR - VOTE
	300	AGREED RESOLUTIONS
	302	ADJOURNMENT
	302	PERFUNCTORY SESSION
	302	MESSAGES FROM SENATE
	317	MESSAGES FROM SENATE
	317	PERFUNCTORY SESSION - ADJOURNMENT

DATE	PAGE	SUBJECT
05/27/83	1	HOUSE TO ORDER - SPEAKER MADIGAN
	1	PRAYER - REVEREND PAUL J. EVANS
	1	PLEDGE OF ALLEGIANCE
	1	ROLL CALL FOR ATTENDANCE
	15	REPRESENTATIVE MATIJEVICH IN CHAIR
	56	SPEAKER MADIGAN IN CHAIR
	109	REPRESENTATIVE MATIJEVICH IN CHAIR
	134	SPEAKER MADIGAN IN CHAIR
	172	REPRESENTATIVE MATIJEVICH IN CHAIR
	180	SPEAKER MADIGAN IN CHAIR
	231	ADJOURNMENT
	231	PERFUNCTORY SESSION
	232	MESSAGES FROM SENATE
	244	PERFUNCTORY SESSION - ADJOURNMENT
06/01/83	1	HOUSE TO ORDER - SPEAKER MADIGAN
	1	PRAYER - FATHER JOHN SPREEN
	2	PLEDGE OF ALLEGIANCE
	2	ROLL CALL FOR ATTENDANCE
	2	MESSAGES FROM SENATE
	8	COMMITTEE REPORTS
	9	AGREED RESOLUTIONS
	10	GENERAL RESOLUTIONS
	11	ADJOURNMENT
06/02/83	1	HOUSE TO ORDER - SPEAKER MADIGAN
	1	PRAYER - FATHER EUGENE COSTA
	1	PLEDGE OF ALLEGIANCE
	1	ROLL CALL FOR ATTENDANCE
	8	GENERAL RESOLUTIONS
	8	AGREED RESOLUTIONS
	9	DEATH RESOLUTION
	18	REPRESENTATIVE GREIMAN IN CHAIR
	19	ADJOURNMENT
	19	PERFUNCTORY SESSION
	19	COMMITTEE REPORTS
	21	PERFUNCTORY SESSION - ADJOURNMENT
06/03/83	1	HOUSE TO ORDER - SPEAKER MADIGAN
	1	PRAYER - RABBI ISRAEL ZOBERMAN
	1	PLEDGE OF ALLEGIANCE
	1	ROLL CALL FOR ATTENDANCE
	2	MESSAGE FROM SENATE
	2	COMMITTEE REPORTS
	9	AGREED RESOLUTIONS
	10	GENERAL RESOLUTIONS
	10	COMMITTEE REPORT
	11	ADJOURNMENT
	11	PERFUNCTORY SESSION
	15	PERFUNCTORY SESSION - ADJOURNMENT

DATE	PAGE	SUBJECT
06/07/83	1	HOUSE TO ORDER - SPEAKER MADIGAN
	1	ROLL CALL FOR ATTENDANCE
	1	MESSAGES FROM SENATE
	1	COMMITTEE REPORTS
	8	RECESS
	8	HOUSE RECONVENES - MADIGAN IN CHAIR
	32	ADJOURNMENT
06/08/83	1	HOUSE TO ORDER - SPEAKER MCPIKE
	1	PRAYER - REVEREND DR. JAMES H. HARGETT
	1	PLEDGE OF ALLEGIANCE
	1	ROLL CALL FOR ATTENDANCE
	48	AGREED RESOLUTIONS
	50	GENERAL RESOLUTIONS
	50	DEATH RESOLUTION
	51	COMMITTEE REPORT
	52	ADJOURNMENT
06/09/83	1	HOUSE TO ORDER - SPEAKER MADIGAN
	1	PRAYER - FATHER ANTHONY TZORTZIS
	1	PLEDGE OF ALLEGIANCE
	4	REPRESENTATIVE MATIJEVICH IN CHAIR
	34	ADJOURNMENT
	34	PERFUNCTORY SESSION
	34	COMMITTEE REPORTS
	37	PERFUNCTORY SESSION - ADJOURNMENT
06/10/83	1	HOUSE TO ORDER - SPEAKER MADIGAN
	1	PRAYER - RABBI ISRAEL ZOBERMAN
	1	PLEDGE OF ALLEGIANCE
	2	ROLL CALL FOR ATTENDANCE
	2	COMMITTEE REPORTS
	40	AGREED RESOLUTIONS
	40	GENERAL RESOLUTIONS
	41	DEATH RESOLUTIONS
	42	ADJOURNMENT
	42	PERFUNCTORY SESSION
	42	COMMITTEE REPORTS
	44	PERFUNCTORY SESSION - ADJOURNMENT
06/14/83	1	HOUSE TO ORDER - SPEAKER MCPIKE
	1	PRAYER - REVEREND JOHN C. FERGUSON
	2	PLEDGE OF ALLEGIANCE
	2	ROLL CALL FOR ATTENDANCE
	3	COMMITTEE REPORT
	28	RECESS
	28	HOUSE RECONVENES - REPRESENTATIVE GREIMAN IN CH
	63	CONSENT CALENDAR - THIRD READING VOTE
	64	COMMITTEE REPORT

PROGRAM-LRTRNMST
08/20/85

LEGISLATIVE INFORMATION SYSTEM   PAGE 355
HOUSE OF REPRESENTATIVES

MASTER TRANSCRIPT INDEX

PROGRAM-LRTRNMST
08/20/85

LEGISLATIVE INFORMATION SYSTEM   PAGE 356
HOUSE OF REPRESENTATIVES

MASTER TRANSCRIPT INDEX

DATE	PAGE	SUBJECT
06/14/83 (cont'd)	64	AGREED RESOLUTIONS
	64	GENERAL RESOLUTIONS
	64	DEATH RESOLUTION
	65	ADJOURNMENT
06/15/83	1	HOUSE TO ORDER - REPRESENTATIVE MCPIKE
	1	PRAYER - REVEREND JAMES HOLIMAN
	2	PLEDGE OF ALLEGIANCE
	2	ROLL CALL FOR ATTENDANCE
	4	COMMITTEE REPORT
	4	MESSAGE FROM SENATE
	4	RECESS
	4	HOUSE RECONVENES - REPRESENTATIVE MCPIKE IN CHAIR
	18	REPRESENTATIVE MATIJEVICH IN CHAIR
	80	REPRESENTATIVE YOURELL IN CHAIR
	124	RECESS
	124	COMMITTEE REPORTS
	125	HOUSE TO ORDER - REPRESENTATIVE YOURELL IN CHAIR
	180	AGREED RESOLUTIONS
	181	DEATH RESOLUTION
	184	ADJOURNMENT
06/16/83	1	HOUSE TO ORDER - REPRESENTATIVE MCPIKE
	1	PRAYER - FATHER JOSEPH CERNICM
	1	PLEDGE OF ALLEGIANCE
	1	ROLL CALL FOR ATTENDANCE
	2	RECESS
	2	PERFUNCTORY SESSION
	2	COMMITTEE REPORT
	3	CONSENT CALENDAR THIRD READING - SECOND DAY
	7	PERFUNCTORY SESSION - ADJOURNMENT
	7	HOUSE RECONVENES - REPRESENTATIVE MCPIKE IN CHAIR
	7	COMMITTEE REPORT
	11	REPRESENTATIVE BRESLIN IN CHAIR
	139	REPRESENTATIVE BRAUN IN CHAIR
	185	ADJOURNMENT
06/17/83	1	HOUSE TO ORDER - REPRESENTATIVE MCPIKE
	1	PRAYER - RABBI ISREAL ZOBERMAN
	1	PLEDGE OF ALLEGIANCE
	1	ROLL CALL FOR ATTENDANCE
	11	SPEAKER MADIGAN IN CHAIR
	12	RECESS
	12	HOUSE RECONVENES - SPEAKER MADIGAN IN CHAIR
	39	REPRESENTATIVE MATIJEVICH IN CHAIR
	99	COMMITTEE REPORTS
	99	AGREED RESOLUTIONS
	100	GENERAL RESOLUTIONS
	101	ADJOURNMENT
06/20/83	1	HOUSE TO ORDER - REPRESENTATIVE MCPIKE

DATE	PAGE	SUBJECT
06/20/83 (cont'd)	1	PRAYER - REVEREND OPHILIS MCCOY
	2	PLEDGE OF ALLEGIANCE
	2	ROLL CALL FOR ATTENDANCE
	17	SPEAKER MADIGAN IN CHAIR
	18	CONSUL GENERAL OF ITALY - DR. CLAUDIO FERRARI
	46	REPRESENTATIVE GREIMAN IN CHAIR
	125	REPRESENTATIVE MATIJEVICH IN CHAIR
	192	ADJOURNMENT
06/21/83	1	HOUSE TO ORDER - SPEAKER MADIGAN
	1	PRAYER - DR. ARNO Q. WENIGER
	1	PLEDGE OF ALLEGIANCE
	1	ROLL CALL FOR ATTENDANCE
	2	MESSAGE FROM SENATE
	15	REPRESENTATIVE MCPIKE IN CHAIR
	55	CONSENT CALENDAR - VOTE
	71	REPRESENTATIVE GREIMAN IN CHAIR
	77	REPRESENTATIVE MCPIKE IN CHAIR
	109	REPRESENTATIVE GREIMAN IN CHAIR
	140	REPRESENTATIVE BRESLIN IN CHAIR
	142	REPRESENTATIVE YOURELL IN CHAIR
	145	REPRESENTATIVE MATIJEVICH IN CHAIR
	147	REPRESENTATIVE YOURELL IN CHAIR
	196	REPRESENTATIVE MATIJEVICH IN CHAIR
	208	REPRESENTATIVE YOURELL IN CHAIR
	228	AGREED RESOLUTIONS
	229	GENERAL RESOLUTIONS
	232	ADJOURNMENT
06/22/83	1	HOUSE TO ORDER - REPRESENTATIVE MCPIKE
	1	PRAYER - REVEREND PHILIP KAUFMAN
	1	PLEDGE OF ALLEGIANCE
	2	ROLL CALL FOR ATTENDANCE
	2	MESSAGE FROM SENATE
	6	REPRESENTATIVE CAPPARELLI IN CHAIR
	13	SPEAKER MADIGAN IN CHAIR
	14	REPRESENTATIVE CAPPARELLI IN CHAIR
	31	REPRESENTATIVE YOURELL IN CHAIR
	66	REPRESENTATIVE MATIJEVICH IN CHAIR
	109	REPRESENTATIVE GREIMAN IN CHAIR
	168	COMMITTEE REPORT
	179	RECESS
	181	HOUSE RECONVENES - REP. GREIMAN IN CHAIR
	263	REPRESENTATIVE MCPIKE IN CHAIR
	278	ADJOURNMENT
	278	PERFUNCTORY SESSION
	278	CONSENT CALENDAR - 3RD READING - 1ST LEG. DAY
	279	PERFUNCTORY SESSION - ADJOURNMENT
06/23/83	1	HOUSE TO ORDER - REPRESENTATIVE MCPIKE
	1	PRAYER - FATHER ANTHONY TZORTZIS

DATE	PAGE	SUBJECT
06/23/83 (cont'd)	1	PLEDGE OF ALLEGIANCE
	1	ROLL CALL FOR ATTENDANCE
	1	AGREED RESOLUTIONS
	2	DEATH RESOLUTION
	8	MESSAGE FROM SENATE
	8	REPRESENTATIVE MATIJEVICH IN CHAIR
	112	REPRESENTATIVE BRESLIN IN CHAIR
	208	REPRESENTATIVE MATIJEVICH IN CHAIR
	315	ADJOURNMENT
	315	PERFUNCTORY SESSION
	315	CONSENT CALENDAR - 3RD READING - 2ND DAY
	315	PERFUNCTORY SESSION - ADJOURNMENT
06/24/83	1	HOUSE TO ORDER - REPRESENTATIVE MCPIKE
	1	PRAYER - FATHER JOHN SPREEN
	1	PLEDGE OF ALLEGIANCE
	1	ROLL CALL FOR ATTENDANCE
	18	REPRESENTATIVE MATIJEVICH IN CHAIR
	113	REPRESENTATIVE BRESLIN IN CHAIR
	176	REPRESENTATIVE MATIJEVICH IN CHAIR
	224	RECESS
	225	HOUSE RECONVENES - REP. MATIJEVICH IN CHAIR
	225	MESSAGE FROM SENATE
	298	ADJOURNMENT
	298	PERFUNCTORY SESSION
	298	CONSENT CALENDAR - THIRD READING - ROLL CALLS
	300	PERFUNCTORY SESSION - ADJOURNMENT
06/25/83	1	HOUSE TO ORDER - REPRESENTATIVE MCPIKE
	1	PRAYER - FATHER JOHN BEVERIDGE
	1	PLEDGE OF ALLEGIANCE
	2	ROLL CALL FOR ATTENDANCE
	3	AGREED RESOLUTIONS
	9	MESSAGE FROM SENATE
	9	GENERAL RESOLUTIONS
	9	DEATH RESOLUTION
	12	REPRESENTATIVE GREIMAN IN CHAIR
	122	REPRESENTATIVE MCPIKE IN CHAIR
	129	REPRESENTATIVE BRESLIN IN CHAIR
	167	ADJOURNMENT
	167	PERFUNCTORY SESSION
	167	MESSAGE FROM SENATE
	168	PERFUNCTORY SESSION - ADJOURNMENT
06/26/83	1	HOUSE TO ORDER - REPRESENTATIVE MCPIKE
	1	PRAYER - FATHER JOHN BEVERIDGE
	1	PLEDGE OF ALLEGIANCE
	2	ROLL CALL FOR ATTENDANCE
	3	MESSAGE FROM SENATE
	4	REPRESENTATIVE GREIMAN IN CHAIR
	64	REPRESENTATIVE MCPIKE IN CHAIR

DATE	PAGE	SUBJECT
06/26/83 (cont'd)	96	ADJOURNMENT
06/27/83	1	HOUSE TO ORDER - SPEAKER MATIJEVICH
	1	PRAYER - REVEREND RUBEN CRUZ
	2	PLEDGE OF ALLEGIANCE
	2	ROLL CALL FOR ATTENDANCE
	3	AGREED RESOLUTIONS
	3	DEATH RESOLUTION
	98	REPRESENTATIVE GREIMAN IN CHAIR
	161	REPRESENTATIVE YOURELL IN CHAIR
	256	REPRESENTATIVE GREIMAN IN CHAIR
	304	REPRESENTATIVE MATIJEVICH IN CHAIR
	388	COMMITTEE REPORTS
	388	ADJOURNMENT
06/28/83	1	HOUSE TO ORDER - REPRESENTATIVE MATIJEVICH
	1	PRAYER - RABBI ISRAEL ZOBERMAN
	1	PLEDGE OF ALLEGIANCE
	1	ROLL CALL FOR ATTENDANCE
	2	MESSAGE FROM SENATE
	125	REPRESENTATIVE YOURELL IN CHAIR
	128	REPRESENTATIVE MATIJEVICH IN CHAIR
	138	MESSAGES FROM SENATE
	139	COMMITTEE REPORT
	149	MESSAGE FROM SENATE
	150	RECESS
	151	HOUSE RECONVENES - REP. MATIJEVICH IN CHAIR
	151	MESSAGE FROM SENATE
	204	RECESS
	204	HOUSE RECONVENES - REP. MATIJEVICH IN CHAIR
	250	ADJOURNMENT
06/29/83	1	HOUSE TO ORDER - REPRESENTATIVE MATIJEVICH
	1	PRAYER - REVEREND PAUL E. FLESNER
	1	PLEDGE OF ALLEGIANCE
	1	ROLL CALL FOR ATTENDANCE
	2	AGREED RESOLUTIONS
	2	GENERAL RESOLUTIONS
	123	REPRESENTATIVE BRESLIN IN CHAIR
	188	REPRESENTATIVE MATIJEVICH IN CHAIR
	213	HOUSE APPROP. BILLS ON SUPP. CALENDAR
	226	RECESS
	226	HOUSE RECONVENES - SPEAKER MADIGAN IN CHAIR
	231	REPRESENTATIVE MATIJEVICH IN CHAIR
	279	ADJOURNMENT
06/30/83	1	HOUSE TO ORDER - SPEAKER MCPIKE IN CHAIR
	1	SPEAKER MATIJEVICH IN CHAIR
	1	PRAYER - GARY MCCANTS
	1	PLEDGE OF ALLEGIANCE
	2	ROLL CALL FOR ATTENDANCE

MST

LEGISLATIVE INFORMATION SYSTEM   PAGE 359
HOUSE OF REPRESENTATIVES

MASTER TRANSCRIPT INDEX

PROGRAM-LRTRNMST
08/20/85

LEGISLATIVE INFORMATION SYSTEM   PAGE 360
HOUSE OF REPRESENTATIVES

MASTER TRANSCRIPT INDEX

(CONT'D)

PAGE	SUBJECT
2	AGREED RESOLUTIONS
2	GENERAL RESOLUTIONS
3	DEATH RESOLUTION
3	REPRESENTATIVE YOURELL IN CHAIR
4	REPRESENTATIVE MATIJEVICH IN CHAIR
11	COMMITTEE REPORTS
15	SPEAKER MADIGAN IN CHAIR
92	REPRESENTATIVE MATIJEVICH IN CHAIR
173	SPEAKER MADIGAN IN CHAIR
175	MESSAGE FROM SENATE
176	ADJOURNMENT
1	HOUSE TO ORDER - REPRESENTATIVE MATIJEVICH
1	PRAYER - REVEREND WILLIAM J. PECKHAM
1	PLEDGE OF ALLEGIANCE
1	ROLL CALL FOR ATTENDANCE
2	AGREED RESOLUTIONS
2	DEATH RESOLUTION
2	RECESS
3	HOUSE RECONVENES - REP. MATIJEVICH IN CHAIR
3	COMMITTEE REPORT
85	REPRESENTATIVE BRESLIN IN CHAIR
203	REPRESENTATIVE MATIJEVICH IN CHAIR
296	SPEAKER MADIGAN IN CHAIR
296	ADJOURNMENT
1	HOUSE TO ORDER - REP. MATIJEVICH IN CHAIR
1	PRAYER - REPRESENTATIVE RICE
1	PLEDGE OF ALLEGIANCE
1	ROLL CALL FOR ATTENDANCE
1	AGREED RESOLUTIONS
2	GENERAL RESOLUTION
2	DEATH RESOLUTIONS
112	REPRESENTATIVE BRESLIN IN CHAIR
154	REPRESENTATIVE MATIJEVICH IN CHAIR
159	AGREED RESOLUTIONS
159	GENERAL RESOLUTION
159	DEATH RESOLUTION
165	SPEAKER MADIGAN IN CHAIR
176	ADJOURNMENT
1	PERFUNCTORY SESSION
1	HOUSE TO ORDER - REPRESENTATIVE CURRIE IN CHAIR
1	PRAYER - CLERK JACK O'BRIEN
1	PLEDGE OF ALLEGIANCE
1	MESSAGES FROM GOVERNOR
3	GENERAL RESOLUTION
3	MESSAGES FROM SENATE
5	MESSAGES FROM SENATE
5	PERFUNCTORY SESSION - ADJOURNMENT

DATE	PAGE	SUBJECT
10/17/83	1	PERFUNCTORY SESSION
	1	HOUSE TO ORDER - REPRESENTATIVE GIORGI IN CHAIR
	1	PRAYER - CLERK JACK O'BRIEN
	1	PLEDGE OF ALLEGIANCE
	1	COMMITTEE REPORTS
	2	PERFUNCTORY SESSION - ADJOURNMENT
10/18/83	1	HOUSE TO ORDER - SPEAKER MADIGAN
	1	PRAYER - SISTER BERNADETT MCMANIGAL
	2	PLEDGE OF ALLEGIANCE
	2	ROLL CALL FOR ATTENDANCE
	2	OATH OF OFFICE - REPRESENTATIVE MARKETTE
	3	INTRODUCTION OF REPRESENTATIVE RYDER
	6	RECESS
	6	HOUSE RECONVENES - REP. MATIJEVICH IN CHAIR
	6	COMMITTEE REPORT
	7	AGREED RESOLUTIONS
	36	REPRESENTATIVE GREIMAN IN CHAIR
	143	DEATH RESOLUTION
	146	ADJOURNMENT
10/19/83	1	HOUSE TO ORDER - REPRESENTATIVE MCPIKE
	1	PRAYER - RABBI ISRAEL ZOBERMAN
	1	PLEDGE OF ALLEGIANCE
	1	ROLL CALL FOR ATTENDANCE
	2	AGREED RESOLUTIONS
	3	GENERAL RESOLUTION
	7	REPRESENTATIVE BRESLIN IN CHAIR
	61	REPRESENTATIVE MATIJEVICH IN CHAIR
	95	RECESS
	95	HOUSE RECONVENES - REPRESENTATIVE MCPIKE IN CHAIR
	98	REPRESENTATIVE YOURELL IN CHAIR
	235	ADJOURNMENT
10/20/83	1	HOUSE TO ORDER - REPRESENTATIVE MCPIKE
	1	PRAYER - FATHER ANTHONY TZORTZIS
	1	PLEDGE OF ALLEGIANCE
	1	ROLL CALL FOR ATTENDANCE
	2	AGREED RESOLUTIONS
	2	REPRESENTATIVE GREIMAN IN CHAIR
	3	AGREED RESOLUTIONS
	3	DEATH RESOLUTIONS
	54	REPRESENTATIVE MATIJEVICH IN CHAIR
	173	AGREED RESOLUTIONS
	174	DEATH RESOLUTIONS
	174	GENERAL RESOLUTION
	176	ADJOURNMENT
	176	PERFUNCTORY SESSION
	176	MESSAGES FROM THE SENATE
	179	PERFUNCTORY SESSION - ADJOURNMENT

DATE	PAGE	SUBJECT
11/01/83	1	HOUSE TO ORDER - REPRESENTATIVE MCPIKE
	1	PRAYER - REVEREND WILLIAM J. PECKHAM
	1	PLEDGE OF ALLEGIANCE
	1	ROLL CALL FOR ATTENDANCE
	3	RECESS
	3	HOUSE RECONVENES - REPRESENTATIVE MCPIKE IN CHAIR
	4	REPRESENTATIVE MATIJEVICH IN CHAIR
	85	REPRESENTATIVE YOURELL IN CHAIR
	102	DEATH RESOLUTIONS
	103	ADJOURNMENT
11/02/83	1	HOUSE TO ORDER - REPRESENTATIVE MCPIKE
	1	PRAYER - RABBI ISRAEL ZOBERMAN
	1	PLEDGE OF ALLEGIANCE
	1	ROLL CALL FOR ATTENDANCE
	2	REPRESENTATIVE GREIMAN IN CHAIR
	2	AGREED RESOLUTIONS
	4	COMMITTEE REPORT
	32	REPRESENTATIVE YOURELL IN CHAIR
	117	REPRESENTATIVE BRESLIN IN CHAIR
	164	RECESS
	164	HOUSE RECONVENES - REP. BRESLIN IN CHAIR
	242	ADJOURNMENT
11/03/83	1	HOUSE TO ORDER - REPRESENTATIVE MCPIKE
	1	PRAYER - REVEREND JOHN C. MORTON
	1	PLEDGE OF ALLEGIANCE
	2	ROLL CALL FOR ATTENDANCE
	2	REPRESENTATIVE GREIMAN IN CHAIR
	5	AGREED RESOLUTIONS
	6	GENERAL RESOLUTIONS
	6	DEATH RESOLUTIONS
	41	REPRESENTATIVE MCPIKE IN CHAIR
	42	RECESS
	42	HOUSE RECONVENES - REPRESENTATIVE MCPIKE IN CHAIR
	42	MESSAGE FROM SENATE
	42	RECESS
	43	HOUSE RECONVENES - REPRESENTATIVE MCPIKE IN CHAIR
	43	ADJOURNMENT
11/04/83	1	HOUSE TO ORDER - REPRESENTATIVE MCPIKE
	1	PRAYER - FATHER TZORTZIS
	1	PLEDGE OF ALLEGIANCE
	1	ROLL CALL FOR ATTENDANCE
	2	RPRESENTATIVE BRESLIN IN CHAIR
	4	MESSAGE FROM SENATE
	5	RECESS
	5	HOUSE RECONVENES - REP. MATIJEVICH IN CHAIR
	30	REPRESENTATIVE BRAUN IN CHAIR
	33	REPRESENTATIVE MATIJEVICH IN CHAIR
	102	MESSAGES FROM SENATE

DATE	PAGE	SUBJECT
11/04/83 (cont'd)	103	AGREED RESOLUTIONS
	105	DEATH RESOLUTIONS
	105	GENERAL RESOLUTION
	108	MESSAGE FROM SENATE
	140	REPRESENTATIVE GREIMAN IN CHAIR
	149	COMMITTEE REPORT
	205	ADJOURNMENT
01/10/84	1	HOUSE TO ORDER - REPRESENTATIVE CURRAN
	1	PRAYER - CLERK JACK O'BRIEN
	1	PLEDGE OF ALLEGIANCE
	1	MESSAGES FROM GOVERNOR
	2	ADJOURNMENT
01/11/84	1	HOUSE TO ORDER - REPRESENTATIVE CURRAN IN CHAIR
	1	PRAYER - CLERK JACK O'BRIEN
	1	PLEDGE OF ALLEGIANCE
	1	MESSAGE FROM SENATE
02/07/84	1	PERFUNCTORY SESSION
	1	HOUSE TO ORDER - REPRESENTATIVE CURRAN
	1	PRAYER - CLERK O'BRIEN
	1	PLEDGE OF ALLEGIANCE
	3	RECESS
	3	HOUSE RECONVENES - JOHN LYONS, SPEAKER OF THE DAY
	4	ADJOURNMENT - PERFUNCTORY SESSION
02/08/84	1	HOUSE TO ORDER - SPEAKER MADIGAN
	1	ROLL CALL FOR ATTENDANCE
	1	MESSAGE FROM SENATE
	5	JOINT SESSION CONVENED
	5	PRAYER - BISHOP DANIEL RYAN
	5	PLEDGE OF ALLEGIANCE
	7	STATE OF THE STATE MESSAGE - GOV. THOMPSON
	25	JOINT SESSION ADJOURNED
	26	RECESS
	26	HOUSE RECONVENES - SPEAKER MADIGAN IN CHAIR
	28	AGREED RESOLUTIONS
	32	DEATH RESOLUTIONS
	33	AGREED RESOLUTIONS
	34	GENERAL RESOLUTIONS
	37	ADJOURNMENT
	37	PERFUNCTORY SESSION
	42	PERFUNCTORY SESSION - ADJOURNMENT
03/06/84	1	HOUSE TO ORDER-SPEAKER MADIGAN
	1	PRAYER - REVEREND PHILLIP SCHNEIDER
	1	PLEDGE OF ALLEGIANCE
	2	ROLL CALL FOR ATTENDANCE
	2	COMMITTEE REPORT
	5	ADJOURNMENT

LEGISLATIVE INFORMATION SYSTEM   PAGE 363
HOUSE OF REPRESENTATIVES

PROGRAM-LRTRNMST   LEGISLATIVE INFORMATION SYSTEM   PAGE 364
08/20/85   HOUSE OF REPRESENTATIVES

MASTER TRANSCRIPT INDEX

MASTER TRANSCRIPT INDEX

PAGE	SUBJECT	DATE	PAGE	SUBJECT
5	PERFUNCTORY SESSION	03/29/84 (cont'd)	8	COMMITTEE REPORTS
12	PERFUNCTORY SESSION - ADJOURNMENT		9	ADJOURNMENT
			9	PERFUNCTORY SESSION
1	HOUSE TO ORDER - SPEAKER MADIGAN		10	PERFUNCTORY SESSION - ADJOURNMENT
1	PRAYER - REVEREND WENDALL WEBSTER			
1	PLEDGE OF ALLEGIANCE	04/03/84	1	HOUSE TO ORDER - MCPIKE
1	ROLL CALL FOR ATTENDANCE		1	PRAYER - REVEREND JEREMIAH A WRIGHT
2	COMMITTEE REPORT		1	PLEDGE OF ALLEGIANCE
6	JOINT SESSION		1	ROLL CALL FOR ATTENDANCE
7	BUDGET MESSAGE - GOV JAMES THOMPSON		7	AGREED RESOLUTIONS
22	JOINT SESSION - ADJOURNMENT		7	DEATH RESOLUTION
22	REPRESENTATIVE MCPIKE IN CHAIR		8	ADJOURNMENT
22	AGREED RESOLUTIONS		8	PERFUNCTORY SESSION
25	GENERAL RESOLUTIONS		8	PERFUNCTORY SESSION - ADJOURNMENT
25	DEATH RESOLUTIONS			
26	ADJOURNMENT	04/04/84	1	HOUSE TO ORDER - REPRESENTATIVE MCPIKE
26	PERFUNCTORY SESSION		1	PRAYER - REVEREND JAMES A. JOHNSON
28	PERFUNCTORY SESSION - ADJOURNMENT		1	PLEDGE OF ALLEGIANCE
			1	ROLL CALL FOR ATTENDANCE
1	HOUSE TO ORDER - REPRESENTATIVE MCPIKE		2	COMMITTEE REPORTS
1	PRAYER - RABBI ISRAEL ZOBERMAN		3	REPRESENTATIVE GREIMAN IN CHAIR
1	PLEDGE OF ALLEGIANCE		37	AGREED RESOLUTIONS
1	ROLL CALL FOR ATTENDANCE		38	GENERAL RESOLUTION
2	JOHN COUNTRYMAN - SWEARING IN		38	COMMITTEE REPORT
4	AGREED RESOLUTIONS		39	ADJOURNMENT
11	ADJOURNMENT		39	PERFUNCTORY SESSION
11	PERFUNCTORY SESSION		44	PERFUNCTORY SESSION - ADJOURNMENT
16	PERFUNCTORY SESSION - ADJOURNMENT			
		04/05/84	1	HOUSE TO ORDER - REPRESENTATIVE GREIMAN
1	HOUSE TO ORDER - REPRESENTATIVE GREIMAN		1	PRAYER - FATHER ANTHONY TZORTZIS
1	PRAYER - REVEREND FARRIES H. MORRISON, SR.		1	PLEDGE OF ALLEGIANCE
2	PLEDGE OF ALLEGIANCE		1	ROLL CALL FOR ATTENDANCE
2	ROLL CALL FOR ATTENDANCE		6	SPEAKER MADIGAN IN CHAIR
2	COMMITTEE REPORTS		8	AGREED RESOLUTIONS
3	AGREED RESOLUTIONS		9	ADJOURNMENT
5	MESSAGE FROM SENATE		9	PERFUNCTORY SESSION
9	MESSAGES FROM SENATE		9	COMMITTEE REPORTS
11	AGREED RESOLUTIONS		16	PERFUNCTORY SESSION - ADJOURNMENT
13	GENERAL RESOLUTION			
13	DEATH RESOLUTIONS	04/10/84	1	HOUSE TO ORDER - REPRESENTATIVE MCPIKE
14	ADJOURNMENT		1	PRAYER - REVEREND RICHARD MAY
14	PERFUNCTORY SESSION		1	PLEDGE OF ALLEGIANCE
22	PERFUNCTORY SESSION - ADJOURNMENT		2	ROLL CALL FOR ATTENDANCE
			2	SPEAKER MADIGAN IN CHAIR
1	HOUSE TO ORDER - REPRESENTATIVE GREIMAN		17	AGREED RESOLUTIONS
1	PRAYER - REV DR. J. SOLOMON BENN III		17	GENERAL RESOLUTIONS
1	PLEDGE OF ALLEGIANCE		19	DEATH RESOLUTIONS
1	ROLL CALL FOR ATTENDANCE		19	ADJOURNMENT
2	COMMITTEE REPORTS		19	PERFUNCTORY SESSION
5	AGREED RESOLUTIONS		22	PERFUNCTORY SESSION - ADJOURNMENT
6	DEATH RESOLUTIONS			

DATE	PAGE	SUBJECT
04/11/84	1	HOUSE TO ORDER - SPEAKER MADIGAN
	1	PRAYER - REVEREND BARRY L. WEST
	1	PLEDGE OF ALLEGIANCE
	1	ROLL CALL FOR ATTENDANCE
	2	COMMITTEE REPORTS
	23	REPRESENTATIVE PIERCE IN CHAIR
	29	REPRESENTATIVE MADIGAN IN CHAIR
	31	REPRESENTATIVE MATIJEVICH IN CHAIR
	34	REPRESENTATIVE MADIGAN IN CHAIR
	39	AGREED RESOLUTIONS
	42	GENERAL RESOLUTIONS
	44	ADJOURNMENT
	44	PERFUNCTORY SESSION
	44	COMMITTEE REPORTS
	49	COMMITTEE REPORTS
	53	PERFUNCTORY SESSION - ADJOURNMENT
04/12/84	1	PERFUNCTORY SESSION - REPRESENTATIVE CURRAN
	1	PRAYER - CLERK O'BRIEN
	1	PLEDGE OF ALLEGIANCE
	1	PERFUNCTORY SESSION - ADJOURNMENT
04/13/84	1	PERFUNCTORY SESSION
	1	HOUSE TO ORDER - REPRESENTATIVE CURRAN
	1	PRAYER - TONY LEONE
	1	PLEDGE OF ALLEGIANCE
	11	PERFUNCTORY SESSION - ADJOURNMENT
04/19/84	1	PERFUNCTORY SESSION
	1	HOUSE TO ORDER - REPRESENTATIVE CURRAN
	1	PRAYER - CLERK JACK O'BRIEN
	1	PLEDGE OF ALLEGIANCE
	14	PERFUNCTORY SESSION - ADJOURNMENT
04/24/84	1	HOUSE TO ORDER - REPRESENTATIVE MCPIKE
	1	PRAYER - HARRY A. MANN
	1	PLEDGE OF ALLEGIANCE
	1	ROLL CALL FOR ATTENDANCE
	2	OATH OF OFFICE - MARGARET PARCELLS
	21	AGREED RESOLUTIONS
	23	GENERAL RESOLUTIONS
	23	DEATH RESOLUTION
	24	ADJOURNMENT
	24	PERFUNCTORY SESSION
	24	PERFUNCTORY SESSION - ADJOURNMENT
04/25/84	1	HOUSE TO ORDER - SPEAKER MADIGAN IN CHAIR
	1	PRAYER - CLERK O'BRIEN
	1	PLEDGE OF ALLEGIANCE
	1	ROLL CALL FOR ATTENDANCE
	3	COMMITTEE REPORTS

DATE	PAGE	SUBJECT
04/25/84 (cont'd)	4	REPRESENTATIVE MATIJEVICH IN CHAIR
	18	REPRESENTATIVE GREIMAN IN CHAIR
	25	AGREED RESOLUTIONS
	26	GENERAL RESOLUTIONS
	27	RECESS
	27	PERFUNCTORY SESSION
	28	COMMITTEE REPORTS
	28	PERFUNCTORY SESSION - ADJOURNMENT
	28	HOUSE RECONVENES - REP GREIMAN IN CHAIR
	29	COMMITTEE REPORT
	30	ADJOURNMENT
04/26/84	1	HOUSE TO ORDER - SPEAKER MADIGAN
	1	PRAYER - REVEREND SAMMY L. HOOKS
	1	PLEDGE OF ALLEGIANCE
	1	ROLL CALL FOR ATTENDANCE
	2	COMMITTEE REPORTS
	4	MESSAGE FROM SENATE
	30	REPRESENTATIVE MATIJEVICH IN CHAIR
	70	SPEAKER MADIGAN IN CHAIR
	92	AGREED RESOLUTIONS
	93	DEATH RESOLUTIONS
	93	ADJOURNMENT
	93	PERFUNCTORY SESSION
	93	COMMITTEE REPORTS
	100	PERFUNCTORY SESSION - ADJOURNMENT
04/27/84	1	PERFUNCTORY SESSION
	1	HOUSE TO ORDER - REPRESENTATIVE CURRAN
	1	PRAYER - CLERK JACK O'BRIEN
	1	PLEDGE OF ALLEGIANCE
	4	PERFUNCTORY SESSION - ADJOURNMENT
04/30/84	1	PERFUNCTORY SESSION
	1	HOUSE TO ORDER - REPRESENTATIVE CURRAN
	1	PRAYER - CLERK TONY LEONE
	1	PLEDGE OF ALLEGIANCE
	7	PERFUNCTORY SESSION - ADJOURNMENT
05/01/84	1	HOUSE TO ORDER - SPEAKER MADIGAN
	1	PRAYER - REVEREND DR. RUDOLPH SHOULTZ
	1	PLEDGE OF ALLEGIANCE
	1	ROLL CALL FOR ATTENDANCE
	4	MESSAGES FROM SENATE
	45	AGREED RESOLUTIONS
	46	DEATH RESOLUTION
	51	MESSAGE FROM SENATE
	52	ADJOURNMENT
05/02/84	1	HOUSE TO ORDER - SPEAKER MADIGAN
	1	PRAYER - REVEREND MCCOY

PAGE	SUBJECT
2	PLEDGE OF ALLEGIANCE
2	ROLL CALL FOR ATTENDANCE
2	COMMITTEE REPORTS
58	AGREED RESOLUTIONS
59	DEATH RESOLUTION
61	ADJOURNMENT
61	PERFUNCTORY SESSION
61	COMMITTEE REPORTS
62	MESSAGE FROM SENATE
62	PERFUNCTORY SESSION - ADJOURNMENT
1	HOUSE TO ORDER - SPEAKER MADIGAN
1	PRAYER - REVEREND JAMES WISMER
1	PLEDGE OF ALLEGIANCE
1	ROLL CALL FOR ATTENDANCE
2	COMMITTEE REPORTS
5	COMMITTEE REPORTS
42	REPRESENTATIVE MATIJEVICH IN CHAIR
52	AGREED RESOLUTIONS
53	DEATH RESOLUTION
55	ADJOURNMENT
55	PERFUNCTORY SESSION
55	COMMITTEE REPORTS
55	MESSAGE FROM SENATE
58	COMMITTEE REPORT
58	PERFUNCTORY SESSION - ADJOURNMENT
1	HOUSE TO ORDER - SPEAKER MADIGAN
1	PRAYER - RABBI ISRAEL ZOBERMAN
1	PLEDGE OF ALLEGIANCE
1	ROLL CALL FOR ATTENDANCE
2	COMMITTEE REPORTS
57	AGREED RESOLUTIONS
57	DEATH RESOLUTION
58	ADJOURNMENT
58	PERFUNCTORY SESSION
58	COMMITTEE REPORTS
59	PERFUNCTORY SESSION - ADJOURNMENT
1	HOUSE TO ORDER - SPEAKER MADIGAN
1	PRAYER - REVEREND FOREST HAGOOD
1	PLEDGE OF ALLEGIANCE
1	ROLL CALL FOR ATTENDANCE
31	RECESS
31	HOUSE RECONVENES - SPEAKER MADIGAN IN CHAIR
45	REPRESENTATIVE MATIJEVICH IN CHAIR
56	DEATH RESOLUTION
57	AGREED RESOLUTIONS
57	ADJOURNMENT
1	HOUSE TO ORDER - REPRESENTATIVE MCPIKE

DATE	PAGE	SUBJECT
05/09/84 (cont'd)	1	PRAYER - RABBI ISRAEL ZOBERMAN
	1	PLEDGE OF ALLEGIANCE
	1	ROLL CALL FOR ATTENDANCE
	9	COMMITTEE OF THE WHOLE
	10	REPRESENTATIVE KEANE IN CHAIR
	25	COMMITTEE OF THE WHOLE - ADJOURNMENT
	25	REPRESENTATIVE GREIMAN IN CHAIR
	26	SPEAKER MADIGAN IN CHAIR
	75	REPRESENTATIVE MCPIKE IN CHAIR
	145	COMMITTEE REPORTS
	151	AGREED RESOLUTIONS
	152	DEATH RESOLUTION
	152	GENERAL RESOLUTIONS
	152	ADJOURNMENT
05/10/84	1	HOUSE TO ORDER - REPRESENTATIVE MCPIKE
	1	PRAYER - FATHER ANTHONY TZORTOZIS
	1	PLEDGE OF ALLEGIANCE
	1	ROLL CALL FOR ATTENDANCE
	2	AGREED RESOLUTION
	18	REPRESENTATIVE BRESLIN IN CHAIR
	99	REPRESENTATIVE GREIMAN IN CHAIR
	160	REPRESENTATIVE MCPIKE IN CHAIR
	165	REPRESENTATIVE GREIMAN IN CHAIR
	181	AGREED RESOLUTIONS
	182	MESSAGES FROM SENATE
	184	ADJOURNMENT
05/15/84	1	HOUSE TO ORDER - REPRESENTATIVE MCPIKE
	1	PRAYER - REVEREND RICHARD MILLER
	1	PLEDGE OF ALLEGIANCE
	1	ROLL CALL FOR ATTENDANCE
	2	AGREED RESOLUTIONS
	25	REPRESENTATIVE BRESLIN IN CHAIR
	64	REPRESENTATIVE MATIJEVICH IN CHAIR
	68	REPRESENTATIVE BRESLIN IN CHAIR
	137	SPEAKER MADIGAN IN CHAIR
	150	REPRESENTATIVE MATIJEVICH IN CHAIR
	195	AGREED RESOLUTIONS
	198	DEATH RESOLUTION
	199	ADJOURNMENT
05/16/84	1	HOUSE TO ORDER - REPRESENTATIVE MCPIKE
	1	PRAYER - REVEREND HAROLD SIMPKINS, JR.
	1	PLEDGE OF ALLEGIANCE
	1	ROLL CALL FOR ATTENDANCE
	2	SPEAKER MADIGAN IN CHAIR
	2	RESIGNATION - HARRY "BOS" YOURELL
	3	OATH OF OFFICE - JOHN J. MCNAMARA
	70	REPRESENTATIVE MATIJEVICH IN CHAIR
	84	COMMITTEE REPORTS

DATE	PAGE	SUBJECT
05/16/84 (cont'd)	143	MESSAGE FROM SENATE
	168	REPRESENTATIVE GREIMAN IN CHAIR
	258	REPRESENTATIVE BRESLIN IN CHAIR
	285	AGREED RESOLUTIONS
	286	DEATH RESOLUTIONS
	286	ADJOURNMENT
05/17/84	1	HOUSE TO ORDER - SPEAKER MADIGAN
	1	PRAYER - REVEREND THOMAS HUBBELL
	2	PLEDGE OF ALLEGIANCE
	2	ROLL CALL FOR ATTENDANCE
	22	REPRESENTATIVE MCPIKE IN CHAIR
	70	REPRESENTATIVE BRESLIN IN CHAIR
	174	REPRESENTATIVE MATIJEVICH IN CHAIR
	246	RECESS
	246	HOUSE RECONVENES - SPEAKER MADIGAN IN CHAIR
	247	MESSAGE FROM SENATE
	248	AGREED RESOLUTIONS
	248	GENERAL RESOLUTIONS
	248	DEATH RESOLUTIONS
	249	ADJOURNMENT
05/18/84	1	HOUSE TO ORDER - REPRESENTATIVE MCPIKE
	1	PRAYER - REVEREND ALVIN RODECK
	1	PLEDGE OF ALLEGIANCE
	1	ROLL CALL FOR ATTENDANCE
	21	REPRESENTATIVE BRESLIN IN CHAIR
	94	REPRESENTATIVE GREIMAN IN CHAIR
	147	SPEAKER MADIGAN IN CHAIR
	151	REPRESENTATIVE GREIMAN IN CHAIR
	157	AGREED RESOLUTIONS
	157	GENERAL RESOLUTION
	157	ADJOURNMENT
05/22/84	1	HOUSE TO ORDER - SPEAKER MADIGAN
	1	PRAYER - REVEREND JOHN C. MARTIN
	1	PLEDGE OF ALLEGIANCE
	1	ROLL CALL FOR ATTENDANCE
	2	AGREED RESOLUTIONS
	29	REPRESENTATIVE MATIJEVICH IN CHAIR
	112	REPRESENTATIVE GREIMAN IN CHAIR
	173	AGREED RESOLUTIONS
	174	ADJOURNMENT
	174	PERFUNCTORY SESSION
	174	MESSAGES FROM SENATE
	176	PERFUNCTORY SESSION - ADJOURNMENT
05/23/84	1	HOUSE TO ORDER - REPRESENTATIVE MCPIKE
	1	PRAYER - REVEREND PAUL E. FLESNER
	1	PLEDGE OF ALLEGIANCE
	1	ROLL CALL FOR ATTENDANCE

DATE	PAGE	SUBJECT
05/23/84 (cont'd)	14	REPRESENTATIVE MATIJEVICH IN CHAIR
	102	REPRESENTATIVE GREIMAN IN CHAIR
	161	REPRESENTATIVE MCPIKE IN CHAIR
	185	REPRESENTATIVE MATIJEVICH IN CHAIR
	194	REPRESENTATIVE BRESLIN IN CHAIR
	306	AGREED RESOLUTIONS
	307	GENERAL RESOLUTION
	308	ADJOURNMENT
	308	PERFUNCTORY SESSION
	308	MESSAGES FROM SENATE
	312	PERFUNCTORY SESSION - ADJOURNMENT
05/24/84	1	HOUSE TO ORDER - REPRESENTATIVE MCPIKE
	1	PRAYER - FATHER JAMES LENNON
	1	PLEDGE OF ALLEGIANCE
	1	ROLL CALL FOR ATTENDANCE
	25	REPRESENTATIVE BRESLIN IN CHAIR
	72	REPRESENTATIVE MATIJEVICH IN CHAIR
	73	REPRESENTATIVE BRESLIN IN CHAIR
	122	REPRESENTATIVE GREIMAN IN CHAIR
	174	REPRESENTATIVE MCPIKE IN CHAIR
	181	REPRESENTATIVE GREIMAN IN CHAIR
	235	REPRESENTATIVE MATIJEVICH IN CHAIR
	254	COMMITTEE REPORT
	254	MESSAGES FROM SENATE
	310	AGREED RESOLUTIONS
	311	GENERAL RESOLUTION
	311	DEATH RESOLUTION
	311	ADJOURNMENT
	311	PERFUNCTORY SESSION
	311	MESSAGE FROM SENATE
	314	PERFUNCTORY SESSION - ADJOURNMENT
05/25/84	1	HOUSE TO ORDER - REPRESENTATIVE MCPIKE
	1	PRAYER - RABBI ISRAEL ZOBERMAN
	1	PLEDGE OF ALLEGIANCE
	1	ROLL CALL FOR ATTENDANCE
	31	REPRESENTATIVE GREIMAN IN CHAIR
	86	REPRESENTATIVE BRESLIN IN CHAIR
	185	AGREED RESOLUTIONS
	186	MESSAGES FROM SENATE
	186	ADJOURNMENT
	186	PERFUNCTORY SESSION
	187	MESSAGE FROM SENATE
	189	PERFUNCTORY SESSION - ADJOURNMENT
05/29/84	1	HOUSE TO ORDER - REPRESENTATIVE MCPIKE
	1	PRAYER - REVEREND RICHARD CHRISMAN
	2	PLEDGE OF ALLEGIANCE
	2	ROLL CALL FOR ATTENDANCE
	3	AGREED RESOLUTIONS

PAGE	SUBJECT
t'd) 34	AGREED RESOLUTIONS
35	DEATH RESOLUTION
35	ADJOURNMENT
1	HOUSE TO ORDER - REPRESENTATIVE MCPIKE
1	PRAYER - REVEREND FRANK GRADY
1	PLEDGE OF ALLEGIANCE
1	ROLL CALL FOR ATTENDANCE
1	MESSAGE FROM SENATE
2	COMMITTEE REPORTS
4	AGREED RESOLUTIONS
21	REPRESENTATIVE DIPRIMA IN CHAIR
21	MEMORIAL DAY OBSERVANCE
36	REPRESENTATIVE MCPIKE IN CHAIR
45	REPRESENTATIVE GREIMAN IN CHAIR
83	AGREED RESOLUTIONS
84	DEATH RESOLUTION
88	ADJOURNMENT
88	PERFUNCTORY SESSION
88	MESSAGE FROM SENATE
88	COMMITTEE REPORTS
90	PERFUNCTORY SESSION - ADJOURNMENT
1	HOUSE TO ORDER - REPRESENTATIVE MCPIKE
1	PRAYER - REVEREND MERWIN MASTERS
1	PLEDGE OF ALLEGIANCE
2	ROLL CALL FOR ATTENDANCE
4	AGREED RESOLUTION
19	REPRESENTATIVE BRESLIN IN CHAIR
83	RESOLUTION - QUINCY NOTRE DAME LADY RAIDERS
118	AGREED RESOLUTIONS
119	GENERAL RESOLUTIONS
120	COMMITTEE REPORTS
120	ADJOURNMENT
120	PERFUNCTORY SESSION
120	MESSAGE FROM SENATE
121	PERFUNCTORY SESSION - ADJOURNMENT
1	HOUSE TO ORDER - REPRESENTATIVE MCPIKE
1	PRAYER - FATHER ROBERT SPRIGGS
1	PLEDGE OF ALLEGIANCE
1	ROLL CALL FOR ATTENDANCE
3	AGREED RESOLUTIONS
3	DEATH RESOLUTION
20	ADJOURNMENT
21	PERFUNCTORY SESSION
21	PERUNCTORY SESSION - ADJOURNMENT
1	HOUSE TO ORDER - REPRESENTATIVE MCPIKE
1	PRAYER - REVEREND R. DAVID GOODELL
1	PLEDGE OF ALLEGIANCE

DATE	PAGE	SUBJECT
06/06/84 (cont'd)	1	ROLL CALL FOR ATTENDANCE
	2	COMMITTEE REPORTS
	5	AGREED RESOLUTIONS
	5	DEATH RESOLUTION
	9	REPRESENTATIVE GREIMAN IN CHAIR
	57	AGREED RESOLUTIONS
	58	GENERAL RESOLUTION
	59	ADJOURNMENT
	59	PERFUNCTORY SESSION
	59	COMMITTEE REPORTS
	59	PERFUNCTORY SESSION - ADJOURNMENT
06/07/84	1	HOUSE TO ORDER - REPRESENTATIVE MCPIKE
	1	PRAYER - REVEREND ELMER FAWLER
	2	PLEDGE OF ALLEGIANCE
	2	ROLL CALL FOR ATTENDANCE
	2	COMMITTEE REPORTS
	4	REPRESENTATIVE GREIMAN IN CHAIR
	5	COMMITTEE REPORT
	20	AGREED RESOLUTIONS
	21	GENERAL RESOLUTION
	39	COMMITTEE REPORT
	40	AGREED RESOLUTIONS
	40	ADJOURNMENT
	40	PERFUNCTORY SESSION
	40	COMMITTEE REPORT
	41	PERFUNCTORY SESSION - ADJOURNMENT
06/12/84	1	HOUSE TO ORDER - REPRESENTATIVE MCPIKE
	2	PRAYER - REVEREND BROOKS MARTIN
	3	PLEDGE OF ALLEGIANCE
	3	ROLL CALL FOR ATTENDANCE
	3	AGREED RESOLUTIONS
	3	GENERAL RESOLUTION
	3	DEATH RESOLUTION
	32	REPRESENTATIVE BRESLIN IN CHAIR
	39	ADJOURNMENT
06/13/84	1	HOUSE TO ORDER - REPRESENTATIVE MCPIKE
	1	PRAYER - REVEREND WAYNE MEYER
	1	PLEDGE OF ALLEGIANCE
	1	ROLL CALL FOR ATTENDANCE
	2	COMMITTEE REPORTS
	2	APPROVAL OF JOURNALS
	6	REPRESENTATIVE BRESLIN IN CHAIR
	6	AGREED RESOLUTIONS
	69	REPRESENTATIVE BRAUN IN CHAIR
	85	ADJOURNMENT
	86	PERFUNCTORY SESSION
	86	COMMITTEE REPORTS
	86	MESSAGE FROM SENATE

DATE	PAGE	SUBJECT
06/13/84 (cont'd)	86	PERFUNCTORY SESSION - ADJOURNMENT
06/18/84	1	HOUSE TO ORDER - REPRESENTATIVE GREIMAN
	1	PRAYER - REVEREND ROBERT BROEDER
	1	PLEDGE OF ALLEGIANCE
	1	ROLL CALL FOR ATTENDANCE
	2	COMMITTEE REPORT
	48	COMMITTEE REPORT
	91	REPRESENTATIVE MATIJEVICH IN CHAIR
	137	AGREED RESOLUTIONS
	137	GENERAL RESOLUTION
	138	ADJOURNMENT
	138	PERFUNCTORY SESSION
	138	MESSAGE FROM SENATE
	138	PERFUNCTORY SESSION - ADJOURNMENT
06/19/84	1	HOUSE TO ORDER - REPRESENTATIVE MCPIKE
	1	PRAYER - REVEREND DARRELL B. HARRISON
	1	PLEDGE OF ALLEGIANCE
	2	ROLL CALL FOR ATTENDANCE
	2	MESSAGE FROM GOVERNOR
	2	MESSAGE FROM SENATE
	21	RECESS
	21	HOUSE RECONVENES - REP. GREIMAN IN CHAIR
	61	REPRESENTATIVE MATIJEVICH IN CHAIR
	87	REPRESENTATIVE BRESLIN IN CHAIR
	99	ADJOURNMENT
06/20/84	1	HOUSE TO ORDER - REPRESENTATIVE MCPIKE
	1	PRAYER - FATHER JAMES HILL
	1	PRAYER - REVEREND TYRONE HENDERSON
	2	PLEDGE OF ALLEGIANCE
	2	ROLL CALL FOR ATTENDANCE
	2	MESSAGE FROM SENATE
	2	AGREED RESOLUTIONS
	3	GENERAL RESOLUTION
	3	DEATH RESOLUTION
	4	APPROVAL OF THE JOURNALS
	11	SPEAKER MADIGAN IN CHAIR
	15	REPRESENTATIVE BRESLIN IN CHAIR
	74	GENERAL RESOLUTIONS
	74	SPEAKER MADIGAN IN CHAIR
	80	ADJOURNMENT
06/21/84	1	HOUSE TO ORDER - REPRESENTATIVE GREIMAN
	1	PRAYER - REVEREND CHARLES NICHOLSON
	1	PLEDGE OF ALLEGIANCE
	1	ROLL CALL FOR ATTENDANCE
	2	MESSAGE FROM SENATE
	2	COMMITTEE REPORTS
	2	AGREED RESOLUTIONS

DATE	PAGE	SUBJECT
06/21/84 (cont'd)	17	REPRESENTATIVE BRESLIN IN CHAIR
	23	REPRESENTATIVE GREIMAN IN CHAIR
	29	REPRESENTATIVE BRESLIN IN CHAIR
	59	REPRESENTATIVE MATIJEVICH IN CHAIR
	64	REPRESENTATIVE BRESLIN IN CHAIR
	68	REPRESENTATIVE GREIMAN IN CHAIR
	111	REPRESENTATIVE MATIJEVICH IN CHAIR
	137	MESSAGE FROM SENATE
	137	AGREED RESOLUTIONS
	141	SPEAKER MADIGAN IN CHAIR
	141	COMMITTEE OF THE WHOLE - SCHOOL FINANCES
	178	COMMITTEE OF THE WHOLE - ADJOURNMENT
	178	REPRESENTATIVE GREIMAN IN CHAIR
	178	MESSAGES FROM SENATE
	178	AGREED RESOLUTION
	179	DEATH RESOLUTIONS
	182	ADJOURNMENT
06/22/84	1	HOUSE TO ORDER - SPEAKER MADIGAN
	1	PRAYER - REVEREND CARL J. CLARK
	1	PLEDGE OF ALLEGIANCE
	2	ROLL CALL FOR ATTENDANCE
	2	MESSAGE FROM SENATE
	2	AGREED RESOLUTIONS
	68	RECESS
	68	HOUSE RECONVENES - SPEAKER MADIGAN IN CHAIR
	107	REPRESENTATIVE MCPIKE IN CHAIR
	155	AGREED RESOLUTIONS
	156	SPEAKER MADIGAN IN CHAIR
	157	GENERAL RESOLUTION
	157	DEATH RESOLUTIONS
	157	ADJOURNMENT
06/25/84	1	HOUSE TO ORDER - REPRESENTATIVE GREIMAN
	1	PRAYER - REVEREND DAVID ASHBY
	1	PLEDGE OF ALLEGIANCE
	1	ROLL CALL FOR ATTENDANCE
	23	REPRESENTATIVE MATIJEVICH IN CHAIR
	41	SPEAKER MADIGAN IN CHAIR
	42	RECESS
	42	HOUSE RECONVENES - SPEAKER MADIGAN IN CHAIR
	68	REPRESENTATIVE GREIMAN IN CHAIR
	78	REPRESENTATIVE MATIJEVICH IN CHAIR
	237	AGREED RESOLUTIONS
	238	GENERAL RESOLUTION
	238	DEATH RESOLUTION
	238	MESSAGE FROM SENATE
	242	ADJOURNMENT
06/26/84	1	HOUSE TO ORDER - REPRESENTATIVE GREIMAN
	1	PRAYER - REVEREND SIMON A. SIMON

MASTER TRANSCRIPT INDEX

PAGE	SUBJECT
2	PLEDGE OF ALLEGIANCE
2	ROLL CALL FOR ATTENDANCE
2	MESSAGE FROM SENATE
6	AGREED RESOLUTIONS
7	DEATH RESOLUTION
91	RECESS
92	HOUSE RECONVENES - REP. GREIMAN IN CHAIR
110	REPRESENTATIVE BRESLIN IN CHAIR
183	AGREED RESOLUTIONS
185	DEATH RESOLUTION
186	ADJOURNMENT
1	HOUSE TO ORDER - REPRESENTATIVE GREIMAN
1	PRAYER - REVEREND WAYNE VAN GELDREN, JR.
1	PLEDGE OF ALLEGIANCE
1	ROLL CALL FOR ATTENDANCE
6	REPRESENTATIVE MATIJEVICH IN CHAIR
9	REPRESENTATIVE GREIMAN IN CHAIR
10	RECESS
10	HOUSE RECONVENES - REP. GREIMAN IN CHAIR
83	REPRESENTATIVE BRESLIN IN CHAIR
97	REPRESENTATIVE GREIMAN IN CHAIR
114	REPRESENTATIVE BRESLIN IN CHAIR
206	AGREED RESOLUTIONS
207	MESSAGES FROM SENATE
208	ADJOURNMENT
1	HOUSE TO ORDER - REPRESENTATIVE GREIMAN
1	PRAYER - REVEREND DON GLENN
1	PLEDGE OF ALLEGIANCE
1	ROLL CALL FOR ATTENDANCE
37	SPEAKER MADIGAN IN CHAIR
42	RECESS
42	HOUSE RECONVENES - SPEAKER MADIGAN IN CHAIR
42	AGREED RESOLUTIONS
43	DEATH RESOLUTION
73	REPRESENTATIVE GREIMAN IN CHAIR
86	SPEAKER MADIGAN IN CHAIR
127	RECESS
128	MESSAGE FROM SENATE
128	HOUSE RECONVENES - SPEAKER MADIGAN IN CHAIR
128	REPRESENTATIVE GREIMAN IN CHAIR
163	AGREED RESOLUTIONS
164	GENERAL RESOLUTIONS
164	SPEAKER MADIGAN IN CHAIR
166	ADJOURNMENT
1	HOUSE TO ORDER - REPRESENTATIVE GREIMAN
1	PRAYER - REVEREND SAUGHKEYSY SMALL
1	PLEDGE OF ALLEGIANCE

PROGRAM-LRTRNMST
08/20/85

MASTER TRANSCRIPT INDEX

DATE	PAGE	SUBJECT
06/29/84 (cont'd)	1	ROLL CALL FOR ATTENDANCE
	2	MESSAGE FROM SENATE
	20	RECESS
	20	HOUSE RECONVENES - SPEAKER MADIGAN IN CHAIR
	23	INTRODUCTION OF STAPLE SINGERS
	49	REPRESENTATIVE GREIMAN IN CHAIR
	49	MESSAGE FROM SENATE
	50	SPEAKER MADIGAN IN CHAIR
	64	REPRESENTATIVE GREIMAN IN CHAIR
	85	AGREED RESOLUTIONS
	86	GENERAL RESOLUTIONS
	86	DEATH RESOLUTIONS
	110	MESSAGE FROM SENATE
	120	ADJOURNMENT
06/30/84	1	HOUSE TO ORDER - REPRESENTATIVE MCPIKE
	1	PRAYER - REVEREND GARY MCCANTS
	1	PLEDGE OF ALLEGIANCE
	1	ROLL CALL FOR ATTENDANCE
	2	REPRESENTATIVE MATIJEVICH IN CHAIR
	2	MESSAGE FROM SENATE
	2	AGREED RESOLUTIONS
	6	RECESS
	6	HOUSE RECONVENES - REP. MATIJEVICH IN CHAIR
	6	MESSAGE FROM SENATE
	20	AGREED RESOLUTIONS
	21	GENERAL RESOLUTIONS
	21	DEATH RESOLUTION
	80	REPRESENTATIVE GREIMAN IN CHAIR
	103	MESSAGE FROM SENATE
	138	REPRESENTATIVE BRESLIN IN CHAIR
	142	REPRESENTATIVE GREIMAN IN CHAIR
	238	REPRESENTATIVE BRESLIN IN CHAIR
	254	RECESS
07/01/84	1	HOUSE TO ORDER - REPRESENTATIVE GREIMAN
	1	PRAYER - CLERK O'BRIEN
	1	PLEDGE OF ALLEGIANCE
	1	ROLL CALL FOR ATTENDANCE
	55	REPRESENTATIVE BRESLIN IN CHAIR
	137	AGREED RESOLUTIONS
	137	GENERAL RESOLUTIONS
	140	REPRESENTATIVE GREIMAN IN CHAIR
	155	SPEAKER MADIGAN IN CHAIR
	155	ADJOURNMENT
11/14/84	1	PERFUNCTORY SESSION
	1	HOUSE TO ORDER - REPRESENTATIVE BOWMAN
	1	PRAYER - CLERK O'BRIEN
	1	PLEDGE OF ALLEGIANCE
	1	MESSAGES FROM GOVERNOR

DATE	PAGE	SUBJECT
11/14/84 (cont'd)	3	MESSAGES FROM SENATE
	3	PERFUNCTORY SESSION - ADJOURNMENT
11/27/84	1	HOUSE TO ORDER - REPRESENTATIVE MCPIKE IN CHAIR
	1	PRAYER - REVEREND GARY MCCANTS
	1	PLEDGE OF ALLEGIANCE
	1	ROLL CALL FOR ATTENDANCE
	2	AGREED RESOLUTIONS
	4	DEATH RESOLUTIONS
	15	RECESS
	15	HOUSE RECONVENES - REP. MCPIKE IN CHAIR
	25	SPEAKER MADIGAN IN CHAIR
	31	REPRESENTATIVE MCPIKE IN CHAIR
	32	REPRESENTATIVE BRESLIN IN CHAIR
	50	COMMITTEE REPORT
	74	ADJOURNMENT
11/28/84	1	HOUSE TO ORDER - REPRESENTATIVE MCPIKE
	1	PRAYER - REVEREND JAMES LOWERY
	2	PLEDGE OF ALLEGIANCE
	2	ROLL CALL FOR ATTENDANCE
	2	AGREED RESOLUTIONS
	4	DEATH RESOLUTIONS
	5	GENERAL RESOLUTION
	5	APPROVAL OF JOURNALS
	27	REPRESENTATIVE BRESLIN IN CHAIR
	71	COMMITTEE REPORT
	73	AGREED RESOLUTIONS
	74	GENERAL RESOLUTIONS
	74	DEATH RESOLUTION
	76	REPRESENTATIVE GREIMAN IN CHAIR
	81	MESSAGE FROM SENATE
	83	AGREED RESOLUTIONS
	84	DEATH RESOLUTIONS
	84	ADJOURNMENT
11/29/84	1	PERFUNCTORY SESSION
	1	REPRESENTATIVE CURRAN IN CHAIR
	1	PRAYER - CLERK O'BRIEN
	1	PLEDGE OF ALLEGIANCE
	1	MESSAGES FROM SENATE
	2	PERFUNCTORY SESSION - ADJOURNMENT
12/11/84	1	HOUSE TO ORDER - REPRESENTATIVE MCPIKE
	1	PRAYER - REVEREND DANNY O'GUINN
	1	PLEDGE OF ALLEGIANCE
	1	ROLL CALL FOR ATTENDANCE
	3	AGREED RESOLUTIONS
	8	DEATH RESOLUTION
	42	REPRESENTATIVE BRESLIN IN CHAIR
		RECESS

DATE	PAGE	SUBJECT
12/11/84 (cont'd)	43	HOUSE RECONVENES - REP. BRESLIN IN CHAIR
	48	AGREED RESOLUTIONS
	49	GENERAL RESOLUTION
	51	DEATH RESOLUTION
	51	ADJOURNMENT
12/12/84	1	HOUSE TO ORDER - SPEAKER MADIGAN
	1	PRAYER - REVEREND HUBERT ENTWISLE
	1	PLEDGE OF ALLEGIANCE
	2	ROLL CALL FOR ATTENDANCE
	2	MESSAGE FROM GOVERNOR
	5	MESSAGE FROM SENATE
	10	RECESS
	10	HOUSE RECONVENES - REP. MCPIKE IN CHAIR
	10	COMMITTEE REPORT
	10	AGREED RESOLUTIONS
	10	DEATH RESOLUTIONS
	14	JOINT SESSION
	14	CHIEF JUSTICE RYAN
	22	GOVERNOR JIM THOMPSON
	25	JUSTICE ROBERT C. UNDERWOOD
	28	JOINT SESSION - ADJOURNMENT
	32	SPEAKER MADIGAN IN CHAIR
	37	REPRESENTATIVE BRESLIN IN CHAIR
	66	RECESS
	66	HOUSE RECONVENES - REP. GREIMAN IN CHAIR
	67	COMMITTEE REPORT
	67	SPEAKER MADIGAN IN CHAIR
	70	REPRESENTATIVE GREIMAN IN CHAIR
	160	AGREED RESOLUTIONS
	161	DEATH RESOLUTION
	164	ADJOURNMENT
01/09/85	1	HOUSE TO ORDER - REPRESENTATIVE MCPIKE
	1	PRAYER - REVEREND ARCHIE GRIGG
	1	PLEDGE OF ALLEGIANCE
	1	ROLL CALL FOR ATTENDANCE
	24	AGREED RESOLUTIONS
	26	GENERAL RESOLUTION
	27	DEATH RESOLUTIONS
	27	APPROVAL OF JOURNALS
	28	SPEAKER MADIGAN IN CHAIR
	29	REPRESENTATIVE GREIMAN IN CHAIR
	39	AGREED RESOLUTIONS
	41	AGREED RESOLUTION
	63	ADJOURNMENT - SINE DIE

CONVERSION TABLE: LEGISLATIVE DAY TO DATE

CONVERSION TABLE: LEGISLATIVE DAY TO DATE

Legislative Day	Calendar Day	Legislative Day	Calendar Day	Legislative Day	Calendar Day	Legislative Day	Calendar Day
1	January 12, 1983	26	April 5, 1983	51	May 24, 1983	76	June 30, 1983
2	January 13, 1983	27	April 6, 1983	52	May 25, 1983	77	July 1, 1983
3	January 25, 1983	28	April 7, 1983	53	May 26, 1983	78	July 2, 1983
4	January 26, 1983	29	April 13, 1983	54	May 27, 1983	79	October 5, 1983
5	January 27, 1983	30	April 14, 1983	55	June 1, 1983	80	October 17, 1983
6	February 2, 1983	31	April 15, 1983	56	June 2, 1983	81	October 18, 1983
7	February 3, 1983	32	April 19, 1983	57	June 3, 1983	82	October 19, 1983
8	February 8, 1983	33	April 20, 1983	58	June 7, 1983	83	October 20, 1983
9	February 9, 1983	34	April 21, 1983	59	June 8, 1983	84	October 31, 1983
10	February 16, 1983	35	April 26, 1983	60	June 9, 1983	85	November 1, 1983
11	February 17, 1983	36	April 27, 1983	61	June 10, 1983	86	November 2, 1983
12	February 23, 1983	37	April 28, 1983	62	June 14, 1983	87	November 3, 1983
13	February 24, 1983	38	May 3, 1983	63	June 15, 1983	88	November 4, 1983
14	March 1, 1983	39	May 4, 1983	64	June 16, 1983	89	January 10, 1984
15	March 2, 1983	40	May 5, 1983	65	June 17, 1983	90	January 11, 1984
16	March 3, 1983	41	May 6, 1983	66	June 20, 1983	91	February 7, 1984
17	March 8, 1983	42	May 10, 1983	67	June 21, 1983	92	February 9, 1984
18	March 9, 1983	43	May 11, 1983	68	June 22, 1983	93	March 6, 1984
19	March 10, 1983	44	May 12, 1983	69	June 23, 1983	94	March 7, 1984
20	March 14, 1983	45	May 13, 1983	70	June 24, 1983	95	March 27, 1984
21	March 15, 1983	46	May 17, 1983	71	June 25, 1983	96	March 28, 1984
22	March 16, 1983	47	May 18, 1983	72	June 26, 1983	97	March 29, 1984
23	March 22, 1983	48	May 19, 1983	73	June 27, 1983	98	April 3, 1984
24	March 23, 1983	49	May 20, 1983	74	June 28, 1983	99	April 4, 1984
25	March 24, 1983	50	May 23, 1983	75	June 29, 1983	100	April 5, 1984

CONVERSION TABLE: LEGISLATIVE DAY TO DATE

Legislative Day	Calendar Day	Legislative Day	Calendar Day
101	April 10, 1984	127	May 30, 1984
102	April 11, 1984	128	May 31, 1984
103	April 12, 1984	129	June 5, 1984
104	April 13, 1984	130	June 6, 1984
105	April 19, 1984	131	June 7, 1984
106	April 24, 1984	132	June 12, 1984
107	April 25, 1984	133	June 13, 1984
108	April 26, 1984	134	June 14, 1984
109	April 27, 1984	135	June 19, 1984
110	April 30, 1984	136	June 20, 1984
111	May 1, 1984	137	June 21, 1984
112	May 2, 1984	138	June 22, 1984
113	May 3, 1984	139	June 25, 1984
114	May 4, 1984	140	June 26, 1984
115	May 8, 1984	141	June 27, 1984
116	May 9, 1984	142	June 28, 1984
117	May 10, 1984	143	June 29, 1984
118	May 15, 1984	144	June 30, 1984
119	May 16, 1984	145	July 1, 1984
120	May 17, 1984	146	November 14, 1984
121	May 18, 1984	147	November 27, 1984
122	May 22, 1984	148	November 28, 1984
123	May 23, 1984	149	November 29, 1984
124	May 24, 1984	150	December 11, 1984
125	May 25, 1984	151	December 12, 1984
126	May 29, 1984	152	January 9, 1985

MICROFICHE FRAME LOCATIONS

Legislative Day	Fiche Number	Legislative Day	Fiche Number
1	1	27	13
2	1	28	14
3	1	29	15
4	2	30	16
5	3	31	17
6	3	32	19
7	3	33	19
8	3	34	20
9	4	35	21
10	4	36	22
11	4	37	22
12	5	38	24
13	5	39	24
14	5	40	25
15	5	41	26
16	6	42	26
17	6	43	28
18	7	44	30
19	8	45	33
20	8	46	35
21	9	47	37
22	9	48	40
23	10	49	43
24	11	50	45
25	12	51	48
26	12	52	51

MICROFICHE FRAME LOCATIONS

Legislative Day	Fiche Number	Legislative Day	Fiche Number
53	54	77	99
54	58	78	102
55	60	79	104
56	61	80	104
57	61	81	104
58	61	82	106
59	62	83	108
60	62	84	110
61	63	85	110
62	63	86	111
63	64	87	114
64	66	88	115
65	68	89	117
66	69	90	117
67	71	91	1
68	75	92	1
69	78	93	1
70	81	94	1
71	84	95	2
72	86	96	2
73	87	97	2
74	91	98	3
75	94	99	3
76	97	100	3

MICROFICHE FRAME LOCATIONS

Legislative Day	Fiche Number	Legislative Day	Fiche Number
101	4	127	35
102	4	128	36
103	5	129	38
104	5	130	38
105	5	131	39
106	5	132	39
107	6	133	40
108	6	134	41
109	7	135	42
110	7	136	43
111	8	137	44
112	8	138	46
113	9	139	48
114	10	140	51
115	10	141	53
116	11	142	55
117	13	143	57
118	15	144	58
119	17	145	61
120	20	146	62
121	23	147	62
122	24	148	63
123	26	149	64
124	29	150	64
125	33	151	65
126	35	152	67

184

APPENDIX A

ILLINOIS DOCUMENTS DEPOSITORY LIBRARIES

Augustana College
Denkman Memorial Library
35th Street & 7th Avenue
Documents Division
Rock Island, Illinois 61201
309-794-7266

Bradley University
Cullom-Davis Library
Peoria, Illinois 61625
309-676-7611 X534

California State Library
Government Publications Section
P.O. Box 2037
Sacramento, California 95809
916-445-4027

Center for Research Libraries
5721 Cottage Grove Avenue
Chicago, Illinois 60637
312-995-4545

Chicago Public Library
Government Publications Department
425 N. Michigan Avenue
Chicago, Illinois 60611
312-269-2900

Chicago State University
Douglas Library
95th & Martin Luther King Dr.
Chicago, Illinois 60628
312-995-2245

Council of State Governments
Interstate Loan Library
P.O. Box 11910
Iron Works Pike
Lexington, Kentucky 40511
606-252-2291

Eastern Illinois University
Booth Library
Charleston, Illinois 61920
217-581-2210

Governors State University
University Library
Park Forest South, Illinois 60466
312-534-5000

Illinois State University
Milner Library
Normal, Illinois 61761
309-438-3675

Illinois Valley Community College
Learning Resources Center
Rural Route One
Oglesby, Illinois 61438
815-224-2720

Library of Congress
Exchange & Gift Division
10 First Street SE
Washington, D.C. 20540

Library of Michigan
Government Documents Unit
P.O. Box 30007
735 E. Michigan Avenue
Lansing, Michigan 48909
517-373-1580

Loyola University
E.M. Cudahy Memorial Library
6525 North Sheridan Road
Chicago, Illinois 60626
312-274-3000 X771

New York State Library
Gift & Exchange Section
Albany, New York 12230
518-474-7860

North Suburban Library System
200 West Dundee Road
Wheeling, Illinois 60090
312-459-1300

185

ILLINOIS DOCUMENT DEPOSITORY LIBRARIES

Northeastern Illinois University
Library
5500 North St. Louis Avenue
Chicago, Illinois 60625
312-583-4050

Northern Illinois University
Founders Memorial Library
DeKalb, Illinois 60115
815-753-1094

Northwestern University Library
Government Publications Department
1935 Sheridan Road
Evanston, Illinois 60201
312-492-5290

Overseas English Section
British Library
Great Russell Street
London, England WC1B 3DG

Poplar Creek Public Library
1405 South Park Blvd.
Streamwood, Illinois 60103
312-837-6800

Quincy Public Library
526 Jersey Street
Quincy, Illinois 62301
217-223-1309

Rockford Public Library
215 N. Wyman Street
Rockford, Illinois 61101
815-965-6731

Sangamon State University
Brookens Library
Springfield, Illinois 62708
217-786-6597

Southern Illinois University
Delyte W. Morris Library
Carbondale, Illinois 62901
618-453-2522

Southern Illinois University
Law Library
Carbondale, Illinois 62901
618-536-7711

Southern Illinois University
Lovejoy Library
Edwardsville, Illinois 62026
618-692-2713

State Library of Massachusetts
Documents Section
341 State House
Boston, Massachusetts 02137
617-727-2590

State Library of Pennsylvania
Technical Services
Box 1601
Harrisburg, Pennsylvania 17126
717-787-2646

University of Illinois
Documents Division
1408 W. Gregory
230 Library
Urbana, Illinois 61801
217-333-0792

University of Illinois
Institute of Government & Public Affairs
1201 West Nevada
Urbana, Illinois 61801
217-333-3340

University of Illinois
Law Library
504 East Pennsylvania Avenue
Champaign, Illinois 61820
217-333-2914

Lightning Source UK Ltd.
Milton Keynes UK
UKHW041152150219
337137UK00013B/1455/P